# A NEW HISTORY OF
# JAPANESE
# CINEMA

**Also available from Continuum:**

Peter Bondanella: *Italian Cinema, 3rd Edition: From Neorealism to the Present*

Rémi Fournier-Lanzoni: *French Cinema: From its Beginnings to the Present*

Joseph G. Kickasola: *The Films of Krzysztof Kieslowski*

David Schroeder: *Cinema's Illusions, Opera's Allure*

Alyn Shipton: *A New History of Jazz*

Takemae Eiji: *The Allied Occupation of Japan*

# A NEW HISTORY OF JAPANESE CINEMA

## A CENTURY OF NARRATIVE FILM

ISOLDE STANDISH

**continuum**

NEW YORK • LONDON

2006

The Continuum International Publishing Group Inc
80 Maiden Lane, New York, NY 10038

The Continuum International Publishing Group Ltd
The Tower Building, 11 York Road, London SE1 7NX

www.continuumbooks.com

Printed in the United States of America

Library of Congress Cataloging-in-Publication Data

Standish, Isolde.
  A new history of Japanese cinema : a century of narrative film / Isolde Standish.
       p. cm.
  Filmography:
  Includes bibliographical references and index.
  ISBN 0-8264-1709-4 (hardcover : alk. paper) 0-8264-1790-6 (paperback : alk.
paper)
  1. Motion pictures—Japan—History.  I. Title.
PN1993.5.J3S72    2005
791.43`0952—dc22
                                                              2004023894

*For Michael*
*2 December 1966–1 June 2001*

# CONTENTS

# PREFACE AND ACKNOWLEDGMENTS

THE WRITING of this study of Japanese narrative cinema in the twentieth century has been a humbling exercise that, upon reflection, makes me marvel at the arrogance with which I first took on the task. This became increasingly obvious as I confronted the breadth of the field to be addressed and the great scholarship of Japanese film historians and critics in whose wake I have followed. However, I feel now as I did when I first put pen to paper, that a new study, and perhaps more important a new approach, was called for, not only in the attempt to come to some sort of terms with the genealogy of what is broadly referred to as Japanese cinema, but more generally, to questions of how we should address the idea of 'national cinema'.

In the contemporary age, when film production is dominated by transnational conglomerations and changing technologies, eloquently discussed by Toby Miller et al. (2001), the question of what constitutes a 'national cinema' provides an alternative paradigm through which to reach a new understanding of cinema's symbiotic relationship to nation. Therefore, however inadequate, it is hoped that these reflections on what is one of the world's great cinematic traditions will open up new debates and new avenues for further profitable exploration of not only Japanese films but also the very idea of 'national cinema'.

In the title of this study I have used the word 'narrative' to make a somewhat arbitrary distinction between what we broadly conceive of as 'fictional' and 'documentary' films. I fully accept that 'documentary' films are just as much narrative-based as that of mainstream 'fictional' cinema, however, as Brian Winston (1995) specifies in his introduction to *Claiming the Real*, definitions of documentary cinema tend to hinge on the relationship between 'image and reality' through claims to 'truth'. Therefore, in this study I am basing this distinction on the documentary filmmakers' motivational claims to 'truth' and, as such, the reader will find no references to such noted Japanese documentary filmmakers as Ogawa

Shinsuke (1935–1992), who is renowned for a series of films documenting the local farmers' struggles in the Narita Airport dispute. However, full mention will be made of directors such as Fukasaku Kinji, who, through style, incorporated elements of documentary filmmaking practices into his fictional films of the late 1960s and 1970s.

Due to the great breadth of a topic of this nature, I cannot claim to be an expert on every aspect of Japanese filmmaking practice over the last one hundred years. Therefore, I fully acknowledge that during the past twenty years I have spent watching films and reading about Japanese cinema, I have absorbed and been influenced by many sources, both second- and in some instances thirdhand, making it difficult to trace back ideas and suggestions to their origins. Hence I have limited my references to actual quotations and in some instances to the authority for statements which may appear controversial. However, in terms of acknowledgements, I would like to thank both Brian Powell and Mark Morris for their support for the project from its inception, when I was first approached by Athlone Press (during the course of the writing Athlone was absorbed into the Continuum International Publishing Group), and for their subsequent references, which secured an AHRB Fellowship. The AHRB Fellowship, combined with a generous two-term sabbatical granted by the School of Oriental and African Studies, gave me an invaluable academic year free to focus on writing in 2001–2002. I should also acknowledge a grant of £2000 made by the Japan Foundation Endowment Committee, which contributed to expenses incurred in Japan researching trade journals in the spring of 2000. I am indebted to my editors, David Barker and Gabriella Page-Fort at Continuum, who took over the project from Athlone with great enthusiasm and efficiency. I am also grateful to Jay Sakomoto of Shōchiku for giving me permission to publish the photograph of his grandfather, Kido Shirō. Thanks are also due to the support staff at SOAS, in particular Lisa McSweeney and her team, who took over the time-consuming duties associated with the exchange programme in the summer of 2003 and thus freed up time to complete the final chapters. Finally, acknowledgement should be made to the students whose great enthusiasm for Japanese films generated many lively and inspiring discussions.

# NOTES ON TRANSLATION

JAPANESE NAMES are given in the Japanese order of surname and first name. In the case of film titles, where standard known English translations exist I have followed custom. However, in some instances films have been released abroad under numerous titles; for example, the first film in the series *Jingi naki tatakai* was originally released as *Battles Without Morality,* but more recently re-released on DVD in the U.K. under the title *Yakuza Papers.* In such cases, I have included all the possible permutations in the first reference to the film in each chapter. I have done this as some readers may wish to read a chapter as a discrete entity. In other cases, the films referred to in the study have not been released in the West and I have translated the titles myself. In the Select Filmography I have attempted to include all the possible titles, and in order to help reduce the level of ambiguity, and indeed frustration, I have included the Japanese titles in *kanji* (Chinese ideograms). In most cases I have taken the Japanese readings for the romanization of film titles from the *Pia Cinemakurabu Nihon Eiga Hen 2004–2005* annual film reference. I have also drawn primarily on this source for the readings of names, the birth and, where applicable, death dates of filmmakers and actors. Alternative sources included the *Kinema Junpō* publications of the complete directory for directors (1988), actors (1991) and actresses (1991). However, in a very few cases the death date of some early actors/directors is unclear; these I have marked with an asterisk. As with film titles, I have included the dates of filmmakers and actors in the first reference to them in each chapter. Regarding the dates of historical and literary figures, I have drawn primarily on the fifth edition of the *Kōjien* (Iwanami Shoten) and the *Nihon Daihyakka Zensho Nipponica Lite Pack* CD-ROM (Shogakukan 2003).

I have made use of macrons to indicate long vowel sounds when transliterating Japanese names and words. Only in the case of film titles when the film was released in the West with the original Japanese title, minus the macron—as in, for example, *Yojimbo the Bodyguard* (*Yōjinbō*)—have I excluded them. I have also excluded them from well-known place names such as Tokyo and Kyoto. The only other case relates to references to two characters who appear in films based on the classic tale *The Loyal Forty-seven Retainers* (*Chūshingura*); in both cases I have followed custom and transliterated the long 'e' as 'ei' in *Yasubei* and *Yahei*. Finally, all translations from the Japanese are my own unless otherwise stated. Quotations from Japanese films were taken directly from the videos/DVDs during repeated viewing, as only in a few rare cases—as in the films of avant-garde filmmakers—are screenplays readily available. In the case of, for example, the films of Miike Takashi, which often involve a mix of languages, for the various scenes involving Chinese dialogue I have relied on the subtitled DVD versions released in the U.K. by Tartan Asia Extreme.

# INTRODUCTION

## Towards a Politics of Cinema

[F]or the first time in world history, mechanical reproduction emancipates the work of art from its parasitical dependence on ritual . . . From a photographic negative, for example, one can make any number of prints; to ask for the 'authentic' print makes no sense. But the instant the criterion of authenticity ceases to be applicable to artistic production, the total function of art is reversed. Instead of being based on ritual, it begins to be based on another practice—politics. (Benjamin 1992: 218)

The real communicative 'products' which are usable signs are . . . living evidence of a continuing social process, into which individuals are born and within which they are shaped, but to which they then also actively contribute, in a continuing process. This is at once their socialization and their individuation . . . (Williams 1977: 37)

[T]he history of 'deep focus', like that of the 'closeup', cannot be constructed without bringing into play a system of determinations which *are not exclusively technical.* They are rather economic and ideological, and as such they break down the boundaries of the specifically cinematic field, extending and therefore transforming it with a series of additional areas; they bring the field of cinema to bear on other scenes and integrate these other scenes into that of the cinema. They break apart the fiction of an autonomous history of the cinema—that is, of 'styles and techniques'. They produce the complex relationships which link the field and history of the cinema to other fields and other histories. (Comolli 1986: 430–431)

If art were only, or mainly, an expression of personal vision, there would be no history of art. (Gombrich 1996: 3)

The modern and the postmodern ages of globalization raise many questions regarding how history functions as a mechanism for structuring shared social and national identities and how narrative modes play an instrumental role as explanatory paradigms, facilitating those shared understandings (Hobsbawn 1992, 1997; Gellner 1999; Frye 1957; and Standish 2000). The role of the historian as recorder of 'empirical facts' has thus, in the modern age, rightly been challenged (Carr 1990, White 1985, Comolli 1986). But still the question remains: How are we to understand the present without some rudimentary understanding of the past? As Colin MacCabe points out in his introduction to Fredric Jameson's *The Geopolitical Aesthetic: Cinema and Space in the World System* (1991), cinema as a medium is often comprised of a combination of 'the most ancient and local artistic traditions with the most modern and global advertising campaign.' Furthermore, it can be argued that non-Hollywood cinematic traditions often reflect a tension between what was in many instances an imported form (cinematic technology and techniques) and content (the 'most ancient and local artistic traditions'). Therefore, without an understanding of the adaptation of the form (the techniques and grammar of cinema) to the local market, or the historical context of the development of the content and narrative modes, it is impossible to reach an understanding of a national cinema, other than at its simplest level of mere spectacle.

This study focuses on the historical development of Japanese cinema as a nexus, a point where a multiplicity of, at times, competing and merging forces from the traditional arts, sociopolitical trends and Western technology came to be adopted, adapted and altered to produce a cinematic tradition. As a result this study, mindful of the challenges to traditional academic discourses of history, does not claim to be *the* definitive history of Japanese narrative cinema. In this context, the use of the word 'history' is perhaps misleading; 'histories' might be more appropriate, as this study takes the view that there is no 'grand narrative' of history that neatly collates all the facts and puts them into place. There are, however, identifiable discourses of history that link political, social and cultural trends to specific time frames. Therefore, this volume is restricted to a detailed study of some of the dominant historical discourses of the last century— modernism, nationalism, imperialism, transgression and gender—and cinema's role as a mechanism of mediation that is both constitutive of, and constituted by, these same sociopolitical discourses.

Utilizing Raymond Williams's (1977) study of language and his analysis of the historical development of linguistics as a starting point, this study takes the view that images, like language, form part of a continuous social process that both shapes individual consciousness and to which spectators and viewing audiences, to a limited extent, actively contribute through their acceptance or non-acceptance of dramatic, stylistic and technical innovations. Thus, in the last century, image production through cinema should be understood as forming an increasingly important role as social practice. As Williams argues from the context of language, this approach to the study of national cinemas becomes 'one of the decisive arguments against reduction of the key fact of social determination to the idea of determination by a system' (Williams 1977: 40). E. H. Gombrich concludes his study of the development of pictorial style in art on a similar note.

> Romanticism has taught us to talk of art in terms of inspiration and creativity . . . The very existence of styles and traditions has made us doubtful of the value of this approach to the history of art. It is here that the tradition of rhetoric is such a useful corrective because it supplies a philosophy of language. In this tradition the hierarchy of modes, the language of art, exists independent of the individual. It is the young artist who is born into this system and who has to make his choice. To do so he must study himself and follow his own bent, and in so far as he succeeds he will also express his personality. (Gombrich 1996: 322)

This volume is effectively divided into six chapters loosely covering the time frame from the end of the nineteenth century, when cinema first arrived in Japan, to the end of the twentieth century. The themes taken up in each chapter are defined and related to one another both structurally and historically; however, my approach to these topics may best be described as essayistic and exploratory. While chapter one looks at cinema's symbolic position in society in the 1930s as both a metaphor and a motor of 'modernity', chapter two takes up the question of cinema's relationship to nationalism and empire building in the late 1930s and early 1940s. Chapter three extends this theme by taking up the question of cinema's relationship with the state, focusing on, in particular, the war and occupation periods. In this chapter, I attempt to move beyond deterministic theories of propaganda to examine some of the heterogeneous elements of film practice evident under the conditions of state control. Chapter four moves into the post-occupation period and examines the films of the 'humanists' and the structuring of 'romance' (a theme discouraged under the censorship regulations of the 1939 Film Law) as the antithesis of war in mainstream films of the immediate post-occupation period; chapter five takes up questions of 'transgression' in the works of the avant-garde directors of the 1960s and early 1970s. This latter chapter links concepts of *daraku* (decadence), put forward in the writings of Japanese intellectuals such as Sakaguchi Ango (1906–1955), and the political use of pornography in the works of directors such as Ōshima Nagisa and Suzuki Seijun. Chapter six returns again to mainstream cinema, taking up the question of genre and gender. As the crisis in the industry developed in the 1970s, Nikkatsu turned exclusively to *romanporuno*[1], while Tōei continued to specialize in producing yakuza (Japanese mafia) films. Considering the collapse of Daiei and the fragile state of Shōchiku, this, in fact, meant that the majority of Japanese films produced at this time were being made exclusively for male audiences. It was only during the short holiday seasons in summer and winter that programmes changed for family viewing. Finally, the study concludes with a consideration of a century of Japanese narrative cinema from a cross-cultural perspective. This final chapter asks the question raised by Ōshima, 'Do Japanese films exist?' One further point regarding the structure of this study: Japanese cinema history, in particular, and the histories of national cinemas in general (other than those of Hollywood and Europe), have been areas of study much neglected until recently and it is therefore hoped that this volume might provide a possible theoretical and expository basis to extend contemporary research.

In grappling with Japanese film history and criticism, most Western commentators have concentrated on offering 'interpretations' of what have come to be considered 'classics' produced by selected directors designated as *auteurs* (McDonald 1994; 2000; Richie 1974; and Yoshimoto 2000). Susan Sontag, in 'Against Interpretation', argues that, since Plato, Western art criticism has been based on mimetic theory that privileges 'content' over 'form'. She goes on to explain what this 'overemphasis on the idea of content entails is the perennial, never-consummated project of *interpretation*' (Sontag: 1983: 96–97). This focus on content has been more than evident within Western approaches to the study of Japanese cinema—an approach, one should add, supported by Japanese views of the 'uniqueness' of their culture, what Brian Moeran (1989) has described as a form of inverted 'orientalism'. The obverse side of this argument is the view held by many Japanese of foreigners' inability to understand the complexities of their 'unique' culture. 'Interpretation thus presupposes a discrepancy between the clear meaning of the text and the demands of (later) readers' (Sontag 1983: 97) or, in the case of Japanese cinema, non-Japanese spectators.

Equally, histories of the development of Japanese cinema have tended to follow two trajectories: one can be labelled the 'progressive' version. This version sees the stylistic development of cinema from the invention of simple forms of technology and the related unsophisticated techniques of filmmakers through to the development of sound, colour, wide-screen and other advanced forms of technology and an accompanying sophistication of technical expertise on the part of filmmakers.[2] Joseph Anderson and Donald Richie's 1959 text and, perhaps to a lesser extent, Richie's more recent 2001 history are examples.

The second version argues that one particular era was the 'golden age'. This argument follows a development, achievement and decline pattern. This latter paradigm was adopted by Noël Burch (1979) in his use of the Japanese silent cinema for his wider political purpose as an example of an alternative to mainstream Hollywood modes of representation, or, to use his term, the International Mode of Representation. Within his case study of Japan, Burch argues that the Japanese silent cinema developed in a geographical and cultural vacuum, thanks to various historical factors that cut Japan off from the rest of the world for prolonged periods (the Tokugawa policy of *sakoku* or closed country, which was in force from 1639 to 1854, and the rise of militarism in the 1930s). As a result, Burch traces the stylistic influences on early Japanese cinema to artistic traditions dating back to the Heian period (794–1185). It was only after 1945 and the arrival of the Allied Occupation Forces that Japanese cinema was 'corrupted' and under the postwar studio system at last brought into line with the International Mode of Representation.

Although Burch offers many poignant observations in his detailed studies of individual films and filmmakers, his basic historical assumptions are flawed. Certainly Japan did maintain a policy of isolation for over two hundred years. However, with the Meiji Restoration of 1868, the Japanese ruling elite rushed headlong into a policy of 'modernization' through a programme of state-sponsored industrialization under slogans such as 'Eastern ethics, Western science' (*tōyō no dōtoku seiyō no gakugei*).[3] The realization that national autonomy was dependent on the maintenance of an advanced industrial economy (highlighted by, amongst other things, the division of China into spheres of foreign influence, the bombardment of Kagoshima in August 1863 and Shimonoseki in September 1864) spurred this enthusiasm. Trends, evident in the late Tokugawa period towards mercantile capitalism and urbanization, grew to unprecedented levels during the Meiji (1868–1912), Taishō (1912–1926) and early Shōwa periods (1926–1989).[4] By the time of the Meiji emperor's death in 1912, Japan was a nation state with a strong economy, a modern army that had been victorious in two wars (Sino-Japanese 1894–1895 and Russo-Japanese 1904–1905), and a national political structure. Universal education and rapid expansion of the print media ensured that, for the first time in Japan's history, all Japanese were aware of the emperor and the national polity, the *kokutai*.

The Meiji, Taishō and early Shōwa periods were dynamic and innovative times when the new and the modern often clashed with tradition. Cinema, which first arrived in Japan in 1896 with the Kinetoscope prototype,[5] came at the very time that Japan was transforming its economic base and society into that of a major international power. During these turbulent times of social change, cinema became both a force and a metaphor for change, as concepts such as 'progress' and 'achievement' were increasingly linked to individual endeavour. The first cinema, the Asakusa Denkikan, was opened in Tokyo in 1903 and, in the short space of thirteen years, the number of movie houses had grown to three hundred throughout the country.[6] The outbreak of the Russo-Japanese War in 1904 generated enormous public interest, becoming Japan's first media event with cinema instrumental in publicizing the war. The Yoshizawa Shōten film company, which had in the previous year opened the Asakusa Denkikan, dispatched a camera team to follow the fortunes of the armed forces. As a result of this public interest, Yoshizawa Shōten was able to expand its operation, building many more theatres in and around Asakusa. With the increase in theatres and the subsequent demand for new films, the company had to formalize its business and, in 1909, built Japan's first film production studio in Tokyo at Meguro. The site included a glass stage, which allowed for maximum light and protection from the weather. Prior to this, films had been produced inside a tent on the same site. When the new studio was built, a planning department was incorporated and was headed by the novelist and *shinpa* (literally 'new school') playwright Satō Kōroku (1874–1949).

To further capitalize on the burgeoning mass urban entertainment market, the head of Yoshizawa Shōten visited New York and was greatly impressed by Coney Island. Upon his return, he set about building the Asakusa Luna Park (*Runa pāku*), which was opened in 1910. Similarly, the Yokota Shōkai company was established in Osaka on the strength of public interest in the Russo-Japanese War. In 1907 they opened the Sen'-nichimae Denkikan, a former theatre that specialized in *misemono* (vaudeville) and touring theatre troupes. With the decline in interest in these entertainment forms and a rise of interest in film, the theatre was converted into Osaka's first permanent cinema. By 1912 four independent film companies with interests in production, importation, distribution and exhibition had been established: Yoshizawa Shōten, Yokota Shōkai, M. Pathé (totally unrelated to the French company of the same name) and Fukudo. These four companies were to merge on 10 September 1912 to form the Nihon Katsudō Shashin (Nikkatsu) Studios. This merger occurred after an acrimonious round of talks that followed various arson incidents resulting in the gutting of several theatres and the Asakusa Luna Park, just eight months after it opened.

## A Dialectic of Form and Content

> The best criticism, and it is uncommon, is of [the] sort that dissolves considerations of content into those of form. (Sontag 1983: 103)

While I do not want to take an overtly technological determinist line, there are various implications that need to be considered in relation to cinema as a Western technological invention and the historicity of the juncture in time when it was invented. Cinema began in the age of Freudian psychoanalysis, the rise of nationalism and the emergence of consumerism. As Ella Shohat and Robert Stam remind us,

> The first film screenings by Lumiere and Edison in the 1890s closely followed the 'scramble for Africa' that erupted in the 1870s, the Battle of 'Rorke's Drift' (1879) which opposed the British to the Zulus . . . , the British occupation of Egypt in 1882, the Berlin Conference of 1884 that carved up Africa into European 'spheres of influence', the massacre of the Sioux at Wounded Knee in 1890, and countless other imperial misadventures. (Shohat and Stam 1996: 152)

Comolli[7] has argued that the development of the camera obscura as a 'machine' is not neutral, but comes imbued with certain ideological assumptions that underpinned its development. '[T]he technology is produced in large part by a socially derived conception of [the] world and how we know it . . . [Comolli] finds the origin of cinema not in scientific inquiry but in nineteenth-century ideological pressures to represent "life as it is" and in economic desires to exploit a new spectacle' (Bordwell, Staiger and Thompson 1999: 250). This desire to re-present 'life as it is' stems from the Renaissance project that attempted to reproduce reality through mimesis. The invention of the camera and the development of photography was a direct result of this aim—an aim compatible with a Western ideological/aesthetic tradition, which, since the Renaissance and later the Enlightenment, sought to distance humanity's understanding of the natural world and civil society from a purely metaphysical and reli-gious context, and to locate that understanding in the real, this worldly study of the sciences. As the landscape painter John Constable remarked, '[P]ainting is a science and should be pursued as an inquiry into the laws of nature' (quoted in Gombrich 1996: 29). The development of the camera was a progression in this ideological/aesthetic tradition that pursued art as science. This development freed artists from the need to re-present reality and can be related to the reactionary development of expressionist and im-pressionist art movements of the twentieth century. The transference of the drive to (re)present reality to the world of film extends to the presenta-tion of 'historical authenticity,' as Anthony Smith (2000) reminds us in his study of the relationship between historical paintings and historical films.[8]

Comolli's analysis of 'deep focus' clearly links the development of camera lenses to Western 'pictorial, theatrical and photographic' codes and representational styles. The lenses and focal lengths (f35 and f50) selected were those which clearly corresponded to 'normal vision'.

> These lenses themselves were thus dictated by the codes of analogy and realism (other codes corresponding to other social demands would have produced other types of lenses). The depth of field which they allowed was thus also what authorized them, was the basis for their utilization and exis-tence. It wasn't therefore just a supplementary effect whose use could be passed up as a matter of indifference. On the contrary, it was what *had* to be obtained, and it had been necessary to strive for its production. (Comolli 1986: 433)

As the Japanese in the early days of cinema were dependent on the impor-tation of film stock, cameras and projection equipment from the West, it follows that they were constrained by the ideological motivations that led to the development and use of specific technologies and the rejection of others. As the reminiscences of Ōbora Gengo (1899–1975),[9] a cameraman working in 1912, confirm, the imported film stock from the United States relied heavily upon natural light, and the best lens to use with this stock was f35 (quoted in Satō 1995 vol. i).

Comolli tackles the question of the relationship between cinematic style and technological innovation from the ideological or collective perspective; Gombrich, in a different context, tackles the question of the development of pictorial style (the language of art) from the psychological perspective of the individual artist. Both approaches are compatible as they provide methodological tools to analyse the place of the artist and/or work of art in the sociohistorical context of their production and reception. The study of the role of the *auteur* is decentred to make way for a study of the artist and/ or work as a part of a collective tradition. Gombrich, drawing on the findings of psychologists' studies of human perception, argues that individual artists do not begin the act of creation from the object as seen, but from an internalized schemata held in the mind's eye. In other words, through cultural habituation, we all hold mental conceptualizations of the basic forms of objects. Artists begin with this conception and then fill in the distinguishing features that will increase the mimetic effect on the actual object before them. In distancing his position from that of the cultural determinist, Gombrich goes on to define the 'art' of artists in their ability to extend and indeed challenge existing schemata. 'I believe . . . that the artist's gift is of this order. He is the man who has learnt to look critically, to probe his perceptions by trying alternative interpretations . . .' (Gombrich 1996: 264).

The re-presentation of 'scientific naturalism' had never been a priority of the traditional Japanese visual arts. Rather the Muromachi (1333–1568) and Tokugawa period (1600–1868) screen paintings, with the sky and clouds that act as a barrier or dividing line separating the human world from the heavenly, are representations of the world and universe according to Confucian precepts.[10] Similarly the seasonal *kakejiku* (hanging picture scrolls) that adorned the walls of the affluent classes, depicting humans in miniature proportions to the landscape, reflect a mode of seeing the world based on an Eastern view of the human being's significance in relation to the natural world. Within this basically Confucian conception of 'reality', deep focus, that selectively privileges people and, at times, objects, is superfluous.[11] Therefore, at a simplistic level it can be argued that when the Japanese adopted film technology, they also imported with it an inherent way of re-presenting the world, a conceptual mode that was not neutral but ideological (in its broadest sense). As David Bordwell argues, drawing on a quotation from a speech made in 1934 by A. N. Goldsmith, the President for the (American) Society of Motion Picture Engineers,

'Showmanship', realism, invisibility: such canons guided the SMPE members toward understanding the acceptable and unacceptable choices in technical innovation, and these too became teleological. In another industry, the engineer's goal might be an unbreakable glass or lighter alloy. In the film industry, the goals were not only increased efficiency, economy, and flexibility but also spectacle, concealment of artifice, and what Goldsmith called 'the production of an acceptable semblance of reality'. (Bordwell, Staiger and Thompson 1999: 258)

As the following study of popular Japanese narrative cinema in the early part of the twentieth century will demonstrate, these qualities of 'spectacle, concealment of artifice' and 'an acceptable semblance of reality' came to dominate the local product.[12] However, this is not to argue that local Japanese artistic or sociocultural practices did not have an equal or greater influence on these films.

The centrality of the *benshi/katsuben* (film narrator) to Japanese films up to the mid-1930s is a case in point, whereby the intervention of the local into the content of the foreign acts as a medium to facilitate understanding. The vocabulary used in Japanese discourse clearly distinguishes the role of the film narrator in films derived from kabuki (*kyūgeki*) as providing literally the shadow dialogue (*kagezerifu*) and the narrator's role as mediator of imported films. The following article published in English for the benefit of foreign readers in one of Japan's early film trade journals, *Kinema Record,* published in August 1915, defines the role of *benshi/katsuben* as a 'photo-interpreter'. (Errors in spelling and grammar reproduced in the following quotation are as in the original.)

> We are sure our foreign readers may wonder at the word 'Photo-interpreters'. Indeed they are found only in the picture-theatres in Japan. What do you think is their business? Why as the word 'Photo-interpreter' may convey its meaning to some extent, they interprete [sic] the spectators the picture-drama's synopsis before the picture appears on the screen or while the picture is shown moving on the white cloth. Sometimes they act as dialogists for the players in the picture and some of them make dialogue so skillfully [sic] as if the players in the picture were really speaking. So in some cases the moving picture plays shown to the Japanese spectators are not the *silent drama* at all the *ture play* [sic] with the help of these photo-interpreters. It is, therefore, natural that we have many eloquent photo-interpreter and often the spectators is influence by the dialogue by them. So important has become their position in the picture-theatres of Japan.
>
>     Such being the case, any photo-play-house in Japan has two or three 'interpreters' at least, so the total number reach to above three thousand in all throughout Japan, the number of photo-play-house being more than nine hundred. Most of them are educated and have the knowledge of a foreign language—English at least. Because they must read and explain the specta-

tors the synopsis in a foreign language shown at the beginning of every scene. As you know the picture-theatres in Japan exhibit chiefly the pictures made in foreign countries and owing to this fact the need of some interpreters sprang up to make the spectators understand what was the scene and what was taking place. Such has gradually developed and has made the present 'Photo-interpreters.'

Despite the exaggerations (the number of cinemas in Japan at the time), from the translation of the terms *benshi/katsuben* as 'photo-interpreters' and the subsequent explanation as to their role, it is clear that the *benshi* were instrumental as mediators between the familiar and the foreign. Western commentators on Japanese cinema have generally attributed the inclusion of *benshi* in the early silent Japanese cinema experience to 'the traditions and peculiarities of Japanese culture' and cited their existence as proof of Japan's difference from Western cinematic traditions. Anderson, in his seminal essay on *katsuben,* saw their role as '(1) *an extension of an indigenous narrative practice which I call commingled media,* and (2) *a modern variation of vocal storytelling traditions*' (italics in the original Anderson 1992: 261). However, in their analysis of the *benshi* tradition, Hiroshi Komatsu and Charles Musser make the following astute observation: '[T]he benshi cannot be characterized in terms of an oppositional or alternative practice vis à vis Western and particularly Hollywood cinema but rather as an accommodation with these dominant Western cinemas' (Komatsu and Musser 1987: 83). Furthermore, economic factors contributed to the central position held by *benshi* in the Japanese cinema experience. Due to the relatively small number of prints sold, it was uneconomical for American and European producers to translate intertitles into Japanese. Equally, Japanese cinemas tended to be large, unlike the American nickelodeons, and this helped offset the cost to Japanese distributors of employing *benshi*. Komatsu and Musser conclude, 'the benshis' position required them to mediate between Japanese audiences that were comparatively unfamiliar with Western representational methods and some Japanese producers who wanted to embrace the most extreme practices of Western cinema' (Komatsu and Musser 1987: 88).

As Gombrich's study indicates, the artist interprets the world in terms of known schemata, but equally the beholder and spectator are complicit in the act of creation in their capacity to collaborate with the artist to make sense of, or read, the image. The *benshi* were crucial as intermediaries in this process. Not only did they attempt to explain the often new and unfamiliar 'schemata' that drove the creative side of the foreign narratives, in the early days at least they also explained the principles of film technology itself.

What one has, as the case of the *benshi* illustrates, is a process of modification and alteration to a new technology and related worldview, which through the passage of time and adaptation conformed to and informed local taste. Therefore, a deterministic view of form (the technology and techniques of filmmaking) has to be tempered with an understanding of the 'content', which as Colin MacCabe (1991) aptly describes, is often derived from the 'most ancient and local artistic traditions'. This dialectic of the form and content is appropriately illustrated by Jacques Rivette's comments in the *Cahiers du Cinéma* in 1958 after the European release of two of Mizoguchi Kenji's (1898–1956) films, *The Life of Oharu* aka *The Life of a Woman by Saikaku (Saikaku ichidai onna)* (1952) and *Ugetsu monogatari* (1953). 'These films, in a language we do not know, presenting stories totally foreign to our customs and habits, in fact speak to us in a very familiar language. Which one? The only one to which a director must aspire: that of *mise en scène*' (quoted in Bordwell 1997: 79). In other words, if we take the example of Comolli's analysis of 'deep focus' as an ideologically determined expression of perspective commensurate with 'normal vision', we have to allow for its modification through its adaptation and application to indigenous contextual forms. However, to ignore the historical and political factors influencing the development of the technology and techniques of its use leaves the film historian with a catalogue of, at the least, empirical facts (dates, names and places) and, at worst, an endless stream of plot summaries. Raymond Williams, in his writings on the development of linguistics as an academic discipline, makes a similar observation to Comolli, in that both linguistics and the study of film style have become self-reflexive. '[H]istory in its most specific, active, and connecting senses, has disappeared (in one tendency has been theoretically excluded) from this account of so central a human activity . . .' (Williams 1977: 28). Edward Said has similarly derided the fact that an emphasis on 'textuality' in the analysis of (literary) texts has had the effect of divorcing texts from the context of their production and reception. 'As it is practiced in the American academy today, literary theory has for the most part isolated textuality from the circumstances, the events, the physical senses that made it possible and render it intelligible as the result of human work' (Said 1991: 4).

In Comolli's critique of Bazin and Mitry, he argues that the 'search for the first time' a particular technique or stylistic innovation was used creates an ahistorical debate that never confronts the 'why' of its development. The result of this tendency to focus on a naturalized evolutionary process has lead to an abstraction of the historical processes by which certain techniques were adopted and others rejected. Images and cinema should be understood as part of the social process of the creation of meaning. Therefore, this study aims to affirm the link between films, their content, production and reception and the 'existential actualities of human life, politics, societies and events'.

In Japan at the turn of the century, discourses of 'modernism', 'imperialism' and 'nationalism' were introduced through the burgeoning mass media and cinema. The early adoption of cinema by the excluded members of the 'legitimate' theatre and entertainment industries and later by left-leaning graduates unable to find employment in mainstream companies increased cinema's poignancy as a challenge to traditional entertainment forms. It therefore became emblematic of the 'difficult and contested transition from feudal to bourgeoisie society'. 'What can then be seen as happening . . . is a historical development of social language itself: finding new means, new forms and then new definitions of a changing practical consciousness' (Williams 1977: 54).

One final problem related to the study of a national cinema is the criteria by which films are selected for discussion. As Kristin Thompson and David Bordwell remind us, 'movies were [often] seen as products with a temporary commercial value, and companies did little to ensure their preservation' (Thompson and Bordwell 1994: xxix). In fact, Japanese film companies produced many popular films in two and three parts. After the initial release, these were then re-edited into one shortened version. Until 1950, the original full-length version was often destroyed in this process, leaving only the shortened (*sōshūhen*) version. The 1938 production *The Love-Troth Tree* aka *The Compassionate Buddha Tree* (*Aizen katsura*, directed by Nomura Hiromasa [1905–1979]) and the 1935 *An Actor's Revenge* aka *The Revenge of Yukinojo* (*Yukinojō henge*, directed by Kinugasa Teinosuke [1896–1982]) both suffered this fate, while Mizoguchi Kenji's two-part *The Loyal Forty-seven Rōnin* aka *The Forty-seven Rōnin of the Genroku Era* (*Genroku Chūshingura* [1941–1942]) survived intact. Due to its failure at the box office on initial release, it was never re-released in a shortened version. Also the instability of nitrate film stock and its vulnerability to fire has severely limited the number of early films still extant[13], particularly in the case of countries such as Japan and Korea where whole cities were decimated by blanket bombing during wartime.[14] Also, in the case of Japan, many films deemed inappropriate to the dictates of Western 'democratic' reforms were destroyed by the Allied Occupation Forces (1945–1952).

One further point raised in relation to popular Japanese films from the early part of the twentieth century is that they rarely survived the ravages of repeated screenings. In some quarters, it is even suggested that the abundance of Ozu Yasujirō's (1903–1963) early films from the silent era can be attributed to their lack of popular success, while the scarcity of extant examples of prewar films directed by Saitō Torajirō (1905–1982) and Gosho Heinosuke (1902–1981) can similarly be attributed to their greater popularity with the cinema-going populace. However, the sheer numbers of films still available to researchers is greater than any single scholar or one volume can encompass. Therefore, the films chosen for discussion in this volume have been limited to films still widely available within the public domain in Japan, that is, through video, and increasingly DVD outlets (both rental and retail) and television. The approximately 1,500 films that formed the basis of this study were collected, and or viewed, between 1984 and 2004. During this twenty-year period, technology came to play an increasingly important role in the Japanese people's re-evaluation of their national cinema, as NHK satellite TV began broadcasting and instituted various themed series of 'classic' film broadcasts under the title The Satellite Cinema (*Eisei Hōsō Eigakan*). A little later Shōchiku, capitalizing on this renewed public interest, began re-releasing early films on video at affordable prices under their Best Selection label. The Tōei and Daiei studios have recently followed suit with the Tōei Jidaigeki Best Selection series and the Daiei Video Museum series. It remains to be seen which films will survive the most recent technology-driven format change to DVD. By following these principles of popularity and availability, it is hoped that this study will reflect cinema history as it is understood by general Japanese audiences who have maintained an interest in their cinematic traditions, and not be an account of the views of the few academics permitted into the rarefied crevices of national archives.

In this introduction I have attempted to elaborate on specific theoretical issues relevant to the study of national cinemas and to lay the foundations for a methodological approach to the study of cinema history that goes beyond the cataloguing of empirical 'facts' and 'interpretation' and to look at cinema as social practice. In short, I am proposing a politics of cinema. However, this statement should perhaps be tempered as I also recognize the inevitability that this methodological approach to the study of cinema will reflect my own personal history within this larger discourse. As such, I have tried not to succumb to the 'illusion of bringing the pure gaze of some absolute spectator to bear on the world' (Lecourt 2001: 134). I have attempted to follow Hayden White's advice:

> [W]hen it is a matter of speaking about human consciousness, we have no absolute theory to guide us; everything is under contention. It therefore becomes a matter of choice as to which model we should use to mark out, and constitute entries into, the problem of consciousness in general. Such choices should be self-conscious rather than unconscious ones, and they should be made with a full understanding of the kind of human nature to the constitution of which they will contribute if they are taken as valid. (White 1985: 22–23)

## CHAPTER 1

# Cinema, Modernity and the Shōchiku Tokyo Studios

One of the propagandists of the [Meiji] enlightenment, in *A Country Dialogue on Civilization*, tells a sceptical peasant, 'In human society (*ningen nakama*) all men, from prince and minister at the top to peasant and merchant at the bottom, are human beings of equal worth. A prince, for all he is a prince, is not by virtue of his position born with three eyes; a commoner does not have one ear less than other people just because he is a commoner. Stripped to the skin, what is the difference between the feudal baron's daughter and the kitchen maid, except that one is white-skinned and the other tanned in the sun? The only distinction of worth among human beings is between those who, having learning and ability, are useful to society, and those who are not'. (Quoted in Dore 1963: 195)

If one starts out from Baudelaire's notion of modernity as the fleeting, the transitory and the arbitrary, then there can be no fixed, secure object of study in the accepted sense. The object of study is thus determined not merely by a particular mode of viewing modern life but by the new mode of experiencing a new social reality itself. (Frisby 1985: 6)

Modern environments and experiences cut across all boundaries of geography and ethnicity, of class and nationality, of religion and ideology: in this sense, modernity can be said to unite all mankind. But it is a paradoxical unity, a unity of disunity: it pours us all into a maelstrom of perpetual disintegration and renewal, of struggle and contradiction, of ambiguity and anguish. To be modern is to be part of a universe in which, as Marx said, 'all that is solid melts into air'." (Berman 1993: 15)

In Western academic discourse the historical periodization of 'modernity' is much debated.[1] However, in general terms, 'modernism' has been linked to the new modes of perception and experience associated with the historical development of industrial capitalism. As such, it should be understood not only as an historical period, but also and perhaps more important for this study, as 'a quality of social experience' (Osborne 1992).[2] Stephen Vlastos contends that in 'Japan the beginnings of industrial capitalism can be dated to the last decade of the nineteenth century, [and] consumer capitalism to the decade following World War I' (Vlastos 1998:9). Therefore, in the Japanese con-

text, the development of modernism as a 'structure of feeling' evident in
the early 1900s is clearly linked to the conscious intervention of the ruling
elite who, following the lead of the instigators of the Meiji Restoration of
1868, advocated a policy of rapid state-sponsored industrialization as a
means of retaining national autonomy. In this sense 'modernism' as a cultural concept, derived from the vision of the Western Enlightenment philosophers, accompanied the importation and adaptation of the technology
that underpinned the development of industrial capitalism. Despite the fact
that the Meiji oligarchs attempted to resist this trend through a policy of
'Eastern ethics and Western science/technology', at the ideological level,
'modernism' became linked to a qualitative transformation in that claims
of progress offered the prospect of improvement upon the past. Progress,
in the social context, was defined in terms of the projection of western
societies' present onto Japan's potential future, and in terms of the individual, onto concepts such as 'the cult of success' (*risshin shusse shugi*). In
Tokugawa Neo-Confucianist terms, this conception of social progress
through individual success was antithetical to the established world order,
which posited the 'ideal' in some past ancient age.

As became evident, the slogan 'Eastern ethics and Western science/
technology' was fundamentally flawed. As I argue in my introductory
chapter, science and technology are not neutral; they carry with them the
aspirations, assumptions and ideologies of the societies that invented, produced and accepted them. Thus cinema, itself a new technology, intervened and, as will become evident, was a fundamental medium in helping
to fill the gap between the adoption of 'Western sciences and technologies'
and the adaptation of the implicit ideological structures inherent in the
technologies themselves to the Japanese situation. This occurred on several levels: at its most basic, popular films of the late 1920s and early
1930s showcased new technology (*He and Life/Kare to jinsei* [1929], *The
Big City:Labour/Daitokai: Rōdōhen* [1929] and *Marching On* aka *The
Army Advances/ Shingun* [1930])[3]; and on more complex levels, through
the development of various narrative themes, character types, genres and
variations on the stylistic uses of film technology; and through the structure and personnel relations within the industry itself. As the Shōchiku
example illustrates, Kido Shiro (1894–1977) who became head of the
Tokyo Kamata Studios in 1924, broke with the rigid hierarchical systems
that governed the traditional theatrical arts by encouraging an open environment where young filmmakers could freely discuss and criticize the
works of other directors. In this environment Sato Tadao argues that merit

was recognized and rewarded. 'In front of Kido assistant directors such as Saitō Torajirō (1905–1982) and Ozu Yasujirō (1903–1963) could talk freely about veteran directors' productions such as those of Ōkubo Tadamoto (1894–*), saying how they would have filmed it etc. In this way their genius was recognized and they were quickly promoted to full director status. Out of this freedom of expression new plans and techniques emerged . . .' (Satō 1995 vol. i: 216). It was in this atmosphere of debate and openness that the foundations of the Shōchiku house style was laid.

At the level of the individual, progress increasingly became linked to individual endeavour and achievement[4] as premodern social institutions came into conflict with the existential realities of a growing urban industrial society. The effects of this transformation were felt most keenly in the changing nature of the family, which had to be propped up legally by the Civil Code of 1890. In the Tokugawa period (1600–1868), the family had been the principal unit of production and had been underpinned by the Confucian precept of primogeniture. Under this system the family was understood not in terms of the individual, but as an economic institution, the maintenance and continuance of which was the responsibility of each individual member. Property rights were invested in the family and not in individuals. The family head, despite his apparently powerful position, was only invested with a transitory authority, which could be passed to his eldest son once he came of age. As R. P. Dore points out, the institutional nature of the family is clearly evident in much of the vocabulary used to articulate concepts central to family concerns. 'The frequent use of words like *kagyoo, kasan, kafuu* [family enterprize, family property, family customs] and so on, and the importance attached to the ancestors, not only serves to strengthen a sense of the continuity of the family group. It also serves to emphasize the importance of the group over that of the individual. Neither occupation, property, house tradition nor ancestors belong to the individual, but to the family as a whole' (Dore 1963: 99–100).

With the advent of industrialization, in many instances, the family no longer functioned as a self-sufficient sphere of production, weakening bonds between parents and children, fathers and sons. As Satō comments, increasingly in the modern age 'young people were trained (*kitaeru*) not so much by their fathers but rather by teachers in cram schools (*juku*) and temple primary schools (*terakoya*), by their bosses at work, by their seniors in dormitories and in the army' (Satō 2000: 238). Accompanying the growth in bureaucratic institutions, factories and commercial enterprises, education became the primary means of social advancement. Ability rather than seniority or age became an increasingly important criterion in modern Japan. 'The ideal of [sons] following in father's footsteps [was] replaced by the ideal of doing better than father' (Dore 1963: 113). Thus economic trends simultaneously undermined the group structure of the family while encouraging a process of individuation. At its most basic level, wages are paid to individuals and not the family unit. This accompanying shift from *gemeinschaft* to *gesellschaft* relations became linked in popular consciousness to a country/city binary opposition, which became a central discourse played out in film narratives lingering on into the postwar period of disruption and regeneration.

The linguistic distinction made in Japanese between the Chinese ideogram (*kanji*) derived concept for 'modernism' associated with the term *kindaishugi* and the *katakana* neologism *modanizumu* illustrates a clear division of meaning in terms of the intellectual/academic and a more general 'structure of feeling' that accompanied the social changes brought about by Japan's embrace of industrial capitalism. The film historian Iwamoto Kenji argues that in the 1920s and 1930s these meanings became fixed and *kindaishugi* came to be associated with European rationalism (*gōrishugi*) derived from political philosophy and the sciences, while the term *modanizumu* carried a far lighter sense of frivolity, cheerfulness and the new. It was this latter meaning that was conveyed through spectacle and became a central theme of films produced by Shōchiku in their Tokyo Studios in the second half of the 1920s and in the 1930s. Kobayashi Kyūzo argues that the Kantō Earthquake of 1923 marked a crucial cut-off point in Japanese popular consciousness marking this transition. 'As a result of the Kantō Earthquake there was a change in the structure of society and popular consciousness. The films produced under Nomura Hōtei [head of the Shōchiku Kamata Studios in Tokyo in the early 1920s] were mainly *shinpa*-derived melodramas. However, gradually salarymen had become central to life in the cities. The earthquake speeded up this trend. Furthermore, the psychological impact of the earthquake had effected a subtle change in audience preferences. Rather than gloom, they wanted brightness' (Kobayashi 1999: 21). Kido Shirō, at the time of his appointment as head of the Shōchiku Kamata Studios in 1924, is reported as saying: '[I]t is uninteresting to make films for audiences who happily come along to the cinema clutching their hankies to watch tragedies. Entertainment must be bright and healthy, while laughing at society's ironies and contradictions, we can study life (quoted in Suzuki 1984: 234 and Kobayashi 1999: 21). As the 1930s progressed, this articulation of 'modernism' took on the added connotation of 'Americanism', a theme increasingly resisted by censors as the country moved closer to war and the cinema came under government scrutiny with the introduction of the film laws of the 1930s.

The 1930s were also characterized by a contradictory dystopic vision of the consequences of modernity and the establishment of conventions that have come to be labelled 'social realist'. In Japan, it is possible to trace the development of realist conventions to the late 1920s and the influences of the 'proletarian film movement' as well as *matatabimono* (wanderer) films such as *The Serpent* (*Orochi*) (1925). These conventions were formalized in mainstream cinema in the 1930s with the development of the Shōchiku Studio's in-house style, which I shall define as 'behaviouralist'. Films directed by Ozu Yasujirō are some of the most representative extant examples of this quasi-documentary style of verisimilitude that depicted the experiential realities of ordinary people's lives in recession-hit Japan of the 1930s. 'Social realism' as a set of narrational conventions can also be found in the works of Uchida Tomu (1898–1970), Tasaka Tomotaka (1902–1974), Mizoguchi Kenji (1898–1956) and Yamamoto Kajirō (1902–1974).

In historical terms, the development within Japan of a concept of modernism was concomitant with the importation of cinema; the first equipment, the Thomas Edison Kinetoscope, arriving in Japan in 1896 less than thirty years after the Meiji Restoration. In this chapter, I shall explore the proposition that cinema as a technological product came to be seen as one of the new technologies that embodied modernity (along with the introduction of the telegraph, and new and improved modes of transport: cars, trains and planes, etc.). Also, I examine the assertion that cinema was instrumental in defining, through representations of modernity, a social aesthetic of what it was to be modern. I shall also argue that the United States, through Hollywood, undoubtedly had a paradigmatic function within this discourse. In short, this chapter is structured around two overriding concerns related to content and form in relation to the studio system. First, as stated above, an analysis of dominant thematic trends and their relationship to society and, second, a discussion of certain stylistic conventions that came to form extrinsic norms that continued to dominate studio genre films well into the postwar period. However, before launching into a discussion of these themes, it is useful to contextualize them within a short outline of the development of the film industry in the first half of the twentieth century.

**Backgrounds**

*[handwritten annotations: conflict, studio profit vs artistic control]*

Popular films, as commercial products, are produced in a studio system designed to maximize efficiency in order to produce profits. As a result, a tension is evident between economic practices, that is, product standardization (the development of popular genres and the star system) and the craft-based traditions of individual filmmakers who seek a degree of artistic control and autonomy over the films and images they produce. Broadly speaking, the period of time between the introduction of film into Japan and the end of the occupation in 1952 can be divided into three overlapping phases that reflect the domination of particular interests between competing groups within the industry.

The first phase can be linked to the *benshi* and to the emergence of a star system. In this early period of film production, dominated in the main by Nikkatsu (Nihon Katsudō Shashin) Studios founded in 1912, a star system emerged which, in terms of public popularity, both challenged and coexisted with the *benshi* tradition. Under this system stars increasingly gained control over their image and how it was projected onto the screen. As a result, a tension is evident between those who were concerned with the economic interests of the studios and the stars who increasingly sought autonomy over their image and, through their popularity, gained an understanding of their financial worth. This led to a trend in the mid-1920s for the major *jidaigeki* (period drama) stars to form their own production companies (Bandō Tsumasaburō [1901–1953] in 1925, Kataoka Chiezō [1903–1983] in 1926, Ichikawa Utaemon [1907–1999] in 1927 and Arashi Kanjūrō [1903–1980] in 1928). The independent star system peaked between 1925 and 1935.

The second phase can be dated from the late 1910s and the emergence of an 'intellectual' approach to filmmaking symbolized by the 'pure film movement' (*jun'eiga undō*) that manifested in the director-centred system of the Shōchiku Studios founded in 1920 and instituted by Kido Shirō in the mid-1920s. This system represented both a culmination of the efforts of young innovative filmmakers to establish cinema as an artistic medium in its own right, and from a commercial point of view, an attempt to curb stars who were seen as being too powerful and therefore too expensive.[5] Under this system directors were to replace stars as the main signature of a film.[6]

The final phase, the economic rationalization of the industry along Western contractual lines and the adoption of the Hollywood 'continuity system' (albeit in modified form), corresponded to a period of heretofore unprecedented growth in the second half of the 1930s. 'In 1935, there were 1,586 movie theatres nationwide, with a total of 185 million admissions annually. By 1940, 2,363 theatres were selling 400 million tickets' (quoted in High 2003:149). The need for large capital investment in the newly developing technology of sound further encouraged trends towards the establishment of vertical integrated systems in an attempt to control not only production but also distribution. This process became institutionalized across the industry in the late 1930s. The establishment of the Tōhō Film Company in 1937 catalyzed this process of change during this period. The dictates of the military-centred governments further reinforced this process in the early 1940s, as did the authorities attached to the Supreme Command for the Allied Powers (SCAP) in the immediate postwar period.

The development of the studio system in the early 1900s can only be grasped from within the wider context of social changes occurring in Japan at the turn of century. At the economic level, the race to industrialize and become a world power altered traditional patterns of rural and merchant household relations as people flocked to the expanding urban centres in search of employment. The mass entertainment industries that developed and prospered with urbanization and the democratization of leisure in and around the former pleasure quarters of the large urban areas of Tokyo and Osaka were, until the 1920s, largely controlled by yakuza (Japanese mafia) organizations under the patriarchal *oyabun/kobun* system (a quasi-familial father/son relationship) of sub-contracting. This holdover from premodern society reflected the inherent time lag between the official adoption of 'modern' capitalist economic structures and their accommodation to existing social structures. Satō Tadao (1995 vol. i: 36) places the time frame of Japan's actual transition to modern capitalist modes of labour relations to the early 1900s, in particular around the time of the Manchurian Incident (September 1931–January 1933) and the beginnings of the Sino-Japanese War (1937–1945). War encouraged the rationalization of production as companies expanded to meet the requirements of the armed forces.

In the entertainment world, strong class distinctions existed both between actors and producers in the 'legitimate' theatres of the major cities and those who worked in touring companies performing at festivals, shrines and in the smaller theatres of the urban amusement districts. The former performed on the *hinoki* (cypress) stage while the latter performed on the 'dirt' ground. Talent was not always the most important criterion within a Confucian tradition that stressed lineage. When cinema first arrived in Japan, it was absorbed into the vaudeville world (*yose*) of the *mis-emono* (spectacle) attraction show, coming directly under the control of the yakuza. Makino Masahiro (1908–1993) in his autobiography recalls his father, Makino Shōzō's (1878–1929) relationship with a Kyoto yakuza group. Makino Shōzō (see figure 1), often referred to as one of the 'the fathers of Japanese cinema',[7] was related through his mother to a prominent yakuza who operated in an area of Kyoto (Makino 1977: 16). It was through the support of his organization, the Senbon-*gumi*, that Makino senior, the manager of the Senbonza theatre, was able to begin producing films in 1907 (Makino 1977: 13). The Senbonza theatre had originally been home to a small touring kabuki troupe; it was also used by the Yokota Shōkai film importation company to screen foreign films. Yokota Einosuke (1872–1943), who was later to head the Nikkatsu Studios, supplied the equipment and raw film stock, all of which had to be imported. In 1909 Onoe Matsunosuke (1875–1926),[8] later to become Japan's first screen idol, joined the cast for these early productions, thereby expanding the operations of Yokota Shōkai to include production.

In part due to the yakuza connection, the newly emerging mass entertainment industries were held in low esteem, and film companies in this early period held little attraction for graduates from the main universities. Therefore, they drew most of their staff from the often talented members of touring kabuki and *shinpa* (new school) theatre troupes, all of whom were excluded from the established theatre companies. For example, the director Kinugasa Teinosuke (1896–1982) began his professional career as an *onnagata* (an actor specializing in female roles) with a *shinpa* company; the director and screenwriter Itami Mansaku (1900–1946) was only educated to middle-school level; and the director Inagaki Hiroshi (1905–1980) came from a family of *shinpa* actors and was himself a child actor. Cinema provided a new and socially liberating medium that broke with the class-riddled system of the traditional theatres. Later in the mid-1930s, following anti-socialist crackdowns, the cinema industry also became a bastion for left-wing graduates who were, due to their political beliefs, unable to find employment in mainstream companies. In this early period, it was this mix of talented theatrical people relegated to the margins of the mass entertainment venues and left-leaning intellectuals that gave the early Japanese film industry a special dynamic.

## Shōchiku and the Movement for Reform

From the first the Shōchiku Kinema Company, a subsidiary of the Shōchiku Theatre Company, was committed to the experimentation and adaptation of Western cinematic techniques and technologies to the Japanese domestic market. Founded in 1920 by Shirai Matsujirō after his trip to Europe and the United States of America, which included a visit to Hollywood, Shōchiku Kinema Company, with the solid financial backing of the theatre company, launched itself into the mainstream domestic cinema market. By the 1930s they had created a style of filmmaking that gave the viewing public a glimpse at a visually defined concept of modernism, later to be equated with 'Americanism', that had been adapted to meet the demands of the rapidly changing society.

Apart from establishing an actors' school headed by one of the leaders of the *shingeki* (new drama) theatre movement Osanai Kaoru (1881–1928), the company sent a former journalist to Hollywood to study filmmaking techniques, to purchase the latest equipment and to hire staff. Through the recommendations of Cecil B. DeMille (1881–1959), he hired the cameraman Henry Kotani. Henry Kotani, born in 1892 in Hiroshima, had migrated with his parents to Hawaii when he was nine years old. He began his film career as an actor during Hollywood's early 'oriental' boom period, appearing in Thomas H. Ince's (1882–1924) productions. Upon his return to Japan in 1920, Kotani was appointed head of the technical department of the Shōchiku Kamata Studios (in the process of being built at that time). He was appointed on a two-year contract at the exorbitant salary of 1,500 yen per month. His knowledge and experience of filmmaking techniques surpassed that of his Japanese colleagues and he soon became a central figure in the filmmaking process, being responsible for the Kamata Studios' first production *Women of the Island* aka *Island Women* (*Shima no onna*) (1920). The following year Kotani became involved in all aspects of filmmaking, from screen writing to direction. Satō (1995 vol. i: 198) argues that Kotani's greatest contribution to Japanese filmmaking practices was to teach the Shōchiku camera crews the art of artificial lighting, in particular, the use of reflectors.

In his reminiscences of this period Shirai Shigeru (1899–1984), a cameraman employed at Shōchiku in the 1920s, states that it was around this time that the studio began the transition from a star-centred system to a directorial system (Iwamoto and Saiki 1988:56). This transition reached its culmination with the appointment of Kido Shiro as head of the studios in 1924. Kido (see figure 2), a star baseball player, had graduated from the Tokyo Imperial (Teikoku) University in English law in 1919 and had worked in the world of finance and trading before joining Shōchiku in 1922. Under his leadership, Shōchiku has been attributed with developing a distinctive style known first as the Kamata-*chō* and later as the Ōfuna-*chō*.

At the time of his appointment, Kido and the director Ushihara Kyo-hiko (1897–1985), first employed as a cameraman in 1920 and going on to become a leading director, were the only two university graduates employed by Shōchiku. They were to form a nucleus of what would become an elite group of filmmakers committed to the development of the film industry along Western, in particular Hollywood, lines. Both Kido and Ushihara had studied English and had a strong interest in American literature. Satō (1995 vol. i: 216) argues that this fact had great consequences for the development of a style of filmmaking distinct from the majority of Japanese filmmakers of the time who had very little formal education, having come to cinema from the kabuki and *shinpa* traditions. Ushihara states in an interview based on his experiences at Shōchiku in the early 1920s that he and other filmmakers including Ozu Yasujirō, an assistant director at this time, formed a study group to analyse foreign films.

> At that time, I participated in a study group that would analyse outstanding foreign films being screened in and around Tokyo. We would arrange it with the people at the cinema in advance and at night after the public screening at about nine we would go to the cinema. In the projection room, while looking at the film, we transcribed the continuity. When a ship leaves port people throw streamers and that is what we used to write on. While using a pocket torch to throw light on the negative, we filled in the whole film—this shot is x number of feet with x number of scenes etc. At the top and bottom of each section we recorded camera movements, pans etc. It would take about three nights working through half the night. (quoted in Iwamoto and Saiki 1988: 118–119)

The films studied were not only those produced in Hollywood but also European productions. In the same interview Ushihara mentions Abel Gance (1898–1981), one of the foremost directors of the French silent cinema.

In 1930, to commemorate the tenth anniversary of the founding of the Shōchiku Studios, *Marching On (Shingun)*, directed by Ushihara, opened at the Asakusa Denkikan. *Marching On,* starring the Far Eastern Olympic (1923) swimmer turned actor Suzuki Denmei (1900–1985) and Tanaka Kinuyo (1909–1977), took a record ten thousand yen at the box office on its first day (Kobayashi 1999:60). A year later Japan's first 'talkie', *The Neighbour's Wife and Mine* aka *The Lady Next Door and My Wife (Madamu to nyōbō)*, also starring Tanaka Kinuyo as the wife and Date Satoko (1910–1972) as the 'madam', was released by Shōchiku to great public acclaim. In both films abstract discourses of modernity are given a corpo-reality through the bodies of the characters. In this respect, both films are exemplary of cinema's role in early 1930s Japan, as both a metaphor and a force for change: in metaphorical terms, through the successful inclusion of sophisticated cinematic techniques and new technological develop-ments, aerial shots, superimposition and subjective camera work in the case of *Marching On*, and the inclusion of sound in the case of *The Neigh-bour's Wife and Mine*; and as a force for change, through the narrative, in the depiction of the successful 'goal-orientated hero' in the case of *March-ing On*, and in the example of *The Neighbour's Wife and Mine*, a challenge to traditional femininity through the depiction of a new conception of womanhood, the *modan gāru* (modern girl). In both films, through the pro-tagonists and by extension the star personas of Suzuki Denmei and Tanaka Kinuyo (the Charles Farrell and Janet Gaynor of Japan), narrativized dis-courses, centring on social issues linked to modernity, were set in place that would dominate Japanese cinema until at least the end of the Pacific War in August 1945. In short, a 'structured feeling' indicative of moder-nity pervades these films. Therefore, in the following sections I shall at-tempt to analyse how modernism as a concept was defined in early-1930s Japan through its cinema.

## The 'Goal-Orientated Hero' and the 'Cult of Success'

The silent film *Marching On* challenged traditional class and hierarchical social structures established in Confucian-based premodern Japanese soci-ety through the depiction of the 'goal-orientated hero'. By linking the country boy hero's social advancement to the mastery of technology and not to status or birth, the narrative makes the clear break between socially determining family occupations and sons' futures. The hero's advance-ment is linked not only to his technical competence but also, as the title suggests, to the opportunities associated with the military and heroism in war. The literal translation of the title *Marching On (Shingun)* is Advanc-ing Army. Within this discourse, physical action is a prerequisite to the mastery of technology, and the athlete turned actor, Suzuki Denmei, be-came the embodiment of this style. He was one of the first star personas to bridge the gap between the weak romantic hero of the *shinpa*-derived melodramas and the action hero of the period genres (*jidaigeki/chanbara*). In cinematic terms, his athletic body is the site of action represented through metaphors of speed and movement and, through the inclusion of the romantic element, a sexual imperative (see figure 3).

The plotline is simple: a country boy, Kōichi (Suzuki Denmei), dreams of becoming a pilot. After feeling he has been slighted by a neighbouring wealthy landowner's daughter (Tanaka Kinuyo), he pleads with his father to allow him to go to Tokyo to study to become a pilot. The film is structured in three clear stages of advancement. First, the country boy at home on the farm playing with model aeroplanes, saving the local landowner's daughter from a bolting horse, and falling in love with her, and then feeling inferior when he compares himself to her brother and his military friends. This prompts his subsequent determination to go to Tokyo and prove himself. His father, understanding this slight to his son's manhood, agrees saying, 'Well, then off you go to Tokyo and study. You'll show them in the big house on the hill'. After which he goes to Tokyo and, through hard work, achieves his goal of becoming a pilot. This middle segment culminates in his triumphal return to the home village after having mastered the art of flying. He proudly returns performing aerobatics over his home village. This scene clearly illustrates the sensual imperative of the thrill of flying. The parallel editing cuts between reaction shots of the village crowd and of his father (providing a comic line as he upbraids his son for performing such dangerous feats), with shots of Tanaka Kinuyo running to try to see Kōichi as he lands. In the final long segment, Kōichi goes off to war and heroically saves his copilot after they are shot down behind enemy lines. He also saves his rival for the hand of Tanaka Kinuyo, a friend of her brother's, by making an incredible escape on various forms of transport: gun tractor, motorbike and horse. Thus through his competence, more specifically his mastery of technology, and heroism, he wins the hand of the girl he loves, his rival conveniently dying in a Red Cross hospital.

In the narrative of *Marching On*, there are two very clearly related discourses, which are linked to the Meiji ideal of equality, set out in the epigraph at the beginning of this chapter: the idea that Confucian class divisions can now be breached, and that lowly birth is not an obstacle to advancement. The old father, purportedly a poor farmer, has no compunction about taking on the chauffeur from the big house when he runs over his chicken, nor does he think it unreasonable that his son should fall in love with the daughter of a wealthy landowner. Equally, Kobayashi, a friend of Tanaka Kinuyo's brother, encourages Kōichi to go to Tokyo and learn to fly despite Kōichi's protestations that he is a 'humble farmer' (*mizunomi hyakushō*).

> **Kōichi**: I am from a poor farming family, I don't have the right (*shikaku*) to become a pilot.
> **Kobayashi**: What are you saying? It doesn't mean that you can't become a pilot just because you are the son of a farmer.

Modern Japan is meritocratic and education, in particular the mastery of technology, is the way for young men from farming/peasant backgrounds to improve their lot. Equally, the play on Kōichi's name (clearly visible to audiences in the intertitles), the *kō* of filial piety and the *ichi* indicating that he is a first son, challenges the contradictory expectation that filial sons should stay at home and take over the property, looking after their parents in old age. In traditional discourses, secondary sons left home and entered society establishing new households or marrying into families with no sons. As Stephen Vlastos's analysis of farming magazines of this period indicates, concern over 'out-migration of village youths' was one of the major social topics of concern in rural Japan at this time. He explains,

> the prosperity and luxury of cities represented more than wealth gained by an economic exploitation of the countryside. Cities stole away village youths by proffering a more exciting and easier way of life. An anonymous poem, 'Guarding the Village,' in the inaugural issue of *Nōson kenkyū*, for example, expressed the profound feeling of loss experienced by a family whose only son fled the ancestral home for 'the bright lights of the city'. (Vlastos 1998: 89–90)

*Marching On*, with its utopian view of the successful 'goal-orientated hero', clearly contributed to this discourse of the attractions of the city. A sharp contrast is drawn between the parochialism of the country compared to the sophistication of the city through, among other things, Kōichi's body. His triumphal return to his village after completing his pilot training is contrasted, through his physical appearance, with his departure. When he leaves the village, sitting on the deck of a paddle steamer, he is clad in an ill-fitting suit and clutching an old carpetbag; he returns as a confident and sophisticated young man wearing jodhpurs and a flying jacket with a wristwatch and slicked-back hair. His triumph over the people in the 'big house on the hill' is complete as Tanaka Kinuyo runs falteringly in her

kimono to see him, only to be spurned. A clear opposition between city
and country is structured into the narrative through the body of Kōichi.

## Ozu Yasujirō and the Politics of Cinema: the James Maki Collaborations

The city, and Tokyo in particular, as site of 'modernity' plays a crucial
role in films of this period as the titles of many films attests—Ozu Yasujirō's *Tokyo Chorus* aka *Chorus of Tokyo* (*Tōkyō no kōrasu* aka *Le Chorus
de Tokyo*) (1931), *Women of Tokyo* (*Tōkyō no onna*) (1933),[9] and Mizoguchi Kenji's *Osaka Elegy* (*Naniwa erejii*) (1936) and *Sisters of Gion*
(*Gion no kyōdai*) (1936). Satō Tadao comments on the significance of
Tokyo in 1930, just seven years after the Kantō Earthquake: '[T]he re-
building of Tokyo meant that the city changed from a city of wooden
buildings destroyed in the earthquake to a city of modern buildings, mo-
torized public transport, and the appearance of cars. *Izakaya* [small intimate bars] became cafes, *enka* [popular sentimental songs] singers were
replaced by records, and small theatres became cinemas. One should consider these changes in popular entertainment as the onset of modernization
(*kindaika*) and at the same time Americanism (*amerikanizumu*)'. (Satō
2000:220) Thus by the 1930s Tokyo had become the physical embodiment
of a modern consciousness.

Within the story line of *Marching On*, Tokyo is inflected with a positive image of the land of opportunities. However, in other films of the
1930s it is presented as a dystopic space in which characters find themselves lost simultaneously in scenes of family disunity and emergent contractual social relations. In many of the films directed by Ozu Yasujirō
during this period, Tokyo becomes the *mise-en-scène* of modernity in all
its negative aspects. These films, also produced by the Shōchiku Studios,
were billed under the pen name of James Maki for the original stories,
but were in fact the result of a collaboration between Ozu Yasujirō, Kus-
hima Akira and Ikeda Tadao. They included *I Was Born But . . .* (*Umarete
wa mitakeredo*) (1932), *Dragnet Girl* (*Hijōsen no onna*) (1933), *Passing
Fancy* (*Dekigokoro*) 1933, *The Story of Floating Weeds* (*Ukikusa monogatari*) (1934) and *The Only Son* (*Hitori musuko*) (1936) among others.[10]
Satō (2000) states that the films produced under this pen name were intended to represent a new sophisticated 'modern' style of filmmaking.

However, as will become clear from the analysis below, these films came to be associated with a 'social realist' questioning of 1930s Japanese society.

One of the defining characteristics of these films is the *mise-en-scène,* which locates the action in the urban wasteland of suburban development sites (*I Was Born But . . .* ) where garbage treatment plants and gas storage tanks loom large (*The Only Son*). *The Story of Floating Weeds* is the only film of this group to be set in a rural location. When, in the first sound film to be directed by Ozu, *The Only Son,* the hero Ryōsuke's mother comes to visit him in Tokyo, we are given a shot of Tokyo Station as the train pulls in and then low-angle shots of tall buildings from the car's front mudguard as it takes them over the bridge and out of the city into the periphery of the suburbs. Hashimoto Osamu explains the significance of the location of Tokyo Station as the place where the 'spatial axis of the centre-periphery was reinterpreted in the simple temporal antimony of modern and pre-modern.

> As the only 'terminal station,' Tokyo Station connected every locale to the center; at the same time, the Imperial Palace presided as the sole center of Japan, surrounded by the modern city and counterpoised to Tokyo Station. When people from the countryside arrived at Tokyo Station, they saw in front of them the Imperial Palace, 'the true Japan,' transcending modern Japan and integrating the whole. This was the point where all time and space in Japan was concentrated. (Hashimoto 1989: 141)

After taking his mother on a sightseeing trip, Ryōsuke (Himori Shin'i-chi 1907–1959) recounts to his wife the famous amusement districts and sights they visited (Asakusa's Kaminari Gate and Ueno Park), but what is depicted in the *mise-en-scène* is an urban wasteland of municipal rubbish incinerators. The structured absence of scenes of the bright amusement districts of Tokyo emphasizes the reality of the urban peripheries where the majority of people lived their lives. Even in the postwar film *Tokyo Story,* directed by Ozu, when their daughter-in-law, Noriko (Hara Setsuko 1920–), takes the old parents on a tour of Tokyo, we are given shots of the sprawl of the city from the Tokyo Tower; again it is the peripheries where ordinary people live that is emphasized. Within these films the portrayal of depressing urban landscapes is political in that it sets up a counterimage to the idealized, but not depicted, image of the *furusato,* the rural country home.[11]

In these 'social realist' films, location and absence assume diegetic significance beyond that of mere settings. The inclusion of apparently incidental location shots of washing lines, smoking chimneys and gas tanks are crucial in establishing location as 'place' in the narrative. As the causal function of these shots to the progression of the narrative is limited, the spectator must focus on their rhetorical implications. Apparently insignificant actions provide the pretext for a visual display of place. In *The Only Son* when Ryōsuke asks his mother if she is disappointed in him, they are sitting in an open space with the municipal garbage incinerators smoking behind them; this location underlines the dialogue based on Ryōsuke's inability to succeed in Tokyo. The urban wasteland of Tokyo's conurbation impinges on the lives of the characters. In contrast in *Marching On*, location functions as setting. In the final segment of the film this latter location shifts to a battlefield setting. We are not given any indication in the intertitles or images of which war, or where, or against whom the Japanese army is fighting. All that matters is that it is a war setting. In this setting the 'goal-orientated hero', Kōichi, is given the opportunity to display his heroism.

In films directed by Ozu in this period, industrial capitalism is linked to the fissures opening up in the family through recurring motifs. In *The Only Son* the expansion of the rural silk factory and the development of the looms becomes a narrative device indicating the passage of time (the narrative spans the thirteen-year period from 1923 to 1936, the year the film was made). The sophisticated machines in the second half of the film are contrasted with those seen in the first half. Kōichi's mother's career in the silk factory is similarly documented, as in the first half of the film she works the looms. However, by the second half of the film, younger women are working the new looms and Kōichi's mother is seen scrubbing floors. Her financial decline is linked to this factory where she is forced to work. During the time span covered in the film and unbeknownst to Ryōsuke, his mother sells the family house and land in order to pay for his education in Tokyo. The final sequence when she returns to the factory is paralleled with the scene of Ryōsuke and his wife as they find the note and the money she has left for them. Within the narrative of the film Ryōsuke has broken all the principles that were seen to have underpinned the Japanese family until the advent of industrial capitalism. He leaves the family home, which as a first son he was expected to take over; his ambition to make something of himself drains the family of its capital and property; he marries without even discussing his intentions with his mother (she arrives in Tokyo to find he has a wife and child); and finally, it is obvious that he will not be able to provide for his mother in her old age. However, despite his transgressions, the film does not place the blame for the disunity of the family on Ryōsuke. Instead, blame is placed on the environment, more specifically, on Tokyo and all it stands for. Within the narrative, Ryōsuke's experiences are foreshadowed through the parallel plot line of his teacher Ōkubo (Ryū Chishū 1904–1993), who also leaves the village to continue his studies in Tokyo, only to end up running a pork-cutlet restaurant. As Ryōsuke attempts to explain to his mother when she tackles him on this issue,

> **Ryōsuke**: From your perspective I probably appear a good-for-nothing, but Mr Ōkubo when he came to Tokyo, he had big plans and look at him running a pork-cutlet restaurant. Mother, there are lots of people in Tokyo, there is nothing one can do.
> **Mother**: Mr Ōkubo is Mr Ōkubo.
> **Ryōsuke**: No, it is the same for me. There is nothing one can do. This is just Tokyo.

The point that comes out of the film is a belief and re-affirmation in the fundamental goodness of simple people. The mother accepts the fact that Ryōsuke has perhaps not been sufficiently ambitious to get ahead in the highly competitive environment of Tokyo. However, he redeems himself in her eyes when she sees him give some money to a poor neighbour whose son had been kicked by a horse and has to spend several days in hospital. She comes to value his generosity in the face of his own hardship. Equally, when she returns to the silk factory after her visit to Tokyo, she does not admit her disappointment but accepts the fate that circumstances have decreed for her, foreshadowing the disappointment of the aging parents in the postwar film *Tokyo Story*. Whereas the parents in *Tokyo Story* are financially secure in the early days of Japan's postwar economic revival, Ryōsuke's mother faces an insecure future dependent on the silk factory in the recession-hit days of the post-Wall Street crash (1929). In this sense Ozu, as a 'realist' filmmaker, rises above the potential for melodramatic effect and places the blame for the predicaments in which his characters find themselves onto the socioeconomic circumstances of their *mise-en-scène*.

On another level, films directed by Ozu and scripted by the James Maki collaboration extend the theme of the breakdown in social relations onto questions of masculinity and patriarchal authority. The black comedy

*I Was Born But . . .* links boyhood ideals and ambition to the perceived humiliation of salarymen in 1930s Japan; and within a working class setting, patriarchal authority is questioned in *Passing Fancy* (1933) and its sequel *The Story of Floating Weeds* (1934), while the 1932 film *Where Are the Dreams of Our Youth?* (*Seishun no yume ima izuko*) explores the breakdown of relations between male friends.

The narrative of *I Was Born But . . .* is centred on the 'rite of passage' of two young sons of a salaryman (Saitō Tatsuo 1902–1968) who have recently moved to the suburbs of Tokyo. The two brothers must establish themselves within the local boys' gang. The film therefore deals with complex questions of masculinity and male social organization. This is compounded as the two brothers' bid to define masculine power is paralleled through the secondary plot of their father's role as a subservient salaryman. The power game the boys play, whereby the weaker boys lie down when a signal is given and do not rise until another signal is given, is a childish play version of the power relationship between Iwasaki (Sakamoto Takeshi 1899–1974), the company director, and their father. Their father, mirroring the actions of the subservient boys, has to play the fool in Iwasaki's home movies. However, the criteria that determine the power positions in the boys' gang and the father's company are different. In the case of the boys' gang, it is based largely on the ability of the two brothers to manipulate the politics of the group in their favour. One of the brothers, aware that it is his father's pay-day, tips off the sake merchant's boy that his mother is likely to buy some beer. The sake shop boy is then enlisted to warn off the principal bully. The bully, Kamikichi, who had relied simply on his physical strength to dominate the group, is displaced in terms of the leadership of the gang. Thus mental ability and not pure force become the criterion of domination. However, in the father's company, power is based purely in monetary terms: Salarymen are dependent on their monthly salary to survive. The film makes this point at the very basic level of food, as the two brothers protest by going on a hunger strike after a violent scene in which they challenge their father's right, as their father, to their respect.[12]

> **Ryōichi**: (the elder brother): Father, you always tell us to distinguish ourselves (*eraku nare*) but you're not distinguished. Why do you have to bow and scrape like that to Tarō's father?
> **Father**: Because Tarō's father is a company director.
> **Ryōichi**: Well, why don't you become a director?

**Father**: It is not as simple as that. I am an employee of Mr Iwasaki's company. That is, I receive a salary from Tarō's father.

**Ryōichi**: Don't get a salary then.

**Younger brother**: Yes, if that's the case, don't get a salary.

**Father**: If I didn't get a salary, you wouldn't be able to go to school and you wouldn't have anything to eat.

**Ryōichi**: Why is Tarō's father a director and you're not?

**Father**: Because Tarō's family is wealthy.

**Ryōichi**: Because they have money they are distinguished?

**Father**: In the world there are people who don't have money, but are distinguished.

**Ryōichi**: Father, which are you then?

The two brothers integrate themselves as autonomous individuals who assert their power over the other boys through merit. They also learn that the rules governing boyhood power relations will no longer apply when they reach adulthood. The film makes a powerful statement to this effect by using a series of tracking shots to connect school as a process of socialization for the future salaryman. During a scene at the school during physical training, the students are lined up in a regimental fashion and begin marching off left, as the camera tracks right, cutting to a line of salarymen sitting yawning at their desks. The camera pauses on one bored salaryman before continuing down the line and halting on a group of men including Yoshii, the father of the two boys, engaged in conversation. They are discussing Yoshii's recent move to the suburbs. Yoshii is then called into Iwasaki's office, where Iwasaki is seated at his desk fiddling with his new home movie camera. The scene then shifts back to the salarymen, who are scathing in their assessment of why Yoshii moved to the suburbs—to be near the boss.

The camera, through the use of tracking and graphic-match-on-action editing as continuity devices, clearly links the regimentation of the boys' marching with the monotony and boredom of the salarymen confined to their desks. Finally, the camera tracks left, back down the line of the salarymen before continuing, with a graphic-match, the same leftward track along the line of schoolboys sitting at their desks practising calligraphy. In time, the boys will replace school desks with the office desks of the salarymen. After stopping, as a teacher admonishes one boy, the camera tracks right back along the line of desks before cutting to the open space where the two brothers, having played truant from school, are lying in the grass attempting to practise their calligraphy. In this way the three parallel worlds of the school, the office and the brothers are linked in time and action. The brothers have for the moment escaped the monotony that will sap and thus contain their masculinity, rendering it harmless through boredom and the constraints imposed on the salaryman.

While the central theme of *I Was Born But . . .* is the stress and strain placed on the father/son relationship and changing cultural definitions of masculinity due to the changing economic foundations of the family in suburban Tokyo, the 1932 film *Where Are the Dreams of Our Youth?* portrays the breakdown of relationships between men, similarly brought about by the changing economic basis of society. The plotline of *Where Are the Dreams of Our Youth?* also utilizes comic elements to heighten the poignancy of the more serious social issues taken up in the film. Unlike *I Was Born But . . .* , which integrates the comic and the serious, *Where Are the Dreams of Our Youth?* is clearly structured into two segments. The first covers the student days of Horino Tetsuo (Egawa Ureo 1902–1970) and his three friends. The second part shifts to the world of the salaryman as Horino inherits the chairmanship of the family business upon the death of his father and his three friends come to work for him. The various incidents that make up the narrative in the first half of the film all work to establish the relationship between Horino and the other three members of the group. Through humour, the film creates a sense of the equality and intimacy that, in a traditionally hierarchical society, is only possible amongst equals or *dōkyūsei* (classmates of the same age and grade). However, even in this utopian student world, the economic realities, which will threaten the stability of the group in the second half of the film, are already evident. Saiki (Saitō Tatsuo), a young student from a disadvantaged background, does not enter into the group as fully as the others. Saiki's position on the margins of the group is evident in the first scene. As the others, part of the university cheer squad, go through their routine, Saiki strolls along with his nose in a book. When Oshige (Tanaka Kinuyo) asks why he studies so hard and does not join in with the others, Saiki explains that he and his mother live alone and therefore he has to rely on his ability (i.e., not on patronage nor wealth) in order to get a good job. The reason for his disadvantage is clearly linked to the absence of a father.

In the second half of the film, when the four friends enter the modern corporate world, the strains economic necessity places on their relationships become apparent. Horino attempts to continue their relationship as before, helping his three friends, amongst other things, to cheat in the company entrance examination. However, he gradually becomes aware of the fact that the others are treating him more and more as their boss and not as their friend. Oshige, the young girl who worked at the Blue Hawaii Bakery where they, as students, used to meet, becomes the catalyst that sparks off the crisis of the denouement. Horino had been fond of Oshige since his student days but, unbeknown to him, she had agreed to marry Saiki. Horino, finding out about the engagement by accident through Saiki's mother, is deeply hurt by the betrayal of his friends who were not honest enough to tell him of the engagement, letting him continue with his own plans. After confronting Oshige, who tells him that she had dreamt of marrying him, but realizing the difference in their social positions, had agreed to marry Saiki, he goes off to confront the three friends in a climactic scene:

> **Horino**: What did you mean when you gave your approval to my marriage to Oshige? Do you think that I am the sort of man who would enjoy stealing his friend's girl? Saiki, stop shilly-shallying about and give me a direct answer.
>
> **Shimazaki**: Look, Saiki thought he was doing you a favour. Don't you think it's wrong to attack him like this?
>
> **Horino**: There are a few things I have to say to you both, too. Do you consider yourselves my friends? You stand before me like dogs wagging their tails—is that friendship? When did I ever ask you to behave like that? When have I ever been pleased by that sort of behaviour? Where has the feeling of fellowship (*yūjō*) gone that we had as students?
>
> **Saiki**: Our families' livelihoods are dependent on you. If we offend you, our boss, we risk losing our livelihood. (Horino strikes Saiki.)
>
> **Horino**: Are you therefore the kind of fellow to just hand over his girlfriend? Idiot! (He continues hitting Saiki; the others attempt to restrain him.) I shall beat this servility out of him . . . (They release him.) This is the clenched fist of fellowship (*yūjō no tekken da*) . . . (Horino continues hitting Saiki until he sinks to the ground in tears. By this time Horino is also crying. The other two apologize and the three of them embrace. Horino, wiping the tears from his eyes, bends down and asks Saiki to forgive him.)

The bonds of fellowship thus restored, the camera cuts to a daytime shot of the roof of Horino's office building. The brightness of the open roof space is in sharp contrast to the dark nighttime *mise-en-scène* of the penultimate confrontation. In this final sequence, unison shots predominate as harmony within the group has been restored. First, there is a shot of two office girls sitting on a wall powdering their noses. This is followed by a shot of two men standing in dark suits smoking. The film concludes with a series of unison shots of the three friends as they wave at a passing train taking Saiki and Oshige on their honeymoon.

In many of the films of the 1930s directed by Ozu and scripted by the James Maki collaboration, the social system, as it had developed from the economic base of industrial capitalism, is brought into question. From a deconstructionist standpoint, this is clearly evident in the development of new narrative structures based on a portrayal of the group, increasingly the family group. These films appear revolutionary because they included new characters (the lower middle classes *shōshimin* and the working class) who are placed in new locations (the office, the suburban wastelands of Tokyo and the factory) facing new problems. Unlike films based on the 'goal-orientated hero' whose actions and desires propel the narrative forward towards an acceptable closure, the plotlines of Ozu's films are complicated in that we follow multiple parallel lines of interactive action. They offer a documentary-style 'slice-of-life' view of a segment of the life course of a group of people caught up in the maelstrom of modernity. The effects of this form of narrative structure is to distance the spectator from a purely emotional response to the characters, to see them as autonomous individuals and to examine the situations making up the plot analytically. This is reinforced visually through Ozu's self-imposed restrictions on camera movement, camera placement and a rigidly controlled editing technique.[13]

David Bordwell rejects the earlier position adopted by some critics that Ozu's low camera placement represents the viewpoint of some unseen observer on the following grounds: Ozu's camera is 'almost never at the literal height of a seated observer; . . . what sort of observing entity is almost always lower than anything it sees, even in streets, train aisles, and office corridors? . . . if the frame represented an invisible, squatting witness, it should remain constant. It does not . . . [and finally, there are instances when] Ozu changes the camera's height even when filming the same object' (Bordwell 1988:77). He goes on to interpret the significance of Ozu's camera position, 'exactly because the camera cannot be presenting the viewpoint of an intelligent agent, either a character or a person-like invisible witness, it can serve as the basis of an *impersonal* narrational style' (emphasis in original Bordwell 1988: 79)—that is, a narrational style that weakens the spectator's emotional identification with particular characters and supports the loosely motivated plotline. This is in marked contrast to the cinematic techniques used by Ushihara in *Marching On,* which attempt to draw the spectator into an empathetic response to Kōichi. Ozu's camera position, on the other hand, is always impersonal and his refusal to use close-up reaction shots, combined with his insistence on actor restraint and impassiveness in the expression of emotions, are further examples of techniques that limit the spectator's emotional responses to the characters. As Bordwell concludes, 'Ozu's directing thus ruled out empathetic interpretation: the actor became a repository of pictorial behaviors'. [To quote Ozu,] "You are not supposed to feel, you are supposed to do'" (Bordwell 1988:85). Furthermore, the eye line of medium close-up shots of characters is rarely if ever directed at the spectator, even in the most emotional scenes such as the *onsen* (spa town) scene from the 1942 film *There Was a Father* (*Chichi ariki*). Due to the low position of the camera, the glances of the characters pass over the top of the camera or, alternatively, the eye line is directed slightly to the right or left of the camera's lens. Ozu's technique of editing each scene according to time further lessens the emotional buildup of his films. 'For the spectator, such repetitive meter creates a subliminal norm. There will be no sudden accelerations, no flurry of rapid shots; the calm pace of cutting will match the unfolding syuzhet events' (Bordwell 1988:75).

By limiting the potential for spectator identification with one particular character through the narrative structure, camera position and editing techniques, Ozu, on the one hand, forces his spectator into an analytic mode of response and, on the other hand, to view the group as a whole. One could argue that like Kōichi (*Marching On*), Ryōsuke's (*The Only Son*) social ambition to move beyond his country origins and study in Tokyo drives the narrative. However, the inclusion of the parallel plotline around Ōkubo (Ryōsuke's former teacher) and his inability to make it in Tokyo, ending up as the proprietor of a pork-cutlet restaurant, shifts the blame for Ryōsuke's failure away from his personal traits to a more generalized problem of city life; that is, the economic reality that there were just not sufficient jobs for university graduates in 1930s Tokyo. Thus problems raised by the films are not just problems for the individual but are social and/or economic. This is reinforced by the fact that there is no sense of narrative closure, only an all-pervading sense of the characters' resignation to their fates. The Meiji 'dream' of equality, outlined in the epigraph that opens this chapter, is just that, a dream, and it is with the nightmare realities of daily life in recession-hit Japan that the protagonists have to contend.

## The Body in Question: the *Modan gāru*

A Portrait of the *mogā* and *mobo*: The image of the modern girl and modern boy is one of lightness as they swagger at the vanguard of public morality. This lightness was connected to frivolity and became disparaging. However, the modern girl and modern boy in films, were exposed to a look from audiences that was half yearning and half jealous. There were also those modern girls and modern boys who were indifferent to frivolity and decadence. These were the young people who devoted themselves to sport. In particular, the 'bathing beauties' displaying both health through exercise and a sense of the erotic. (Iwamoto 1991: 50)

I often used phrases like 'mix with Westerners' and 'like a Westerner'. Clearly this pleased her [Naomi]. 'What do you think?' she'd say, trying out different expressions in the mirror. 'Don't you think I look like a Westerner when I do this?' Apparently she studied the actresses' movements when we went to the movies, because she was very good at imitating them. In an instant she could capture the mood and idiosyncrasies of an actress. Pickford laughs like this, she'd say; Pina Menicheli moves her eyes like this; Geraldine Farrar does her hair up this way. Loosening her hair, she'd push it into this shape and that. (Tanizaki Jun'ichirō, *Naomi,* translated by Anthony H. Chambers 1986: 34)

When we say the Modern Girl exists in our era we are not in particular referring to individuals named Miss So-and-so-*ko* or Mrs Such-and-such-*e*.[14] Rather, we are talking about the fact that somehow, from the midst of the lives of all sorts of women of our era, we can feel the air of a new era, different from that of yesterday. That's right; where can you folks clearly say there is a typical modern girl? That is to say that the Modern Girl is but a term that abstractly alludes to one new flavor sensed from the air of the life of all women in society. (Kataoka Teppei from his 1927 study 'Modan gāru no kenkyū' quoted in Silverberg 1991: 250)

The advent of modernism in Japan of the 1920s and 1930s precipitated a change in 'public morals' particularly evident in the cities. This change came to be associated in popular consciousness with a new image of womanhood. Women were increasingly breaking out of their traditional space as *okusan* (wives within the home) and entering society for the first time

in significant numbers. Figures for white-collar workers employed in
Tokyo's Marunouchi district in 1924 suggest that of the 30,000 employees
3,500 were women and that '[b]y the second half of the 1920s, approximately 8,200 women were employed at secretarial and service jobs in Japan's urban centres' (Silverberg 1991: 256–257). As Margit Nagy's study
of middle-class working women indicates, the term *shokugyō fujin* (working woman) only came into use in the 1910s and 1920s and even then its
usage was not clearly defined. However, various surveys of the period tend
to link it to white-collar workers. For example, a survey conducted by the
Hiroshima Bureau of Social Affairs in 1926 'applied the term solely to the
"intellectual laborers" (*chiteki rōdōsha*) among women in the labor force.
These included female teachers, office workers, telephone operators, mid-
wives, and nurses, but excluded factory workers and domestic servants'
(Nagy 1991:201–202). Women from working-class and rural backgrounds
had, since the late nineteenth century, formed an important labour source
for the newly industrializing Japan.[15] However, in the early 1900s, women
from middle-class backgrounds increasingly found employment outside
the home, precipitating a masculine backlash that manifested itself in a
media-generated image of what came to be known as the *modan gāru*.
Within this context she became the corporeal expression of the destabiliza-
tion of traditional ideologies of gender. In cinematic terms, a complex discourse of containment surrounded the body of the *modan gāru*. The female
star was at the centre of this discourse, for as Deguchi Takehito reminds
us, actresses, formerly banned from the theatre, became an increasingly
important symbol of this emergent femininity: '1919 was the year when
film actresses first made their entrance. It was just at the beginning of the
modern period, the very existence of actresses in themselves became one
manifestation of modernity' (Deguchi 1991:116).

The Shōchiku Studios, through the policies of the head of the Tokyo
studio, Kido Shirō, played an important role in the creation and establishment of the *modan gāru*. Aware of women's growing spending power and
the need to foster new audiences, he saw the commercial potential in attracting women into cinemas[16] and as a concomitance Shōchiku was instrumental in providing female audiences with an iconology of the
'modern women'. As a result of this policy during this period, a clear narrational and stylistic shift is evident: a move away from the 'pathetic'
*shinpa*-derived melodramas chronicling women's suffering towards an alternative conception of womanhood. This phenomenon is well illustrated
in the 1938 release *The Love-Troth Tree* aka *The Compassionate Buddha*

*Tree (Aizen katsura: sōshūhen)*. Kobayashi Kyūzō explains, 'Vulgar *shinpa* melodramas were overwhelmingly popular, but the nature of these films and the trite way in which women were portrayed was old fashioned. They supported a conventional morality, were restrictive and did not portray women with any sense of vivacity. It was against this kind of *shinpa*-style that Kido Shirō conceived of what became known as the Kamata-style female line' (Kobayashi 1999:66).

*The Love-Troth Tree,* directed by Nomura Hiromasa, was based on a popular novel by Kawaguchi Matsutarō (1899–1985) and serialized between 1936 and 1938 in the women's magazine *The Wives Club (Fujin kurabu)*. At the time of its release, *The Love-Troth Tree* was slated by the critics but hugely popular with the public. Suzuki Kazutoshi suggests that the film's popularity can be attributed to several factors. First, at the time of its release Japan had already invaded China. Men were being conscripted into the military and there was a general sense of unease. People were facing tremendous difficulties in recession-hit cities and in the countryside extreme poverty as crops failed and weather conditions deteriorated. By the second half of the 1930s, the sale of daughters into prostitution had become commonplace in northern regions of the country. *The Love-Troth Tree* appealed to people because it put love above all else *(ren'ai shijōshugi)*; no obstacles were allowed to stand between the heroine (Tanaka Kinuyo) and the hero (Uehara Ken 1909–1991). Second, the *Cinderella*-like happy ending was based on a 'success story'. The heroine, faced with providing for her child after the death of her husband, chooses a modern rationalist approach to her existence at a time when influences of an earlier order were still widely prevalent. Suzuki reminds readers of the entrenched class system maintained into the modern age through such social institutions as the *koseki* (family register). *The Love-Troth Tree* presented the power of love as the vehicle through which the heroine achieved success. Her status as positive and competent is reinforced through her occupation as a nurse. Nursing, at the time the film was made, was held in high regard partly because of the difficulty of the examinations and partly due to the associations made with the white uniform which came to symbolize *eigyō* (a vocation), *junshin* (pure heartedness), *otome* (virginity), *seiso* (neatness) and *seiketsu* (cleanliness).

This radical innovation of the success story with a happy ending challenged the punishment theme of traditional *shinpa* 'women's weepies', such as the often filmed *Golden Demon (Konjikiyasha)*, literally *The Usurer*[17], *The Downfall of Osen* aka *Osen of the Paper Cranes (Orizuru Osen)* and *The Story of the Last Chrysanthemum* (*Zangiku monogatari*), the latter two both directed by Mizoguchi Kenji. Within these *shinpa*-derived films female characters have little constitution of their own as individuals; they exist merely within a masculine consciousness, and when they transgress traditionally defined roles of the feminine they are punished, as is the hapless Miya in one of the last screen adaptations, the 1937 Shōchiku version of *The Usurer,* directed by Shimizu Hiroshi (1903–1966).

In this romantic tragedy, the hero Kaiichi (Natsukawa Daijirō 1913–*) is spurned in love by Miya (Kawasaki Hiroko 1912–1976) who chooses to marry the wealthy Toriyama. In an early scene, Miya gives her reasons for rejecting Kaiichi as (a) he is still only a student and it will be another three to four years before he graduates; and (b) in the current economic climate he cannot be sure of getting a good job even after graduation. Kaiichi, who believes that love can surmount all obstacles, says that if Miya loved Toriyama, he could understand and he would not stand in her way. If, however, she were basing her decision on purely economic reasons, then he would oppose the match. Kaiichi then offers to give up his studies so that they could be married sooner, but Miya rejects this, saying she does not want to live such a 'miserable life' (*mijimena seikatsu*), at which point Kaiichi strikes her. As he strides off, he knocks Miya down as she tries to follow him. After Miya's marriage to Toriyama, Kaiichi gives up his studies and begins work in his father's loan company. He becomes totally ruthless, rejecting all human relationships in the pursuit of profit and ultimately revenge, as after many twists and turns in the narrative, Miya's husband becomes indebted to Kaiichi.

Kaiichi's rejection of Miya is acceptable because in the opening scenes we, the spectators, have been made aware of the duplicity of Miya's character. After an evening out with Toriyama, she is shown in the back of his car with him as he drives her home. He asks about Kaiichi only to be told that he is like a brother to her, at which point Kaiichi comes into view through the windscreen, also on his way home. Miya then asks to be dropped off, as she wants to walk the rest of the way. It is as she and Kaiichi walk home together that the true nature of their relationship, and thus the lie, becomes evident. As such, the film brings her character as a 'good' woman into doubt from the first scene.

In a parody of this questioning of the 'good' woman, *The Love-Troth Tree* includes a self-reflexive scene taken from *The Usurer*, depicting the fatal scene in Atami when the hapless Miya rejects Kaiichi and chooses economic security over love. This scene is given greater poignancy as it is

played to great comic effect by two nurses in an amateur theatrical entertainment. The nurse operating the sea sound effects misses her cue and the
moon shoots up the painted backdrop. The inclusion of this scene invites
an intertextual comparison between the positive image of the *modan gāru*
as professional nurse and the pathetic figure of a *shinpa* heroine: Miya.
The scene relies for its effectiveness on the audience of the day's familiarity with the narrative of *The Usurer*.

Upon Kido Shirō's return to Japan in 1929 after his extensive tour of Europe and the United States, he was keen to introduce two new policies to
the Shōchiku Kinema Co. Surprised by the extent to which 'talkies' had
been taken up abroad, Kido was eager to introduce sound into Japanese
film, and he set about establishing a connection with a record company.
His second policy was related specifically to actresses. Affected by Hollywood's glamorization of the female star, Kido sent out talent scouts
throughout the country looking for new actresses with, in particular,
shapely legs who could wear Western-style clothes (*kyakusenbi joyū*). 'In
kimono the shape of the body and the line of the legs are hidden, but in
western clothes this is not the case. From that time on it was not sufficient
for women to have only a beautiful face, they had to have a beautiful body
and shapely legs' (Kobayashi 1999: 95). By 1931 Shōchiku had successfully combined both policies in Japan's first major sound production, *The
Neighbour's Wife and Mine*. Date Satoko took the part of the seductive
jazz singing *modan gāru*, living next door to the hero, a struggling writer
(see figure 4).

As the quotation taken from Kataoka at the beginning of this section
indicates, the term *modan gāru* is an abstract term used to capture a 'new
flavor sensed from the air of the life of all women in society'. Shōchiku,
through its dual policy of targeting female audiences and glamorizing actresses, was instrumental in the 1930s in setting the terms of reference for
how femininity would be defined in this period. The film world's emphasis
on the glamorization of actresses meant that, in its abstract sense, the body
of the cinematic *modan gāru* often became the site upon which eroticized
fears of the disunity of the traditional family were played out. As such,
their image within popular films of the period is at times ambiguous, reflecting masculine insecurity and the destabilising effect these trends had
on the traditional family. While at other times, the figure of the *modan
gāru* re-inscribes female characters back into maternal roles by adjusting
these roles to the contingencies of modern society as in the 1938 block-

buster *The Love-Troth Tree*. In this film Tanaka Kinuyo plays a young widowed nurse with a small child who, after many misadventures, marries the
wealthy son and heir apparent of the hospital where she works. Although
depicted as a skilled nurse, the heroine still remains circumscribed by the
universality of her maternal role established in the opening sequences. It
is this normative quality that encourages her colleagues to support her, and
it is ultimately this quality that attracts the hero to her. It is her maternal
feelings that give her the strength to abandon the hero in the first instance
at the station when they are due to leave for Kyoto. Her modesty and re-
serve reaffirm her sexually non-threatening nature, as her maternal feelings remain dominant. Thus, despite her modern status as an independent
working woman, she also becomes a signifier of the traditional. It was this
ability to bridge the contradiction between the modern and the traditional
that came to define Tanaka Kinuyo's star persona in the 1930s.

Like her Hollywood counterpart, the flapper, the *modan gāru* was both
erotic and threatening. In the 1933 film directed by Ozu, *Dragnet Girl*,
there is a playful parody of a Dietrichesque erotic ambiguity as Tanaka
Kinuyo, the *modan gāru*, herself the object of her boxer/gangster boyfriend's desire, feels threatened by a traditional kimono-clad rival. She
confronts the rival with a pistol only to conclude that she is being foolish.
The camera cuts to a shot of her calves and stiletto heels as she walks
towards the rival, there follows another cut as Tanaka Kinuyo pulls back,
leaning against the fence and laughing. Then a series of reverse-cut shots
as the rival raises her hand and caresses her cheek before a cut to Tanaka
Kinuyo as she walks off down the street. This hint of sexual ambiguity is
reinforced when Tanaka Kinuyo arrives back at her boxer lover's room
and tells him that she can understand why he has fallen for the rival. Date
Satoko, in an earlier film also directed by Ozu, *Walk Cheerfully* (*Hogaraka
ni ayume*) (1930), lures men from clubs for her boxer/gangster lover to
threaten and steal their wallets (see figure 5).

The *modan gāru*'s proclivity for Western-style fashions and behaviour
extended her symbolic meaning as a challenge, not only to traditional feminine gender stereotypes of the 'good wife and wise mother', but also to
questions of cultural difference. In cinematic narratives, the social response to the new femininity was to contain it within a 'masculine point
of view' or masculine voice, either directly through the *onnagata* (an actor
who specializes in women's roles) or indirectly through cinematic techniques, such as point of view or more pervasively through omniscient narration. Susan Jeffords defines the 'masculine point of view' as that 'which

represents the disembodied voice of masculinity, that which no individual man or woman can realize yet which influences each individually. In this way, it is possible to identify the voice through which dominance is enacted in a narrative representation, though it may not consistently be spoken by any one character' (Jeffords 1989: xiii). This is particularly evident in 'wanderer' films (*matatabimono*) of the late 1920s and early 1930s, as during this period they increasingly became the bastion of besieged masculinity. In the 1928 *matatabimono* film *The Wandering Gambler (Hōrō zanmai)*, directed by Inagaki Hiroshi, the love of the hero, played by Kataoka Chiezō, for his wife is intensified and simultaneously contained within the narrative through a universal masculine point of view by cinematic devices, such as flash-forwards into the hero's imagination. The hero, returning from Edo as part of the *sankin kōtai* policy[18], imagines in a series of flash-forwards what will happen when he first greets his wife and young son. In his mind's eye he also elaborates on all the preparations she has made for his long-awaited return. The expectations these scenes build up in the spectator who, unlike the hero, is partially aware of the disaster to follow, heightens the dramatic impact of the climactic scene. In this scene, he returns home to find his wife, having committed suicide, drawing her last breath in front of the the Buddhist family altar (*butsudan*). The extreme melodrama of this death scene allows the hero to express his love for his wife in a physical embrace as he cradles her in his arms. His wife had been the victim of the implied sexual advances of a senior official of the clan and had accordingly committed suicide, so proving herself worthy of the hero's love within the traditions of the code of the samurai (*bushidō*) of loyalty and purity. In this way, the hero's masculine status as a samurai who, in the latter half of the film, becomes a masterless samurai (*rōnin*) is not compromised. In the first half of the film the discourses of love, through the mechanisms of flash-forwards into the hero's thoughts and the suicide of the wife, are enunciated solely from within the masculine voice of the hero and the *bushidō* tradition. The character of the wife is thus constructed from the idealized image of her held in her husband's imagination. While *The Wandering Gambler* effectively contains the female character within an idealized feminine image, the hero's estranged mother in the 1931 film *The Mother He Never Knew (Banba no Chūtarō mabuta no haha)*, also directed by Inagaki Hiroshi, is in the reality of the film's narrative found to be very different from the image the hero held of her in his mind's eye (*mabuta*). Inverting a staple *shinpa*-theme, the separation of mother and child, by taking the lost (now adult) child's perspective, this film offers a sharp critique of the successful entrepreneur mother figure. Although set in the late Tokugawa period, the film reflects the unpredictability of changing social roles brought about by rapid modernization. The title, freely translated in Burch (1979) as *The Mother He Never Knew*, in fact carries greater diegetic meaning when *mabuta*, which literally means eyelid, is read in its metaphorical sense as in phrases such as *mabuta ni nokoru* (live in one's memory) or *mabuta ni ukabu* (float back into one's memory). It is this sense of memory that the images, dialogue, intertitles and the *benshi*'s 'stream-of-consciousness' narration dwell on in the final climactic scenes when Chūtarō, after many months searching, finally finds his mother, only to be rejected by her before a tainted reconciliation is reached.[19]

In considering the symbolic meaning of the *modan gāru* in the cinema of 1930s Japan, it is important to consider the following questions: Why did so many middle-class women feel the need to work outside the home; and why had the government deemed it necessary to establish the Rinji Hōsei Shingikai, a special investigative committee established in 1919 to review the provisions for the family in the Civil Code of 1898? Margit Nagy, from her study of middle-class working women in Japan in the early twentieth century, concludes that three factors came into play at this time: 'economic necessity, awakened women's consciousness, and job availability'. Economic need, Nagy argues, was foremost (Nagy 1991:204). The economic boom years of the First World War had encouraged many middle-class families to extend their daughters' education beyond the compulsory level into further education. Also during these boom years, many men were tempted out of such professions as teaching and nursing by the higher salaries offered in the private sector. Women increasingly moved in to fill these vacancies. However, with the subsequent postwar recession, many middle-class families began to experience difficulties. This was exacerbated by high rents brought about by a housing shortage in Tokyo and other major urban centres. The Kantō Earthquake of 1923 and the Wall Street crash of 1929 also plunged Japan into a deep economic recession. As a result, it became increasingly common for young women to work for the period between graduation and marriage. Their earnings were used to either supplement the family income directly or were saved to help offset expenses incurred when they married. Capitalizing on this trend, in 1934, Shōchiku's top ten releases were based on plotlines that involved women entering the workforce.

In this section I shall put forward the argument that the *modan gāru* of the cinema of the 1930s, like her male counterpart, the 'goal-orientated hero', became symbolic of Japan's transition from a focus on the rural *ie* (household), as a structure for organizing the family as an economic and social unit, to a stress on the individual and individual success as the motor of industrial production and the exchange of wealth. The *modan gāru* thus crossed the boundaries of the public and private becoming a symbolic figure of the city, which is both modern and degenerate. Film titles make this connection clear—*Women of Tokyo* and *Osaka Elegy*. The prostitute, the geisha and the office lady, all of dubious morality, are depicted as the principal female figures in the iconography of the city landscape, thereby linking notions of the pleasure quarters of Edo and Kyoto to modern myths of the licentious city. Narratives centring on the victimization of women and the pathetic nobility of a woman's self-sacrifice had long been evident in the *shinpa* theatrical tradition and, from the early days of Japanese cinema, been an important genre. However, in the late 1920s and 1930s this theme took a dramatic turn. Suffering in the *shinpa* tradition had been equated with family loyalty or loyalty for the male love interest. The heroes in this tradition were known as *nimaime* (weak romantic heroes) and were inspired by the heroine to courageous acts or inspired to go on with their studies and make something of themselves (Sōkichi in *The Downfall of Osen* and Kikunosuke in *The Story of the Last Chrysanthemum*). The suffering on the part of the heroine is thus given purpose. However, in many films of the 1930s, heroines are betrayed by their men and their suffering denied purpose. Equally, in many of these films, these women do not accept their suffering as fate: they resist it and fight against it. An analysis of some of the films directed by Mizoguchi Kenji during the 1930s is instructive on this transition. Mizoguchi, who joined Nikkatsu in 1920 as assistant director to Tanaka Eizō (1886–1968) amongst others before moving to Daiichi Eiga Studios in 1933 and then to Shōchiku in 1939, was nurtured in the *shinpa* tradition. The films he directed in the 1930s reflect the stylistic variations of the period. *The Downfall of Osen* (1935) and *The Story of the Last Chrysanthemum* (1939) both echo the *shinpa* tradition, while *Osaka Elegy* and *Sisters of Gion*, both made in 1936, reflect the changing nature of narrative themes and stylistic conventions during this dynamic period.

The narrative structure of many of these films centring on female characters was set within a simple triangular framework comprised of a male character, the subject of the narrative; a traditional woman (wearing a kimono); and a *modan gāru* (dressed in Western-style clothes and sporting a perm or short bobbed hairstyle) who usually worked in an office as a typist, telephonist or in a hospital as a nurse, or in the entertainment industry either as a singer or in the more traditional geisha quarters. This structure had become established by 1931 in Shōchiku's first 'talkie', *The Neighbour's Wife and Mine*. As the title implies, this triangular structure of the narrative (along with such cinematic devices as point of view) invites the spectator to identify with the main male protagonist to make a comparison between the traditional woman and the *modan gāru*. Therefore, through the title, we are invited to view these characters not as individuals but as social types representing competing social values. The Japanese title of the lighthearted *The Neighbour's Wife and Mine* invites us to make this comparison between the 'madam' next door, written in *katakana* (a syllabic script used solely to transcribe foreign loan words) emphasizing her foreignness; and the *nyōbō*, the traditional familiar term for wife (a husband uses *nyōbō* when referring to his own wife), which literally means 'woman of the house'. Similarly the title of Ozu's film *Women of Tokyo* (1933) invites a comparison between women of Tokyo and women from the country, that is, traditional women. The narrative of Mizoguchi's *Sisters of Gion* (1936) is also structured around two women working as low-ranking geisha in the pleasure quarters of Gion in Kyoto. The elder believes in the traditional values of *giri* (duty/obligation), which in theory governed the relationship between a geisha and her client, while the younger girl (Yamada Isuzu 1917–), a *modan gāru* and a graduate from high school, espouses a cynical view of the relationship, which she regards as being based purely on exploitation. However, the point of view taken up by these films differs considerably as it focuses on the female characters who are surrounded not by the handsome physically active gangster/ boxers of Ozu's films but by weak men who betray them. In both *Osaka Elegy* and *Sisters of Gion*, the main female characters end up being betrayed and, in the case of the younger sister in *Sisters of Gion*, the *modan gāru*, being kidnapped and thrown from a moving car, thereby sustaining serious bodily injuries. Within all these films the *modan gāru* is punished, often physically as above. In *Women of Tokyo*, Chikako (Okada Yoshiko 1902–1992) receives a severe beating from her younger brother (Egawa Ureo) before his suicide, and in *Osaka Elegy* the heroine (Yamada Isuzu) is thrown out of her family home and left to wander across a bridge on the edge of Osaka's pleasure quarters. Within both of the films, patriarchal masculinity is being criticized for its inability to come to terms with the modern world.

Japanese films of the late 1920s and the 1930s, reflecting the instabilities of modernity, projected two highly contradictory visions of the modern present, incorporated within which were changing concepts of gender. It was through cinema that the *mogā* and *mobo* (modern girl and modern boy) first entered Japanese society. The USA, through Hollywood, undoubtedly had a paradigmatic function within these discourses that often broke with tradition and permitted happy endings—in *Marching On*, which was based on an American novel by James Boyd, the hero saves the day on the battlefield and wins the hand of the girl he loves; in *The Neighbour's Wife and Mine,* marital harmony is restored by the end of the film; and in *The Love-Troth Tree* the heroine marries the young, handsome, wealthy man she loves. Alternatively, films of the period, which have come to be labelled 'social realist', at least implicitly and often explicitly, depict a dystopic view of the changes in social relations brought about by the upheavals of rapid industrialization and competitive individualism. Centred on the metropolis and surrounding conurbation, narratives focus on the disjunctions, dislocations and disorientations of individuals' lives. Within this worldview, social relations become increasingly transitory and arbitrary. Inhumane and corrupt corporations govern life and individuals have to suppress their natural 'manhood/womanhood' to survive. The fate of the heroes/heroines of these films is either resignation to the realities of modern life, or if they refuse to accept the world as it is, as do the heroes of the *matatabimono,* death or incarceration in gaol is the only alternative as there is no legitimate place in civil society for them.[20] Satō Tadao argues that these films are evidence of the emergence of a sense of 'social realism' in Japanese cinema: '[I]t was not just a case of presenting reality as it was, but within that reality was included a sense of defiance, a spirit of resistance to its beautification and its role as escapism . . .' (Satō 1995 vol. i: 360). He cites the works of directors such as Ozu Yasujirō, Gosho Heinosuke (1902–1981) and Mizoguchi Kenji as exemplary directors of this period who infused their films with this sense of critical resistance.

## Style: Narrational Norms and Modes

> You are not supposed to feel, you are supposed to do. (Ozu directing actors, quoted in Bordwell 1988: 85)

Humanity is defined in terms of an appeal to human feelings . . . (Kido
Shirō in Yamada [ed.] 1978: 79)

In the preceding section I set out some of the dominant narrative themes
evident in films produced by the Shōchiku Tokyo Studios of the 1930s and
attempted to locate these themes within wider social trends and discourses
of their day. In this section I intend to explore film style,[21] as it was manifested in this period, as a means by which these narrative themes were
interpreted and expressed.

   In his *auteur*-based analysis of Ozu Yasujirō's film style, David Bordwell makes the following observations: 'Ozu never presents such subjective states as dreams, memories, fantasies or hallucinations. We know the
human agents only "behaviorally" through their words, gestures, expressions, routines and decisions'. Bordwell goes on to observe that in films
directed by Ozu no background information is given about the characters'
lives before the time frame of the narrative. 'This narrational tactic contributes to some of the most commonly felt effects of the Ozu film; its realism (as in real life, characters don't explain all) and its intimacy (we come
to "know" these characters because their existence is almost completely
circumscribed by the span of the film)' (Bordwell 1988:53–54). In this
section I shall argue that these characteristics are not only representative
of films directed by Ozu, but are in fact representative of the in-house style
of Shōchiku Studios where Ozu spent his working career.

   In the Japanese literature this style was first known as the Kamata-*chō*
and later the Ōfuna-*chō*, so named after the locations of the two Shōchiku
Tokyo Studios. Kido Shirō outlines the philosophical principles upon which
the Kamata-style was based. He defines this style as an alternative to the
'gloom' of the *shinpa*-derived melodramas that it ultimately superseded:

   At this point it would be helpful to explain clearly what the Kamata-style
   is, briefly, it conveys the familiar happenings that frequently occur in
   human society, out of these we can plainly see the truth of humanity. In
   other words, human beings are not gods, no matter how much time passes
   human beings will not become gods, but supposing we define the word god
   as a human being who has achieved perfection, then out of the effort to
   become perfect, that passion, the culture of human society is born. There,
   in my opinion, lies the essence of human beings in our eternal shortcomings. It is here also that art is born, as are the difficulties of this world,
   the emergence of hubris, conversely, the opposite may occur, one may be
   indifferent to attractions, solitary, in any case humans have a variety of fac-

ets. And yet, this is the form human reality takes, there is nothing to be
done it is a truth. It is art that delves into this true form, but there are two
ways we can view it, with a warmth and brightness, or with a feeling of
gloom . . . Religion and revolution derive from the search for hope through
ways of thinking that stem from viewing gloomy things as they are. But at
Shōchiku, we try to view human life with a sense of warm aspiration and
brightness. In concluding, the basis of a film must be hope. It must not
impart to the spectator a sense of despair. This, in other words, is the base
line of the Kamata-style . . . (Kido 1956:39–40, also quoted in abbreviated
form in Kobayashi 1999:65)

In the above quotation, Kido Shirō like many Japanese film historians, is
defining this style in terms of film content rather than in terms of the development of a distinctive cinematic style. Through a deconstructionist analysis of films from the late 1920s and the 1930s, I shall put forward the view
that there emerged within Japanese cinema what I shall define as a 'behavouralist' style of narration, which as an expressive style was allied to the
'social realist' narrative themes discussed above. This stylistic shift can be
attributed to three related factors: first, as a backlash against the *shinpa*-
derived, *benshi*-driven, melodramatic traditions of filmmaking; second, to
the esoteric experimentation of the *jun'eiga undō* (pure film movement),
represented by such films as Kinugasa Teinosuke's (1896–1982) *A Page
of Madness* aka *A Page Out of Order (Kurutta ichipeiji)* (1926); and third,
as a response to the introduction of sound technology. Therefore this section will explore the role of the *benshi* as a crucial factor in the film experience of the *shinpa*-derived melodrama and *matatabimono* films, before
going on to consider the implications of the introduction of sound technology to narrational norms established before the *benshi*'s demise. These
narrational modes will then be considered in light of the development, in
the late 1920s and the 1930s, of the distinctive melodrama style spearheaded by Shōchiku. For the discussion of narrational norms and the *benshi*, I have drawn heavily on a set of video releases of early Japanese films
produced by the Matsuda Film Library in the early 1990s. These releases
come complete with *benshi* narration by Matsuda Shinsui (1925–1987)
and Sawato Midori.

## The *Jun'eiga Undō* and the Call for Reform

Up until the mid-1920s Japanese cinema audiences were divided into the
'educated', who patronized foreign films and spurned local productions,

and women and children, who respectively patronized films derived from the *shinpa*-melodrama tradition and the *kyūgeki/chanbara* (swordplay) tradition. These latter groups were referred to disparagingly as 'nursing mothers' (*komori onna*) and 'runny-nose brats' (*hanatare kozō*).[22] This division in audiences was reflected in a tension between filmmakers who were influenced by Western cinematic techniques, and those who were content to stay within the bounds of the existing studio system. The innovation and implementation of new techniques requires investment and was at first resisted by Nikkatsu. The *benshi*, who had installed themselves as the principal attraction of the cinema, also resisted change. They found it difficult to adapt their narration to films with fast editing. D.W. Griffith's 1916 multi-plotline film *Intolerance* was screened in Japan, giving *benshi* a clear indication of the difficulties to be resisted. Equally, the inclusion of dialogue inter-titles was similarly seen as a threat to the *benshis'* autonomy and role as an instrumental component of the overall film experience.

Writing in the *Kinema Record* magazine in 1916, Kaeriyama Norimasa (1893–1964), an intellectual who had graduated from the Tokyo Engineering University (Tokyo Kōtō Kōgyō Gakkō), summed up the mood of progressive filmmakers and 'educated' audiences with a catalogue of complaints under the title 'Why are Japanese productions uninteresting?' His first complaint was regarding the relationship of characters to the screen; as the camera was positioned at a distance from the action, the characters appeared small. 'It does not matter what the shot; characters appear overwhelmed by the interiors . . .'[23] Kaeriyama also criticised plotlines, arguing that very often the overall time of a film could be reduced by a third. In particular, he is most disparaging of films in which Onoe Matsunosuke appeared. 'If reforms are not made and characters filmed from the waist up or in a three-quarter pose, and superfluous material not deleted from scenes, Japanese productions will become unwatchable. Also, it would be a great help if we did not have to look at unnatural scenery that had been cheaply knocked together'.[24] Kaeriyama continues, attacking the *benshi* system, which allowed actors to remain expressionless: '[U]nder the current system, as actors have the support of the *benshi* dialogue the audience can follow the plot, but, if we were to watch these films in the ideal situation without *benshi* narration, I doubt we would understand what was being expressed'. Next he questions the role of the *onnagata*:

> Inoe Masahiro's *shingeki* theatre group employs actresses. It is a mistake of the times for the most eminent company in Japan, Nikkatsu Tokyo Stu-

dio, to employ *onnagata*. Generally speaking, on the stage with colour and intonation, it is possible to conceal the fact they are men, but in cinema it is impossible for a man to become a woman . . . Rather than an *onnagata* of skilful expression, an actress with no expression is preferable in the cinema . . . The dramatic plot lines of Japanese films are vulgar. We need good original stories . . . Only vulgar novels from the newspapers and magazines are used, there is no sense of pride.

By the late 1910s, as indicated by the above, there was a call amongst serious filmmakers and 'educated' audiences increasingly exposed to imported films to explore the expressive possibilities of cinema. Kaeriyama Norimasa was one of the first to call for a reform of the domestic film industry as part of a bid to produce Japanese films for export. In 1917, after an extensive study of American sources, Kaeriyama published a book entitled *The Production of Narrative Cinema and the Laws of Photography* (*Katsudō Shashingeki no Sōsaku to Satsueihō*). That same year he began working for Tenkatsu Film Company, as Tenkatsu were at this time experimenting with the production of Japanese films for export.

With the First World War, Hollywood came to the fore as the major exporter of films, taking over from the two leading countries, France and Italy. After the First World War, some European countries attempted to re-establish their film industries, and as a means of competing with Hollywood's domination experimented with alternative styles of filmmaking—the French Impressionist movement (1918–1929), German Expressionism (1920–1927) and Soviet Montage (1928–1933). As Hollywood films were produced with a view to sales beyond the domestic market, their budgets were invariably high; this also added to the burden of smaller film-producing countries and affected the export potential of these countries' industries.

In the late 1910s and early 1920s Japanese filmmakers also attempted to produce films for export. In an interview, Shirai Shigeru, who joined Shōchiku in 1920 as a cameraman, gives an example whereby several Japanese filmmakers formed a partnership with Universal Studios to distribute Japanese films abroad. Shirai attributes the failure of the enterprise to a lack of foresight on the part of the Japanese companies engaged in churning out one period (*jidaigeki*) film per week: The films were simply not of sufficient quality. Similarly, the actor Nakano Eiji, who also joined Shōchiku in the 1920s, cites the example of Murata Minoru (1894–1937), who attempted to export his 1925 expressionist film *The Street Magician*

(*Machi no tejinashi*) to Germany. In this latter case it can be argued that the reason for the negative criticism was related to the fact that films set in the contemporary era (*gendaigeki*) were attempts at emulating Western cinematic techniques and narrative structures. The failure of exports at this time can therefore be attributed to a failure to ensure quality productions on the one hand, and an inability to tap into the 'novelty' factor of local colour so successfully exploited by Kurosawa Akira (1910–1998) and Mizoguchi Kenji in the early 1950s. However, one positive effect of the attempt at exports was to give some local filmmakers, such as Kaeriyama Norimasa, the opportunity to experiment with alternative styles of filmmaking, and in the late 1910s he became involved in the production of two films, *The Virgin of Fukayama* (*Fukayama no otome*) (1918) and *The Brilliance of Life* (*Iki no kagayaki*) (1919). Unfortunately neither film has survived. However, from a study of the screenplays, Satō Tadao explains the revolutionary nature of the techniques employed in their production.

> With both productions, Kaeriyama Norimasa first carefully wrote the screenplay and had the production crew and the actors study it. The lead, Hanayagi Harumi [1896–1962], was the first actress to play the part of a woman. Essential dialogue was inserted using inter-titles. Even without *benshi* narration the story could be understood. Scenes were divided into shots of various sizes as close-ups and long-shots were used . . . (Satō 1995 vol. i: 160).

Due to Tenkatsu's fear of a *benshi* revolt, both films were held back and released in Japan some eighteen months after production.

As stated above, following the First World War, several European countries attempted to re-establish their filmmaking industries by turning to alternative techniques of cinematic expression. Some French impressionists advocated a theory of *cinéma pur* or 'pure cinema'. This movement was based on the development of abstract films, which concentrated on graphic and temporal forms, often with no clearly defined narrative. Some reformist Japanese filmmakers such as Kaeriyama appropriated this term 'pure cinema' (*jun'eiga*) in a looser context to distinguish their theoretical movement from traditional theatrically (*shinpa* and kabuki) derived filmmaking practices of the pre-1920s.

*Shinpa*-derived films of the early Japanese cinema would be described in Western film studies' terms as melodramas. Generally speaking, the melodramatic narrational mode is structured to convey the 'inner states' of the characters and as such, it subordinates all else to emotional impact. All the cinematic aspects of filmmaking, from *mise-en-scène*, lighting, setting, camera placement and 'point of view', work to convey the 'inner states' of the protagonists, and we, the spectators, are encouraged to focus on the protagonists within the various developing situations of the *syuzhet* rather than on one single character. This is quite different from the structure of films based on, for example, the 'goal-orientated hero' or the *chanbara* film, where we are clearly encouraged to identify with the main characters whose actions motivate the causal chain of events making up the *fabula*. The melodrama narrational mode is omniscient, in that we, the spectators, know more about the emerging situation than any one single character, thus the narrational mode supports a situation rather than a character-centred perspective. In the pre-'talkie' films of the late 1920s and the 1930s, the *benshi* and the inclusion of intertitles were important devices through which omniscient narration was conveyed. The *benshi* also provided a 'stream-of-consciousness' narration that, increasingly combined with the sophisticated use of subjective cinematic techniques, such as point of view, flashbacks, hallucinations and imaginings, provided protagonists with a degree of psychological depth that went far beyond intertitles in terms of dramatic impact.

This role of the *benshi* as voice-over narration of 'inner states' was used to great effect in the development of the *matatabimono* (the wandering yakuza or masterless samurai) film, which could be alternatively subtitled as 'men's weepies'. The *matatabimono* film is closely related to the *chanbara* genre; its main difference is that the principal protagonists, while being men of action are given, primarily through the *benshi*'s 'stream of consciousness' narration, an inner psychological depth denied to their *chanbara* counterparts. This 'stream-of-consciousness' narration successfully overcomes the contradiction that men of action should not show their feelings. The *benshi* provides a soliloquized articulation of the man of action's emotions. Similar techniques were later adapted to the 1960s 'drifter' (*nagaremono*) films where 'voice-over' narration of inner thoughts and the inclusion of verses from sentimental songs sung by the hero on the sound track conveyed 'inner states'. In films of the late 1920s and early 1930s, such as *The Serpent* (*Orochi*) (1925), *The Wandering Gambler* (1928) and *The Mother He Never Knew* (1931), what can be described as the *benshi*'s many cadenzas are clearly built into the structure of the films. Shots of poignant scenes of the heroes' contemplative musings are held for lengthy periods, clearly allowing sufficient time for the *benshi*'s extemporization. In this way the emphasis of the causal chain of events is shifted from the hero's actions, as in the *chanbara* films, to his emotional states. In *The Serpent* it is clearly the hero, Heizaburō's (Bandō Tsumasaburō), sense of the injustices of a society that favours privilege above honesty and merit; while in *The Wandering Gambler,* in the first instance, it is the hero's love for his wife and his desire to avenge her death; and finally, in *The Mother He Never Knew,* it is Chūtarō's sense of loneliness at not having a mother and a family that drives the causal chain of events that make up the *syuzhet*. Naturally, cinematic techniques play an important role in the depiction of 'inner states' and to illustrate this point I shall draw in detail on the example of *The Downfall of Osen* produced by Daiichi Eiga. A late production, 1935, *shinpa*-derived melodrama employing many of the conventions of the pre-'talkie' style, directed by Mizoguchi Kenji, it is based on the short story 'Osen and Sōkichi' by Izumi Kyōka (1873–1939). The film's framing through flashback, told as a story from the main protagonists' point of view through the sophisticated use of cinematic techniques and complex parallel plot structures, makes it exemplary within the *benshi*-driven *shinpa*-derived tradition.

Contained within the highly sophisticated structure of the *fabula* are two parallel lines of action, the relationship between Osen (Yamada Isuzu) and Sōkichi (Natsukawa Daijirō) and an attempted crime, a fraud scheme perpetrated against a group of Buddhist monks. The film begins *in medias res* before moving to a series of flashback sequences, which establish the action of the film as past memory. Despite the implied subjectivity of the opening sequences, the parallel structure of the *syuzhet* presents an omniscient survey of the events. The parallel plotting structure of the narrative impedes the revelation of *fabula* events; as one scene ends on a question, the *mise-en-scène* shifts to the other plotline suspending our knowledge, thus providing dramatic intrigue and drawing the spectator into the drama by apparently telling all, while withholding some information. The question follows: How does this apparently contradictory structure work? The opening sequences at the train station are crucial, being comprised of a series of flashback sequences that apparently frame the body of the narrative within Sōkichi's point of view. Due to delays Sōkichi stands waiting on a crowded platform while, unbeknownst to him, Osen sits in the waiting room. He is held in medium close-up as he stands gazing out to the right of the frame. This is followed by a cut to a point-of-view shot of a Shintō shrine on a hill, the object of Sōkichi's gaze. This sequence of shots is repeated, allowing sufficient time for the *benshi*'s 'stream of conscious-ness' cadenza. This is followed by a shot of leaves being blown in the wind, an intrinsic norm established in these opening sequences that trig-gers flashback sequences. This same shot will be used in the final scenes of the film; however, in this instance it is from Osen's point of view. Dur-ing the opening sequences, Osen is highlighted by the key light while sit-ting in a dazed state also gazing out of the frame to the right. The point-of-view cut between Osen, held in medium close-up, and the Shintō shrine visually links Osen and Sōkichi, as does the camera through a right track along the platform where Sōkichi is standing, to the waiting room and a medium close-up of Osen. They are linked through framing, lighting and camera movement, and despite their different physical positions on the platform (he is standing and she sitting some distance away in the waiting room), the point-of-view shot of the shrine is taken from the same angle. Both are thus visually conjoined as the main characters of the film. As the film moves into the main narrative with a flashback from Sōkichi's point of view, the camera follows his gaze from the *genkan*, the entrance hall of the antique shop, and entering the house peers behind the screen. The cam-era tracks forward along the corridor before a sharp swish-pan left as it focuses on Osen. Hereafter the narrational mode shifts to omniscience and the introduction of the crime plotline.

Thus two narrational strategies are used: one the subjective, supporting the Osen/Sōkichi plotline through the *benshi*'s 'stream of consciousness' narration, point of view and flashback sequences that are centred on Sōki-chi's psychological motivation in his relationship with Osen; and two, the omniscient narrational style characteristic of the crime plot. Despite the inclusion of flashback sequences from Osen's point of view in the opening scenes, in neither of the plotlines is her character given much in the way of psychological depth, that is, until the final sequences when she is in hospital where superimpositions reveal her deranged mental state. In the early scenes through the dual plot structure, various questions are raised about Osen's moral status, and it is the investigation into this character and her relationship with Sōkichi that motivates the causal chain of events that maintains, in large part, spectator interest. From the first scene, Sōki-chi's character as an important man is established, first by his attire and demeanour; this is then confirmed when a group of university students greet him. On the other hand, Osen's character, as a woman of dubious morals, is also established as a group of drunken revellers make lurid as-persions. The visual linking of the two main characters through cinematic devices, point of view, framing, lighting and camera movement sets up a contradiction in relation to the norms of social expectations. What type of woman is Osen and how can she and Sōkichi be connected? For most of the film Osen is held at a distance and her actions are observed either from Sōkichi's point of view or through the omniscient narration. The narrative during the rest of the film sets out to disprove the initial inferences drawn from these opening scenes and structures her character as a 'good' woman, despite her apparent circumstances. This is done through both the crime plotline—she is opposed to the villains' plan to cheat the monks and it is she who eventually foils their plans and has them arrested—and through Sōkichi's recollections. Osen is a fallen woman, but thanks to Sōkichi's memories of her and the depiction of her role in foiling the crime, providing objective 'empirical' support for Sōkichi's subjective memories, we are encouraged towards a realization that circumstances and not some intrinsic evil have drawn her into this state.

The *benshi*'s 'stream of consciousness' narration is central to the subjective portrayal of Sōkichi's memories, both of his relationship with Osen and in providing background information about his circumstances before he came to Tokyo. The *benshi* also helps to guide the spectator through the complex temporal disunity of the ordering of *syuzhet* events. Visually, windswept leaves do denote an intrinsic norm that cues subjective states. However, these cues are established much more quickly in the spectators' minds with the aid of the *benshi*.

Although the thematic concerns of *The Downfall of Osen* are characteristic of films produced at this time (in particular, the structured investigation into the heroine's morality through her actions), the stylistic signifiers that inform the *syuzhet* are very different from those of the 'social realist' film. Where psychological motivation in *The Downfall of Osen* is depicted in terms of Sōkichi's memory, subjective point of view and superimpositions, in 'social realist' films of the same period such as *Women of Tokyo* and *Osaka Elegy,* the dialogue between characters and their actions advances the causal chain of the *syuzhet*. As such it is possible to identify a distinction between a 'behaviour'-centred melodramatic mode and the 'subjective' mode of the *shinpa*-derived tradition. In very broad terms the characteristics of the 'behaviourist' style are summarized below with examples taken primarily from *Women of Tokyo*, a sophisticated melodrama produced by Shōchiku in 1933 centring on the relationship of a young student who is being supported through university by his elder sister; *The Love-Troth Tree* (also produced by Shōchiku in 1938); and *Osaka Elegy* (produced by Daiichi Eiga) directed by Mizoguchi Kenji in 1936, one year after the release of *The Downfall of Osen*:

1. Films of the 'behaviouralist' style are characterized by a linear temporal ordering of time, and flashbacks are rarely used. In *Women of Tokyo* the action takes place over a period of morning, evening and the next morning. The title of the original story upon which the film is based is 'Twenty-six Hours,' and it is safe to assume that the film covers this time frame. The final sequences are set in Harue's (Tanaka Kinuyo) rooms where a wall clock is clearly visible and in a shop selling clocks; both these settings help to underline this point. Where information about a character's past activities or situation is necessary to our understanding of the subsequent action, it is given in dialogue. In *The Love-Troth Tree* the heroine, a nurse, is seen out with her young daughter. Upon her return to the hospital, she is confronted by her colleagues, at which point she apologizes for having deceived them, before going into a lengthy explanation of how she was married at a young age and how her husband died when she was nine months' pregnant. While she was in hospital giving birth, she resolved to work and to raise the child herself, hence her present situation.

2. Protagonists' psychological states, desires and motivations are revealed through dialogue and actions; dream and hallucination sequences are not used nor is 'voice-of-god' or voice-over narration. In *Women of Tokyo* after the young brother Ryōichi learns of the accusations regarding his sister who is suspected of supplementing their income through prostitution, the scene shift is punctuated with a cut to a close-up shot of a kettle boiling on the stove. Ryōichi had lit the stove and placed the kettle there when Harue, his girlfriend, first arrived. After the following scene there is another shot of the kettle, now boiled dry. These shots not only mark the passage of time but are also an indication of Ryōichi's emotional state: he is too distracted by these accusations about his sister to notice the kettle boiling dry. His subsequent suicide is a dramatic response to the circumstance of the plot, clearly indicating his emotional state.

3. Generally speaking characters are held in medium close-up or long shots, and close-up shots are rarely used. The spectator is encouraged to observe characters in the various situations of the narrative.

4. The *mise-en-scène* is central to the narrative as place. In *Osaka Elegy,* Osaka in 1936 is clearly established through shots in the opening sequence of the entertainment district with jazz background music followed by the popular song 'Stairway to the Stars'. Also the inclusion of a scene in the puppet (*bunraku*) theatre and department store locate the action in Osaka in the 'modern' period. Scenes filmed in the underground train system, which opened in 1936, help establish the time frame of the action. The inclusion of Tokyo in the title *Women of Tokyo* also locates the setting as place within the narrative.

As omniscient narration is common to both the *shinpa*-derived melodramas and the 'social realist' film, in the following section, through a detailed analysis of *Women of Tokyo* and reference to *Osaka Elegy,* I shall explore how the stylistic characteristics listed above combined with the omniscient melodramatic narrational mode impacted on the common subject matter of these films. *The Downfall of Osen, Women of Tokyo* and *Osaka Elegy* all share a common basic plot—a sister (or sister surrogate figure in the case of Osen) is drawn into prostitution to help put her brother through university and/or save her father from imprisonment. However, in stylistic terms there are clear differences and it is these differences that alter the way the subject matter is treated and perceived—either as *shinpa*-derived or as 'social realist'[25], which in turn influenced the potential political readings of the films.

As in *The Downfall of Osen,* in the opening scenes of *Women of Tokyo* a similar investigative questioning, through the depiction of socially contradictory images of the character of Chikako, is established as the driving causal force of the first half of the film. In these opening sequences Chikako gives her younger brother Ryōichi money, thus her relationship to her brother as financial provider is clearly established. The following scene shifts to the office where Chikako works as a typist. From the typewriter and later through the dialogue intertitles we can infer that Chikako is educated, as she understands a foreign language. Exactly which language is not specified, but this is unimportant; the important point for the action of the drama is the establishment of her social status as an educated middle-class woman working as an "office lady." In this scene these 'facts' about Chikako are observed through the mediated gaze and dialogue intertitles exchanged between the personnel manager of the company and a police officer, this latter the legitimate social representative of authority. The office, in which they hold this conversation, is partitioned off by a glass wall and glass door, facilitating the processes of observation and investigation. Chikako is unaware of this investigation. Therefore, through the omniscient narration the spectators' gaze is complicit in the investigation. This scene sets up the questions surrounding Chikako's activities and by extension her morality that are answered in the dénouement when it is revealed that she has been supplementing the family income through prostitution. The omniscient narration therefore subordinates her threatening competence in the workplace to an investigation of her sexuality.

In the second half of the film the all-knowing narration shifts, as not only Chikako but Ryōichi is placed in a situation of knowing less than the narration. Ryōichi's girlfriend, Harue, whose brother is a policeman tells Harue of the investigation. Harue, in an attempt to warn Chikako, tells Ryōichi, who refuses to believe these rumours. In anger he breaks off his relationship with Harue and demands that she leave. In the next scene the omniscient narration takes us to a bar where Chikako is depicted putting on lipstick in front of a mirror. Later, we see her telephone Ryōichi to tell him she will be home late before getting into a car with a man. The narration confirms the 'facts', as yet unknown to Ryōichi, of the police investigation. In the final scenes, the diegesis, as a whole, shifts to the feminine perspective as Chikako attempts to explain her motives to an enraged Ryōichi. After beating her, he storms off into the night and the narrative remains focused on the feminine—on the inside worlds of, first, Chikako's room and then Harue's with only a few minor cuts to Ryōichi walking in the street and then sitting on some rubble. We do not see his suicide and only learn of it when Chikako and Harue find out. We, the spectators, empathize with his death through the reactions of Harue, who is silent and tearful, and Chikako, who makes the following statement: 'Ryōichi, until the last you didn't understand me (long pause). To die like this, really (another long pause). You were a weakling (*yowamushi)*'. In this way the film ends in discord and death. Chikako compromises in order to survive in the modern world and is punished through the death of her brother. Ryōichi, who could not bear the dishonour Chikako's behaviour brought upon him, is confirmed through his sister's criticism as being a weak man.

Within the diegesis of both *The Downfall of Osen* and *Women of Tokyo*, the omniscient narration is clearly related to questions of power, both between characters and in relation to social position (as well as between the spectator and characters) through processes of knowledge and the inhibition of knowledge. Individual character positions are strengthened or weakened by their knowledge or lack of knowledge about the situations in which they find themselves. In the case of *Women of Tokyo,* both Chikako and later Ryōichi are weakened as they become isolated in positions of not knowing. Chikako does not know she is being investigated, and Ryōichi becomes a pathetic figure in wanting to believe in his sister's innocence while we the spectators know, through shots of the bar and later scenes of Chikako going off with a man in his car, that the accusations are correct. Within the narrative of *Women of Tokyo*, through the patterns of omniscient narration, the main characters are divested of any control over their lives. The narrational strategies are linked to social forces, which contrive against them. Harue's brother, the policeman and the only character to remain unaffected by the events, is representative of these social forces. Similarly in *Osaka Elegy,* Ayako is unaware of the fact that her father has not told her brother and sister that she had raised the two hundred yen for the brother's tuition fees. She is also unaware of the fact that her father had entered into an agreement with Mr Asai prior to her becoming his mistress. In *The Downfall of Osen*, Sōkichi's position of mediating narrator through his memory ensures that we come to know Osen from his point of view. He, as the main male character, is placed in an all-knowing position of power through flashbacks, *benshi* 'stream-of-consciousness' narration and point of view. The inclusion of the crime subplot serves to verify his subjective memories as 'correct'. Alternatively in films of the 'behavouralist' style, the stylistic conventions adopted by filmmakers shifts the balance of power within the diegesis by limiting the mediating opportunities for any one character to observe and/or control the image of another character. Power is etherealized, it is placed onto the society at large and a business economy, undermining the legitimacy of the traditional family. The fact that the two households depicted in the *Women of Tokyo*, Ryōichi's and Harue's, are both comprised of brother and sister living together, emphasizes the breakdown of the traditional family structure. In this way, the destruction of the traditional family is the precondition for Chikako's need for independence: she could no longer depend on the family or marriage as a means of economic support. The city, Tokyo, of the title figures as the ambivalent site of the 'modern girl's' independence and downfall.

In 'social realist' films of the 1930s the market economy that continued to permit the sale of women's bodies and demanded that men adopt a subservient attitude became, through the narratives and an omniscient narration style adhering to a restrictive use of expressive cinematic techniques, the etherealized cause of the disintegration of social relations. In *Women of Tokyo* the link between the characters' situations and money is reinforced through the self-reflexive insertion of a scene from the Paramount production *If I Had a Million*. In this scene, directed by Ernst Lubitsch (1892–1947), a clerk (Charles Laughton 1899–1962) is seen sitting at his desk in a large office. The layout of Chikako's office in the preceding scene is very similar. In this way both visual and character continuity are maintained. A letter is handed to Charles Laughton, who brushes it aside and continues writing in his ledger. The camera then cuts back to the cinema and a medium close-up of Harue and Ryōichi in the audience. Harue is fumbling for her programme. This shot is followed by a cut back to the screen and the film, by which time Charles Laughton, rising from his desk, proceeds down the aisle between the desks and out of the room. Because of the cut back to Harue and Ryōichi, we do not see Charles Laughton read the letter nor do we see that he has been given a cheque for one million dollars. Also the clip is cut before the end of the sequence and we are returned to the main narrative before we see Charles Laughton walk into the company president's office and make a rude gesture. The inclusion of the intertextual reference from *If I Had a Million* relies for its effectiveness on the audience's knowledge of the film. Both films were released in 1933. However, the link between the two films is clear: All the characters who receive a million dollars in *If I Had a Million* are socially oppressed. Once Charles Laughton has the money, he is able to demonstrate his contempt for the company through its symbolic head, the president, before he resigns.

The opening shots of Osaka's amusement district and the following scenes in the Asai household in *Osaka Elegy* make a similar causal connection between money and the breakdown of social relations. Mr Asai, head of the pharmaceutical company, is a *yōshi*, an adopted son-in-law,[26] a point his wife plays upon. In cinematic terms the financial basis of their marriage is linked visually as the camera, panning right, slowly follows Mrs Asai as she walks along the corridor from the residential quarters through to the company office. She is on her way to ask one of the clerks, Nishimura, to accompany her to the theatre. She is just as exploitative as her husband in manipulating younger, weaker employees through the power of position and money.

In the bleakness of *Women of Tokyo* and *Osaka Elegy,* all the dominant themes of the 1930s 'social realist' films find expression—the city versus country; the absence of the patriarch; an elder sister driven to prostitution to educate a male sibling, and male impotence in the face of modern competitive corporate society.

The 'behavouralist' style was spearheaded by Shōchiku under the leadership of Kido Shirō, whose theories of filmmaking, in particular screenplay writing, are set out in the volume *Wa ga eigaron* (*My Theory of Filmmaking*) edited by the Shōchiku director Yamada Yōji (1931–) and published in 1978. One crucial factor that comes out of this volume is Kido's belief in the centrality of the screenplay to the filmmaking process and to the Shōchiku Studio style. It must be remembered that up until the late 1910s most films were made without the aid of a screenplay, filmmakers giving instructions to actors during the actual filming. At Shōchiku all apprentice directors joining the company began their careers by studying the art of screenplay writing; only after they had produced an acceptable screenplay were they allowed to advance beyond assistant director status. This emphasis on the screenplay ensured that under the Shōchiku Tokyo Studio system, language/dialogue, supported by a minimalist cinematic technique, became the dominant expressive medium.[27] In his writing Kido expresses the importance of the screenplay to filmmaking: '[D]ialogue is most important . . . the portrayal of the protagonist's personality and psychology exerts a strong control over a film and the best way to explain this is through dialogue' (Kido Shirō, in Yamada (ed.) 1978: 86). Yamada Yōji, in his introductory reminiscences, confirms the centrality of character development to the Shōchiku style:

> To portray characters' personalities accurately, that is, objectively capturing a character's personality . . . Realism (*riarizumu*), in truth, that is the brilliant tradition of the Ōfuna Studios. It is possible to say that this tradition of realism constructed by Naruse Mikio, Gosho Heinosuke, Shimizu Hiroshi, Shimizu Yasujirō, Ozu Yasujirō, Kinoshita Keisuke and the many accomplished performers, was based on Kido's principle that the essence of a screenplay is in the construction of the characters' personalities. (Yamada 1978: 56)

In conclusion, this emphasis on character exposition through dialogue as the dominant means of narrative development gained poignancy with the transition to sound. The minimalist filming techniques, the resistance to flashbacks, hallucination and dream sequences, and the preference for medium close-ups and long shots, ensures that we come to know the characters through their speech and their actions. The importance placed on *mise-en-scène* as place and not just as a setting for action creates a sense that location is the depiction of social space, the newly created (post-1923 earthquake) urban spaces of Western-style capitalism on the fringes of Tokyo and Osaka. These are the designated spaces for biological reproduction—the family, in the new cityscapes. In films directed by Ozu, the many punctuating location shots of urban wastelands, smoking chimneys and washing lines document this transitional phase of newly emerging social relations in newly developing landscapes. Through the structured absence of any alternative spaces in these films, the *furusato* (country home) becomes the idealized, longed-for space of a lost world. The omniscient narrational mode and the often complex multiple plotlines of the 'social realist' film locates the causes of the characters' predicaments in the socio-economic climate of recession-hit Japan in the 1930s and the inability of men to live up to the ideals of a past patriarchy.

Industrial capitalism acts upon the body in fundamental ways through speed, movement and regimentation. Charles Chaplin's (1889–1977) 1936 film *Modern Times* is a parody of the relationship of the labouring body to modern industrial practices. Japanese films of this period are also punctuated with symbols of speed and movement, trains and planes; motifs of regimentation; and the ordering of time. However, unlike the Chaplin example, in films of the Japanese *gendaigeki*, industrial capitalism is depicted as impacting on the lower-middle classes (the salaryman in particular) rather than on the labouring classes. In the next chapter, this theme will be expanded as 'speed' and movement will be analysed through the body of the *jidaigeki* star as a mimetic response to the modern mechanical ordering of time.

The emergence of an urban consumer economy and the increase in young educated women from middle-class backgrounds finding employment in clerical positions as 'office ladies', as nurses and as teachers brought women out of the home and into public spaces. Shōchiku, in order to capitalize on women's increased spending power, developed a commercial strategy to attract women into cinemas while simultaneously providing them with an iconology of the 'modern woman'. The *shinpa* tradition of the woman as victim of the vicissitudes of an unjust patriarchal order was challenged by the seemingly autonomous 'modern girl'. Either as the cigarette-smoking, gun-toting *femme fatale* of the Date Satoko style, who exerts control over both her male victims and her male henchmen, or through the star persona of actresses such as Tanaka Kinuyo, who allied autonomy to romance and the maternal instinct as in *The Love-Troth Tree*. Bearing in mind that most marriages were arranged and that women had little choice in the matter of their partner in this period, romance and its connection with choice takes on connotations not always associated with it in a Western context. The *modan gāru,* also as the epitome of the discontinuity of the traditional family, became an erotic and threatening site of the contested terrain of the modern as her body was displayed and her morality investigated. She was put on display in terms of the exotic and the erotic through the revealing foreign fashions she wore and, as in *The Neighbour's Wife and Mine,* where the *modan gāru* appears as a performer, a jazz singer, her frontal address to the camera during the group's rehearsal solicits the audience's gaze and invites this scrutiny (see figure 4).

In this chapter I have argued that cinema as a modern technology intervened and was indeed an important social medium in the discourses of modernism in Japan in the 1930s. Modernism, as a social concept concomitant with the development of industrial society, redefined cultural gender types and the foundations of social relations. Cinema within this context was both a mechanism and a force for change. Through the development of the distinctive style spearheaded by Shōchiku, two contradictory and competing discourses of modernity are played out, one centred on the egalitarian opportunities offered by industrial society and the other, the 'social realist' films depicting the breakdown of traditional 'premodern' or agrarian-based social structures. The two films *Marching On* and *The Only Son* provide examples of the two opposing visions of modernity available to the 'modern boy', while *The Love-Troth Tree* and *Osaka Elegy* depict the extremes of the modern project as it impacted on the 'modern woman'.

# CHAPTER 2

# Cinema, Nationalism and Empire

In Japan, the connection between a person and his . . . *ie* [household] is at the same time the link between the individual and the nation. Today, if we but probe a little, we realise that the faithful subjects and loyal retainers of history are our ancestors, and we are aware, not just vaguely but in a concrete way, of the intentions of our ancestors. The awareness that our ancestors have lived and served under the imperial family for thousands of generations forms the surest basis for the feelings of loyalty and patriotism (*chūkun aiko-kushin*). If the *ie* were to disappear, it might even be difficult for us to explain to ourselves why we should be Japanese. As our individualism flourished, we would come to view our history no differently from the way we view that of foreign countries. (From a speech made by Yanagita Kunio to the Greater Japan Agricultural Association in 1906, quoted in and translated by Irokawa 1985: 288)

Its myths invert reality: it claims to defend folk culture while in fact it is forging a high culture; it claims to protect an old folk society while in fact helping to build up an anonymous mass society. (Gellner on nationalist ideology, 1999: 124)

If you don't understand [*Chūshingura*] you are not a Japanese . . . (Yomota 1999: 182)

While within areas of Japanese popular culture there was an enthusiastic embrace of modernism, there was also, as seen in the 'social realist' films discussed in the previous chapter, a critical backlash against the inherent travails accompanying modernization. The modernism depicted in the films still extant from the late 1920s and the 1930s provides clear evidence of the social contradictions inherent in this period of rapid economic and social change. In this chapter, I shall shift the focus of enquiry to another related concomitant of Japan's industrialization—that of nationalism. Nationalism, as a sociopolitical concept, grew out of the institutions of modernity, universal education, the development of popular media and modern political structures (Gellner 1998 and 1999, Anderson 1993 and Hobsbawn 1992). The irony is that a sense of popular nationalism developed at the very juncture in time when the traditional culture it draws upon was in a state of disintegration due to these same forces of modernity, hence Eric Hobsbawn's and

Terence Ranger's (1992) astute observation regarding the sociopolitical imperative to 'invent tradition' in the modern age. Within Japanese films of the late 1930s and early 1940s, 'the invention of tradition' is clearly manifest in the modern project's continuing re-invention of an apparently historically determined masculinity and re-defined 'group-orientated' society, or to use Benedict Anderson's (1993) term, the 'imagined community'. In the Japanese example, the 'imagined community' of the modern period emerged as a derivation of the Neo-Confucianist ideologies that had so successfully underpinned the Tokugawa regime. Hobsbawn suggests that the imagined community fills an 'emotional void' left by the disintegration of 'real human communities and networks' caused by the economic and social shift from collective agricultural practices to industrial structures of social relations. The group model, characteristic of Japanese society, became in the Meiji period the ideological substitute for the co-operative collective model of the agro-literate society of the early-middle Tokugawa period. The competitive individualizing ethos, inherent in capitalist industrial societies, was subsumed beneath the group ethos as a variant feeling 'of collective belonging which already existed and could operate . . . on the macro-political scale which could fit in with modern . . . nations' (Hobsbawn 1992: 46). In terms of political policy, the connection between the family, village community and the state had been officially promoted since the Meiji period through slogans such as *kazoku kokka* (the family state), as the epigraph taken from a speech made by Yanagita (at the beginning of this chapter) so clearly explicates.

If the films discussed in the previous chapter highlighted the contradictions in the social consequences of modernity, other films offered through allegory an alternative unifying theme that re-inscribed alienated masculinity within the national, re-invented patriarchal structures of a modern industrial society. They offered solutions to contradictions inherent in the valourization of Western, Hollywood-derived heroic individualism and the group ethos of the 'family state' (*kazoku kokka*). It is to an exploration of these films that I now wish to turn before going on to look at the imbricated issue of nationalism, 'imperialism'. In 'national policy' films (*kokusaku eiga*) of the early 1940s, Empire was clearly linked to political policies of 'assimilation' and the outward migration of native Japanese to the colonies. However, it was also an important element as the defining 'other' of the Japanese 'nation-state'. Therefore, this chapter will continue with an analysis of the star persona of Ri Kōran/Li Xianglan (Yamaguchi Yoshiko 1920–) before concluding with a discussion of the 1940s 'spy film', a narrative space where the ideological entities of the Japanese 'nation-state' and Empire form parallel and mutually reinforcing concepts, while the American enemy becomes the defining 'other'.

If the harsh realities of recession-hit Japan in the 1930s exploded the fissures inherent in a policy of rapid state-sponsored industrialization,[1] the Manchurian Incident of 1931 and the Shanghai Incident of 1932 helped turn public resentment away from a disaffection with internal political mechanisms and onto patriotic sentiments that increasingly manifested as popular nationalism.[2] In thematic terms, a form of popular nationalism found expression in cinema in two dominant discourses centring on the depiction of the male hero. These distinct portrayals were divided along the two broad classifications of Japanese cinema, the *jidaimono* (period dramas) and the *gendaigeki* (contemporary drama). The *jidaimono* centred on the depiction of an idealized masculinity that was clearly linked to the star personas of the principal actors of the time (in this chapter, I shall focus on, in particular, the 'three treasures' of Nikkatsu, Bandō Tsumasaburō [1901–1953], Arashi Kanjūrō [1903–1980] and Kataoka Chiezō [1903–1983]).[3] And second, in *gendaigeki* films, one finds a privileging of the male group and the individual's place within the group through the depiction of (a) the sublimation of the individual's will to that of the group, as in *Sanshiro Sugata* (*Sugata Sanshirō*) (1943) and *There Was a Father* (*Chichi Ariki*) (1942); and (b) by creating a personal link between the individual and authority; an authority which in modern society had become increasingly abstract, built around concepts such as the 'nation-state' and the 'imperial institution'. *Submarine Number One* (*Sensuikan ichigō*) (1941), *The War at Sea from Hawaii to Malaya* (*Hawai Marei oki-kaisen*) (1942), *Navy* (*Kaigun*) (1943) and *Army* (*Rikugun*) (1944) are all examples of this latter case. In short, it is a question of emphasis. The individual character played by one of the great *jidaigeki* stars, in that he was often based on some historical or pseudo-historical figure and was therefore exemplary, dominated the world of *jidaimono*. Equally, the star persona of the actor himself, became sufficiently imbued, through multiple appearances as various historical figures, to be exemplary in himself, as in the example of Bandō Tsumasaburō, who plays the lowly rickshaw man in the 1943 Meiji-*mono* film *The Life of Muhō Matsu* aka *The Rickshaw Man/The Life of Matsugorō the Pure/Matsu the Untamed* (*Muhō Matsu no isshō*) directed by Inagaki Hiroshi (1905–1980). In the case of *gendaigeki*, these films were concerned with the politics of the group. Due to the complex nature of this discussion, this chapter is set out following the geopolitical structure of the film industry which, by the mid-1930s, was clearly divided in both geographical terms and in the domination of specific genres along company lines. Nikkatsu held a dominant position in Kyoto making *jidaimono*, period films, and was known colloquially as the 'kingdom of period drama' (*jidaigeki ōkoku*), while the Shōchiku Tokyo Studios dominated the production of *gendaigeki* and was known as the 'kingdom of actresses' (*joyū ōkoku*). To fully appreciate the relationship between popular nationalism and its manifestations in the Japanese cinema from the mid-1930s to the end of the Pacific War in 1945, it is helpful to trace the development of these discourses from the mid-1920s.

## *Jidaimono:* from *Kyūgeki* to *Chanbara*

Period films made prior to the mid-1920s were dominated by the star persona of the kabuki-trained actor Onoe Matsunosuke (1875–1926), Japan's first screen idol. These films were based on popular *kōdan* historical tales, which were conservative in the pre-modern Neo-Confucian morality they endorsed. *Kōdan* storytelling had developed from an earlier genre, that of the *kōshaku* lectures on historical texts, given to people of high rank. *Kōdan* as a popular oral storytelling tradition, which developed in the Meiji period (1868–1912) as part of an anonymous collective tradition, underwent further transformations in its print form as popular literature and in its adaptation to cinema in the Taishō (1912–1926) and early Shōwa (1926–1945) periods. It is thus a good example of Ernest Gellner's (1999) premise that in industrial societies the high culture of the former ruling elite becomes the dominant culture, albeit in a modified form.[4] Jean-Pierre Lehmann in his history of Japan (1982) refers to this process as the samurai-isation of the lower classes, that is, the dissemination of the former samurai values to all levels of society.

The shift from oral storytelling traditions to the publication boom in the early 1900s of popular novels, derived from the *kōdan* tradition, brought with it questions of authorship and originality, as storytelling was brought into the system of property rights in a capitalist market. Concomitant with this process, popular novelists such as Nakazato Kaizan (1885–1944)[5], Osaragi Jirō (1897–1973)[6], Hayashi Fubō (1900–1935)[7] and Hasegawa Shin (1884–1963)[8] came to prominence. These developments had implications for the structure of *jidaimono* films as their works have been repeatedly made into films spanning both the pre- and postwar periods. The increase in print production, the death of Onoe Matsunosuke in 1926, the establishment of independent star production film companies from the mid-1920s and the influences of the *shinkokugeki* theatre movement,[9] in which popular film actors such as Ōkōchi Denjirō (1898–1962), Tsukigata Ryūnosuke (1902–1970) and Ōtomo Ryūtarō (1912–1985) were trained, are cited by Japanese film historians (Tsutsui 2000, Hashimoto 1989, Satō 1995 vol. i) as a conjunction of factors that led to major changes in *jidaimono* films at this time. In terms of content, two trends are clearly discernible: those that adapted and developed the *kōdan*-style drama to the interests of modern audiences, often through the inclusion of a romantic subplot; and those that challenged, at the political level, the moral conservatism of the earlier Onoe Matsunosuke productions. In terms of style, filmmakers experimented with new cinematic techniques in depicting movement. This stylistic shift in the depiction of movement is identified as the historical point in the transition from *kyūgeki* films to *chanbara*, or the more formal term, *jidaigeki*. *Chanbara* is an onomatopoeic expression denoting the rhythm of the climactic sword-fight scenes as expressed by children of the period mimicking the musical accompaniment, '*chan chanbara, chanbara*' (Hashimoto 1989: 224). This semantic expression clearly links rhythm to movement in *jidaimono* and is well illustrated in a scene in the 1928 version of *Kurama Tengu* (re-released in 1991 on video, complete with *benshi* voice-over, by the Matsuda Film Library). Two young boys, bored with their calligraphy practice, use their brushes as mock swords, one boy pretending to be Saigō Takamori[10] and the other boy, the Kurama Tengu. The *benshi*, Matsui Shinsui, takes the part of one of the boys chants—'*chan chanbara chanbara*'—as the boys cross swords. According to Tsutsui (2000: 22–23), the term *jidaigeki*, which literally means period drama, was first used in the publicity material for the 1923 Shōchiku production based on a screenplay by Itō Daisuke (1898–1981) and directed by Nomura Hotei (1880–1934) called *Women Pirates* (*Onna to kaizoku*). *Kyūgeki* refers literally to the 'old drama' derived from the kabuki tradition.

## Bandō Tsumasaburō and the Alienated, Idealistic Hero

In the previous chapter I briefly raised the suggestion that the *matatabimono* (wandering yakuza/masterless samurai) films, a subgenre of *jidaigeki*, took up questions of male alienation. With the egalitarian ideals and the disintegration of the premodern class structures that accompanied the transition from premodern to modern Japan[11] came a counter-side, the de-sanctification of the former elite samurai class. *Rōnin* (masterless samurai), as economically outdated remnants from this previous age, were unable to function in the evolving mercantile capitalist, urban society of the declining years of the Tokugawa hegemony. Excluded from society, in film narratives they become the objects of juridical disciplinary controls. Metaphorically, this process of de-sanctification is played out in film narratives of the late 1920s on the body of the hero, which is beaten and bound (*The Serpent* [*Orochi*]) or mutilated (Tange Sazen, the one-armed, one-eyed *rōnin*). Within film narratives of this period, their very existence questions a social morality that excludes them, 'unjustly' labelling them as outlaws. As the intertitle that opens and concludes *The Serpent* pleads, 'Even amongst fearsome people whom society labels as rogues (*narazumono*), there are right-minded men'. It is against this label *narazumono*, repeated several times throughout the film by the *benshi* mimicking the cruel gossiping crowd, that Heizaburō (Bandō Tsumasaburō) fights. *The Serpent* follows a simple causal trajectory that alternates between violent incidents that provoke a hostile social reaction, followed by Heizaburō's soul-searching. In the first instance, he is unjustly expelled from the local school of Chinese learning (*kangaku*). It is the headmaster of the school's birthday and during the ensuing celebrations a son of a high-ranking official of the clan provokes Heizaburō. He responds violently to the insult and a fight ensues. The headmaster takes the side of the official's son and Heizaburō is expelled. Later he returns to the school to try to explain the true facts of the situation to the daughter of the headmaster with whom he is in love; she calls for assistance and another fracas ensues. This time Heizaburō is expelled from the domain and condemned to wander as a *rōnin* musing on life's injustices.

Within these discourses, the *rōnin*s' masculine encoding of themselves, as a former elite class, comes into conflict with emerging concepts of a national rather than a domain-(*han*) based citizenship. *Rōnin* enter the public world on their own terms, believing in an outdated but still revered morality, becoming in the films' narratives the symbolic 'other' of the modern, now conformist and compromising, citizen. This new class of citizens is protected by the civil police (*yakunin*), who use long poles and ropes to beat, bind and incarcerate Heizaburō. The police thus impose the new social values and morality upon the body of the dispossessed samurai, the *rōnin* (see figures 6 and 7).

The 1925 film *The Serpent* starring Bandō Tsumasaburō is perhaps the best extant example of this group of films labelled by Japanese film historians as the 'rebellious *jidaigeki*' (*hangyaku jidaigeki*), portraying what has often been described as a 'nihilistic' hero. Ishiwari describes the film in the following terms: 'A hero, whose love is destroyed by a feudalistic power and class system, attempts to resist that power and is rejected and cornered by society. Finally, in a fit of discontent and resentment, he explodes and slashes out with his sword' (Ishiwari 2000: 288). Other films most commonly listed by Japanese scholars under this rubric are *The New Publication of the Trials of Magistrate Ōoka* aka *Ōoka Trials* (*Shinpan Ōoka seidan*)[12] (1928) directed by Itō Daisuke and starring Ōkōchi Denjirō, based on the popular novel by Hayashi Fubō about the one-armed, one-eyed *rōnin*, Tange Sazen (this film is no longer extant); and *The Streets of Masterless Samurai* (*Rōningai*), a series of three films (1928–1929) directed by Makino Masahiro (1908–1993), fragments of which remain. In all these examples, the *rōnin* have been betrayed by their lords and their loyalty rejected, and in return they reject society. Certainly when compared to the alternative, and one might add the more popular *jidaigeki* subgenre nascent at this time, constructed around the star persona of Arashi Kanjūrō, in the form of the *Kurama Tengu* series[13] and *The Case Notes of Kondō (Muttsuri) Umon* (*Umon torimonocho*) series[14], the hero of *The Serpent* can be described as nihilistic. However, in thematic terms a more appropriate but perhaps less obvious comparison can be drawn with the themes of the *gendaigeki* 'social realist' films of the period. In this case the hero of *The Serpent*, Heizaburō, is better described as the alienated or idealistic hero. This characterization was to become the defining criterion upon which the star persona of Bandō Tsumasaburō was constructed.

*The Serpent,* produced by Bandō Tsumasaburō's own production company (Bantsuma Productions) based on a screenplay by Suzukita Ryokuhei and directed by Futagawa Buntarō (1899–1966) was, as Suzukita has stated in an article in the journal *Shinario* published in 1954[15], an attempt to elevate *jidaigeki* to attract audiences from the 'educated' classes. The principal strategy used was to give Heizaburō a degree of psychological depth—through the expression of inner conflict—denied other samurai heroes, such as those portrayed by Arashi Kanjūrō, whose star persona, like that of Onoe Matsunosuke, was constructed to appeal to young boys through action. As discussed in the preceding chapter, the depiction of Heizaburō's inner self was achieved using cinematic techniques and, more important through interior monologues, given expression through the *ben-*

*shi*. Unlike their Western counterparts, Japanese filmmakers, due to the *benshi*, were freed from the restrictions of intertitles for character exposition. A scene towards the middle of the film exemplifies this: Heizaburō's yakuza friends kidnap a girl with whom Heizaburō has fallen in love because she physically resembles his first love, Namie, the daughter of the head of the Chinese Classics School. The yakuza leave him alone in the room with Otsu as she pleads with him not to rape her. In a sequence of ten shots Heizaburō, after roughly attempting to undo her *obi* and forcing her cringing into a corner to the left of the screen, proceeds to advance menacingly towards Otsu. During this sequence of reverse shots devoid of intertitles, the *benshi*, Matsuda Shinsui, voices Otsu's pleas as direct dialogue, but in the case of Heizaburō, he voices his inner conflict, his desire for Otsu and his conscience that mitigates against this act of violence.

> **Benshi**: A fiendish voice asks Heizaburō, What are you going to do? [As a social outcast] you don't have to do what society considers right.

The camera cuts between medium close-up shots of Otsu as she pleads and then back to frontal shots of Heizaburō as he slowly moves with each reverse-cut shot closer into the camera until his face, slightly to the left of the screen, fills the frame, with the camera focusing on his eyes. At this point in extreme close-up Heizaburō moves his eyes slightly, signalling his return to consciousness and his realization that he must resist this 'fiendish voice'. In the next shot the camera pulls back, framing Heizaburō again in medium close-up, signalling his retreat from Otsu and the resolution of his moral dilemma. This sequence ends as it began with a shot of the yakuza huddled outside by the sliding door listening to what is going on in the next room. In terms of camera movement, it is interesting to note that Heizaburō physically moves in towards the stationary camera to bring his face into an extreme close-up and that as he appears to pull away, it is in fact the camera that pulls back, altering his position within the frame.[16]

Through the portrayal of Heizaburō's inner conflict, the film offers a critique of a class-based society that unjustly condemns men, through no real fault of their own other than perhaps youthful hotheadedness, to a life as an outcast, a *narazumono*. If the headmaster of the Chinese Classics School had made a fair and 'just' decision, and not favoured the son of a clan official, Heizaburō would not have been expelled from the school. Equally, if the police had accepted Heizaburō's explanation and not judged him by his appearance, he would not have been sent to jail and would not have come into contact with the yakuza. Equally, the film attacks the loyalty ethic of the yakuza gang in a scene when they appear to help an ill samurai and his young wife, who just happens to be Heizaburō's first love, Namie. While the husband is lying ill on his *futon*, the head of the yakuza gang attempts to force himself on Namie sexually. Heizaburō, in the next room, again struggles with his conscience through the *benshi*. 'Why should I help her? She did, after all, reject me.' However, intervene he does. He asks the *oyabun* to let them go, pointing out that the *oyabun* can have any woman he wants. The *oyabun*, rejecting this request, tells Heizaburō to 'shut your eyes . . .' but Heizaburō persists. Ultimately, the *oyabun* reminds Heizaburō of his debt/obligation (*ongi*) to him for taking him in and protecting him from the authorities. Heizaburō replies, 'I have not forgotten my obligations to you, but I cannot for the sake of an obligation ignore justice'. At which point a fight begins that leads to Heizaburō's climactic battle with the police in which his body is beaten, bound and led away through a jeering crowd to his final incarceration. It is only Namie and her samurai husband, now saved thanks to Heizaburō's intervention, who watch sympathetically with heads bowed as he is led away.

Within this narrative Heizaburō as a moral being can find no social space within which he can live. Legitimate society is depicted as class-based and corrupt, and the yakuza group, which takes him in, is shown to be equally devoid of any sense of a humane morality, appealing instead to outdated feudalistic concepts of loyalty that often require the individual to go against his conscience in putting the interests of his gang first. *The Wandering Gambler* (*Hōrō zanmai*) (1928), set in the declining years of the Tokugawa hegemony, offers a similar bleak view of society as the hero (Kataoka Chiezō), after becoming a *rōnin*, is approached by both the Imperial Forces seeking to restore the emperor and by the pro-Tokugawa shogunate faction in Kyoto, the *Shinsengumi*. He concludes that both are corrupt and ultimately rejects both groups, preferring to ruminate on 'human nature' (*shōne*), which he concludes is not about winning and losing. As such, these films went against the grain of many *chanbara* films of the period, which are based on contests and winning and losing. In the case of *The Serpent* and *The Wandering Gambler*, the heroes are attempting to discover their true natures. This theme of male alienation reappears in the postwar period in the 'cruel' (*zankoku*) *jidaigeki* films and the 'drifter' (*nagaremono*) films of the 1960s and will be taken up in a later chapter.

If these *chanbara* films of the late 1920s depicted an alienated masculinity beaten into submission by the forces of the state, by the late 1930s, the death of the hero had become encoded in positive terms as the ultimate expression of loyalty through sacrifice. *Seppuku*—death by one's own hand through ritual disembowelment, as a form of self-mutilation—became the masochistic expression of submission to the social order. Although the open depiction of this theme did not find full expression until the advent of the 'cruel' (*zankoku*) *jidaigeki* films of the 1960s, its roots can be traced back to the late 1920s and 1930s and such classic tales as *The Story of the Forty-seven Loyal Retainers (Chūshingura)*. However, in these prewar films the final *seppuku* scene is rarely depicted; only in Mizoguchi Kenji's (1898–1956) iconoclastic two-part epic *The Loyal Forty-seven Rōnin* aka *The Forty-seven Rōnin of the Genroku Era (Genroku Chūshingura)* (1941–1942), based on the play by Mayama Seika (1878–1948), is it included. The inclusion of the *seppuku* scene in this version shifts the emphasis of the drama away from the triumphal success of the attack, which is not depicted, to an even greater emphasis on the sacrifice of the forty-seven *rōnin* and, perhaps more important, their submission to the rule of law. This shift in emphasis was in keeping with the directives included in the 1939 Film Law and is one of the reasons cited by Japanese film critics for the box-office failure of the films. In the main, *Chūshingura* films end with the *rōnins'* triumphal march through the streets of Edo carrying the severed head of Kira Kōsuke-no-suke, the enemy of their dead lord.

Between 1937 and 1938 Bandō Tsumasaburō appeared in three films based on the *Chūshingura* theme: in 1937 he appeared as Horibe Yasubei in *Duel at Takadanobaba (Kettō Takadanobaba)*, jointly directed by Makino Masahiro and Inagaki Hiroshi, and in 1938 he took the part of Akagaki Genzō[17] in *Akagaki Genzō and the Night Before the Attack on Kira's Mansion (Chūshingura Akagaki Genzō uchiiri zen'ya)*, directed by Ikeda Tomiyasu (1892–1968). Both films form part of a distinct sub-genre of the *jidaigeki* known as the *Chūshingura meimeiden,* that is, the re-telling of aspects of the lives of one of the forty-seven *rōnin*. These films, although based on characters in *Chūshingura*, should not be confused with the ninety-one film versions made between 1908 and 1994 (*Kinema Junpō* 1994: 168–170) ostensibly based on the events of the actual incident. In 1938 Bandō Tsumasaburō went on to play Ōishi Kuranosuke, the leader of the forty-seven *rōnin*, in the all-star production *Chūshingura: the Heavenly Scroll and the Earthly Scroll (Chūshingura: ten no maki, chi no maki*), jointly directed by Makino Masahiro and Ikeda Tomiyasu. This version also stars Kataoka Chiezō in the two roles of Asano Takumi-no-kami and Tachibana, and Arashi Kanjūrō as the shogunate official who carries out the investigation into Asano's attack on Kira. Through an examination of the star persona of Bandō Tsumasaburō, as depicted in relation to the characters he portrays in these films, I shall trace the shift from the socially critical alienated hero of the late 1920s *The Serpent* period to the re-invented and re-inscribed masculinity characteristic of the late 1930s.

*Chūshingura*, due to its great popularity in puppet theatre (*bunraku*), kabuki and cinema, has become, through constant repetition, part of the Japanese collective tradition. In this sense, film versions of *Chūshingura* have come to rely on the 'iconic memory' and the shared cultural knowledge of their viewing audience in the creation of meaning. Jackie Stacey defines 'iconic memory' as memories of a 'frozen moment; a moment removed from its temporal context and captured as pure image' (Stacey 1994: 318). For example, a single shot of the forty-seven *rōnin*s' wooden sandals (*geta*) placed at the entrance to a shop signifies the night of the attack on Kira's mansion. It is generally accepted that in the room above this shop the *rōnin* made their final preparations. Also Kira's character as an ill-tempered old man is often reduced to close-up shots of his contorted face. In the 1994 *Chūshinguragaiden Yotsuyakaidan*, which entwines the *Yotsuyakaidan* ghost story around the *Chūshingura* narrative, Kira is virtually absent from the screen. An aging retainer of Kira's house, who plays a significant role in the ghost subnarrative, is constructed to carry iconic meanings associated with more traditional representations of Kira. As these brief examples illustrate, films based on the *Chūshingura* incident often rely heavily on the audience's 'iconic memory'.

The historical incident took place in Edo between 1701 and 1703. On the fourteenth day of the third month of the year *Genroku* 14 (1701), Asano Takumi-no-kami Naganori, Lord of Akō *han* (estate) in Harima in the eastern section of the Inland Sea, attacked and wounded Kira Kōzuke-no-suke Yoshinaka in the *shōgun*'s castle in Edo. In the subsequent investigation, when questioned, Lord Asano reported it had been a private grievance, and when Kira was similarly questioned, he replied he did not know what had provoked the attack. After the results of this investigation were made known to the *shōgun*, Lord Asano was ordered to commit *seppuku*; his lands were confiscated, his family disinherited, and his retainers dismissed. On the fifteenth day of the twelfth month of *Genroku* 15 (1702), Ōishi Kuranosuke Yoshio and forty-six of Asano's former retainers attacked Kira's home in Edo, beheading him before surrendering to the *bakufu*. On the fourth day of the second month in *Genroku* 16 (1703), the forty-six retainers also committed *seppuku*.

Satō's (1976) detailed study of *Chūshingura* in Japanese popular culture is a useful aid to understanding the cultural significance of this tale, as he sets out the main sociohistorical discourses that have developed around the incident. His main thesis is that, historically within popular discourse, the attack of the forty-seven on Kira's house has been construed in one of two ways. It has been interpreted as (a) an act of extreme loyalty to their dead Lord Asano, or (b) as an act of rebellion against the Tokugawa shogunate. Satō explains the logic surrounding the first interpretation in the following terms: Ōishi Kuranosuke and the forty-six retainers and indeed the Tokugawa shogunate all had a vested interest in promoting the first option. Satō suggests that Ōishi and the forty-six were concerned with their honour. Therefore, if it had been construed that their actions were rebellious, they would have been executed as traitors, and their families would have suffered for generations to come. At this point, historical fact is brought in to support this interpretation. Horibe Yahei and the other forty-six wrote a proclamation to the *shōgun* stating that they accepted the fact that their Lord Asano was at fault in striking Kira within the castle precincts. They went on to say that, had Asano not been restrained at the time, he would surely have killed Kira. Thus, in order to placate the spirit of their dead lord, they felt it was their duty out of loyalty to him to complete the deed. To bring moral backing to their argument, they altered the Confucian precept upon which revenge killings were permitted by law during the Tokugawa period (1600–1868): 'One should not live under heaven with the enemy of one's father' (*chichi no teki totomo ni ten o itadakazu*). This they changed to 'One should not live under heaven with the enemy of one's lord' (*kunpu no teki totomo ni ten o itadakazu*). As Satō goes on to explain, it was commonly accepted that a child or younger brother could seek vengeance against a person who had killed their father or elder brother; however, there were no recorded cases of retainers taking vengeance for their lord. Until the attack of the forty-seven on Kira's house, Japanese Neo-Confucianism laid emphasis on the *kō* of filial piety and not the *chū* of loyalty. Therefore, Satō concludes that it was from this period on that absolute loyalty to one's lord became the central concept of *bushidō* (the code of the samurai). Prior to the events of the *Chūshingura* incident and their immortalization in the *bunraku*/kabuki *Kanadehon* version[18], bravery (*buyū*) and honour (*meiyo*) were central to the *bushi* tradition. To reinforce this line of argument, he points to the many examples of *bushi* who changed their allegiance to lords to advance their own positions during the Sengoku warring states period (1467–1568). 'To the *bushi* the honour and respect of their house was more important than loyalty, but after *Chūshingura*, this ideology descended to the level where honour and respect were equated with loyalty' (Satō 1976: 31). Satō, in this interpretation of the development of *Chūshingura* as a popular narrative, attempts to ground the two dominant themes of loyalty and rebellion in the few historically known facts relating to the incident. However, as with all similar attempts, in the final analysis, it is based on supposition. This in no way detracts from Satō's account, which provides one of the best outlines of the incident as a topic of popular discourse (as opposed to academic accounts). The important point is not whether this interpretation is accurate, but rather that in Japanese popular discourse it is generally accepted as accurate.

Bandō Tsumasaburō's star persona as the pure and honest but misunderstood young *rōnin* running against the current of society became established in the mid-1920s. However, in the 1930s as the symbolic significance of *rōnin* as social outcasts began to change, the rebellious and alienated star persona of Bandō Tsumasaburō became contained within the figures of historically significant *rōnin* of popular myth such as Horibe Yasubei and Akagaki Genzō, each of *Chūshingura* fame. His raw *rōnin* masculinity that once signified social opposition, in these later productions, is representative of loyalty as a positive social force. As Genzō in *Akagaki Genzō and the Night before the Attack on Kira's Mansion,* he must play the profligate younger brother in his brother's house in order to keep secret the plans to attack Kira's mansion. Kira, fearing an attack, has planted spies in the house of Genzō's brother. Thus Genzō must endure the ignominy of being censured by not only his brother, but also he must withstand the vituperations of his brother's wife and young nephew. In this case loyalty to his dead lord transcends even his relationships with members of his own family, re-affirming the altered Confucian precept, 'One should not live under heaven with the enemy of one's lord'. The emotional impact of the film relies for its effect on the audiences' prior knowledge of the events of *Chūshingura* and the heroic status of the forty-seven *rōnin* in Japanese cultural history. Much of the pleasure in the film is derived from watching Genzō's sister-in-law deride Genzō, only to have to admit her error in the final scenes. These scenes draw on the spectator's 'iconic memory', as they are a variation on one of the main scenes depicted in the majority of film versions of *Chūshingura,* when just before the planned attack on Kira's mansion, Ōishi Kuranosuke, the leader of the forty-seven *rōnin,* visits Lord Asano's wife to make his obeisance to his dead lord at the Buddhist family altar on the anniversary of his ritual self-immolation *(seppuku).* Asano's widow and her ladies-in-waiting attempt to question him on his plans for revenge. Ōishi, of course, cannot reveal the plan as again there are spies in the house and, like Genzō, Ōishi must suffer the derision of those around him. The scorn of Genzō's sister-in-law adds also to the loneliness Genzō feels on the night of the attack when he calls at his brother's house to have one final drink with him, only to find that his brother is not at home and his wife refuses to see him. In true filial fashion, he places his brother's kimono on a stand and, kneeling before it, he offers his brother a symbolic cup of *sake.* The brother's face is superimposed on the kimono.

The film thus remains faithful to the dominant loyalty theme of *Chūshingura*-derived narratives of this time and, in so doing, deflects the inner conflict characteristic of Bandō Tsumasaburō's star persona away from a critique of society and onto the 'positive' attribute of loyalty and filial piety, which were central concepts of the *kazoku kokka* ideology of the nation-state as per Yanagita et al. (see epigraph). The raw masculine energy of the *rōnin* is thereby tamed and transformed and used to the advantage of the group.

In cinematic terms, in the late 1920s silent film, the expression of inner conflict so central to the characters portrayed by Bandō Tsumasaburō was, in part, dependent on the *benshi* cadenza. In the era of the 'talkie', there was a shift in emphasis from the *benshi*'s verbal expression of inner monologues, as the main vehicle for the exposition of a character's inner conflict, to action being the outward expression of inner feelings. However, the *benshi*'s interior monologue was to a lesser extent reproduced through the soliloquy. In *Akagaki Genzō and the Night Before the Attack on Kira's Mansion,* on the night of the attack when Genzō makes his offering in front of his brother's kimono, he makes a speech as if the brother were present (the brother's face appears in superimposition over the kimono). He wishes his brother a long life and apologizes for parting on bad terms. Also, in *Duel at Takadanobaba* as Yasubei, in a scene after his father has admonished him in severe terms for his profligate ways, Yasubei is left alone in the room, and taking his father's part, he repeats word for word his father's rebukes.

Although the soliloquy works to great effect in these emotionally charged scenes, in the era of the 'talkie', the focus shifted to the expression of inner conflict through action and a psychological tension maintained by the audience's all-knowing position. At one level, due to the prominence of *Chūshingura* in Japanese popular culture, we are totally familiar with the outcome of the plotline, never doubting the integrity of the hero, and on another level, through the omniscient narration we are privy to the effects the other characters' derisive attitudes have on Genzō. In terms of actions, at one point in the film Genzō and his brother are playing *go* (a board game) and Genzō is losing. His brother, using the black and white stones as metaphors, asks Genzō, Do his white stones not hate the black stones that are killing them? This is a direct reference to the Akō *rōnin* who appear to be standing idly by and not taking the requisite revenge. Genzō, aware that he cannot reveal the truth, excites the anger of his brother, who turns over the *go* table in a rage, inadvertently spilling a cup of tea onto Genzō's sword. As the brother stands up, the camera cuts from a long shot to a close-up of the hilt of Genzō's sword and then to a medium close-up of Genzō as he grabs the sword to see if it has been damaged. The brother misconstrues Genzō's action and reaches for his sword at which point his wife intervenes. Genzō apologizes, saying that he had no intention of drawing his sword against his brother. At that point, the brother leaves the room and stands listening at the door. Throughout the film, the brother is not entirely taken in by Genzō's behaviour. Genzō, now alone, checks his sword and carefully wipes the drops of tea from the blade. The camera, again through an extreme close-up shot of the sword, directs our attention to its significance, as Genzō's concern for his sword negates the accusations of his brother. The sword is after all the 'soul' (*tamashii*) of a samurai. This characterization of Genzō remains faithful to Bandō Tsumasaburō's star persona in that, until the final triumphal scene, he is still the misunderstood social outcast; the son of the next-door neighbour derides him earlier in the film as a 'freeloader' (*isōrō*), which carries strong resonances of the label *narazumono,* so central to Heizaburō's/Bandō's self-image in *The Serpent*.

The inclusion of a romantic parallel plot in *jidaigeki* films of this period also functioned to tame the *rōnin*. Tange Sazen, in the 1935 version directed by Yamanaka Sadao (1909–1938) starring Ōkōchi Denjirō, *Tange Sazen and the Story of the One Million-Ryō Vase* aka *The Million-Ryō Pot* (*Tange Sazen yowa hyakuman-ryō no tsubo*), has a seemingly stable relationship with the woman who runs the archery gallery in the amusement district (in subsequent films she teaches the *shamisen*). When they take in a young boy, whose father was killed and who keeps his goldfish in the sought-after vase, they effectively form a family. Tange Sazen adjusts to the surrogate father role as he shows concern over the boy's education and protects him from the school bullies. *Duel at Takadanobaba* puts a romantic twist on the renowned tale of Yasubei's adoption as a son-in-law by Horibe Yahei. In this version it is Horibe's daughter who first notices Yasubei in a scene when he is fighting off a group of men who had been threatening some of the townspeople: she then tells her father, who sets about looking for Yasubei. When he finally sees Yasubei fight off a large group of men while avenging his dead father in the climactic sword-fight (*tachimawari*) sequence at Takadanobaba, he is impressed, at which point the film ends. The subsequent wedding ceremony, although not depicted, confirms Yasubei's newfound place in society. He has redeemed himself as a filial son by killing his father's enemies and will now take his place in the Horibe household and, as we the audience know, he will go on to distinguish himself in the future as one of the loyal forty-seven. In *Akagaki Genzō and the Night Before the Attack on Kira's Mansion*, Hanayagi Kogiku (1921–) plays the part of the girl next door who is in love with Genzō. In her attempts to reform Genzō, she gives him a hanging scroll of Minamoto no Yoshitsune (1159–1189, a warrior immortalized as a tragic hero) and Benkei (his faithful retainer) for inspiration before giving up and marrying someone else. The final scene of the film is focused on her reaction as she follows Genzō and the other *rōnin* through the snow in their triumphal march. Her emotional state is conveyed through a long left tracking shot in close-up of the lower portion of her legs as she walks through the snow and unconsciously slips out of her wooden clogs (*geta*) and continues barefoot through the snow, finally dropping her umbrella. Even the ever stoic Arashi Kanjūrō, in the 1927 film *The Million-Ryō Secret* (*Hyakuman-ryō hibun*) based on the novel by Mikami Otokichi (1891–1944), has a wife, and in the *Kurama Tengu* he has a female admirer in the 1928 episode. However, unlike Hollywood adventure films of this period in which the hero had to be successful in both his adventure and romance, in most *jidaigeki* films the romantic subplot remains unconsummated. In the films cited above, Heizaburō, in the final sequence of *The Serpent*, is led off to prison as the woman he loves looks on, now fully aware that she had misjudged him. *Akagaki Genzō and the Night Before the Attack* concludes on a similar note. As Genzō marches triumphantly off through the snow, the woman he loves follows distraught in his wake. In both *The Wandering*

*Gambler* and *The Million-Ryō Secret,* the heroes' wives die. In the former case, she kills herself after being violated, and in the latter, she is murdered by a jealous rival with poison. Only in the case of Yasubei in *Duel at Taka-danobaba*, through historical documentation, do we know that he marries Horibe's daughter. However, the film concludes with Yasubei's triumph at Takadanobaba, thus understating the union. In this way these films successfully exploit the novelty of romance as a modern inclusion into the heroic tradition of the *jidaigeki* genre, while in most instances they continue to re-affirm the incompatibility of a heroic masculinity and romance, a theme that reached its apotheosis in the 1940s in films such as *The Life of Muhō Matsu* (1943) and *Sanshiro Sugata* (1943).

Perhaps the ultimate example of the domesticated samurai is Akanishi Kakita in the 1936 film of the same name directed and scripted by Itami Mansaku (1900–1946). *Akanishi Kakita* is based on the historical novel about the Date family disturbance of the 1660s (*Date sōdō*) by Shiga Naoya (1883–1971). The tale surrounding the Date family disturbance had long been a mainstay of the kabuki and *kōdan* traditions, but in the iconoclastic *Akanishi Kakita, chanbara* conventions are parodied. The hero of the title of the film, Akanishi Kakita (Kataoka Chiezō), is in this version the proverbial salaryman. He is unattractive with a wart on his nose, he suffers from stomach troubles, plays chess (*shōgi*) by himself in his room and keeps a cat. In the final scene with the wedding march resounding on the sound track, the film clearly confines him to domestic bliss.

Tsutsui Kiyotada points out that, in the circles of Japanese film critics of the late 1930s and the early 1940s, there was much debate on the relationship of *jidaigeki* films to historical fact. In short, he argues that at this time there was a critical backlash against the lighthearted and frivolous elements that had been incorporated into the genre. These elements, in particular the inclusion of romantic subplots, were criticized in some quarters as being too 'American'. Considerable criticism was levelled at a group of filmmakers who became known as the Nakutaki-*gumi*, so named after the suburb in Kyoto where they lived. Yamanaka Sadao was at the centre of this group, which also included Inagaki Hiroshi. Tsutsui goes on to make the point that members of this group were in contact with directors from Shōchiku, including Shimizu Hiroshi (1903–1966) and Ozu Yasujirō (1903–1963) among others, and that in their *chanbara* films they incorporated elements of light humour of the American Hollywood style of Ernst Lubitsch (1892–1947). The 1935 version *Tange Sazen and the Story of the One Million-Ryō Vase* and *Akanishi Kakita* (1936) came in for considerable criticism on the following grounds, to quote Tsutsui: 'The purpose of *jidaigeki* is to portray the past. *Jidaigeki* films that use contemporary language in the dialogue and put samurai haircuts on contemporary dramas have no meaning. If this is the case, it would be preferable to make contemporary dramas . . .' (Tsutsui 2000: 35). Some filmmakers responded accordingly and fidelity (*chūjitsu*) became a central concern. History, which had previously provided the *mise-en-scène* of *chanbara* films, became the subject of the genre. The *bakumatsu* period (1853–1886) of political revolution took on a symbolic significance beyond that of nostalgia, as in the 1940s a new sensibility was incorporated into an old form.

## Speed and Movement in *Chanbara*: Stylistic Conventions

Within philosophical discourse, Anthony Giddens (1990) argues that the industrialization of the economy led to a re-organization of 'time' in terms of mechanically ordered time: the clock, the universal adoption of the Gregorian calendar and the introduction of timetables. In metaphorical terms, in films of the 1930s this was often depicted as speed. Charles Chaplin's *Modern Times* (1936) is perhaps one of the most famous cinematic explorations of the effects this alteration of time had on the human body. The necessity for the human body to adapt to the speed and regimentation of the conveyor belt provides much of the humour. However, the humour serves to underline the key point which is that the human body, once governed by the seasonal order of life typical of agro-literate societies of the premodern era, must adapt itself in the modern age to the new mechanical re-ordering of time through regimentation and timetables. At one point Chaplin's body, caught in the mechanism, goes round the cogwheels, forming just one more component of the machine driving the belt.

This section shall focus on speed, or more specifically the Japanese transliteration of the English as '*supiido*', as a mimetic response to the mechanical ordering of temporality. However, unlike the 'social realist' films of the 1930s discussed in the previous chapter, these films valourize these processes through spectacle and display. In Japanese *gendaigeki* films of the 1930s this manifests itself in an emphasis on mechanical aids to human movement. In films such as *Marching On* aka *The Army Advances (Shingun)* 1930s' trains, paddle steamers, planes, military tractors used for pulling heavy artillery, cars and motorbikes all form prosthetic extensions to the body of the hero. In fact, the whole of the second half of the film is built around movement—that is, the physical sense of the mili-

tary advance against the unnamed and unidentified enemy as per the title
of the film, *Marching On*. These sequences of shots, built around the
massed movement of troops, are introduced by the animated superimposition of the Chinese ideograms (*kanji*) for *shingun*. The intertitle increases
in size to give the illusion of perspective as it grows larger before flashing
off the screen. The intertitle in this way forms an integral part of the
diegesis. The directional continuity of the subsequent sequences ensures
the sense of movement towards and beyond enemy lines. Thus, the depiction of movement in these sequences underlines the dominant theme of the
film in the tangible sense of the advance of the Japanese army and, in the
allegorical sense, of the fantasy of social mobility. The relentless advance
of the army is also central to the two classic war films set on the Chinese
mainland directed by Tasaka Tomotaka (1902–1974), *The Five Scouts*
(*Gonin no sekkōhei*) (1938) and *Mud and Soldiers* (*Tsuchi to heitai*)
(1939). However, in these films, shot on location, the appeal to an heroic
individualism is not evident, as the homosocial bonding of comrades
forms the overriding political imperative. Even in Ozu's family-centred
melodramas, trains as mechanical aids to human movement are often featured. Here they bridge the spatial gap between the country and the city,
between family members separated by employment and educational com-
mitments. Regimentation is symbolized by workers streaming into office
buildings, hats lined up on racks, children drilled on playgrounds and sitting in row upon row of desks.

In *The Neighbour's Wife and Mine* aka *The Lady Next Door and My
Wife (Madama to nyōbō),* it is only after the hero hears the madam next
door singing a jazz song with the English language chorus of 'Speed up,
speed up' that he overcomes his writer's block and, staying up all night,
completes his commission, thus restoring the family finances and marital
harmony. In the final scene, the hero, his wife, young daughter and the
baby in its carriage are out for a stroll, 'My Blue Heaven' is on the sound
track, and they look up to watch a plane overhead. In fact, speed or the
Japanese transliteration '*supiido*' was one of Kido Shirō's three criteria
of a good film and formed part of the title of popular magazines of the
period, such as *Ze supiido* (*Speed*) and *San-esu* (the three s's: screen,
speed and sex).

In *chanbara* films of the late 1920s and 1930s, due to the nature of the
subject matter, speed was linked to human movement. Hashimoto Osamu
(1989) draws parallels with the depiction of movement in the '*tachimawari*' (climactic sword-fight scenes) of the *chanbara* films of the mid-1920s,
to the adoption of Western sports by Japanese youth. He cites the establish-

ment of the Inter-varsity Baseball League in 1925 as one example.[19] With films such as *The Serpent* (1925) and the *Streets of Masterless Samurai (Rōningai)* series of three films released between 1928 and 1929, Hashimoto goes on to describe the metaphorical meanings associated with the visceral intensity experienced by young men of the period when watching scenes depicting movement. These scenes, he argues, provided subjective moments of corporeal intensity and fantasy. 'He moved and so did I, he was able to move and I thought I could too . . . Young men, while watching these films, were also able to move. Young men caught up in society (*shakai ni makikomarete*) knew that in reality they could not move . . .' (Hashimoto 1989: 247).

Sawada Shōjirō (1892–1929) and his *shinkokugeki* theatre movement are attributed with the introduction of the realistic display of sword-fight (*kengeki*) scenes into Japanese theatre. While Onoe Matsunosuke was performing the stylized display of sword-fight scenes that effectively called for a momentary halt in the dramaturgy, the *mie* (pose), Sawada altered the tempo and fluidity of his dramas as his actors rushed headlong into the mêlée. In the cinema, Japanese film historians cite Bandō Tsumasaburō as being one of the first screen stars to bring this realistic style of sword-fighting to the screen. However, in cinematic terms the depiction of 'speed' and human movement are not only dependant on the actor but are enhanced through both editing and camera movement. It is to an analysis of the depiction of movement in cinematic terms that I now want to turn, as it is through an analysis of editing and camera movement and their relationship to on-screen movement that we can begin to understand Hashimoto's claims quoted above.

Broadly speaking, it is possible to discern a stylistic trajectory from a reliance on rhythmic editing in the depiction of movement in *tachimawari* scenes of the mid-1920s, through to the establishment of sophisticated genre conventions in the expressive uses of rhythmic editing, graphic-match-on-action-shots and camera movement from the late 1920s and the 1930s. In the 1940s there appears to have been a trend towards an emphasis on camera movement and the long take, taken to the extreme by Mizoguchi Kenji in his 1941–1942 *The Loyal Forty-seven Rōnin of the Genroku Era*, which is renowned for its slow tempo 'one scene, one shot' style.

In *chanbara* films the most important sequences are the action scenes, in particular, the final *tachimawari* sequence that concludes the film. This convention is central to the genre as a whole and spans both the pre- and postwar periods. Even iconoclastic films, such as *Akanishi Kakita* (1936), conform to this narrative convention, although stylistically the film challenges codes dominant in more mainstream films by reverting to a highly stylized kabuki-esque (*mie*) display in the *tachimawari*. Although *chanbara* films tell a story, their primary investment is in the display of the male hero's body. Therefore, the focus in sword-fight (*tachimawari*) sequences is on the bodily display of the prowess of the star, and the cinematic techniques employed are all geared to enhance this physical spectacle. In films such as *The Serpent*, camera movement is limited to pans and tracking shots. However, the conventions, which became more pronounced in films of the late 1920s and 1930s, are clearly in evidence. In the *tachimawari* sequences, re-framing of character action is maintained primarily through rhythmic editing, and the graphic-match is employed in tracking shots of chase scenes to great effect. In later films, this was further enhanced through crosscutting between different parallel lines of action, as in the penultimate sequences leading up to Yasubei's climactic *tachimawari* at Takadanobaba in *Duel at Takadanobaba* (1937). This penultimate montage sequence begins at a slow pace as Yasubei returns home drunk to be told by a neighbour that his father had called and, after waiting for some time, had left, leaving a letter for him. Yasubei, too drunk to take in the significance of the letter, brushes it aside. His neighbours, sensing that it is important, press it upon him. Reluctantly he begins to read the letter. The camera holds him in a medium close-up framed by his neighbours, all anxious to know the contents of the letter. As Yasubei begins to realize the import of the letter, the pace of his reading increases while simultaneously the editing and camera position place him in a medium close-up shot before cutting into a close-up revealing his anxious facial expression. After reading the letter, Yasubei finally staggers out and, after dousing himself with water, he rushes off to Takadanobaba where his father, with the aid of one retainer, is now fighting off a large group of men. The race to Takadanobaba is creatively enhanced through a sophisticated mixture of rhythmic editing, graphic-matches-on-action and crosscutting between three concurrent lines of action: Yasubei running to the scene, a group of his neighbours and supporters and the sword fight at Takadanobaba. The montage sequence is as follows:

> **Shot 1**: a group of excited neighbours assemble to follow Yasubei, who has already rushed out of the frame; cut to
>
> **Shot 2**: Yasubei in long shot, tracking left as he runs along and out of the frame—six seconds; graphic-match-on-action to

**Shot 3**: Takadanobaba, as Yasubei's father runs across the frame left, slashing at two of his opponents with his sword—three seconds; graphic-match-on-action to

**Shot 4**: the group of neighbours and supporters held in a tracking shot left, as they run along the same path that Yasubei has just traversed calling *washoi, washoi*—nine seconds; graphic-match-on-action to

**Shot sequence 5**: Yasubei, held in a tracking shot left, as he continues running along the path. This sequence lasts for fourteen seconds and contains five graphic-match inter-sequence cuts, accelerating his running speed and graphic-match-on-action to

**Shot 6**: Takadanobaba, as the father's retainer rushes left and is cut down by an opponent—six seconds; cut to

**Shot sequence 7**: the group now running along the same path that Yasubei has just been along. This sequence lasts for twelve seconds with three graphic-match inter-sequence cuts. In the second inter-sequence cut, Horibe and his daughter join the group, graphic-match-on-action to

**Shot sequence 8**: Yasubei, still running left and held in tracking shot. This sequence lasts for thirty-three seconds and has twenty-five graphic-match inter-sequence cuts, increasing the sense of speed he generates and the urgency of his flight.

At the end of this last sequence of shots, Yasubei arrives at Takadanobaba just in time to see his father cut down and to cradle him in his arms as he takes his last breaths. Just as the father dies, the group of neighbours and supporters burst onto the scene. In this way the spectators' perception is propelled forward with the pace of the editing and camera movement, a fundamental stylistic convention of the genre and precursor to Kurosawa Akira's (1910–1998) famed sequences in *Rashomon* (1950) and later in *The Seven Samurai* (*Shichi-nin no samurai*) (1954).

In *chanbara* films, the relationship between rhythmic editing and narrative form is central to these action sequences, as in many films narrative content is subordinate to the form and stylistic conventions of the genre. This is particularly evident in films constructed around the star persona of Arashi Kanjūrō. One of the best examples I have found from this early period, of this subordination of content to form, is the 1928 episode of the *Kurama Tengu* series. Set in the troubled times of the *bakumatsu* period (1853–1886), when the pro-Imperialist factions fought against the pro-shogunate faction, the *Shinsengumi*, based in Kyoto, this series of adventure films never attains the psychological depths of *The Serpent* and other films from the late 1920s and early 1930s, but offers instead a visual display of an all-powerful and omnipotent masculinity.

Built almost entirely around action, the *Kurama Tengu* series offers spectators a visceral intensity that is linked by the subject matter to an heroic quasi-imperialist tradition. It is perhaps one of the best early examples whereby the form itself, that is, the portrayal of action, determines the content of the narrative, which in the 1928 episode is centred on the Kurama Tengu's escape from the dungeon below the moat of Osaka Castle and a subsequent plot to entrap him. The plotline of this episode, divided into two clear sections, both culminating in a dramatic sword fight (*tachimawari*), can at best be described as minimal, as there is little causal narrative motivation. The character at the centre of the daring rescue is a young boy. Arashi Kanjūrō inherited the mantle of Onoe Matsunosuke, becoming the idol of the 'runny-nosed brats'. Before his death in 1926, Onoe Matsunosuke starred as the Kurama Tengu in the first five films of the series. As with Onoe Matsunosuke, adolescent males often appear as central characters in films built around Arashi Kanjūrō's star persona. In the 1928 episode, the sophisticated use of stylistic cinematic techniques totally overshadows the narrative as the film is entirely devoted to the Kurama Tengu's flight from Osaka Castle and his subsequent entrapment and escape. The pace of the action is built up and sustained by camera movement in conjunction with rhythmic editing. Chase scenes are enhanced by tracking shots from the back of moving vehicles as the Kurama Tengu attempts to outrun his pursuers. High-angle crane shots place the Kurama Tengu in the centre of the action as the police (*yakunin*) encircle him. Rapid 360-degree swish-pans from the Kurama Tengu's point of view emphasize the number of attackers he must fight off. In the final entrapment sequence, three further parallel lines of action are established as various groups rush to join the fray. As this is an episode from a series, this final sequence culminates with these various hostile groups meeting and facing each other off. Thus, as the parallel strands come together into a final frame, a question mark appears on the screen, leaving the outcome of these confrontations tantalizingly open until the next episode.

In the late 1930s and early 1940s, as the calls increased for *jidaigeki* films to become more 'authentic' and to be based on history, episodes of the *Kurama Tengu* series along with other *jidaigeki* films became more content-orientated. And as the emphasis shifted from action to plot through dialogue, the conventions of filming style also moved from an emphasis on expressive rhythmic editing to that of camera movement matched to dialogue. In plot terms, the displays of speed and action are subordinate to narrative content in films such as *The Last Days of Edo* (*Edo saigo no hi*) (1941), directed by Inagaki Hiroshi and starring Bandō Tsumasaburō, based on the life of Katsu Kaishū (1823–1899)[20]; *Aviators* (*Chōjin*) (1940), directed by Marune Santarō (1912–1994) and starring Arashi Kanjūrō; and *The Loyal Forty-seven Rōnin of the Genroku Era* (1941–1942), directed by Mizoguchi Kenji. In part, this may be attributed to the age of the principal stars, as Bandō Tsumasaburō had reached thirty-nine by 1940 and Arashi Kanjūrō was thirty-seven. Clearly their advance in years necessitated changes in types of roles and stylistic changes in filming techniques. However, this is clearly not the sole reason, as Kataoka Chiezō was thirty-seven when he starred in the 1940 film based on the early life of Oda Nobunaga (1534–1582), *The Story of an Adventurer in Troubled Times* (*Fūunji: Nobunaga*), directed by Makino Masahiro. However, within other 'historical' films of the 1940s, there is a clear stylistic shift to a reliance on camera movement and the long take. Mizoguchi took this to extremes in his 'one scene, one shot' style. This term historically linked to Mizoguchi's style is perhaps misleading, as an emphasis on long takes does not preclude cutting within the sequence. Brian Henderson (1976) refers to this editing technique as the 'intra-sequence cut' and this should not be confused with the rhythmic editing so central to the *chanbara* genre. As has long been pointed out by such film scholars as Andre Bazin, there is a seeming similitude between the long take and the representation of real time, or to use Bazin's term, a 'temporal realism'. At the stylistic level, it is this linking of 'temporal realism' to calls for historical authenticity that distinguishes *The Loyal Forty-seven Rōnin of the Genroku Era* from the action-orientated *chanbara* films of the late 1920s and 1930s. Darrell William Davis has defined the style of historical films of the 1940s as 'monumental' (he lists *The Loyal Forty-seven Rōnin of the Genroku Era/Genroku Chūshingura* under this rubric as the 'classic example'), arguing that it 'turns the dramatic spotlight on Japanese period design, behavior, and ethics and renders them, as much as the characters and situations based upon them, objects of reverence and respect.' He goes on to add that the 'aura of traditional forms permeates the films and gives them their epic scale, hieratic gravity, stately camera movements, and long takes' (Davis 1996: 43–44). In fact the opposite is the case: it is the 'stately camera movements and long takes' that give the illusion of a traditional aura permeating these films. It is the invention of tradition, through the adaptation of stylistic conventions, within the nationalist context of the needs and exigencies of the period; for it must be remembered that all forms of cinematic style, in terms of editing and camera movement, break down and analyse events. There can be no pure form of filmed historical reality, only the illusion of it. So the question is, How have filmmakers broken down the events and according to what style? As Henderson reminds us, '[I]n the long-take sequence, rhythm is achieved not by the lengths of the shots themselves . . . , but rather *within* each shot, through movement—or lack of it—by camera, or both' (Henderson 1976: 318–319). In Japanese historical films, the early 1940s expressive cutting is geared to enhance the dialogue, as stories deemed to be exemplary take precedence over displays of action and speed that emulate Hollywood 'slapstick' and Keystone Kops.

As with earlier *jidaigeki* films such as *The Serpent*, Mizoguchi Kenji's two-part epic *The Loyal Forty-seven Rōnin of the Genroku Era,* which is based on the ten-play cycle by Mayama Seika, is a complex mediation between values and exigencies of two different systems of social exchange: on the one hand, the aristocratic samurai tradition and on the other, the legitimate sociopolitical structures of civil society. It is on the bodies of the principal characters, Ōishi and the other forty-six *rōnin,* that this discourse is played out. However, unlike Heizaburō in *The Serpent* and Tange Sazen in *The New Publication of the Trials of Magistrate Ōoka,* the physical punishment and mutilation inflicted on the bodies of Ōishi (Kawarasaki Chūjūrō 1902–*) and the forty-six *rōnin* is portrayed through symbolism. As stated above in *The Loyal Forty-seven Rōnin of the Genroku Era,* the emphasis of the drama is shifted from the triumphal execution of the revenge on Kira and his house by the forty-seven to questions of sacrifice. Sacrifice, through this interpretation of the drama, becomes thus firmly rooted in the samurai group tradition the film purports to uphold. And this is one of the crucial factors that separates *The Loyal Forty-seven Rōnin of the Genroku Era* from the *Kanadehon*-derived versions— that is, the emphasis on group action as opposed to an individualizing heroism. Therefore, sacrifice is depicted and imparted through symbolism and dialogue rather than displayed through direct action. When, in the first half of the film, Asano commits self-immolation (*seppuku*), the camera cuts from the scene in the courtyard, as he walks to the site of his *seppuku,* to the inside of his Edo residence, where Lady Asano and her maids are preparing to cut her hair as she renounces the world. 'Temporal realism' is maintained as the gong sounds just after Lady Asano's hair is cut, signal-

ling the moment Asano drove the knife into his stomach. Equally, in the
second half of the film, the main act of the drama, the attack on Kira's
residence and his beheading, is played out in the early dawn in Lady
Asano's house, as her companion, Lady Toda, reads an account of the attack of the previous night. The following scene cuts to the arrival of the
forty-seven at Asano's grave at Sengoku temple carrying the severed head
of Kira. Again 'temporal realism' is maintained and again dialogue is the
means through which the drama progresses. In this scene, after placing
Kira's severed head before the grave and making their obeisance, Ōishi
goes into a long speech on their sufferings over the last few years. This
suffering has now come to fruition, as they have demonstrated the true
samurai spirit. But now they must acknowledge that they have violated the
law and must submit themselves to the rule of law. Thus the emphasis of
the drama is shifted from vengeance to sacrifice. By submitting to the *shōgun*'s judgement and committing *seppuku*, Ōishi places the personal griev-
ances of the *rōnin* within the public domain. Their vengeance thus dealt
with within the law negates its potential revolutionary status. Thus the emphasis on sacrifice, not only the sacrifices of the forty-seven but also of
the other people affected by Asano's actions, overrides the potential disruption of the rebellion theme.

The world of the *shōgun*'s court is corrupt, as the decision to label
Asano's attack on Kira as *ninjō* rather than *kenka* indicates. *Ninjō*, under
these circumstances, refers literally to an attack and means punishment for
one party only, while under the *kenka ryōseibai* system, which places
blame for quarrels equally between the two parties, Kira would also have
been subject to punishment. In this respect the film version differs from
the play, in that the play opens seconds after the attack with the bustle of
the feudal lords (*daimyō*). In this way, as Brian Powell elucidates, the play
remains faithful to history as the true reason for Asano's attack is not
known. Powell argues that in the play, it is through the actions of Okado
Denpachirō, the court official in charge of the investigation, that the audience becomes aware of the potential injustice being done to Asano. In the
scene when the judgement is being handed down by the *shōgun*'s top ad-
visers, 'Okada subverts the enormous status difference between him and
them by protesting . . . Here the audience knows that Okado may be risking
his job by acting as he does. A man who does that must have a serious
reason, and Mayama utilises this logic to enlist the sympathy of his audiences in Asano's cause. Asano too must have had a serious reason for acting as he did, and this becomes the major motivation for the *rōnin* in their

quest for vengeance' (Powell 1990: 168–169). In the film version Okada also makes strong protestations, which threaten his career. However, the film does not allow for any potential ambiguity regarding the heroes and villains of the drama, as it opens just before the attack on Kira with Asano overhearing Kira's rude aspersions, thus providing the motive for the attack. In this way the film remains within the *Kanadehon*-derived tradition of clearly labelling Kira as the villain. The 1938 all-star Nikkatsu version, *Chūshingura: The Heavenly Scroll and The Earthly Scroll*, opens with Asano's appointment as organizer of the ceremonies for the Imperial Envoys under the direction of Kira. During these early scenes, much is made of Kira as a bad-tempered old man and his refusal to give Asano the correct information.

The film version of *The Loyal Forty-seven Rōnin of the Genroku Era*, and it would seem the play, straddle the two dominant themes of *Chūshingura*, loyalty and rebellion, through the homosocial codes of loyalty, depicted through the actions of the forty-seven, while containing the rebellion theme to a rebellion against the shogunate's judgement on Asano. The knowledge that those associated with the higher authority of the emperor's court admitted sympathy for Asano justifies Ōishi and the forty-six *rōnin*s' actions. This version of the drama lays emphasis, through allegory, on the abstract dichotomy between a premodern morality and the rule of law of a centralized state. The body of the state, the body politic (*kokutai*), is constituted from the self-mutilated (*seppuku*) physical bodies of Asano, Ōishi and the other *rōnin*. In the final part of the drama when the shogunate's judgement is handed down to Ōishi and the other *rōnin*, it is made clear Kira's house has been discontinued. The *shōgun*'s government has been forced, through the actions of the Akō *rōnin* and popular opinion, to inadvertently acknowledge the error of their initial judgement on Asano. Unlike other film versions of *Chūshingura*, which often focus on a country/city dichotomy or simply good versus evil, this complex schematization of the physical bodies of the forty-seven *rōnin* in *The Loyal Forty-seven Rōnin of the Genroku Era* re-defines corporeality in terms of the body politic and not individual subjectivity. The complex nature of the drama as perceived through Mayama's play and the lack of visceral intensity of the mainstream formula *Chūshingura* productions may, in part, explain the failure of the film version, despite the popularity of some of the plays in the cycle in the theatre.

In summary, *jidaigeki* films, with their origins in the popular fiction of the *kōdan* storytelling/popular novel tradition, took root in the Japanese national consciousness in the early years of the twentieth century at a time when the forces of modernity impelled the Japanese to establish a national identity. Hashimoto Osamu (1989) argues that with the Meiji Restoration of 1868 came the imposition of foreign culture and this left a gap in the indigenous culture. He goes on to say that this gap was filled through the invention of the Edo period as a time-space configuration, a *mise-en-scène* of popular culture, first through *kōdan* novels and later in *chanbara* films. Therefore, the Edo period should be distinguished from the term Tokugawa period used as an historical, temporal classification in academic discourse, as the Edo of popular culture refers to a time-space configuration of social relations (Edo as a term can refer to both the historical name of Tokyo while also referring to an historical period). Hashimoto clearly links the origins of these discourses to the early twentieth century when he states, '[D]espite the fact that with Meiji came a world of [Western] civilization and enlightenment (*bunmei kaika*), the overwhelming majority of the people lived according to the patterns of life that had continued since the Edo period—but Edo had no value, and therein lay the dilemma, the Meiji period meant the end of Edo. In order to solve this dilemma somehow, the people had to invent an "ideal Edo Period" (*risō no Edo jidai*). Regarding the mass of the people, they needed splendid stories (*rippana monogatari*) that they could support and that corresponded to their lives' (Hashimoto 1989: 59).

One of the earliest developments of the *chanbara* genre was the portrayal of the alienated hero. These films centred on an introspective analysis of the alienation of man in the modern society through the character of the dispossessed *rōnin*. In these early examples, the myths of an omniscient patriarchy, re-affirmed through such star personas as that of Arashi Kanjūrō, are challenged. This alienation theme, so clearly linked to recession, faded in the early 1930s to re-emerge in the 1960s in the *zankoku* (cruel) *jidaigeki* films, when the myths of the samurai ideal are criticized as part of the 1960s' 'cinema of transgression': *Harakiri (Seppuku)* (1962), *A Story of Cruelty of the Bakumatsu Period (Bakumatsu zankoku monogatari)* (1964), and *The Great Bodhisattva Pass* aka *The Sword of Doom (Daibosatsu tōge)* (1966). Allied to the changes in character types in the genre, in the late 1920s and early 1930s, was an aesthetic shift in the depiction of human movement, particularly in the spectacle of the sword fight (*tachimawari*), through the incorporation of expressive forms of editing and camera movement.

**Allegory: Fathers, Sons and the Politics of the Collective**

If the social realist *gendaigeki* films of the 1930s depicted an alienated and besieged masculinity struggling to cope with the competitive demands of recession-hit Japanese urban society (*I Was Born But . . . /Umarete wa mita keredo* and *The Only Son/Hitori musuko*), mainstream *jidaigeki* films of the same period, framed within a Neo-Confucian morality, centred on the authoritative but benevolent patriarch. In the 1940s this theme extended into the Meiji-*mono* in films such as *The Life of Muhō Matsu* (1943) and *Sanshiro Sugata* (1943), and into *gendaigeki* films such as Ozu Yasujirō's (1903–1963) 1942 film *There Was a Father*.

*The Life of Muhō Matsu,* based on a screenplay by Itami Mansaku and directed by Inagaki Hiroshi, is centred on the relationship between a young boy, Toshio, and a rickshaw man, Matsugorō (Bandō Tsumasaburō), who, after the death of the boy's biological father, effectively takes over the role of surrogate father. The character of Matsugorō, as an ideal masculine type, is predicated on his physical strength and allied to this is his independent working-class status. Unlike the salaryman father in *I Was Born But . . .* he maintains a moral integrity through his independence. He can choose when he works and whom he will take in his rickshaw. His character is honest and upright and as such he has no need to bow and scrape to his superiors. In one scene before Toshio's father dies, he describes Matsugorō as being like a piece of split bamboo—a straightforward fellow (*take o wattayōna otoko*). These attributes are implied in the title of the film. *Muhō* is usually translated as 'untamed' (Barrett 1989); however, used in this context in relation to Matsugorō and by extension the star persona of Bandō Tsumasaburō, it carries far greater connotations of 'purity' in the sense that he has not been corrupted by modern society.[21] Therefore, the title may more appropriately be translated along the lines of *The Life of Matsugorō the Pure.* In this sense too, the film, by giving a rickshaw man, a socially low position, such a positive role conforms to the egalitarian ideals of earlier films such as *Marching On* (1930) that admitted a young country boy into the heroic tradition. As such, both films fit into the social discourse of the 'samurai-isation of the lower classes'. The fact that, unlike the *chanbara* heroes, Matsugorō is a mere rickshaw man and Kōichi the son of a peasant intensifies the potential for spectator identification and opens up the possibility for the lower orders of Japanese society to become part of an elite tradition. As such, Matsugorō has remained popular right through the postwar period, occasionally being screened on television and included in special screenings on the NHK satellite channels. The film is also still being listed by Japanese critics amongst the best top ten Japanese war films[22] and in the Kodansha *Japan: an Illustrated Encyclopaedia* in the top twenty Japanese films ever.

In contrast, the 1942 film *There Was a Father*, directed by Ozu Yasujirō, is concerned not with a natural spontaneous masculinity as is *The Life of Muhō Matsu* but with patriarchal authority and responsibility in a transitional age when the extended family is increasingly being superseded by the nuclear family. It also has an important paradigmatic function as a model for the maintenance of the 'ideals' of the traditional family, despite the physical separation and reduced size of the family—father and son. In this way the contradictions, inherent in the spatial distanciation of modern social relations as reflected in trends towards the establishment of nuclear families as against the traditional multigenerational extended family, are in a certain sense overcome. As in *The Life of Muhō Matsu*, the narrative revolves around the relationship between a man and, in this case, his natural son. This relationship between father and son represents in microcosm the symbolic relationship between the individual and authority within the familial nation state, the *kazoku kokka*. The film received a Bureau of Information award as an outstanding 'national policy' film (Bordwell 1988: 292).

The father, Horikawa, played by Ryū Chishū (1904–1993), is a widowed schoolteacher living in Kanezawa with his only son, Ryōhei, played as an adult by Sano Shūji (1912–1978). While on a school sightseeing excursion to Tokyo including visits to the Meiji and Yasukuni shrines, the Great Buddha at Kamakura, and Hakone from which Mount Fuji can be seen, one of the students drowns in a boating accident. Horikawa feels that he must accept responsibility for the accident and, placing Ryōhei in a dormitory, resigns from his teaching post and goes to work in a Tokyo textile factory. Thus begins the long years of separation the two must endure.

It is not until the second half of the film when Ryōhei has grown up and is himself a teacher that the aging Horikawa puts into words the philosophy that has guided his reactions to the chain of events that make up the plot of the film. The two meet in Shinbara Onsen (a hot spring resort), where after bathing they have lunch. Ryōhei suggests he should give up his teaching job in Akita and come to Tokyo with his father, as he says, 'I can't bear any more this living apart from you'. His father interrupts him, telling him that his job is a vocation (*tenshoku*) and that he must devote his life to it. Ryōhei silently bows his head in assent, swallowing back his disappointment. After lunch, the two go fishing together, thereby duplicating a scene from earlier in the film when Ryōhei was still a child, during which Horikawa told the young Ryōhei he would have to live in a dormitory. Up until this moment, the movement of the two fishing lines had been perfectly synchronized. Momentarily, the young Ryōhei falters. However, after accepting his father's decision, his line again falls into sync. In this latter scene, again the mature Ryōhei has accepted his father's decision and is again depicted casting his line in unison with his father's line, emphasizing the total harmony between them.

Contained within these narratives, based on the relationships between fathers/surrogate fathers and sons, on the one hand, is the portrayal of an idealized masculinity in the depiction of the father, and on the other, the implicit 'rite of passage' to manhood and citizenship of the son through the example of the father. In the Meiji-*mono Sanshiro Sugata*, directed by Kurosawa Akira and starring Ōkōchi Denjirō as Yanō and Fujita Susumu (1912–1990) as Sugata, this is portrayed as a spiritual development. In the case of Sugata, in a variation on the narrative conventions established in many of the adaptations made about the seventeenth century warrior *Miyamoto Musashi*, his raw masculinity (in both the physical and spiritual senses) is tempered through his training in the newly invented martial art of judo. The film thus operates on two levels: the personal, in that Sugata must find his rightful place within the *bushidō* tradition (the judo school hierarchy), and the wider framework of the establishment of the Kōdōkan judo school within the martial arts world. Within this latter context the *Miyamoto Musashi* theme is made relevant to the 'modern' world. Inoue Shun, in his study of the 'invention' of Kōdōkan judo in the late nineteenth century by Kanō Jigorō (1860–1938) (the historical figure upon whom the character Yanō is based in the film), states that,

> *Budō* [a collective term for judo, kendo, aikido and *kyūdō*], of which Kōdō-kan judo was the prototype, was originally conceived as a hybrid cultural form produced by modernizing "traditional" practice. With the rise of militarism and ultranationalism, however, *budō* was reinvented as a counter to Western values and to infuse Japan's modern sports culture with "Japanese spirit" (Inoue 1998: 164).

It is this story, the establishment of the Kōdōkan judo school and its rise to prominence in the competitions hosted by the Metropolitan Police Department between the Kōdōkan school and various *jūjutsu* schools for the contract to train police, that forms the framework for the personal narrative of Sugata. The pseudo-biographical plot is based on the popular novel published in 1942 of the same title by Tomita Tsuneo. He was the son of Tomita Tsunejirō, one of the early proponents of the sport, and his novel is based on the life of one of Kanō Jigorō's most accomplished disciples, Saigō Shirō.

Kanō placed much emphasis on the philosophical side of the sport, arguing that 'energy', which he saw as being at the centre of judo, had both a physical and a mental component, and that the 'most efficient use of energy "entailed both not wasting energy and promoting goodness". "Goodness", as conceived by Kanō, "is something that promotes the continuing development of collective and social life'" (quoted in Inoue 1998: 168). Inoue goes on to explain that 'Kanō frequently stressed in his writing that spiritual cultivation was as important as physical mastery of technique' (Inoue 1998: 168). In the film this philosophy of promoting the good of the collective is shifted onto the Neo-Confucian principles of 'loyalty and filial piety'. In the early part of the film, Sugata becomes involved in a street brawl. Yanō reprimands him by accusing him of not understanding 'the way of humanity' (*ningen no michi*). Yanō goes on to define 'the way of humanity' in terms of 'loyalty and filial piety,' which he argues is 'the truth that governs heaven and earth' (*tennen shizen no shinri de aru*). Sugata's subsequent enlightenment in the temple pond ties enlightenment to suffering. Therefore, to know 'the way of humanity' is to have suffered.

The control of Sugata's emotions is depicted in his relationship with the two daughters of his two principal opponents. The first daughter, through her hatred and attempted revenge on Sugata, after he has killed her father in a match, is impressed upon his mind. Cinematically, this is depicted both on the soundtrack, as a woman's scream pierces the silence after the fatal throw, and visually, by a long close-up held on the face of the daughter of the dead opponent. It was she who let out the scream, and it is her face held in close-up that returns in flashbacks to haunt Sugata when he is in training to take on Murai (Shimura Takashi 1905–1985) from a rival *jūjutsu* school at the next police-sponsored tournament. Sugata has in the interim met Murai's daughter and grown fond of her. Women thus are representative of emotional weakness, a weakness that Sugata overcomes in order to advance the fortunes of the judo school. He goes on to win the match, at which point his ego becomes one with the group. The concepts of 'loyalty and filial piety' that Yanō had stressed come to the fore, as Sugata overcomes his inner conflict—a conflict that had threatened the position of the school and was played out in his mind

through his disturbed relationship with Murai's daughter. The righteousness of Sugata's position is vindicated in the final scenes as Murai recognizes his superior ability and they become friends, thus opening up the
possibility for Sugata, at some future date, to enter into a relationship with
his daughter. However, as with all potential romance subplots, the relationship is not consummated and the film ends with Sugata leaving to begin
his travels. His most intimate moment with Murai's daughter comes when
he removes a fragment of engine smut from her eye in the train, as she
accompanies him to Yokohama to see him off.

   In the 1940s, these discourses of father and son or male homosocial
bonding also formed an important element in *gendaigeki* commemorative
films (*kinen eiga*). These films, described as 'national policy films,' were
designed to boost recruitment and allay the fears of parents who might
have been hesitant in allowing their young sons to transfer to the various
military academies after graduating from middle school. *Submarine Number One* (1941), *The War at Sea from Hawaii to Malaya* (1942), *Navy*
(1943), *My Favourite Plane Flies South* aka *Our Planes Fly South* (*Aiki
minami e tobu*) (1943), and *Army* (1944) are all representative examples.
All these films centre on the 'rite of passage' of individual youths who,
advancing through the education system, transfer after middle school to a
military academy, successfully progressing to take their place as valued
members of Japan's new militaristic citizenship. As in *Sanshiro Sugata,*
there is a harnessing of history through a docudrama format to the primary
narratives of individual youths. The docudrama form thus legitimates present political expediency and also places the main characters within a genealogical trajectory that defines their being in terms of some spiritual
essence of belonging, of sharing a unique sensibility of 'Japaneseness',
symbolized through the military.

   *Army*, directed by Kinoshita Keisuke (1912–1998), adapts this docudrama format to the primary narrative, following the lives of three generations of a Chōshū merchant family (Chōshū was one of the clans
instrumental in the events of the Meiji Restoration and therefore carries
strong connotations of loyalty to the emperor) from the battle of Kokura
in 1866 and the bombardment of Shimonoseki, through to the grandson's
departure for the front in China in the 1930s. The opening title sequences
instantly inform the spectator this is not a film about high-ranking military
officers but is about the ordinary foot soldiers who make up the overwhelming majority of the army. The first shot is of a close-up at a low
angle of a young soldier standing to attention. At the command to present

arms, the camera cuts to a high-angle shot of the parade ground as the title *Army* is superimposed on the screen. In this sequence, while acknowledging the army as a massive body of men, the images draw attention to the individual, quickly establishing the subject matter of the film. Events from the lives of each generation of the Takagi family are depicted against a backdrop of historically significant events, such as the public protests against the Triple Intervention of 1895, the Russo-Japanese War and finally, the war in China. The authenticity of these events is verified through the inclusion of newspaper headlines from the *Asahi Shinbun* and actual newsreel footage of the Japanese bombardment of Shanghai. In the final sequences Shintarō, now a regular soldier, merges back into the massed body of the advancing army as they march through the cheering crowds on their way to the war front. For a brief moment, Shintarō's mother (Tanaka Kinuyo 1909–1977), desperately searching for her son amongst the columns of marching men, gains a glimpse of him. She runs beside him for a few brief moments before being knocked down by the crowd as he disappears, merging, lost, in the vast body of the group, the army. The film thus ends as it had begun by first singling out the individual, only to lose him in the last scenes in the sea of marching men.

Where *Army* traces a genealogical connection between individuals and major historical events, in both *Navy*, directed by Tasaka Tomotaka, and *Submarine Number One*, directed by Igayama Masamitsu (1905–*), place is significant as the geo-historical connection between famous military heroes and the principal characters in the films. The young hero, Makoto, in *Navy* is portrayed as a son of Kagoshima, following in the footsteps of another famous son of Kagoshima, Tōgō Heihachirō (1848–1934), commander of the fleet during the Russo-Japanese War. Katagi and, to a lesser extent, his young school friend Hidaka, are the heroes in *Submarine Number One*, sons of Mikata in Fukui prefecture; likewise they are following in the footsteps of Sakuma Tsutomu (1879–1910), a naval man instrumental in the early development of Japan's submarine fleet. Katagi advances to the naval academy and then on to the special submarine training centre, eventually becoming a submarine commander, while his young school friend Hidaka goes to university and studies shipbuilding and design. In the final sequences the two friends are reunited as Katagi takes command of the new submarine, *Submarine Number One* of the film's title, designed by his friend. Within this scenario, the two friends live up to the promise they made to each other as children, and the military and industry represented by these two friends are seen to work together in perfect harmony to further Japan's collective goals, following the example set by Sakuma Tsutomu.

In stylistic terms, these films all draw on iconographic images of a prominent historical figure as an inspiration to later generations. In the absence of biological fathers, their symbolic presence, still echoed through photographs placed prominently in the family altars (*butsudan*), allows the young heroes of the films to create symbolic relationships with the dead heroes of generations and wars past, through repeated trips to their graves and memorial sites. Cinematically, these exchanges are filmed using the shot-reverse-shot convention of classical cinema, usually associated with scenes of inter-human exchange. In these films the youth's face is held in close-up, looking up at a statue or memorial headstone, before a cut directs us to the object of their gaze and then back to the youth's face.[23] Photographs are also central in signifying, through absence, the continued importance of the past for the present, as they are hung prominently above the desk where Makoto works, or in the school classroom where Katagi and his friend study as children. The docudrama format allows for the use of actual footage filmed in the various military academies featured in the films. Subtitles are sometimes supplied, giving basic information on the topics studied by the cadets. Much time is given to massed displays of physical exercises in the form of gymnastics and massed formations of marching cadets. Regimentation, which had been criticized through parody in Ozu Yasujirō's films of the 1930s, in these films is valourized. Portrayed in positive terms, it offers a sense of fellowship, community and common purpose.

Japanese 'national policy' films of the 1940s took their basic theme, the social advancement of youths from the lower classes through the military, from films derived from a Western heroic individualism such as *Marching On*, one of the earliest manifestations. Within these narratives, the military institutions provide a seemingly meritocratic environment through which an individual, by means of dedication, effort and skill, could achieve great feats. This theme of heroic individualism, which in *Marching On* had been sufficient in and of itself, in the 'national policy' films of the early 1940s underwent a modification, in that personal achievement, through character motivation, became cloaked in the national good, thereby overcoming the inherent contradiction between heroic individualism and a consensual group ethos. As the father in *My Favourite Plane Flies South* (1943) says to his wife in a conversation about their young son, Takeshi, 'I shall be content if he is of service to the

nation' (*kokka ni yakunitatsu koto dake ii desu*). This conversation frames
the principal narrative of the film as, towards the end of the film, when
Takeshi has grown up and achieved great feats as a reconnaissance pilot
for the army in Taiwan, his mother, as justification for her efforts, repeats
these words of the now deceased father.

In war films, the theme of battlefield camaraderie also draws on the
father/son patriarchal allegory and was central to the films of Tasaka Tomotaka in the late 1930s and early 1940s, *The Five Scouts* and *Mud and
Soldiers*, and was carried over to films based on the lives of heroic military
figures, such as the ace pilot Katō Hayabusa in *Katō's Falcon Fighters
(Katō Hayabusa sentōtai)* (1944), directed by Yamamoto Kajirō (1902–
1974). Again, these films overcome the inherent contradiction between a
meritocratic system, based on competitive heroic individualism, and a
group ethos through the sacrifice of the individual for the greater good.
Through an emphasis on the portrayal of a homosocial ethos, these films
override the rivalry and bullying inevitable in a situation of competitive
individualism. It was in the postwar period in war-retro films that the negative sides of competitive individualism were emphasized and linked to antiwar sentiments as in *The Sacrifice of the Human Torpedos* (*Ningen
gyorai kaiten*) (1955).

At the heart of many *gendaigeki* films of this period is the re-negotiation and re-affirmation of a patriarchal ideal. In *The Life of Muhō Matsu,
There Was a Father, Sanshiro Sugata* and *Army*, various forms of the ideal
are portrayed through the father figures. However, in other films such as
*My Favourite Plane Flies South, Navy* and *Brothers and Sisters of the
Toda Family* (*Todake no kyōdai*) (1941), the ideal is maintained through
absence by symbolism. In *My Favourite Plane Flies South*, the father's
words resound throughout the film, affecting first the widowed mother's
behaviour towards her son (after the death of her husband, she had initially
intended to leave her son with her parents and to go to Tokyo to work) and
second, the son's life and eventual career in the military. In *Navy,* the absent father's place is taken by such past heroes as Tōgō Heihachirō and
Saigō Takamori (1827–1877). The linking of these images to the hero of
the film, Makoto, harness an historically defined image of masculinity to
the events of Pearl Harbour.

*Brothers and Sisters of the Toda Family* (1941), directed by Ozu Yasujirō, takes an alternative approach to the father/son allegory by depicting
the consequences of the breakdown of the patriarchal structure of the family after the sudden and unexpected death of the father and the failure of

the eldest son (Saitō Tatsuo 1902–1968) to fulfil his obligations as head of the family. The narrative line of *Brothers and Sisters of the Toda Family* continues in the same vein as the 'social realist' and proletarian traditions of the 1930s, in that class and material privilege are condemned as the causes of the family breakdown. This is made explicit towards the end of the film in a speech the younger brother, Shōjirō (Saburi Shin 1909–1982), makes in which he castigates his brother and sisters for not looking after their mother and younger sister, Setsuko (Tsubouchi Yoshiko 1915–1985), in the period after the death of their father. Due to financial problems, the main house is sold and the elderly mother and Setsuko, the youngest daughter, whose marriage proposal was cancelled after the death of the father, are condemned to wander Lear-like from household to household, until, in desperation, they retreat to the dilapidated family seaside holiday house. Shōjirō takes up the question of filial piety:

> **Shōjirō:** People living at bare subsistence levels have a warmer relationship between parent and child. We were all born from the same womb; is it too much to then care for our mother? It is not that long. Just one year has passed. To think that this could have happened and on the memorial day of Father's death . . .

Within all these examples, the modern heroic tradition of individualism is harnessed for the sake of the good of the nation. Women are also subsumed within this ethos, in films such as Kurosawa Akira's *The Most Beautiful* (*Ichiban utsukushiku*) (1944), *The Flower of Patriotism* aka *A Patriotic Flower* (*Aikoku no hana*) (1942), directed by Sasaki Keisuke (1901–1967) and starring Kogure Michiyo (1918–1990) and *The Night Before the Outbreak of War* aka *On the Eve of War* (*Kaisen no zen'ya*) (1943), starring Tanaka Kinuyo. Within *jidaigeki* films, the very structure of films made, based on *Chūshingura,* overcomes this inherent contradiction. The division of the narrative into discrete segments or scenes centring on one character ensures that the individual hero is allowed to shine in the knowledge that he is advancing the group cause. This was taken further with the introduction of the *meimeiden* or *gaiden* biographical films recounting the life and experiences of one of the forty-seven (Yasubei in *Duel at Takadanobaba* and Genzō in *Akagaki Genzō and the Night Before the Attack on Kira's Mansion*). The establishment of this structure as dominant can be attributed to the star system in the theatre and later in the film studios. *Chūshingura* provided the perfect vehicle for the celebratory all-star New

Year release. Yomota Inuhiko goes further by linking the act of watching *Chūshingura* to the raising of a nationalist consciousness. He argues that, due to the importance of *Chūshingura* to the New Year celebrations, it has achieved a quasireligious status, which he relates to nationalist sentiments. 'When a story that has become established over many years as popular entertainment and that everyone knows the outline of is made into a film, it is almost an act of courtesy, as a way of re-affirming one's sense of belonging to a nation, to a national audience, to gather at the cinema to watch the film' (Yomota 1999: 182). In the above, Yomota echoes the views published in an article in the journal *Der Deutsche Film* (December 1937) on the efficacy of Germany's wartime film policy in instilling a sense of collective belonging in the populace:

> [O]nly when a 'strong sense of community' has been established could film truly become a vital experience, that is, 'only when the audience thinks homogeneously, when—how should one put it—it shares the same view of the world; and when a film is shown, its point of view mirrors that of the community.' Film gives expression to the forces that go to form a community, but only 'when the [idea of] a community has already been planted in viewers' minds and only when film acts to enhance that community,' i.e., when it has an ideological message to communicate. (Quoted in Hoffmann 1996: 101)

Relying on the audiences 'iconic memory', filmed versions of *Chūshingura* shift from scene to scene with little explanation. Display supersedes causal motivation in the forwarding of the narrative. The narrative becomes a mere vehicle for the studios to display their wares—the stars and, to a lesser extent, the directors and screenplay writers. In the moving interchange between Bandō Tsumasaburō and Kataoka Chiezō in the all-star Nikkatsu 1938 New Year release, *Chūshingura: The Heavenly Scroll and the Earthly Scroll*, jointly directed by Makino Masahiro (*The Heavenly Scroll*) and Ikeda Tomiyasu (*The Earthly Scroll*), there is a strong element of ambiguity in the overlap of character and star persona. In this production, Bandō Tsumasaburō is Ōishi Kuranosuke and Kataoka Chiezō is both Asano in the first half of the film and then Tachibana in the second half. In this latter half, the moving exchange between Ōishi and Tachibana in a *ryokan* near the Hakone barrier can be read in one of two ways: first, as an exchange between Ōishi and Asano, despite the fact that Asano is dead, the star persona of Kataoka transcends his roles, leaving this as a possible interpretation, or second, this scene can be understood as a moment of intense bonding between the two stars. In either case it is the homosocial bonding between the two that is at the centre of the scene, as the dialogue is limited and the exchange consists of a series of close-up reverse-shot sequences between the two, often looking deeply into each others eyes and at one point holding hands. The soundtrack places this scene within the theatrical conventions of display and pose (*mie*) through the *jōruri* chant.

In popular films produced in a studio system, character traits follow established conventions appropriate to the genre, the series, or in the case of *Chūshingura*, conventions established through repetition of the same story line. Added to these are individual traits and characteristics, which enhance the character's function in the narrative. Star personas, as Bordwell, Staiger and Thompson remind us, reinforce 'the tendency toward strongly profiled and unified characterization' (Bordwell et al. 1999: 14). This can in part be attributed to the phenomenon of the 'stars' themselves. As Richard Dyer points out, '[S]tars have an existence in the world independent from their actual screen . . . appearances, [and] it is possible to believe . . . that as people they are more real than the characters in stories' (Dyer: 1992: 22). This I would argue works both ways; just as stars embody certain cultural values, those values are then automatically transferred to the screen characters portrayed, helping to consolidate the character as real and believable. Stars therefore, 'serve to disguise the fact that they are just as much produced images, constructed personalities as "characters" are. Thus the value embodied by a star is as it were harder to reject as "impossible" or "false", because the star's existence guarantees the existence of the value he or she embodies' (Dyer 1992: 22).

In the analysis of the films above, I have argued that by the late 1930s and early 1940s, alienated masculinity had become re-inscribed within a group ethos which, taken at its most significant, encompassed clear notions of what it was to be a man in modern Japanese society. Through allegory, in a changing modern, imperial-industrial age, patriarchal structures were re-negotiated to accommodate the political imperatives of the times. Moreover, individualism, a concomitant of modernity, was at odds with the collective national ideal that politicians, such as Yanagita Kunio (1875–1962), sought to instil in the population. Within these discourses, heroic individualism is valourized in the Hollywood tradition through films such as *Marching On*, which was based on an American novel. In films produced in the first half of the 1940s, it is tempered through the sacrifice of the self for the general good. This discourse crossed genre boundaries, finding expression in *jidaigeki*, first and foremost, in the many versions of *Chūshingura*, and in *gendaigeki*, in the 'national policy' films of the first half of the 1940s. Masculinity in these discourses is linked to progress through the mastery of technology, technology, becoming a prosthetic extension of the man. The male 'rite of passage' follows the trajectory of a senior or paternal figure as role model, through the various training stages both in terms of the correct 'spirit' (*gunjin seishin* and *Yamato damashii*) and the mastery of technology—planes and submarines. These discourses were further inscribed and given credence through the personas of the principal stars. In a highly competitive industry, stars are one of the principal arenas of product differentiation, an important marketing strategy. Therefore, in seeking to understand the significance of these films in relation to the discourses surrounding the collective consciousness of the nation, one must acknowledge the multivalent nature of the images of masculinity on offer, both in terms of character traits and in terms of the star personas as marketable products.

## Empire, Aesthetics and Assimilation

[I]n realist fiction personal relationships are the medium in which social issues become active and incarnate. Such relationships are in fact metonymic of society as a whole; but it is the nature of realist writing to convert this metonym into metaphor, recasting social processes as personal transactions. This literary convention then holds open the perpetual ideological possibility of *reducing* social questions to interpersonal ones . . . (Eagleton 1996: 181)

Just as steel navies, constitutions, machine guns, rationalized tax structures, and steam locomotives seemed part of modernity and efficiency, acquisition of a colonial empire in the late nineteenth century was a mark of national eminence, the ultimate status symbol upon the world scene. (Peattie 1984: 10)

The relationship between modernity and empire . . . was dialectical: just as modernization conditioned the growth of empire, the process of imperialism shaped the conditions of modern life. (Young 1998: 12)

To view those who are in essence unequal as if they were equal is in itself inequitable. To treat those who are unequal unequally is to realize equality.

(Taken from a report published in 1943 entitled *An Investigation of Global Policy with the Yamato Race as Nucleus* quoted in Dower 1986: 264)

Cinema, total war and the imbricated issue of imperialism all came into being in the mechanical age of modernity. As one of the many weapons of war and as a tool in the management of empire, the Japanese were quick to realize the potential of film as far back as the Russo-Japanese War of 1904–1905. The outbreak of the Russo-Japanese War generated enormous public interest, becoming Japan's first media event. The Yoshizawa Shōten film company, which had in the previous year opened Japan's first permanent cinema in the popular Tokyo amusement district Asakusa, dispatched a camera team to follow the Japanese forces. Cinema was thus instrumental in publicizing the war and it was based on the popularity of these war 'topicals' that many Japanese film production and distribution agencies gained a foothold in the newly emerging entertainment market. In fact, so successful was Japan at this time that the British made an extensive study of Japan's propaganda policy during the Russo-Japanese War and utilized this knowledge when forming their own policy during the early days of the First World War.

In terms of empire building, Japanese politicians were quick to realize the potential of cinema as a political tool in the management of empire. Prior to the formal annexation of Korea in 1910, Itō Hirobumi (1841–1909), one of the original Meiji oligarchs, invited the Korean crown prince to Japan in 1908. In Korea, rumours were being spread by anti-Japanese elements that the Japanese would attempt to assassinate the crown prince during this visit. To counter these rumours and to try to win over Korean public opinion, Itō asked the Yoshizawa Shōten film company to make a documentary about the crown prince's stay in Japan. As such, the crown prince was filmed enjoying all the delights of Japan. This film was then sent to Korea where it was widely disseminated. At the same time, Itō arranged for the Yokota Shōkai film company to make a film about his own tour of Korea. This was subsequently shown in Japan (unfortunately neither film is extant).

Due to the nature of Japanese colonial policy, all film companies established in the colonies under their auspices were quasi-national, as in the examples of Taiwan and Korea until 1940, or 'national' (*kokusaku kaisha*) as in the case of the Manchurian Motion Picture Association (*Manshū Eiga Kyōkai* or shortened to *Man'ei*).[24] In the case of Taiwan/Formosa, Japan's first colony founded in 1895 after the Sino-Japanese War, a film department, the Taiwan Motion Picture Association (Taiwan *Eiga Kyōkai*), was attached in 1941 to the existing Taiwan Education Society (*Kyōikukai*), a society founded by the colonial government to promote Japanese culture in Taiwan. As a result of the founding of this department, Japanese films were widely circulated throughout Taiwan with the aim of promoting Japanese culture and the use of the Japanese Language.[25] Later in 1941, as the war situation became more imperative, the Taiwan Motion Picture Association expanded operations to include a production unit that made newsreel and cultural films for the domestic market. One of the main themes, at this time, under the *kōminka* policy of the 'imperialization of colonial subjects', was to encourage native Taiwanese to enlist as volunteers to serve in the Japanese armed forces. Under this policy, the 'obligations' of colonial people to the Imperial institution were emphasized as opposed to the 'privileges'. Satō Tadao (1995 vol. ii) cites *Sayon's Bell* (*Sayon no kane*), made in 1943, as one of the most important films of this type.

Where the essence of Japanese nationalism was defined in popular cinema of the late 1930s and first half of the 1940s in terms of an idealized masculinity, the essence of empire, on mainland China and Taiwan, was defined in terms of its opposite, femininity, through the body of the principal actress of the Manchurian Motion Picture Association (*Man'ei*), Yamaguchi Yoshiko, alias Ri Kōran/Li Xianglan. Financed equally by the Manchukuo government and South Manchurian Railway (*Mantetsu*)[26] and founded in 1937, the Manchurian Motion Picture Association (*Man'ei*) had a mandate to produce films for the local native population of the newly established 'puppet state' of Manchukuo (1932–1945). Yokochi Takeshi and Aida Fusako (1999), in their comprehensive history of the company, argue that *Man'ei* was first and foremost designed as a medium for the dissemination of propaganda. The premises upon which it was founded can be linked to various issues that were central to discussions being held in Japan during the 1930s on the relationship between cinema and the state, following a proposal put forward in the Diet (Japanese Parliament) in 1933 to implement a 'national film law'. This law was finally put into effect in 1939; a full discussion of this law is taken up in the following chapter. According to *Man'ei*'s charter, the statement of mission was as follows:

> The Manchurian Motion Picture Association is a national company of Manchukuo. It is founded on ethical principles for the mutual advancement of Japan and Manchukuo; in discharging our duties in the true spirit of East Asian peace, to bear the great responsibility of the spiritual building of

Manchukuo in times of peace. To inform the people of Japan and the various regions of China of the true circumstances of Manchukuo and gain their full understanding, and furthermore, to present material of a high cultural standard from Manchukuo. In times of emergency, these responsibilities will be enlarged. That is, we will become one with Japan, and use film in the ideological and propaganda wars both inside and outside the country. (Quoted in Yokochi and Aida 1999: 37)

Prior to the establishment of *Man'ei*, documentary films had been produced since 1923 under the auspices of the South Manchurian Railway Company. Yokochi and Aida (1999) argue that this film unit was in fact employed as the propaganda arm of the Kantō (Guandong/Kwantung) Army. They were instrumental in gaining public support in Japan for the military action taken by the army in China, by filming the various incidents that collectively form the Manchurian Incident. This footage was ultimately compiled into three feature films, all of which were widely distributed in Japan and throughout the colonies. The first film in the trilogy was also released in English and various European languages for overseas release.

In the early 1940s the romance genre, as a space for the exploration of alterity, or otherness, became the narrative paradigm through which colonial relations were portrayed in popular films, in the simplistic terms of the active male/passive female binary schema. Staying within cultural metaphors of gender, the relationship between Japanese and colonial men was portrayed in quasi-Neo-Confucian familial terms of the relationship between the elder brother and younger brother. Within this hierarchical conception of the family structure, founded on the economic imperative of primogeniture, the elder brother/younger brother relationship places younger brothers in a secondary position, occupying an ambiguous place somewhere between the 'masculine' and the 'feminine'. Just how this quasi-familial system should work at the level of the Japanese community and the wider community of empire was expounded as follows in the *Cardinal Principles of the National Polity* (*Kokutai no Hongi*) published in 1937.

In our country, under a unique family system, parent and child and husband and wife live together, supporting and helping each other . . . [T]his harmony must also be able to materialize in communal life . . . In each community there are those who take the upper places while there are those who work below them. Through each one fulfilling his position is the harmony of a community obtained. To fulfill one's part means to do one's appointed task with the utmost faithfulness each in his own sphere; and by this means do those above receive help from inferiors, and inferiors are loved by superiors; and in working together harmoniously is beautiful concord manifested and creative work carried out. This applies both to the community and to the State. (Quoted in Dower 1986: 280)

As Terry Eagleton, in the epigraph opening this section, reminds us, in the case of 'realist writing' (here read realist cinema), metonym is converted into metaphor, 'recasting social processes as personal transactions'. In this way the inscription of colonial subjects within quasi-Neo-Confucian precepts in 'national policy' films of the early 1940s, located colonial subjects within the patriarchal structure of the 'family state' (*kazoku kokka*), through the narrativization of political doctrines of 'assimilation' (*dōka*). These were later expanded to concepts such as 'impartiality and equal favour' (*isshi dōjin*), under the Imperial institution through such nebulous slogans as 'the imperialization of colonial subjects' (*kōminka*). Mark Peattie outlines the political rationale that underpinned this policy.

Affinities of race and culture between Japan and her colonial peoples [*dōbun dōshū* 'same script, same race'] (excepting the islanders of the South Pacific) made possible the idea of a fusion of the two and suggested that ultimately Japanese colonial territories had no separate, autonomous identities of their own, but only a destiny which was entirely Japanese. (Peattie 1984: 96)

John Dower goes further in his analysis of a report published in 1943 under the title *An Investigation of Global Policy with the Yamato Race as Nucleus*, which he describes as 'an unusually frank statement of the relationship between Japan's expansionist policies and its assumptions of racial and cultural supremacy—that is, of the assumptions of permanent hierarchy and inequality among peoples and nations . . .' (Dower 1986: 265). He argues that this conception of an interracial hierarchy lay at the heart of slogans such as 'Pan-Asianism' and 'co-prosperity'. This model of racism, as revealed in the report, is analogous with Western patterns of 'supremacism'. As such, it represents a fusion of indigenous attitudes and Western supremacist theories, which found fitting allegories in the Confucian family structure. Should film audiences fail to make the appropriate links between the political policy of assimilation and the events depicted on the screen, films such as the 1943 'national policy' film set in Taiwan, *Sayon's Bell*, hammered them home with the following opening intertitles.

> In Taiwan, there is a native mountain race that was once referred to as unenlightened (*keigai no min*) and uncivilized (*seiban*), but now they are all Imperial subjects (*kōka*), and as subjects of the Emperor they are fighting in the front line for their homeland. This film is dedicated to the patriotism of the Imperial subjects of Taiwan, to the regional government and to the devoted police officers.

## Tropes of Empire

In the early 1940s, romance as a theme in popular films produced in Manchuria and Taiwan took an overtly political turn with the instant popularity of Yamaguchi Yoshiko (alias Ri Kōran in the Japanese transliteration and Li Xianglan in the Chinese rendering). Born to Japanese parents living in Manchuria in 1920, she joined *Man'ei* in 1938. Her name was changed to Ri Kōran/Li Xianglan, and in the company publicity material the mystery and speculation on her true origins formed a major part of her star persona. As well as regularly broadcasting on radio and appearing live in musical reviews with the Takarazuka Theatre in Tokyo, as a Chinese film star of *Man'ei*, Ri Kōran appeared in nineteen films between 1938 and 1945. It was only after the war when, after being indicted as a collaborator in Shanghai and after she was repatriated to Japan, that the truth about her parentage was finally revealed.

In the films in which Ri Kōran appeared during the war, it is possible to discern a discourse of an inter-Asian 'Orientalism' of the kind described by Edward Said (1991)[27] in that Ri Kōran's body is invested with a sexualised image of what the colonies represented to the Japanese at the time of their attempt at continental expansion. Shimizu Akira elaborates: 'Ri Kōran, through her attractive Chinese style, her captivating singing voice and her fluency in Japanese, embodied an idealized image of China that appealed to Japanese people' (Shimizu 1994: 62). The Japanese male leads who starred alongside Ri Kōran, Hasegawa Kazuo (1908–1984) and Sano Shūji, similarly embodied the positive characteristics associated with colonial expansion, such as the bringing of civilization through science and technology to backward societies (see figure 10). The popularity, in Japan, of Ri Kōran and of these films attests to the efficacy of romance as a metaphor for relations between the Japanese and the Chinese and for the policy of an Asian Co-Prosperity Sphere (*Daitōa Kyōeiken*).

In the 1942 film *Suchow Nights* (*Soshū no yoru*), directed by Nomura Hiromasa (1905–1979), Ri Kōran plays the part of a young Chinese woman who works at an orphanage in Shanghai. In the early scenes, she is hostile to the young Japanese doctor (Sano Shūji) who comes to examine one of the children. She tells him the child is Chinese and that Chinese people know best how to look after Chinese children. However, after he saves one of the children from drowning in the river, her attitude changes and she apologizes for her behaviour. In this scene, while they wait for the child to regain consciousness, she explains why she had hated the Japanese. She tells the young doctor that with the war,

> our lives had been thrown into confusion. My home was in the country in Suchow. I lived there with my brother and cousins, we were happy and our world was peaceful. Then the war began and rough Chinese soldiers came and our family scattered. The men went into hiding. Parents and children were separated, it was terrible. I came alone to Shanghai; you wouldn't understand how lonely I was. All I could think of was my mother and all I wanted was to see her again . . .

Here the doctor interrupts, explaining that he understands how she feels, but that the Japanese came to China to help the Chinese and, echoing Pan-Asianist policies, that it is the responsibility of Asians to help each other. He continues saying that it is not only people working in the medical profession, but Japanese soldiers, the technicians and the tradespeople; they all came to China to help the Chinese. The fact that Ri Kōran changes her opinion of the young doctor after he has physically intervened to save the child illustrates how the narrative is completely contained within a Japanese social logic that values actions far more than words. In popular films, romantic relations between men and women and love as a sentiment is rarely expressed in the dialogue but is expressed through the narrative in terms of actions; for example, in the silent era the knitting of socks for a man was often used as an expression of romantic interest, as in *Days of Youth* (*Gakusei romansu: wakaki hi*) (1929), directed by Ozu Yasujirō. So it becomes logical within this aesthetic convention of the portrayal of male/female relations that Ri Kōran should accept the doctor's sincerity at this juncture in the narrative.

In keeping with the feminization of China through the body of Ri Kōran, no attractive or heroic Chinese male characters appear in the film. As the child is drowning, some Chinese men look on, but none attempts to save her. The camera dwells on the doctor's body as he swims out to the child, thereby investing his body with all the positive meanings of masculinity denied to the Chinese male characters. Also, Ri Kōran's Chinese fiancé is described by his father as a 'weak man'. This is confirmed when he attempts to shoot the doctor in the back out of jealousy. The fact that the fiancé and other Chinese men depicted in the film all wear traditional Chinese dress further feminizes them, as they are constantly compared to the smart suits replete with padded shoulders worn by the Japanese doctors.

Ri Kōran's body/femininity is constantly linked to nature and a fertile penetrability. As she works in an orphanage, she is often depicted surrounded by children. In the crucial scene in which the young doctor's feelings for her first move towards romance, the camera, taking his point of view and unknown to Ri Kōran, shows her in a vast field bordered by mountains in the distance, singing amidst a flock of sheep. The fact that this scene is repeated in flashback in the doctor's imagination when he is ill and feverish underlines its significance as an iconic, natural/uncultivated landscape full of appealing potential. This scene invites comparison between the vastness and implied fertility of the new colony with the mountainous claustrophobic order of Japanese rural landscape. In both the actual scene and the flashback, the spectator makes this comparison through the desiring gaze of the young doctor as he watches Ri Kōran. This investment of Ri Kōran's body with connotations of nature/fertility is even more pronounced in the 1943 film directed by Shimizu Hiroshi (1903–1966), *Sayon's Bell*, in which Ri Kōran plays the part of a young native girl living in an isolated mountain village in Taiwan. Again, she is constantly associated with young children and animals. In both these films, Ri Kōran's body/femininity is equated with fertility and nature and displayed as a defining other in relation to an idealized Japanese masculinity that is associated with modernity and science.

The young doctor's ultimate rejection of Ri Kōran in the final scenes of *Suchow Nights* reaffirms his purity and therefore reconciles an heroic masculine ideal which spurned love (*ren'ai*) and romance. It also overcomes the inherent contradiction in the use of romance as a metaphor for the relationship between Japan and colonial subjects and a national policy that frowned on interracial marriage. The doctor's earlier rejection of his Japanese fiancée similarly functions at one level to maintain his purity, but also is significant as a rejection of claustrophobic Japanese social relations in favour of the more open spontaneous ones the film depicts as being possible in Manchuria, thus further reinforcing the iconic significance of the landscape and Ri Kōran's body as sites of freedom.

The fact that, in the final scene, the doctor has left the hospital in Shanghai and is on a boat heading inland to some remote clinic wearing a safari hat and carrying a water bottle implies his newfound freedom and the possibility of future adventure. This image of the doctor is contrasted with intermittent shots of Ri Kōran's wedding. The film ends with the re-inscription (and therefore, taming) of Ri Kōran into traditional family relations, while the hero remains free to pursue future adventures.

The narrative of *Brothers and Sisters of the Toda Family* is given a similar 'imperialist' twist as it is Shōjirō, the youngest son, who, after transferring to Tientsin (Tenshin) and through finding fulfilment in his work, goes through a 'rite of passage', returning to Japan as the most responsible member of his family. He castigates his brothers and sisters for their lack of filial piety in neglecting their duty to their mother. Implicit within Shōjirō's reform is the utopian view of Manchuria as a meritocratic land of opportunities where the old values of class and society do not apply, as he later tells his sister, Setsuko, and their mother when he persuades them to return to Manchuria with him.

> **Shōjirō:** Setsuko could work there. Nobody would object. . . No one sets any store by things like 'reputation' (*taimen*), 'form' (*teisai*) or 'appearances' (*sekentai*) . . .'

Earlier in the film, Setsuko had wanted to work in a department store like her friend Toshiko, but her sister-in-law had forbidden this as she felt it was too demeaning. The national policy of Manchurian settlement, in the film, is thus portrayed in terms of personal fulfilment, and the homeland Japan is presented as a class-based society that has lost its moral purpose through affluence.

Washitani Hana (2001) argues that Ri Kōran's fluid identity as structured through her film roles and publicity material—the speculation on her birth: is she Chinese, Manchurian, Taiwanese or Japanese?; her fluency in foreign languages, Chinese (various dialects), French and Japanese; and the media's constant reportage of her movements between China, Manchuria, Taiwan, Korea and Japan—meant that she came to embody in a tangible sense the multifaceted cultural aspects of Empire. I would go further, and suggest that the fluidity of her identity placed Empire as the natural concomitant of modernity in popular consciousness. Empire, within popular conceptions, can be seen as an extension of the disorientation and disunity of modernity. The geographical re-shaping and cultural re-mapping of the 'native land' (*kyōdo*) through Ri Kōran's body became one of the tropes that incorporated the alien other of the colonies into the nation-state, in much the same way as the series of theatrical reviews held at the Nihon Theatre (Nihon Gekijō) in the late 1930s and early 1940s.[28] In eroticizing and exoticizing colonial subjects through the body of Ri Kōran, these films consolidate the central position of a Japanese masculine nationalism. Either through the bringing of civilization (medicine, science and technology) to backward peoples or through romantic allegorical displays of interracial harmony, these films were important in the formation and legitimization of the Japanese nation-state. As Mark Peattie affirms in the quotation above, '[T]he acquisition of a colonial empire in the late nineteenth century was a mark of national eminence . . .' (Peattie 1984: 10). Empire provided one of the elements confirming the nation-state through the construction of an imaginary homogeneous national community; another strategy was the depiction of the hostile other, the American.

In his study on 'race and power in the Pacific War', John Dower sums up the accepted view on the different cultural conceptions of 'race' between Japan and her Western enemies during the Second World War in the following terms:

> Whatever reasons may be offered to explain differences between the racial and racist thinking of the Japanese and their Western enemies during World War Two, one overarching generalization seems difficult to challenge: whereas racism in the West was markedly characterized by denigration of others, the Japanese were preoccupied far more exclusively with elevating themselves. While the Japanese were not in-adept at belittling other races and saddling them with contemptuous stereotypes, they spent more time wrestling with the question of what it really meant to be 'Japanese', how the 'Yamato race' was unique among the races and cultures of the world, and why this uniqueness made them superior. (Dower 1986: 204–205)

While the above is certainly true in the sense that the Japanese did not demonise their Asian or their Western enemies, it is also clear that representation of the other was an important defining paradigm of difference against which the purity of the Japanese could be measured. In 'national policy' films, as the above analysis has demonstrated, this occurred in a positive depiction of interracial incorporation through romantic allegory embodied in the star personas of Ri Kōran and her leading Japanese male counterparts, Hasegawa Kazuo and Sano Shūji. In its negative sense, the 'spy film' became the paradigm through which the other was portrayed as a threat to the nation-state. In the following discussion I shall draw on two examples directed by Yoshimura Kōzaburō (1911–2000) and produced by Shōchiku, the all-star spy production *The Spy Is Still Alive* aka *The Spy Isn't Dead Yet* (*Kanchō imada shisezu*) (1942) and *The Night Before the Outbreak of War* aka *On the Eve of War* (1943).

*The Spy Is Still Alive*, a sophisticated film scripted by Kinoshita Keisuke, while drawing on Western Hollywood narrative conventions that equate death with metaphorical failure, is structured within a triangular framework of conflict that, through the parallel structuring of differences between racial groups, affirms the superiority of the Japanese through the *kenpeitai*. The *kenpeitai* officers, officers of Japan's gendarmerie concerned with maintaining internal security, played by Saburi Shin (Shōjirō in *The Brothers and Sisters of the Toda Family*) and Uehara Ken (1909–1991) (the young doctor of *The Love-Troth Tree* aka *The Compassionate Buddha Tree / Aizen katsura: sōshūhen*), are the heroes and, through their superior ability in terms of intellect and their access to technology, survive. Their all-knowing and all-powerful positions within the narrative provide a reassuring site of spectator identification. The Chinese spy, a former student who had studied and lived with a family in Japan, and his Filipino counterpart are (albeit too late as they both die by the end of the film) re-claimed within the assimilation strategy of the Confucian family structure, as the Chinese spy dies attempting to disentangle himself from his American masters and escape back to China. The real villains of the narrative, and the cause of the colonial spies' deaths, are therefore the American Embassy staff/journalists/spies who, by the end of the film, are taken into custody by the *kenpeitai* officers. Nara Shin'yō (1896–1977) and Saitō Tatsuo (the hapless father of Ozu's *I Was Born But . . .*) became typecast during this period as American villains. Saitō also appears as an employee/spy at the American Embassy in Tokyo in the 1943 production *The Night Before the Outbreak of War*.

While the colonial spies are contained within the 'family state' as errant younger brothers, the American characters are defined within a discourse of the binary opposition of Western materialism versus Japanese spiritualism. This was not achieved through simplistic attempts at denigration, but far more potently, through the re-appropriation of established

Hollywood conventions of luxury and the glamour associated with the star system. The meanings associated with these Hollywood codes and practices are inverted and re-defined as decadence and excess, characteristics made all the more poignant when contrasted with the frugality of the life-style of the hero, the *kenpeitai* officer, and the luxury of the American Embassy compared to the functional, but spartan, offices of the *kenpeitai* headquarters. The spy films of the 1940s turn Hollywood trademarks of sophistication and refinement, depicted in spectacular sets, and the world of luxury into negative signifiers of decadence and deception.

Actors such as Nara Shinyō and Saitō Tatsuo modelled their personas on Hollywood stars, turning romance into predatory sexual advances as in *The Night Before the Outbreak of War*, or in duplicitous relations with weak colonial subjects, which in the wider context of Pan-Asianist political policies takes on metaphorical connotations of exploitation. Sexuality, within the context of the 'spy film', is posited as the antithesis of the romance of the Ri Kōran films in which her body is coded in terms of nature and fertility, while American sexuality is coded as threatening and destructive.


## Conclusions

In this chapter, I have focused on the portrayal of a psychosocial sensibility of the inclusiveness of the 'family nation-state,' the *kazoku kokka,* and its links, in the first instance, to modernity; and in the second instance to empire. One of the major consequences of modernity was a sense of alienation brought about by the disintegration of, among other things, the network community structures characteristic of premodern, agro-literate societies and the subsequent disunity of the family. Following from Hobsbawn (1992) and Anderson (1993), I argued that, as an ideology of incorporation and assimilation, the 'family nation-state' formed the basis of an imaginary community that filled emotional voids in the experiential reality of people's lives through collective fantasies. In cinematic terms, alienation was depicted through allegory in the 'social realist' *gendaigeki* films of the 1930s (discussed in the previous chapter) and through the metaphor of the dispossessed *rōnin* (unemployed samurai) in *jidaigeki* films of the 1920s, such as *The Serpent*. In these productions Bandō Tsumasaburō's star persona, much the same as Takakura Ken's (1931–) in the 1960s, became synonymous with a revered masculinity out of tune with the modern age. In the 1930s through the inclusion of a romantic subplot and a shift in emphasis from rebellion to loyalty as a theme in, for example, film versions of *Chūshingura,* the alienated *rōnin* is re-inscribed into society through the family and/or the social group.

In terms of style, the links between modernism and speed are played out on the bodies of the *jidaigeki* stars who take on the agility associated with Western athletic sports. In Hashimoto's (1998) account, this display of speed as spectacle rather than the kabuki-esque pose (*mie*), was central to the visceral pleasure on offer to the audience. With the rise of anti-Western/American sentiments and calls for historical authenticity in *jidaigeki* films, a clear change is discernible in the stylistic uses of editing and camera movement. As history was increasingly harnessed to political expediency, the emphasis shifted from action to plot. In the 1940s, with the introduction of the 'national policy' film, this trend was further in evidence in the increasing use of the docudrama format, which became an important framing device in *gendaigeki* productions that harnessed modern history and contemporary events to the political exigencies of the times. As recruitment aids, exercises in public relations and propaganda for the military services, these films placed young men from Japan and also the colonies at the centre of history, providing a genealogical trajectory that clearly inserted the individual in the geo-historical entity defined as the 'nation-state'. Within these films, Hollywood-style heroic individualism is linked to professional advancement through the military institution for the good of the nation.

The final section, through a discussion of two films starring Ri Kōran, *Suchow Nights* (1942), and *Sayon's Bell* (1943), attempted to outline how political discourses of assimilation were encoded on the body of the actress Ri Kōran. The other dominant narrative schema through which these policies were articulated was the representation of relations between Japanese men and colonial men through the elder brother/younger brother metaphor. Contained within these discourses of colonial assimilation was a secondary discourse related to the Japanese government's policy of the mid-1930s to solve Japan's rural crises through mass emigration to the colonies. Under this policy, five million Japanese were to be relocated in Manchuria. Within film narratives of the early 1940s, Manchuria became a utopian space of opportunity where a better society could be created. These themes are also played out on the body of Ri Kōran, which is linked to the land through metaphors of fertility. It is also echoed in films, such as Ozu Yasujirō's 1941 production *Brothers and Sisters of the Toda Family*, in which Japanese class-based society is contrasted through the character of the youngest son with the freedom offered by the meritocratic nature of colonial society.

In films produced in the post-1939 Film Law period, the absence of foreigners, and where depicted, their portrayal by Japanese actors, has led scholars to de-emphasize the unifying role of the other in fictional accounts of the interracial community of nation-state and empire. However, in 'spy films', the depiction of themes of sexual predation and opulent lifestyles, during a period of extreme hardship and austerity, implies cultural decadence that became symptomatic of the West against which Japanese national purity was defined. Within the triangular structure of the 'spy film', the metaphor of the inclusiveness of the 'family nation-state' encompasses colonial subjects and structures the American characters as the threatening other by inverting established Hollywood conventions. The following chapter, from the context of a state-sponsored system of film production (the 'national policy' film and films produced under the auspices of occupation policy), will consider some of the heterogeneous elements of cinema style and practice.

CHAPTER 3

# Cinema and the State

> We are now in an age of economic transition. Development of machine industry and intensification of competition create a gap between rich and poor and this becomes greater and greater; and according to Western history this is an inevitable pattern. Socialism is today accepted by only a few but if it is ignored it will someday spread. Obviously therefore it is necessary to propagate public morals. What we call social policy will prevent socialism from taking root. (Premier Katsura Tarō 1908, quoted in Kasza 1993: 17)

> The water flows, but the river remains. (Quoted in Dower 1988: 325)[1]

In the previous chapter, I explored the relationship between the individual and the social collective as represented in films of the late 1930s and early 1940s in terms of a nationalistic sensibility of belonging to a geo-historical entity, defined as the *kokka,* the nation-state. In this chapter, I want to shift the argument to examine political discourses on the state regulation of cinema. By the state, I am referring to the body politic (*kokutai*) in its legal rather than its ideological sense. While the focus of this chapter is the regulation of cinema by the state up to, and including, the postwar occupation of Japan by the Supreme Command for the Allied Powers (SCAP) under the leadership of General Douglas MacArthur, I want to move beyond deterministic theories of propaganda and ideology to examine some of the heterogeneous elements of cinematic practice that are evident under the conditions of state control permitted, in particular, by the terms of the 1939 Film Law and SCAP film policy. In this way I hope to shed light on some of the continuities of aesthetic and cultural practices that span these political, ideological and historical frames of reference.

Due to the initial incorporation of films into *misemono* (vaudeville) shows, cinema was initially marketed as a new technological novelty. The Japanese film historian Sakuramoto Totomio (1993) dates the emergence of a consciousness of cinema, as more than just another sideshow attraction, to the 1910s and the moral panic that was sparked by the screening of the highly popular French detective film, *Zigoma* (1911), directed by Victorin Jasset. He goes on to explain that following the huge box-office success of

— 133 —

*Zigoma* and the fact that some children were reported as imitating the actions of the hero of the film, there followed a heated debate, sparked by educationists, between pro- and anti-cinema factions. The Imperial Education Association (*Teikoku Kyōikukai*), an association founded in 1896, took up the cause of the anti-cinema position, arguing that films had an adverse effect on youth and should therefore be regulated. They put forward a proposal to the Ministry of Education (*Monbushō*) and the Metropolitan Police Office (*Keishichō*) arguing in favour of the regulation of cinema. This became the basis of the 1917 Regulation. According to Makino Masahiro (1977) in his autobiography, there were also reports of incidents of children copying the daredevil antics of such screen idols as Onoe Matsunosuke (1875–1926) in his highly popular *ninja* films, and that this prompted his father, Makino Shōzō (1878–1929), to resign from Nikkatsu in 1919, following which he established his own company producing *kyōiku* (educational/cultural) films in 1920.[2]

Japanese public concern with the detrimental effects of the cinema experience on audiences, in particular the young, was in tune with worldwide popular concerns at this time. Mica Nava, in her study of Western literature from this period, draws the following conclusions: 'The literature about this period of cinema-going indicates that there was widespread concern about the moral and physical consequences—particularly for the working class and the young—of the content of films and the social and physical environment in which they were shown' (Nava 1996: 61).[3] The Japanese concerns with the physical environment of cinemas extended to various articles published by Kaeriyama Norimasa (1893–1964) in *Kinema Record* during 1915 on the construction of film theatres. One article published in the November issue gives detailed instruction on the installation of a system of centrifugal fans. However, while it is clear from Sakuramoto's study that concern was expressed in the popular press regarding the moral and physical effects of cinema on the young, in order to fully appreciate the underlying political imperatives that foreshadowed the relationship between the cinema and the state in Japan from the late 1910s up until surrender in August 1945, it is necessary to consider the wider political context of the regulation of various aspects of the newly emerging mass media.

Framed within the *min/kan* (civil/bureaucracy) oppositional paradigm prevalent in contemporary academic discourses, Gregory Kasza's analysis of the implementation of media controls in the late 1880s clearly illustrates that the two nebulous justifications for legal sanctions, 'to keep public

order and to safe-guard manners and morals', were applied against the
press. He draws the conclusion that these 'vague prescriptions . . . would
remain at the heart of media censorship until 1945'. The early part of Kasza's study focuses on the 1909 Newspaper Law, which gave extensive
powers over the press to the bureaucracy (*kan*). In effect the bureaucracy
could 'ban particular editions of a journal' and 'seize all copies without
resorting to prosecution'. He concludes his analysis of the support for the
implementation of this law by party politicians (*min*/civil) as follows,
'[party politicians] discovered certain common interests with the Meiji
leadership, above all a shared desire to control labor. They were not averse
to police laws apparently aimed at this new opposition group, and conse-
quently they did not uphold the liberal cause in 1909 as had once been
anticipated (indeed feared) by the constitution's framers' (Kasza 1993:
17). Within the context of Kasza's study, it becomes apparent that nebulous political discourses around 'public order and the safe-guarding of
public manners and morals' were euphemisms for the control of labour
in general and socialist movements in particular. This process reached its
apotheosis with the implementation of the Peace Preservation Law of 1925
(*Chian Iji Hō*) and in its shadow the promulgation of the 1925 Film Regulations. It is from this context, the political regulation of public 'morals',
that the relationship between the state and cinema in Japan should be understood in the first half of the twentieth century and arguably also in the
second half. One further point that needs consideration, with regard to the
state's regulation of cinema, was the concern of Japanese with the country's image in the international arena.

On 16 May 1911, the Ministry of Education (*Monbushô*) established
a committee to investigate 'popular education'—Tsūzoku[4] Kyōiku Chōsa
Iinkai. The founding of this committee, Satō Tadao (1995 vol. i: 318) suggests, was prompted by what became known as High Treason Incident of
1910 (*Taigyaku Jiken*), which involved the execution of twelve people suspected of plotting the assassination of Emperor Meiji. The government,
Satō continues, was concerned with the rise of socialism and the emergence of anti-imperialist movements. The mass media were seen as one
vehicle through which the populace at large could be 'guided along the
right path' (*zendō*). Against this backgound, a subcommittee was formed
to investigate 'magic lantern shows' and 'moving pictures'. This led, in
October of the same year, to the publication of the Regulations for the
Inspection of Magic Lantern and Moving Picture Shows (*Gentō oyobi Katsudō Shashin Firumu Shinsa Kitei*).

During the 1920s there emerged a two-pronged approach to the regulation of film production. First, the production of 'education films' (*kyōiku
eiga*) was to be encouraged; it was at this juncture that Makino Shōzō established his 'education film' company; and second, a strengthening of
film production controls. This was achieved through the enactment of a
further regulation in 1925 that brought responsibility for cinema censorship firmly under the control of the Ministry for Internal Affairs (*Nai-
mushō*). Prior to this, film regulation had fallen under the jurisdiction of
regional police departments, leading to a confused and ad hoc approach to
regulation. The main aims of the 1925 Regulation, which were to dominate
film censorship until 1945, were the preservation of 'the dignity of the
Imperial Institution' (*kōshitsu no songen*) and the 'protection of Japanese
virtue and morals' (*bitoku ryōzoku*). These aims clearly located cinema
within a conservative political discourse of nation building. Under the provisions of the regulation the following themes were outlawed: no character
in a film was to appear to represent a member of the Imperial Family;
imported films which depicted members of a royal household engaged in
a romance were prohibited; scenes of men and women kissing and embracing were to be cut; titles of films that included the word 'kiss' had to be
altered[5]; and films which appeared to deny the right to private property
were also banned (Hamada 1995: 94).

Yanai Yoshio, who by 1927 had compiled a thousand-page volume titled *On the Protection and Administration of Motion Pictures*, headed the
new censorship office under the jurisdiction of the Ministry of Internal
Affairs. Under him were seven other officials, four from the police department and three ministry bureaucrats, all graduates from the Aesthetics Department of Tokyo Imperial University (*Tōkyō Teikoku Daigaku*).
According to Yanai's memoirs, in the early days after the censorship office
was established, there were few problems due to the adoption of a system
of informal pre-production consultations. However, around 1929 due to a
combination of factors censorship became an issue of concern. The formation of the 'proletarian' film movement (known as the *Nihon Puroretaria
Eiga Dōmei* or *Purokino* in its abbreviated form) and an increase in the
production of 'tendency' films (*keikō eiga*/films with a tendency to the
left), combined with the increasing military tension on the continent, lay
at the basis of this concern.

The proletarian film movement was an artistic movement with its roots
in the wider literary and theatrical movements of the early 1920s. The
films themselves, mainly amateur productions, were not particularly so-

phisticated in terms of technical standards, however, in terms of content, they were seen by the authorities as potentially subversive as they focused on topical incidents of the day deemed relevant to the lives of workers. Few examples remain and those few that do are mostly fragments that have withstood the ravages of the censorship officers, war and occupation. Filmed as documentaries, they often depicted strikes and labour unrest. One typical example cited by Satō was filmed during the funeral of the left-wing Diet member Yamamoto Senji (1889–1929) who was assassinated by a right-wing fanatic because of his opposition to government policy in China and the strengthening of the provisions of the 1925 Peace Preservation Law. A member of the Labour and Farmers Party (*Rōdō Nōmintō*), Yamamoto opposed the introduction of the 1929 amendment to the Peace Preservation Law, which made 'subversive' activities punishable by death. In the early 1930s, the police increasingly ordered the dispersal of audiences at proletarian film screenings and the Censorship Office became more active, as the figures for footage cut during this period indicate:

> 1927—10,273 meters cut
> 1929—10,305 meters cut
> 1930—15,687 meters cut
> 1931—18,368 meters cut (cited in NHK 1995: 104)

One of the reasons cited as a catalyst, that signified the beginnings of the crackdown against the movement, was the riot that followed a screening of various films in Tokyo at the Yomiyuri Lecture Hall in 1930. Several factors are listed as contributing to the tensions that arose between the authorities and the audience. Prior to the screenings, members of the audience had been subjected to a body search and the Censorship Office had banned the *benshi* narration. The organizers then played a German recording of the *Internationale* throughout the screenings. According to Satō, this concoction of events created a highly charged atmosphere, eventually erupting in rioting. By 1932 the 'proletarian' film movement had been all but suppressed and the amount of film cut by the censorship office again decreased. By 1934 the principal organizers and filmmakers associated with the movement had been arrested; also by this time all the theatres associated with the Proletarian Theatrical Movement (*Puroretaria Engeki*) had been closed down.

The buildup to the enactment of the infamous 1939 Film Law and its subsequent revisions in the early 1940s should be understood from within the highly charged atmosphere of this crackdown on left-wing activities both in the workplace and in the cultural sphere, and the war in China. In political and legal terms, this process reached a denouement in the revisions to the Peace Preservation Law in 1929, hence the symbolic significance of the assassination of Yamamoto Senji on the day the revision was passed by the Diet. The enactment of the National Mobilization Law (*Kokka Sōdōinhō*) of 1938 further reinforced this policy and provided the structure in which the 1939 Film Law was framed. Kasza explains the political relevance of the National Mobilization Law in the following terms: 'The law was an enabling act for use only during war. It authorized sweeping state controls over labor, industry, and other civil sectors by means of executive imperial decrees, obviating the need for parliamentary laws in each case. It was not, then, just another law itself, but a new legal framework replacing regular constitutional procedures' (Kasza 1993: 195).

Iwasaki Akira (1958a), a film critic imprisoned under the terms of the Peace Preservation Law for opposing the implementation of the 1939 Film Law, dates its origins to the series of military incidents between September 1931 and January 1933 in Manchuria, known collectively as the Manchurian Incident (*Manshū Jihen*). He argues that it was at this time that the government bureaucrats first conceived of the shift in emphasis from purely proscriptive measures in the regulation of cinema to prescriptive measures. As evidence, he cites the large number of newsreel films made with the army in Manchuria in the six months between September 1931 and April the following year. However, this realization of cinema's potential, as a tool in war, should perhaps be seen in the more general international context of the First World War, which first transformed cinema into a national resource. Nicholas Reeves, in his study of British propaganda during the First World War, draws the following conclusion: 'In sum, before the end of 1914, those responsible for official propaganda had reached precisely the same conclusion as the cinema trade: official films had an important and distinctive contribution to make to the war effort' (Reeves 1999: 28).[6]

It was during 1934 and 1935 that the foundations for the 1939 Film Law were being laid by, amongst others, Tatebayashi Mikio. He was a bureaucrat in the Ministry of Internal Affairs Censorship Office and is attributed by Japanese film historians (NHK 1995, Satō 1995 vol. ii)[7], and more recently the American historian Peter B. High (2003), as being the principal architect of the law. Iwasaki Akira (1958a), however, also attributes much of the ideological underpinnings of the law to the interventions of Hayashi Fusao (1903–1975), a novelist and literary critic who started his career in the proletarian literary movement only to shift his position to the conservative right in the 1930s. Hayashi was a friend of Tatebayashi's, and they were both frequent contributors to the journal *Japanese Film* (*Nihon Eiga*) in which they advocated the adoption of a national film policy along the lines of the 1934 German Film Law. *Japanese Film,* which commenced publication in 1936, was the official organ of the conservative Greater Japan Film Association (*Dai Nihon Eiga Kyōkai*). This association had been founded in 1935, having grown out of a committee established in March the previous year by the Ministry of Internal Affairs, the Film Regulation Committee (*Eiga Tōsei Iinkai*), to look into the further regulation of cinema. This committee was originally chaired by Admiral Saitō Makoto (1858–1936), Minister for the Navy, until his assassination during the 26 February 1936 Incident, after which the former cabinet minister Yamamoto Tatsuo succeeded him as chairman. This committee was extremely conservative in nature, and its makeup of representatives from the government and military is cited by Yokochi Takeshi and Aida Fusako (1999) as just one of the examples of the influence the military exerted on film policy at this time.

It is clear from Iwasaki's readings of the *Japan Film* articles, published in the latter half of the 1930s by both Hayashi and Tatebayashi, that this discourse on the relationship between cinema and the state was further complicated by reactionary concerns against the perceived negative consequence of modernity: the 'Westernization/Americanization' of Japanese society. In an article published in September 1938, the term *fukko* is used extensively. *Fukko,* used in this context, signified a call for a return to an essential Japaneseness founded on the Emperor System (*Tennōsei*). Western individualism was reviled and an essential Japanese 'totalitarianism' (*zentaishugi*) advocated. Tatebayashi continues in this vein in an article published in the same journal in October of that year when he states, '[T]he time for reverently following European and American ideologies in the name of world knowledge has passed'. In this sense, this call for reactionary reform of the film industry became confused around two issues. Tatebayshi continues his argument along the following lines: ideology had not kept pace with political and military events. Citing the Meiji oligarchs as historical precedent, he makes the claim that they employed music and the arts in modernizing Japan. He therefore calls for a similar use of cinema in bringing the people's thoughts (*shisō*), sentiments (*kanjō*), and attitudes to life (*seikatsu taido*) to a unity and conformity (*sokuō*) under the Emperor System.

One further issue that was raised in support of a national film policy was concern with Japan's international image. This was manifested in two ways: (a) the desire to promote Japanese films abroad as an intercultural exercise in mutual understanding, and (b) to ensure that Japan's censorship standards met those of other 'advanced nations' (*senshin koku*).

One of the main thrusts of the comparative study of propaganda films of the pre-war and wartime periods carried out by the NHK editors (1995) was Japan's concern with the country's image on the world stage. The editors cite two examples, arguing that Kawakita Nagemasa (1903–1981), who set up the successful Tōwa Shōji Film Distribution company upon his return from Germany in 1928, was motivated by his concerns with what he saw as the 'mis-representation' of Japan abroad.[8] In 1929 he took several Japanese films to Germany for distribution, but, like his two predecessors, he did not meet with great success. In 1925 Murata Minoru (1894–1937) had taken his film *The Street Magician* (*Machi no tejinashi*), a joint production with Mori Iwao, to Germany and in 1929 Kinugasa Teinosuke (1896–1982) took his film *Crossroads* (*Jūjiro*) to Germany via the Soviet Union. In Germany it was released under the title of *Shadows of Yoshiwara*.

In 1932 the Parliamentarian Iwase Akira, who would make the initial proposal for the development of a National Policy on Film (*Eiga Kokusaku Kengian*) in 1933, went to Geneva as part of the Japanese delegation to the League of Nations. As part of the proceedings, newsreel footage from various countries was screened. Iwase was reportedly shocked by the Japanese section, which showed lower-class geisha dancing semi-naked at the Itami hot spring resort near Tokyo. The NHK authors argue that it was this experience that influenced Iwase's decision to support the proposal to parliament for the establishment of a committee to consider the question of a national film policy. They go on to say that he was probably influenced by the actor/politician/sportsman Asaoka Nobuo who, after studying film in America, wrote a report based on his experiences titled, *A Proposal for a National Film Policy* (*Eiga Kokusaku Teishō*). In this report Asaoka advocates the establishment of a centralized policy on film. His main premise is that the Japanese film industry is producing films, which he states are caught between American materialism and the power of Soviet filmmaking techniques.

Today's American commercial films have given rise to materialism and this has potentially harmful effects. On the other hand, Soviet, Russian films that we should be fearful of are encroaching. At this time we Japanese are caught between the materialism that runs through commercial American films and the power of the Soviet film . . . When considering this, it is lamentable that neither our government or thinking people within the populace have little interest in, or are divided, on the question of film.

Indeed, thinking seriously about our country and to save it from crisis, there is a pressing need for a mechanism to make films based on the spirit upon which Japan was founded, that is, we need to establish a mechanism that will supply a unified leadership for the film industry. One that will incorporate those who advocate the rationalization of the industry, those who are calling for ideological guidance (*shisō zendō*), and those who simply love film. (Quoted in NHK 1995: 132)

In 1933 Asaoka was appointed head of the newly founded Imperial Japanese National Film Research Centre (*Dai Nippon Teikoku Eiga Kenkyūjo*).

The excerpts from the preamble, quoted below, to the 1933 proposal for a National Film Policy clearly link these two principal questions: one, reflecting Asaoka's concerns over the influence of film on the Japanese population, and the second again takes up concerns with Japan's national prestige in the world.

It is said that film, in its function as a mechanism for entertainment and propaganda, in other words, as a mechanism for education, could be more widely involved in the life of the people in the modern scientific age. However, if the government leaves the making of films to private companies whose motivation is profit, then we must rely on negative sanctions against infringements, but under the terms of this proposal we would implement a system of positive guidance . . .

On the question of Japan's international image,

In the case of films made by foreign companies to introduce Japan, there are many which brought about unforeseen misunderstandings that have harmed the dignity of our country by portraying strange fabricated customs as if they were the truth. Our principal aim, is to induce commercial film companies to make films to introduce Japan abroad that are genuine (*junsei*) and refined (*kōgana*), in order to prevent the loss of our international standing in this way. In view of this kind of abuse, in the current world situation today, various countries feel the need to implement guidance regulations, in particular, the establishment of an exclusive mechanism dealing with the film industry. (Quoted in NHK 1995: 134–135 and Iwasaki 1958a: 33)

Therefore, the 1939 Film Law and its subsequent amendments should be considered as an end point, a nexus where a series of complex discourses coalesced. On the surface, the Law formed part of Japan's war preparations for total mobilization, linked to which became a reactionary attack on the film industry, which, as we saw in an earlier chapter, had become symbolic both as a metaphor and motor of modernity.

The Law was drafted at a series of meetings held throughout January and February in 1939, in central Tokyo at the Hōsō Building opposite Sakurademon. In attendance were Tatebayashi; Machimura Kingo, the head of the Ministry of Internal Affairs Police Department; three bureaucrats from the Film Censorship Office; and the head of the General Affairs Section of the Ministry of Education. The meetings were chaired by Fuwa Suketoshi, a bureaucrat also from the Ministry of Education, who went on to head the Cabinet Propaganda Office (*Naikaku Jōhōkyoku*) in the early 1940s. The draft of the law was completed by 26 February and presented to the Diet by the then Minister of Internal Affairs, Kido Kōichi (1889–1977), becoming law on 1 October 1939. The shift in policy from a purely proscriptive to prescriptive intervention is clearly laid out in the two main aims of the law: the strengthening of the censorship controls, and the restructuring of the industry, as presented in Kido's speech to the Diet introducing the bill.

> The film industry occupies a most important position as provider of entertainment to the people. In recent years by degrees, film has come to perform a remarkable function even in areas such as religion, propaganda, and the dissemination of news, and the national responsibility for film has gradually assumed great importance. However, government policy towards film has generally been limited to questions of prohibition. In order to employ film in a positive sense, I propose the following plan. We should reform all aspects of our film industry, production, distribution and screening. We should also give due consideration to film content . . . (Quoted in NHK 1995: 172)

The 1939 Law completely restructured the relationship between the film industry and the state by bringing the industry directly under the control of the Cabinet Propaganda Office (*Naikaku Jōhōkyoku*). The main points of the Law as presented to the Diet are paraphrased below:

1. A licensing system will be introduced to regulate film production companies and distribution companies.
2. To improve the quality (*shitsuteki kōjō*) of films produced, all personnel working within the industry are to be registered.
3. For the public good (the prevention of injury, hygiene and education), film production and screenings are to be limited.
4. To improve the level of the national culture, a system for selecting good films will be introduced.
5. To correct (*zesei suru*) the influences of foreign films, their distribution and screenings will be limited.
6. For the benefit of public education (*kyōiku*) and enlightenment (*keihatsu*), film screenings will be controlled, limiting the quantity of films produced and regulating film distribution.
7. To implement the main points of this law, a film advisory committee will be established. (Quoted in Iwasaki 1958a: 50–51)[9]

Censorship controls were strengthened through the introduction of a pre-production system of censorship. As stated above, the industry was initially regulated by a personnel registry system, which continued until December 1940, when the Cabinet Propaganda Office took over responsibility for film. Negotiations took place forming the basis for the complete restructuring of the industry through a series of company mergers. In August 1941 the Propaganda Office summoned the heads of the two largest film companies at this time, Tōhō and Shōchiku, to a preliminary meeting where the need to amend the 1939 Law by rationalizing the industry was put to them in terms of the scarcity of raw film stock. The outcome of the amendments are summarized as follows:

1. The combined production output for all drama and culture film production companies is to be limited to no more than four films per month. Film stock will be distributed accordingly and drama films are to be limited to approximately 8,000 feet of film.
2. The approximately ten existing film companies will merge into two companies and all existing culture film production companies will form one company.
3. The distribution of all films (drama, culture and newsreel) will be handled by a public corporation. A fixed percentage of box office takings will go to the production company and the cinemas. Five prints will be made of each drama and culture film.

4. With regard to film production, under the provisions of this bill, the Propaganda Office will not only have the authority to prohibit certain subject matter, but will also sponsor the production of films. (Quoted in Iwasaki 1958a: 54)

After much lobbying from the two major studios, all existing drama production companies merged into three conglomerates. Two were structured around Shōchiku and Tōhō while the third, Daiei, was formed through the merger of Nikkatsu, Shinkō and Daitō, and each company was restricted to producing two films per month. All existing cultural and education film production companies merged to form one company, and the distribution of all films, both domestic and imported, was controlled by one central company. Newsreel production companies had already merged in 1940 into the Japan News Film Company. Through this stringent system of restructuring it was intended that the number of films produced was to be curtailed and, as a consequence, the 'quality' of the content improved. At this time Japan was producing some 560 films annually. Tatebayashi believed that the quality of film content would improve if the number of films being produced was reduced. Tōhō and Shōchiku had both come under attack for producing highly popular films that were deemed in some quarters to be unsuitable. They were charged with being exploitative in producing 'vulgar' films for commercial gain. In Tōhō's case, it was the series of films starring the highly popular comedian Enomoto Ken'ichi (1904–1970) known as Enoken, and in the case of Shōchiku, the 1938 romance *The Love-Troth Tree* aka *The Compassionate Buddha Tree (Aizen katsura)* was severely criticized. Enoken was criticized for his frivolity and for encouraging a lack of responsibility, while romance (*ren'ai*) was considered to be incompatible with the martial spirit required at the time.

Of the two main planks of the 1939 Law and its subsequent amendments, increased censorship controls and the restructuring of the industry, it is the latter which had the most profound effect on the content and production of films up until August 1945. In stylistic terms, the controls on content through pre-production censorship were unable to completely stamp out plotlines that depicted the cost of war to individuals, as the example of the final scenes from Kinoshita Keisuke's (1912–1998) 1944 'national policy' film sponsored by the army, *Army (Rikugun)*, clearly attests. In this final sequence, the female character (Tanaka Kinuyo 1909–1977) usurps control of the hitherto male-dominated narrative through a complex montage sequence, which caused great controversy amongst film censors and critics at the time of its release. In this final sequence, devoid of dialogue, the pace of the editing, the juxtapositioning of shots and point of view all support the mother's position as she desperately searches through the columns of marching men for one last glimpse of her son before he goes to the front. In the screenplay, presented to the censors prior to production, this sequence is simply described as a mother seeing off her son. However, this emotional final sequence, set as the climax to a narrative that spans three generations of men from the one family through Japanese history from 1866 to the late 1930s, clearly challenges the militaristic patriarchal discourse that dominates the film up to this point.

Neither could censorship alone negate the stylistic influences of the proletarian film movement of the late 1920s, or those of the 'social realist' films of the 1930s. Uchida Tomu's (1898–1970) 1939 film *Earth* (*Tsuchi*) is cited as one of the best examples of this 'realist' tradition. Based on the novel of the same title by Nagatsuka Takashi (1879–1915) and released just before the Film Law came into effect, it follows the lives of a struggling peasant farmer and his family through the seasons. Filmed in secret after Nikkatsu had rejected the initial proposal, the film develops in image form the theoretical principles of Nagatsuka's writings. He strove for a *cinéma direct* style of objectivity known as the *shasei* method. 'Uchida did not make the film from the scenario but from the lives of the people. The original novel has a sense of realism developed from the *shasei* (sketch from nature) method'. Iwasaki (1958b: 243–244) goes on to explain that this involved location shooting over the four seasons of the year, which in fact took two years to complete. In terms of cinematic technique, Uchida's *Earth* also incorporates many of the conventions of the Soviet school of 'montage', being perhaps influenced by Alexander Dovzhenko's 1930 film of the same title. However, where the ideological and aesthetic aims of Dovzhenko's *Earth* are to celebrate the bonds between peasants and nature and, to define socialism as the link between them, Uchida's *Earth*, in contrast, is a critique of capitalism, which acts as the cause that disrupts these very bonds. Kanji (Kosugi Isamu 1904–1983), the main protagonist, is crippled in his efforts to provide for his family because of the debt he inherited when he became head of the household. His father-in-law, in hard times past, had gradually sold off the family lands, forcing the family into tenant farming, while borrowing further amounts from the landlord in times of difficulty. By the time Kanji inherits the position as head of the household, all he can manage to do is pay the interest. Other families in the community as a whole are portrayed in similar predicaments as they sell off their daughters to textile factories. In this way, the mantle of patriarchal family head, so central to the ideologies of the 'family state', is presented as meaningless. Kanji is placed in a position of powerlessness by external circumstances beyond his control, but it is his humanity that transcends the ideological construction of masculinity dominant in a militaristic society. In the latter part of the film, Kanji recants and helps the old father-in-law. Previously, Kanji had held his father-in-law, the instigator of the debt and more recently the perpetrator of the fire that burns Kanji's house to the ground, accountable as the source of all the family's misfortunes.

In stylistic terms, Uchida captures the lyricism of the Soviet school through complex montage sequences that create an evocative sense of the peasants' struggles with nature as, for example, the sequence when Kanji and his daughter cart water to the parched rice paddies before the rains. The sound track provides the continuity, as the *taiko* drumbeat of the previous scene, when the peasants perform a ritual at the shrine for rain, carries over into the next series of shots as Kanji and his daughter struggle with the buckets of water. The incessant drumbeat both reflects the visceral pounding of their heartbeats under the extremes of exertion and heat and sets the rhythmic pace for the elliptical editing, which compresses the work of several days into three minutes. The near futility of their efforts is heightened with punctuating close-up shots of the dry cracked earth and the limp seedlings. This sequence ends as heavy drops of rain hit the earth followed by a cut to a shot of the sky heavy with clouds—the awaited rains have come. This is followed by a high-angle shot of the mature rice plants billowing, wave-like, in the wind.[10] However, the regulation of the industry that culminated in the advent of the 'national policy' film (*kokusaku eiga*) tended to subsume these once oppositional stylistic conventions within a 'total mobilization' ethic that often rendered them benign at best, and supportive of the war effort at worst. One example is Yamamoto Kajirō's (1902–1974) 1941 film *Horse* (*Uma*).

Like *Earth*, *Horse* follows the lives of a family of peasants through the four seasons. Set in a documentary realist style and filmed on location in Iwate Prefecture in northern Honshu, the film brings together two themes central to 'national policy' films of the period. First, mobilization for the war effort; as a peasant family, they raise with great devotion a horse, which is eventually sold at auction to the army. Second, the incorporation of women into the war effort. The young daughter, Ine, played by a youthful Takamine Hideko (1924–), is instrumental in the raising of the horse and therefore is central to the narrative. As the horse is sold for a hand-some price, enabling the family to pay back their debt to the co-operative, both these 'national policy' themes become instrumental in solving the issues of poverty raised by Uchida's earlier film *Earth*: the question of crippling loans and the related issue of the sale of daughters as virtual slave labour to textile factories. In terms of the narrative, the film is clearly divided into two sections: the first, culminating with the illness of the horse, dwells on the suffering and hardships of life as a peasant in the harsh winters of northern Honshu. However, the second half, coinciding with early spring and the thaw, renders the hardships of the winter mean-ingful as they bring in their wake the joys of rural life. Ine plays with the foal and rides the mare through the rich pastures beneath the distant snowcapped mountains. Young girls from the textile factories, with white summer parasols and wicker baskets, return to the village for the *Obon* summer festival. In one sense, by drawing on the documentary-like realis-tic conventions, established and developed in the proletarian and 'social realist' films of the 1920s and 1930s as the means to express this utopian pastoral ideal of rural Japanese life, *Horse* renders these conventions benign.

Just as these realist stylistic conventions were co-opted and re-appro-priated within films produced in the post-1939 Film Law period, so too were the narrative conventions derived from the Shōchiku Kamata/Ōfuna-style romance genre. While films produced under the auspices of the Tōhō Studios often placed women within central roles in the narrative, and by extension emphasized the importance of their contribution to the war ef-fort in films such as *Horse* and Kurosawa Akira's (1910–1998) 1944 'na-tional policy' film *The Most Beautiful* (*Ichiban utsukushiku*), the Shōchiku Studios re-appropriated the heroine's love for the hero, sublimating it to love of country. This then results in selfless heroic actions, as in *The Flower of Patriotism* aka *A Patriotic Flower* (*Aikoku no hana*), and even death, as in the spy film *The Night Before the Outbreak of War* aka *On the Eve of War* (*Kaisen no zen'ya*) (1943).

In the 1942 Shōchiku production, *The Flower of Patriotism* aka *A Pa-triotic Flower*, directed by Sasaki Keisuke (1901–1967), the heroine (Ko-gure Michiyo, 1918–1990), after her father's failed attempt at negotiating a marriage for her, becomes a Red Cross nurse. Ayako's love for the hero (Sano Shuji 1912–1978), the prospective groom of the failed negotiations, is thus deflected onto her work and consummated when Tetsuo, now a sol-dier, is wounded and admitted to a field army hospital where he is nursed

by Ayako. The selfless love Ayako feels for Tetsuo, dramatized by the fact
that Tetsuo's wound has temporarily blinded him, is heightened as he is
unaware that it is Ayako who is tending him. The theme of sublimated
love in *The Flower of Patriotism* extends narrative conventions established
in, for example, the enormously popular trilogy *The Love-Troth Tree*
where the nurse, a single mother, ends up marrying the hospital owner's
handsome son, and accommodates these themes of female independence
onto alternative discourses appropriate to the times: namely that women in
wartime when men are scarce have to find fulfilment through means other
than marriage and children.

The later 1945 Shōchiku production *The Bases Where the Maidens Are*
aka *The Girls of the Air Base* (*Otome no iru kichi*), directed by Sasaki
Yasushi (1908–1994) and made with the support of the Airforce Section
of the Army and the Women's Association (*Fujinkai*), similarly equates
the love which young female ground crew/mechanics feel for individual
pilots with their work. As in the majority of romance films of the prewar
and wartime periods, the expression of love is reflected in the visual narrative through actions and not words. In this example, the little doll mascots
the girls make for the pilots signifies love in an extraordinary time when
the 'normal' expressions of affection between young men and women are
not possible. In one scene, after a pilot has been killed, the girls hold a
funeral service for him and bury a mascot one of the girls had been making
for him. As they are performing the ceremony, by chance another young
pilot sees them and after being told what they are doing exclaims, 'We
pilots are indeed fortunate (*shiawase*) that you all care so much for us'.
This scene becomes even more poignant when, at the end of the film, he
leaves as part of the Special Attack (*kamikaze*) Forces. The burial of the
mascot becomes the substitute for the *kamikaze* pilots' bodies, which are
destined never to return for cremation and burial of the ashes in the family
graves.

In these examples, love is transformed into patriotic sacrifice: the doing
of things for people who are unaware of what is done for them. However,
it is essential for the dramatic effect of the narrative, and therefore an important site of pleasure in the diegesis, that the recipient becomes aware of
what is done for him. Hence, in the scene just described, it is essential that
a young pilot inadvertently sees the girls and acknowledges their affection.
Similarly, in *The Flower of Patriotism,* it is important that Tetsuo finds out
by chance from the doctor that it is Ayako who is nursing him. In *The
Night Before the Outbreak of War*, the sacrifice of the heroine, a geisha

(Tanaka Kinuyo) who helps the *kenpeitai* (gendarmerie) uncover American spies, is acknowledged after her death in the final scenes of the film. Not only does she thwart the sexual advances of the American Embassy official Knox (Nara Shin'yō 1896–1977), but by sacrificing herself, kills Knox and his associate and protects the secrets of Japan. Within the romance element, a powder compact given to the heroine by the *kenpeitai* officer (Uehara Ken 1909–1991) signifies his presence in her thoughts as she resolves to run the car off the road into the sea deep below the cliff. The compact, a love token, signifies their nonconsummated love, which merges into a national theme, the protection of Japan.

There has been a tendency within Japanese film histories to, on the one hand, dismiss films made in the post-1939 period as an aberration, the defining other against which pre-1939 films are measured, or to treat the period as highly problematic when filmmakers were 'forced' post-1939 Film Law to make 'national policy' films against their better judgements. Satō Tadao makes the following statement, typical of the treatment of this period: 'This new policy served to abolish the urban love story or melodrama, one of the most profitable film genres, and resulted in the almost exclusive production of "national policy films" (*kokusaku eiga*). The first of the three main characteristics that *distinguished* these films . . .' (italics mine, Satō translated by Gregory Barrett 1987: 100) Satō then goes on to list and describe the three features that supposedly *distinguish* these films: first, an absence of the enemy, second, a 'concentration on the human side of Japanese soldiers', and third, the 'monotony' of the training and marching scenes. Hirano Kyoko, in her study of the Japanese film industry during occupation, reverts to traditional 'theories of Japaneseness' (*nihonjinron*) to explain this phenomenon, when she argues that the Japanese proverb, *nagai mono niwa makarero*, 'may be roughly translated as "If you can't beat 'em join 'em," reflecting the traditional prizing of harmony over conflict rooted in the nation's geographical and sociological imperatives. This aspect of the Japanese psyche doubtless influenced the behavior of film directors' (Hirano 1992: 204). The entries in the *Kinema Junpō* complete book of actors for the two actors who took on the parts of American spies in 'national policy' films, Nara Shinyō and Saitō Tatsuo (1902–1968), also provide illustrative examples of how this highly problematic period is dealt with in Japanese cinema history. *Warm Current* (*Danryū*), made in 1939, is the last film listed for Saitō Tatsuo after which follows, 'In the period just before Pearl Harbour amongst his performances he appears to hide his talents, unusually the following was expressed in the November issue of *Film Criticism* (*Eiga Hyōron*) "at this time, the roles he took could not possibly fulfil his wishes, however, there is a change in the quality of his acting"' (*Kinema Junpō: Nihon Eiga haiyū zenshū: Danyūhen* 1991: 232). The account then jumps to 1946. In the case of Nara Shinyō, *Kinema Junpō* gives a similar account: 'After 1932, he took many supporting roles and as a reliable performer, after the move from Kamata to Ōfuna he became a central actor. After the war . . .' (*Kinema Junpō: Nihon Eiga haiyū zenshū: Danyūhen* 1991: 431).

As the above brief re-assessment of films produced in the post-1939 Film Law period has demonstrated, these films were part of a popular tradition sustained by well-established genre conventions, studio house styles and a highly developed star system. Furthermore, films produced in the post-1939 period developed through the selective incorporation and re-appropriation of elements of pre-1939 filmmaking practices and, in some instances, even challenged hegemonic images and social discourses. Some Shôchiku productions of the post-1939 period, in redefining female fulfilment through work rather than through marriage and motherhood, contradicted the hegemonic image of the patriarch, as the self-assured autonomous woman is contrasted with the ineffective male. In *The Flower of Patriotism*, Ayako is only free to become a nurse, something she had wanted to do since her brother was killed in action some three years previous, when her father fails in his traditional role as head of the household in finding a suitable husband for her. In a lengthy dialogue with her father after her return from Tokyo, Ayako rejects her father's second marriage proposition telling him that, up to now, she had lived in her own small world, but that in Tokyo she had come to realize that the world for women is now much larger and her eyes had been opened. Her father reluctantly agrees, saying there is nothing more he can say (*mō nani mo iwan*). In *The Night Before the Outbreak of War,* the image of the *kenpeitai* officer (Uehara Ken) reverts back to the more ineffectual weak romantic hero of the *shinpa*-tradition (*nimaime*), as he is not on hand at the crucial moment to save the heroine. Contrary to much popular opinion, post-1939 productions encompassed all popular genres of the period from romance to the sophisticated developments made in the period drama (*jidaigeki*). In keeping with the Film Law guidelines, the post-1939 *jidaigeki* films aimed at distancing the genre from the swashbuckling antics of *chanbara*, and in films such as Mizoguchi Kenji's two-part *The Loyal Forty-seven Ronin* aka *The Ronin of the Genroku Era* (*Genroku Chūshingura*) based their themes on historical 'fact'.

My main thesis is that industry regulation through a centralized production system, and not censorship, is the most effective tool in controlling and containing film content within desirable hegemonic sociopolitical discourses. In Japan in the war period, this was achieved through a restructuring of the industry by the direct interventions of bureaucratic-government institutions: a process that was legitimated by the National Mobilization Law and was effected through the rationing of film stock. In the 1950s and 1960s regulation came in the form of monopoly capital management. The introduction of new technologies is also a factor as they fire audience expectations for even greater spectacles, which in turn require greater capital investment. In 1930s Japan, independent actor-led film production companies were pushed out of business and the stars forced to return to the big studios, due in part, to the high investment required to convert silent studios to sound. In the 1960s controversial filmmakers, such as Ōshima Nagisa (1932–), were forced into virtual exile in an attempt to find external funding in a bid to maintain artistic autonomy, due in part to the major studios' monopoly practices. However, this assertion, that the most effective tool in controlling and containing film content is industry regulation through a centralized production system, and not censorship, should be tempered with the provision that it is not completely effective, as the example of the father image in *The Flower of Patriotism* illustrates. In seeking to incorporate women into a total war mobilization, Shōchiku inadvertently defined women's autonomy against ineffective males. Only in films such as *My Favourite Plane Flies South* aka *Our Planes Fly South* (*Aiki minami e tobu*) (1943), through such strategies as a husband's or father's words posthumously repeated and photographs placed in the family altar, was the patriarchy sustained during the physical absence of the male.

Iwasaki Akira (1958a) argues that in Japan there was a time lag between the adoption of Western-style industrial capitalism and the adaptation of the population to the civil responsibilities associated with 'democracy'. He argues that the Japanese in the Taishō and early Shōwa periods were still operating under a quasi-feudalistic ethos that deterred them from challenging authority, hence the film industries' meek acquiescence in the planning and promulgation of the various film laws that ultimately centralized production and restricted autonomy. Satō Tadao, on the other hand, argues that it was a case of pragmatics. The rationalization of the industry meant assured profits in a highly competitive market, through a system of monopoly production and distribution. He also makes the point that the involvement of government in the production of films gave the industry a respectability it had lacked in the past. Peter B. High's study of Japanese film culture during the fifteen-year war period (1931–1945) further problematizes the impact of the 1939 Film Law, which stipulated under article 15 the mandatory screening of 'culture films', that is, documentary films. This encouraged a profusion of theoretical debates on the nature of the relationship of documentary to fact. Furthermore, according to High's research on the topic, many of the filmmakers formerly engaged in the Proletarian Film Movement responded enthusiastically to the 'Film Law's demand for high quality films capable of serving the "public enlightenment" needs of the nation . . .' (High 2003: 124). While there is merit in all these arguments, it is also profitable to consider the relationship between cinema and the state in Japan in the first half of the century from the world context. It is clear that Japan was not unique in utilizing film as a national resource in both nation building and the domestic war effort. As has been argued above, by 1915 the British were well aware of the important role cinema could play in the domestic war effort, and according to Reeves' study, they were equally concerned to export propaganda films abroad in an attempt to influence, though not always successfully, foreign opinion through the Department of Information and the Ministry of Information. Viewed in this context, Japanese government film policy in the first half of the twentieth century was not an aberration but closely mirrored international trends and explains in part how the SCAP authorities were easily able to adapt existing structures to their own censorship agendas.

## Occupation: August 1945–April 1952: Yoshida Shigeru (1878–1967) and the Banning of *The Tragedy of Japan*

On 2 August 1946, Prime Minister Yoshida Shigeru invited Brigadier General Frayne Baker, a close associate of General MacArthur, and Colonel D. R. Nugent, head of the Civil Information and Education Section, to a private screening at his home of the film *The Tragedy of Japan* (*Nihon no higeki*).[11] This film, although passed by both the occupation civil and military censors in June of the same year, was subsequently withdrawn from cinemas. *The Tragedy of Japan*, directed by Kamei Fumio (1908–1987), a left-wing sympathizer who had been imprisoned during the war for making films contrary to government policy, was a documentary compiled from Japanese and American newsreel footage.[12] It covered fifteen years of Japanese military rule and was obviously critical of the emperor and his role during that period. As Shimizu Akira explains, 'Kamei is an excellent editor. In the last scene of *The Tragedy of Japan*, he slowly superimposed a shot of the Emperor dressed in a suit over a shot of him dressed as a full General of the Army. This montage sequence symbolized the Emperor's statement of humanity [the renunciation of his status as a god], while at the same time giving the impression that the Emperor had simply taken off the uniform, but was still responsible for the war' (Shimizu 1994: 189). Lieutenant Colonel D. S. Tait and Lieutenant Colonel Thomas P. Davis, who actually attended the screening at Yoshida's home, concluded their reports by stating that the film should be banned 'in the interests of public order' as 'its radical treatment of the Emperor might provoke riots and disturbances'. Hirano Kyoko (1992) makes the point that, during the two weeks *The Tragedy of Japan* was shown in cinemas, there was no evidence it provoked disorderly conduct amongst the audiences. Davis later stated that, '[I]t is patently obvious that we had been invited to the showing in the hope that SCAP [Supreme Command for the Allied Powers] might be influenced to take some action in banning this and other films of its kind' (quoted in Hirano 1992: 134). The political machinations leading up to and culminating in the banning of *The Tragedy of Japan* raises two interrelated questions regarding interpretations, both academic and popular, of Japan's modern postwar history. First, why was a film made by the Japanese and critical of the emperor banned by the occupation authorities? Relatedly, to what extent has continuity been a defining concept in postwar Japanese historical interpretations?

In the immediate postwar period, the Americans, in their capacity as leaders of the Allied Occupation Forces, engaged in an hegemonic struggle with conservative elements of Japan's ruling elite led by Yoshida Shigeru, Prime Minister for most of the occupation (May 1946–May 1947, and October 1948–December 1954). General MacArthur's Occupation Forces had a mandate to ensure that 'Japan will not again become a menace to the peace and security of the world . . .' and to establish new and 'democratic' institutions so that Japan could once again become a 'peaceful member of the family of nations . . .' (Beasley 1990: 214).[13] Yoshida and the conservative faction, while apparently supportive of the superficial structural changes the Americans sought to make, was purportedly opposed to any radical change to the ideological principles upon which Japanese social institutions were founded. They saw ideological continuity as a bulwark against radical elements that had sprung up in the social and political chaos that was characteristic of Japanese society in the occupation period. Dower, in his study of Japan in the immediate postwar period, succinctly sums up the position of Japanese 'conservatives' in the following terms.

> To conservatives, the overriding tasks of the post-defeat period were to thwart social upheaval, preserve unchanged the emperor-centered 'national polity', and put the country back on its feet economically. They rejected all arguments about the 'root' causes of militarism, repression, and aggression, choosing instead to depict the recent war as an aberration brought about by irresponsible and conspiratorial elements within the imperial military. This being the case, their argument continued, sweeping structural and institutional reforms were unnecessary. On the contrary, all that needed to be done was to return the state and society to the *status quo ante* of the late 1920s, before the militarists took over. (Dower 1999: 83–84)

## Occupation Film Policy: Prescription and Proscription

At noon on 15 August 1945, Emperor Hirohito's (1901–1989) surrender speech was broadcast to the nation. On the same day the Film Corporation, previously the Film Distribution Corporation established in 1942, closed all cinemas for one week. On 22 August, they issued a voluntary prohibition on the distribution of films 'portraying chauvinistic patriotism and including war scenes, as well as all culture films and current newsreel films; [they] ordered the reopening of theatres that had been closed during the war; and ended restrictions on show times' (Hirano 1992: 37).

These measures were given approval on 18 September by the Ministry of Internal Affairs and the Information Bureau in a communiqué 'Concerning the Guidance and Regulations of Performances and Exhibitions, etc.'. It is interesting to note how quickly the industry responded to changes they saw as inevitable and the skill they showed in pre-empting the changes the Occupation Forces later sought to implement.

In November 1945, and in his capacity as Supreme Commander for the Allied Powers, General MacArthur received a directive from the United States Government that set out in broad terms the objectives of the Occupation Forces. These objectives were to ensure 'the abolition of militarism and ultra-nationalism in all their forms; the disarmament and demilitarization of Japan, with continuing control over Japan's capacity to make war; the strengthening of democratic tendencies and processes in government, economic, and social institutions; and the encouragement and support of liberal political tendencies' (quoted in Beasley 1990: 214).

The Occupation Forces quickly mobilized the popular media as a forum to promote, at the ideological level, the ideals of 'democracy' that they wanted to disseminate. On the day the Occupation Forces first arrived in Japan, 27 August 1945, General MacArthur established the Information Dissemination Section to control the media. On 22 September, this section became known as the Civil Information and Education Section (CIE). The CIE was 'charged with expediting the establishment of freedom of religious worship, freedom of opinion, speech, press and assembly by the dissemination of democratic ideals and principles through all media of public information. [It had] the responsibility of making clear to all levels of the Japanese public *the true facts of their defeat, their war guilt,* the responsibility of the militarists for the present and future Japanese suffering and privation and the reason for the objectives of the military occupation of the Allied Powers' (quoted in Hirano 1992: 34, emphasis mine).

Hirano Kyoko, in her historical study of the Japanese film industry under occupation, states that the CIE followed a dual policy: on the one hand, of promoting suitable themes for film productions and, on the other hand, a policy of rigorous censorship in an attempt to carry out its mandate. The CIE sought to encourage the development of ideals associated with American 'democracy' while preventing the media from disseminating anything considered unsuitable or dangerous to the Occupation Government.

On 22 September 1945 the CIE called a meeting of representatives from all the main film studios to set out its policy. The list of 'desirable subjects' was as follows:

1. Showing Japanese in all walks of life co-operating to build a peaceful nation.
2. Dealing with the resettlement of Japanese soldiers into civilian life.
3. Showing Japanese prisoners of war, formerly in our hands, being restored to favour in the community.
4. Demonstrating individual initiative and enterprise solving the post-war problems of Japan in industry, agriculture, and all phases of national life.
5. Encouraging the peaceful and constructive organization of labour unions.

6. Developing political consciousness and responsibility among the people.
7. Approval of free discussion of political issues.
8. Encouraging respect for the rights of men as individuals.
9. Promoting tolerance and respect among all races and classes.
10. Dramatizing figures in Japanese history who stood for freedom and representative government. (Quoted in Hirano 1992: 38; also listed in Japanese in Shimizu 1994: 157)

Between January 1946 and June 1947 Japanese films were subject to both pre-production and post-production censorship. Although the CIE began to censor films in early October 1945, the system of double censorship officially began when the 'Memorandum Concerning Motion Picture Censorship' was issued on 28 January 1946. The CIE was involved in the pre-production censorship of all scripts and film projects. Although military personnel headed this section, it was staffed by civilians and was therefore considered a civil censorship office. The Civil Censorship Department (CCD), which carried out all post-production censorship, was a subcommittee of military intelligence. Staffed by military personnel and engaged in 'military intelligence and counter intelligence activities', it was considered a military censorship office. After June 1949 and until the end of the occupation in 1952, the CIE section relaxed this policy of double censorship and films were only subject to post-production censorship.

On 19 November 1945 the CIE published a list of thirteen prohibited themes. Any film that contained one or more of the following subjects would not pass the censorship offices. Films would be prohibited if they were:

1. infused with militarism;
2. showing revenge as a legitimate motive;
3. nationalistic;
4. chauvinistic and anti-foreign;
5. distorting historical facts;
6. favouring racial or religious discrimination;
7. portraying feudal loyalty or contempt of life as desirable and honourable;
8. approving of suicide either directly or indirectly;
9. dealing with or approving the subjugation or degradation of women;

10. depicting brutality, violence or evil as triumphant;
11. anti-democratic;
12. condoning the exploitation of children; or
13. at variance with the spirit or letter of the Potsdam Declaration or any SCAP directive. (Quoted in Hirano 1992: 44–45; also in Japanese in Shimizu 1994: 163)

One of the main obstacles in relation to the 'democratization' of Japan was what SCAP officials perceived as an inherent conflict between Japanese Neo-Confucian-derived concepts of loyalty and revenge on the one hand, and the Western-derived concepts of the rule of law based on universal principles of good and bad. This issue had already been raised at an earlier meeting of CIE officials and representatives of the film companies on 22 September when the Americans made the following statement on themes in kabuki narratives.

Kabuki theatre is based on feudalistic loyalty, and sets faith in revenge. The present world does not accept this morality any more. The Japanese will never be able to understand the principles of international society insofar as things such as fraud, murders and betrayals are justified by the principle of revenge, regardless of the law . . . Western morality is based on concepts of good and evil, not feudal loyalty. For Japan to participate in international society, the Japanese people must be made to understand the basic political ideals of law and democratic representative government, respect for the individual, respect for national sovereignty, and the spirit of self-government. The entertainment media and the press should all be used to teach these ideals. (Quoted in Hirano 1992: 38; also in Japanese in Shimizu 1994: 154)

This prohibition on the theme of 'revenge' again featured prominently as number two on the 19 November prohibited subject list (above) and came to dominate the argument over the prohibition of *jidaigeki* films, in particular the prohibition on sword-fight (*kengeki*) scenes, which Japanese filmmakers protested were no different from the gunfights in American westerns. The American censors countered this argument by pointing out that Japanese use swords to exact revenge out of loyalty to a lord as in myriad versions of *The Loyal Forty-seven Retainers* (*Chūshingura*), while cowboys use guns to defend the 'rule of law' and their communities (Hirano 1992: 67). Shimizu Akira elaborates, 'On this point GHQ were particularly insistent, hammering it home. This is because they were afraid that the fanatic sense of loyalty the Japanese people had for the Emperor might stir up resistance against the Americans' (Shimizu 1994: 160).

The initial premise of the occupation officials was flawed. They were indulging in a variant of cultural imperialism, which did not distinguish between feudalism and Neo-Confucianism. Feudalism is a set of economic relations, which came to an end with the fall of the Tokugawa *bakufu* and the Meiji Restoration (1868), when Japan's economy moved towards industrialization. Neo-Confucianism is based on a set of social relations used at various periods in Japanese history to legitimate different political and economic systems. Hence, it was Neo-Confucian ideologies that were carried over into Japanese society after the Meiji Restoration. As with Christianity in the West, Confucianism in Japan has been adapted to support industrial economic structures. Occupation officials completely underestimated the strength of the ideological tradition they were attempting to repress.

The 'Memorandum Concerning the Elimination of Undemocratic Motion Pictures' issued on 16 November 1945 listed 236 Japanese films produced since the Manchurian Incident of 1931 that were to be banned (Shimizu 1994: 164). Many of the films were destroyed by the studios themselves, and the Occupation Forces were also active in destroying many negatives. However, they did retain some master copies, which were submitted to the Library of Congress in Washington.

As Hirano Kyoko points out, it was ironic that officials of the Occupation Forces, in Japan ostensibly to establish a new state founded on 'democratic' principles, should find it necessary to resort to the widespread use of censorship and propaganda as the most effective means to disseminate their ideals. This contradiction between principle and practice meant that the censors had to disguise their operations in order to maintain at least the illusion of democracy. Hirano from her study of the period concludes that

> [H]owever well intentioned censors may be, in reality . . . their judgements [were] often based on arbitrary interpretations, extraneous political considerations, or personal biases. The criteria of the occupation censorship authorities for allowing or prohibiting ideas to be expressed in films in fact changed significantly over the course of the occupation, corresponding to shifts in occupation policy that reflected decisions made in Washington and the overall international climate. (Hirano 1992: 45)

Historical accounts of Japan's immediate postwar period (Dower 1999 and 1988; Kosaka 1982) emphasize the conservative's concern with the maintenance of ideological continuity in the postwar period. According to such accounts, Yoshida Shigeru sought to ensure the continuance of the ideological principles upon which Japanese society had been founded since at least the Meiji Period (or, as myth would have it, since the time of the first Emperor Jimmu, 660 b.c.—considered to be the foundation of the Empire of Japan: Sansom 1983). The epigraph opening this chapter is from a speech made by Kanamori Tokujirō (1886–1959), a member of the Yoshida cabinet, and is indicative of the attitude of the ruling elite to change. Governments may come and go, wars may be won or lost, but the river, symbolic of Japan's immutable *kokutai* (national polity), will remain as it has done since time immemorial.[14]

Yoshida, who first became prime minister in May 1946, was equally concerned to preserve the Imperial Institution, seeing it as the focal point upon which Japan's spiritual and ideological principles were founded. He established himself in opposition to the intellectuals and socialists who were supportive of the changes they thought the Occupation Forces intended to make. As Kosaka Masataka explains, Yoshida believed that through the skilful manipulation of the constantly altering relations between the world powers, Japan could minimize the losses suffered from defeat and 'transform defeat into victory' (Kosaka 1982: 87). As John Dower has shown in his biography of Yoshida, the prime minister's ultimate aims remained consistent with the objectives he had pursued as a career diplomat prior to 1945. These were

1. preservation of the emperor and national polity;
2. repression of the revolutionary potential within Japan, particularly at the mass level;
3. restoration of the old guard and traditional levers of elite rule, a task of structural reconsolidation rather than simply overturning the occupation's purge of personnel;
4. economic reconstruction along capitalist lines, and in the *zaibatsu* [industrial financial combines that dominated Japanese commerce from the Meiji Period to the end of WWII]-dominated mould of the prewar era; and
5. Japan's return to international stature as a partner of Western powers. (Dower 1988: 277)

Yoshida's aims were indicative of the desire of the ruling elite to minimize the effects of change inherent in defeat and reconstruction. He sought
to strengthen the economic base of Japanese society, while simultaneously
attempting to preserve the social structure and ideological belief systems
of the general population, just as the Meiji oligarchs had done before him.
This attitude was obvious in the comments he made to the Diet on 25 June
1946 on the revised constitution, which he states in his memoirs 'was perhaps the most important single reform undertaken after the termination of
the Pacific War'. Yoshida's commentary, worth quoting at some length, is
a clear example of his ability to co-opt American-style 'democratic' ideas
into the existing ideology and therefore, minimize their potential to influence change.

> There was little need to dwell on the fact that democracy, if we were to use
> the word, had always formed a part of the traditions of our country, and
> was not—as some mistakenly imagined—something that was about to be
> introduced with the revision of the Constitution. As for the Imperial House,
> the idea and reality of the Throne had come into being among the Japanese
> people as naturally as the idea of the country itself; no question of antago-
> nism between the Throne and people could possibly arise; and nothing con-
> tained in the new Constitution could change that fact. The word 'symbol'
> had been employed in the definition of the Emperor because we Japanese
> had always regarded the Emperor as the symbol of the country itself—a
> statement which any Japanese considering the issue dispassionately would
> be ready to recognise as irrefutable fact. (Yoshida 1996: 139)

But why did the Occupation Forces go along with Yoshida and agree
to the continued role of the Imperial House in Japanese politics? W. G.
Beasley (1990) states that 'expediency' was the overriding factor in the
early days of the occupation. He goes on to suggest that 'war criminals'
were being viewed as martyrs by the general population, and SCAP did
not want to turn Hirohito into one too and risk the social unrest that might
follow. To support this line of argument, Beasley refers to an opinion poll
held in December 1945 on the issue of the emperor that found ninety-five
percent of those polled were in favour of the Imperial House. A telegram
MacArthur sent to Dwight Eisenhower on 25 January 1946 emphasized
MacArthur's fears that, if the emperor were tried as a war criminal, there
was a serious possibility of civil unrest and the threat of a communist
takeover.[15]

The incident over the banning of *The Tragedy of Japan* would appear to support this line of argument. Whether, as Hirano suggests, it is evidence of the early implementation of the 'reverse course' policy that Beasley (1990) contends came into effect in 1951 after the outbreak of the Korean War, or whether it was a result of 'expediency' and general confusion over policy is not clear. Noam Chomsky (1993) seems to support the 'expediency' argument by dating the 'reverse course' policy from 1947. Alternatively the saving of the Imperial Institution was perhaps, following on from Gore Vidal's interpretation of modern American history, part of the wider American bid for global hegemony, which he dates from 1940 when 'Franklin Delano Roosevelt . . . deliberately provoked the Japanese into attacking us at Pearl Harbour' (Vidal 2003: 74). However, it is certain that the conservative clique's relationship with the top officials of the Occupation Forces was sufficiently strong for Yoshida to override the censors at both the CIE and CCD who had already approved *The Tragedy of Japan* and get it withdrawn from public cinemas and eventually banned. It also indicates the convergence of views between the SCAP censorship policy, which was gradually shifting from an anti-militarist and anti-ultra-nationalist line to an anti-left-wing position, and the Japanese government's conservative position, which had the maintenance of the Imperial Institution at the centre of its 'permanence-amid-change' policy. As a precursor to the problems filmmakers might expect to experience under occupation censorship policy, the arbitrary nature of the banning of *The Tragedy of Japan* provided a valuable lesson. Nichiei, the company that had funded the production of *The Tragedy of Japan*, nearly went into bankruptcy as a result of the banning. As Dower (1999) points out, this provided a 'compelling warning to anyone else who might be contemplating playing with controversy'.

In summary, films produced during the occupation period should be analysed in light of the following contextual issues. First, although the Occupation Forces were ostensibly engaged in an attempt to redefine Japanese ideals along Western 'democratic' lines, they themselves engaged in a system of censorship and propaganda only equalled by the Japanese military government in the latter stages of the war. Second, Prime Minister Yoshida and his conservative elite appeared to have a great influence, not only from the 1950s when the international situation changed and with it American priorities, but, as the banning of *The Tragedy of Japan* indicates, from as early as August 1946. It is my opinion that the influence of Yoshida and his elite group of politicians and bureaucrats on postwar Japanese society cannot be overestimated. This conservative clique saw itself as the guardian of the national polity (*kokutai*), the river that had to be protected from whatever fashionable ideology or political system happened to flow past at the time. Therefore, it is essential that the war not be viewed as an ideological or an institutional caesura, and that the postwar cinema be analysed from an historical perspective of an institutional and political discourse of continuity. It also confirms Ōshima's (1978: 39) position in defending Japanese filmmakers from the criticism of a degree of ideological fickleness in their willingness to cooperate first with Japanese bureaucratic directives under the wartime regime, and then to adapt their position so willingly to occupation imperatives. Filmmakers were used to operating within these politically contingent parameters.

The remainder of this chapter will be given up to an introductory exploration of the complex nature of the issues surrounding the interaction of the opposing forces of continuity and change as they impacted on film content between 1946 and the end of the occupation in 1952. Two aspects of romance will be explored in the following section, forming a foundation for the more detailed analysis of the postwar cinema in subsequent chapters: first, the adaptation of romance as a narrative paradigm for the negotiation and re-definition of the scripts of femininity and masculinity within popular films, and second, the role of the film star as mediator between two ostensibly opposing ideological positions, militarism and democracy.

## Sexual Difference as Structuring Device: the Case of the 'Kiss'

In postwar melodramas, the significance of sexual difference as a structuring device became once again more apparent as women were, after the exigencies of wartime, re-inscribed within patriarchal social structures representative of peacetime. The inclusion of the 'kiss', so central to occupation film policy, became the catalyst around which these discourses coalesced.[16] The terms of reference that defined these discourses within the wider sociopolitical context had, under occupation auspices, changed and with the changes in the postwar Constitution fundamentally altered women's legal position within postwar society. Again as in the 1920s, women and social conceptions of femininity became the focus around which various political discourses associated with economic and social change found representation within popular films.

During the early 1940s sexual difference as a structuring device had been de-emphasized as the image of women, when depicted, was reduced to the demands of the war economy. This was not only evident in the subject matter of the narratives, which often centred on the role of women in the workforce, in particular, taking the place of absent male workers in factories (*The Most Beautiful* [1944]) and as support ground crew on airfields (*The Bases Where the Maidens Are* [1945]), but was also reflected in the androgynous nature of their appearance through their clothing (*monpe*) and hairstyles. It was only in the more glamorous role, as the female counterspy, that sexual difference continued to be a central structuring device. In this context, gendered binary positions shift the primary symbolic meaning of the opposition man/woman from referring to two sides of gender to two sides of the war, as the male is represented by the predatory American male spy. Furthermore, contained within this structure is the hint of an erotic appeal to interracial sexuality and to emotive fears of miscegenation. The counter-side to this discourse was the reversion of the Japanese *kenpeitai* officer to the weak romantic hero (*nimaime*) of the *shinpa* tradition, as he is effectively emasculated by his failure to rescue the heroine who, of course, must die to quash the hint of miscegenation in films such as *The Night Before the Outbreak of War* (1943). Despite her death, the heroine within these narratives is clearly active and in control of her sexuality, outwitting the American spies and saving both her honour and the secrets of Japan.

In films of the late 1930s and early 1940s, in terms of masculinity, the exigencies of the war economy supported an underlying text of sexual repression. This manifested in two interrelated forms: first, a denial of romantic love; and second, the male usurpation of the nurturing role in the family. In Inagaki Hiroshi's (1905–1980) 1943 film *The Life of Muhō Matsu* aka *The Rickshaw Man* (*Muhō Matsu no isshō*) and Ozu Yasujirō's (1903–1963) 1942 film *There Was a Father* (*Chichi ariki*), women are virtually excluded from the narrative and, therefore, from their traditional role as nurturers. Virgin fathers became both role models, as masculine ideals to which sons should aspire, and nurturing figures. Reflected in these films was the conflation of private and public affecting the way Japanese manhood was perceived. The films depicted masculinity in terms of nature, such as the primitive masculinity of Muhō Matsu; in terms of men's interaction with the community, such as the father's role as head of the household, teacher and factory worker in *There Was a Father*; and the role of sons as inheritors of the family business and as sailors and soldiers in Tasaka Tomotaka's (1902–1974) 1943 film *Navy* (*Kaigun*) and Kinoshita Keisuke's (1912–1998) 1944 film *Army* (*Rikugun*). The conflation of social roles and family relations integrated the private into the political as the family was made to represent the smallest unit of the nation-state, emphasizing its primary function as a unit of production. Michel Foucault has pointed out that, in such situations, sexual relations between the sexes becomes repressed, 'because it is incompatible with a general and intensive work imperative' (Foucault 1990: 6). Under this system, affection between family members is converted into duty and obligation.

Hirano Kyoko argues that one of the overriding concerns of the occupation officials was the inclusion of 'kissing scenes' in Japanese films,

> purposely to force the Japanese to express publicly actions and feelings that heretofore had been considered strictly private. The American censors felt that the Japanese in general had a tendency to keep thoughts and actions hidden, and that this was wrong. Ever since the surprise attack on Pearl Harbour, Americans had condemned the Japanese more for their 'sneakiness' than for any other quality . . . They felt uneasy when the Japanese were not expressing themselves openly. Thus, if Japanese kissed in private, they should do it in public, too. (Hirano 1992: 161)

While there is possibly some truth in this explanation, it only goes part of the way in explaining why hardened military censors and occupation officials would go to such lengths to promote romance, and in particular, the public display of kissing in popular films.

From the early days of the Hollywood dual plotline, the 'kiss' is often associated with the narrative closure of the romance element of the plot, signifying in public the act of private sexual consummation associated with marriage. As we saw in *Marching On* aka *The Army Advances* (*Shingun*), the modern Americanized 'goal orientated hero' (Suzuki Denmei 1900–1985) achieves his ambition through 'heroic individualism' within the *mise-en-scène* of war and in the romance element of the plot gets the girl. The girl is thus inscribed into a legitimate family structure defined along the patriarchal principles of marriage. In postwar Japan, in keeping with occupation 'democratic' reforms, both men and women had to relearn the scripts of masculinity and femininity that are at the centre of Western social and capitalist exchange and that had virtually been written out of films in the post-1939 Film Law period. Therefore, in answer to the question, Why did the occupation officials place such an emphasis on the 'kiss'?, the answer must lie in sexuality, and in particular femininity as a structuring social device. As Jane Ussher asserts, echoing Lévi-Strauss, 'The maintenance of the boundaries of sex and sexuality are central to the maintenance of phallocentric order and power, and central to this process is the symbolic meaning of dominant constructions of the sexuality of "woman"' (Ussher 1997: 436). Myths of romance are just one of the vehicles through which the requisite 'dominant constructions of sexuality' are defined, negotiated, learnt and perpetuated and as such, romance was actively re-inscribed within the traditions of Japanese postwar popular culture. And the 'kiss', as the symbolic consummation of the relationship between a man and a woman within a capitalist economy, was central to this discourse.

In premodern Japanese society, the simple exchange of women within the arranged marriage format was both symbolic of, and maintained a patriarchal social order as did the practice of *nanshoku*, homosexual relationships between older (active) men and (passive) youths. (For an interesting analysis of this practice within Japanese samurai society see Ōshima Nagisa's 1999 film *Gohatto/Taboo*.) In the post-Meiji Restoration era of 'enlightenment', the Civil Code of 1890 legally propped up an outdated patriarchal order suffering under the strains of the introduction of industrial capitalism and cultural modernism. In the postwar period under the terms of the 'democratic' Constitution, where freedom of choice and the autonomy of the subject are paramount, the myth of romance becomes one of the principal scripts through which social roles are inscribed in the cultural and economic terms of masculinity and femininity.

## From Yukie in *No Regrets for Our Youth* to Carmen in *Carmen Visits Home*

> To think in this age necessarily means to struggle. Thought must be supported by struggle, and only that thought which is accompanied by struggle will flourish. (From the lecture by Morito Tatsuo quoted in Johnson 1964: 32)

Kurosawa Akira's 1946 production *No Regrets for Our Youth* (*Waga seishun ni kuinashi*) is posited as the quintessential 'democratization film'. It takes up many of the themes associated with occupation social policy, the casting of a strong, independent woman at the centre of the narrative, the links with postwar agrarian reforms and the questions of war responsibility following the opening of the International Military Tribunal for the Far East on 3 May 1946. Related to this was the apparent scarcity of exemplary cases of people resisting militarism and war. With encouragement from David Conde of the CIE, the Tōhō Studios were reportedly urged to make *No Regrets for Our Youth* based on the lives of Kyoto University professor of law Takikawa Yukitoki (1891–1962), who was forced to retire in 1933 on the grounds of his political views, and the suspected Comintern spy and China expert, Ozaki Hotsumi (1901–1944). From the perspective of Japanese popular consciousness, Satō Tadao suggests that, during the occupation,

> [t]he Japanese people in general affirmed the principles of democracy. However, they found it difficult to feel the accompanying emotion that this ideal was theirs. Generally popular culture in various societies is one of the mechanisms through which stories are handed down about people who sacrifice themselves by disregarding their lives in order to found the principles of a good society. In this way people receive an ennobling emotional sense of the principle . . . In the case of Japan, there are many popular stories of brave people connected to the Imperial institution, nationalism and the events of the Meiji Restoration, but there are few stories that give the people a sense of democracy as their own [principle]. (Satō 1995 vol. ii: 175)

Out of this paucity of examples, *No Regrets for Our Youth* has emerged in some historical accounts as exemplary. Ōshima Nagisa (1978), on the other hand, takes a far more critical line with the political aspects of the film, a point to be taken up in a later chapter. However, at this juncture I want to focus on the aspect of romance and the characterization of the heroine, Yukie, acted by Hara Setsuko (1920–), before going on to offer a contrasting analysis of the extremely sophisticated 1951 Shōchiku comedy *Carmen Visits Home* aka *Carmen Comes Home* (*Karumen kokyō ni kaeru*). This latter film, directed by Kinoshita Keisuke within the Shōchiku framework of the depiction of 'active' heroines such as the female counterspy of the early 1940s, offers a far more radical and purposeful image of the autonomous woman who successfully challenges the patriarchal power positions of not only her father but senior village males.

The daughter of Ōkōchi Denjirō (1898–1962), an academic at Kyoto University, Yukie's autonomy is defined through the script of romance, which allows her to choose a husband from amongst the selected group of her father's favoured pupils. The significance of the romance element of the plot is established in the opening sequences set in the mountains around the university. These sequences, aptly described by Ōshima as scenes of 'brilliant youth' (*kagayakashii seishun*), establish Yukie's relationship, as marriageable daughter, to her two central suitors, Noge (Fujita Susumu 1912–1990) and Itokawa. The exchange of reverse-cut shots at the brook, as Yukie hesitates, waiting for one of the two to come forward to help her, not only sets up the triangular structure of the romance plotline but establishes the characters of the two suitors in terms of their opposing political views. Within the political economy of prewar marriage, as Yukie has no brothers, and as an educated daughter from an affluent background, her freedom in the choice of a husband from a selected circle, the future husband ultimately inheriting the mantle of the father-in-law, was not a radical position. In placing Yukie's autonomy within this social framework, the film effectively inscribes her back into the traditional role of dutiful daughter, as she does not attempt to marry outside her father's favoured circle of approved future husbands. And after her marriage, as faithful wife, she does not question Noge's work but dutifully cares for his physical needs and maintains his home. The radical elements of the film, which in turn tinge the character of Yukie, are solely related to her father's and her husband's anti-militarist political stances. As a wife she never questions Noge's work, simply accepting his reassurances that in ten years time the Japanese public will thank them. After his arrest, she stoically resists her interrogators in prison and finally, after his death, as a filial daughter-in-law she returns to his home village and works to help his aging parents who are suffering the stigma of having a son executed/murdered as a spy.

In stylistic terms, the film supports Yukie's position as a dutiful, if somewhat overindulged, daughter in the opening establishing sequences and later as contented wife, the 'kiss' being central to this process of inscription. After having lived and worked in Tokyo for three years, she is still restless and unfulfilled, having changed jobs three times, when she is finally reunited with Noge. After a preliminary conversation in which she vents her dissatisfaction with her life, she runs out of the room. Noge pauses for a moment and, calling her name, follows her. Yukie has only gone as far as the corridor when Noge flies around the corner, knocking her bag out of her hand. The camera follows the trajectory of the handbag, lingering on it lying on the floor, while Noge and Yukie kiss off screen.

The next scene, still set in the same corridor but occurring some time in the future with Yukie now dressed in a married woman's kimono waiting for Noge, begins a montage series symbolizing the harmony of their life together. Their happiness is contrasted with the threat of Noge's potential imminent arrest. In contrast, when Yukie acts independently, she is given an emotional slant that taints her with hysteria and accounts for Iwasaki's observation that as a daughter

> of a zealous academic who is in love with one of her father's pupils, a revolutionary, Yukie leaves home. This beautiful and proud daughter, played by the youthful Hara Setsuko, throws away her comfortable lifestyle and her pride to traverse a thorny path with her lover. Finally, reviled as a traitor and labouring in the fields stained with mud, she becomes an obsessive woman with whom the audience cannot feel any sympathy. (Iwasaki 1958a: 79)

The war and the consequences of her husband's anti-war political stance disrupt the romance element of the plot and affect the mental stability of the heroine. The use of subjective camera work to heighten Yukie's psychological dilemmas alienates her from the audience, turning her into an irrational and hysterical being. The male characters, by contrast, are not subjected to this emotional scrutiny by the camera and their actions appear rational and principled. In this way, through the stylistic use of the camera, a gendered dichotomy between the emotive/female and rational/male is built into the action of the drama.

In contrast, the character of Carmen (Takemine Hideko) in *Carmen Visits Home*, Japan's first major colour production, is framed within the Shōchiku behavouralist style that develops characters' psychological motivations through dialogue and actions. This stylistic convention reinforces Carmen's position as autonomous and in control of her life. This is further reinforced through the absence of a romance element in the narrative. Carmen is therefore free to focus her energies on her 'art', which takes precedence over her concerns about her relationship with her father. The film does set up a series of binary oppositions, however—although these are linked to gender through the bodies of Carmen and her companion Maya—that politicize the sexual. As was the case with the 'modern girl' of the 1930s, Carmen's body becomes the contested terrain where the social dislocations of rapid socioeconomic change, brought about by defeat and occupation, are played out. The main political oppositions represented through the male/female dichotomy are summarized as follows:

| Male | Female |
|------|--------|
| Japaneseness | Westernization |
| Patriarchal authority | Individual autonomy |
| Country | City |
| Traditional arts | Western arts |

In the opening sequences of the film—through the reading of a letter from Carmen by Yuki, Carmen's elder sister, to her father—we are given the background information that frames the narrative of Carmen's visit home. Carmen, after having left home in defiance of her father some years earlier, returns in triumph to flaunt her success in Tokyo as an entertainer in a Western-style review. Male characters in the film, already weakened by the new Constitution giving women equal rights with men (her father), the war (Sano Shūji as a former teacher blinded in the war), and social dislocation (Carmen's brother-in-law, an adopted son-in-law), are further emasculated through the control Carmen exerts on her image as spectacle. In seeking control over her social identity, she changes her name from her Japanese given name Okin to Lily Carmen. In addition, she wears tight-fitting low-cut Western dresses and high-heeled shoes. She affects a sexually provocative swagger of her hips as she walks, asserting an aggressive self-confidence that subverts the signifiers of patriarchal sexuality, turning them into a display of her power and authority over male characters (see figure 11). In the final sequences Carmen and Maya perform their dance for the local villagers and strip naked. At this climactic moment the camera cuts to a parallel sequence of events. Her father (Sakamoto Takeshi 1899–1974), the adopted son-in-law, the school principal (Ryū Chishū 1904–1993), and another male teacher, the object of Maya's advances, are drinking sake, humiliated, as they have all had their authority challenged because they were unable to stop the performance. The father, driven from his own home because he cannot face the humiliation of seeing his daughter, is in tears as he says, 'When I think of my daughter appearing naked in front of everyone at about this time, I feel more ashamed than if it were I dancing naked'.

This sense of masculine humiliation is linked to the changes brought about by the enactment of the postwar Constitution. In an earlier agonizing conversation between the principal and Carmen's father before the performance, her father says, 'If she says she wants to dance, well, why not let her dance. If she becomes a laughingstock or not, I don't care. Anyhow, I am her father and it is a parent's ill fortune to be laughed at as well. It's

well and good to be laughed at. If the dance for the village youth doesn't
go ahead . . . well, if the government permits it in Tokyo, it's all right . . .'
The school principal continues this line of reasoning in the same conversation when he says, 'If she says she wants to dance, to stop her would be a
violation of human rights . . .'

Carmen, under the terms of the Constitution, is politically and legally
autonomous, but more than this, she is in control of the conditions under
which she is viewed. She therefore challenges the very signifiers that determine the power relationship inscribed in the act of looking between active male look/passive female 'to-be-looked-at-ness'. Within this context,
she is not an object given meaning through the male gaze. As John Fiske
explains, 'There can be no voyeurs in spectacle; normal power relations
of looking are inverted, and, as in carnival, the looker and the looked-at
participate equally in the process of looking and the making meanings that
it entails. The carnivalesque element of spectacle denies both class and
gender subordination and thus refuses to acknowledge the social power of
the discourse it uses' (Fiske 1991: 253).

In stylistic terms, the comedy element reinforces the 'carnivalesque'
quality of the spectacle of the dance. The conductor becomes excited by
the performance and speeds up the tempo of the band. The two girls dancing have to keep up, causing the makeshift stage to vibrate, which, in turn,
affects the musicians who are unable to control their instruments. Cuts to
the spectators' comic reactions further heightens this atmosphere. Carmen,
like her wartime geisha counteragent in the spy film, is a rare example
within the Japanese cinematic tradition of the autonomous female who
subverts the signifiers of patriarchal authority. In structuring her character
to appeal to the occupation censor and female audiences, she challenges
and ultimately emasculates patriarchal authority. The dichotomy of the
city and country, as two alien and incompatible worlds, isolates traditional
Japanese men within the world of the idealized 'hometown' (*furusato*) so
clearly articulated in the song composed by the blind returned soldier,
played by Sano Shūji, that punctuates the film at various stages.


**Conclusions**

The implementation of the Film Law in 1939 has become an historical
construct in academic discourses on Japanese film history that marks a
transition to the 'national policy' film and Japan's decline and defeat in

August 1945. However, from a close analysis of the films of this period, it becomes obvious that many of the characteristics that became synonymous with, and defined, 'national policy' films had their origins in the 1930s. As we saw in chapter one, films produced in the 1930s about working women relied on the stereotype of the 'modern girl' as office lady, entertainer and prostitute. In this way, the disruptive effects of women's increased access to education and economic independence, through increased employment opportunities, were played out through the conventions of the melodrama on the body of the 'modern girl'. The Shōchiku Studios were instrumental in this process through the introduction of significant changes in the gendered structure of earlier *shinpa*-derived narrative cinema and through the development of a behaviouralist narrative style that represented a shift from psychological to dramatic modes based on everyday situations. Under the impact of war, 'national policy' films blurred the old binaries of gender positions as androgynous female characters filled the voids in domestic employment left vacant by men away at war. In the 'spy film', gender continued to provide the main binary structure, but the primary symbolic meaning of the opposition man/woman shifted from referring to the two sides of gender to the two opposing sides in the war. In this way, preferred topics in 'national policy' films were framed within the established stylistic conventions of Shōchiku and established paradigms associated with star personas.

Films produced in the post-1939 Film Law period thus mediated between national political imperatives and private fantasies, re-articulating the modern of the 1930s in the negative sense of decadence and materialism. Contained within a discourse of Japanese spiritualism versus a Western materialism, the modern was accordingly re-defined. Attributes such as efficiency, order and regimentation were still very much exalted and became the basis of a military-defined desirable masculinity, while materialism and decadence formally associated with the Americanization of the 'modern girl' and 'modern boy' took on increasingly negative connotations in, for example, the spy film genre. It is possible to trace this trajectory through the star persona of Tanaka Kinuyo—from the quintessential *moga* of Ozu Yasujirō's early 1930s' gangster films, through the working mother image of *The Love-Troth Tree* (1938), and finally the *geisha* counteragent in the 1943 spy film *The Night Before the Outbreak of War*.

In the immediate postwar period, the occupation forces continued to exert a political control over the film industry, using much the same structures of proscription and prescription as those implemented by the Japa-

nese military government post-1939. Japanese filmmakers easily slotted
into these altered modes of production and control. Kurosawa Akira, drawing heavily on the established star personas of Ōkōchi Denjirō and Fujita
Susumu, created the roles of the ousted Kyoto University professor Takikawa Yukitoki and the suspected Comintern spy and China expert Ozaki
Hotsumi, respectively. The relationship between Ōkōchi Denjirō, as Yukie's father in *No Regrets for Our Youth*, and Fujita Susumu as her husband, the spy Noge, bears many of the characteristics of the relationship
between Yanagi/Ōkōchi and Sugata/Fujita of Kurosawa's wartime production *Sanshiro Sugata*; Yanagi, as the sagacious and cautious judo master,
and Sugata as the hotheaded but moral young man undergoing a 'rite of
passage' to full manhood. In *No Regrets for Our Youth,* Ōkōchi, as Yukie's
academic father, urges caution while the youthful Fujita, his student, believes in direct action, which lands him in prison, where, through study,
he goes through a 'rite of passage', emerging as a more principled man
who fights against the militarists. However, contained within this latter relationship, through the death of Noge, is an implicit critique of the parent
generation, which is portrayed as being culpable in that they were not sufficiently active in opposing the military regime. Yukie's father comes to
the realization after Noge's death that perhaps he should have done more
to resist. Withdrawing from public life alone did not exonerate him from
the charge of complicity. As the epigraph taken from a lecture by Morito
Tatsuo (1888–1984), an academic who is purported to have influenced
Ozaki Hotsumi, at the beginning of the section declaims, 'To think in this
age means to struggle'. In other words, passive opposition is not sufficient;
thought must be accompanied by action.

Within this period, women, or the 'new woman' of the immediate postwar period found that she could no longer depend on marriage as a means
of economic survival. In this context, the 'new woman' again became the
site through which socio-economic change was articulated. Within the
Shōchiku framework, female characters such as Carmen briefly claimed
their rights as autonomous individuals under the occupation political reforms. However, increasingly, in films such as *The Gates of Flesh* (*Nikutai
no mon*), based on the popular novel by Tamura Taijirō (1911–1983) first
filmed in 1948, this autonomy became linked to prostitution. Women's
bodies became the site upon which the theoretical issues surrounding the
writings of influential intellectuals such as Sakaguchi Ango (1906–1955)
were articulated. This topic will be taken up again in chapter five.

Within the Shōchiku tradition, by the mid-1950s, romance had again re-inscribed women into passive roles as the scripts of femininity became increasingly linked to the discourses of 'victimization'. This trend first appeared in films such as the 1950 *Until the Day We Meet Again* aka *Till We Meet Again* (*Mata au hi made*), directed by Imai Tadashi (1912–1992), and was consolidated in the 1953–1954 Shōchiku trilogy *What Is Your Name?* (*Kimi no na wa*), directed by Ōba Hideo (1910–1997), the subject of the following chapter.

## CHAPTER 4

# Cinema and Humanism

[C]oncepts of the responsibility of leaders and the concomitant duty of the individual to disobey illegal orders were set forth at the Nuremberg and Tokyo Trials. It is clear that there are many problems with the actual implementation of these concepts. Most people are ordinary citizens and not heroes. To disobey an illegal order is to call for heroic actions, something one cannot unconditionally demand of people. (Onuma 1993: 52)

Nobody thinks of war positively, but the history of war is the history of man. This fact brought inexpressible, deep sadness to us all. Why does mankind do such sad things? (The screenplay writer Hashimoto Shinobu as an epigraph to the film *Storm Over the Pacific/Taiheiyō no arashi* [1960]) quoted in Galbraith 2002: 278)

Contemplation is layered upon experience; for culture to become flesh, first we must remove all our garments and become naked human beings. This is humanism. (Ieki Miyoji [1946] quoted in Iwasaki 1958a: 73–74).

The politics of the death drive, from George Sorel and Patrick Pearse to W. B. Yeats and the apologists of fascism, sees violence as a purifying force, shocking a torpid suburban civilization into new life like the bolts of electricity which the mad scientist sends through his monster. (Eagleton 2003a: 268)

**A**s has been stressed in earlier chapters, popular films, as commercial products, are produced in a studio system designed to maximize efficiency in order to produce profits. As a result, a tension is often evident between economic practices and the craft-based traditions of individual filmmakers. In the light of discourses that stemmed from the criminalization of Japan through the 'war crimes' trials held in the post-defeat period, this dichotomy of interests took on added political connotations as the question of filmmakers' accountability to the public was raised. In the late 1950s and the early 1960s some Japanese filmmakers extended this discourse. A discourse that in terms of the film industry had manifested itself publicly in the series of Tōhō strikes of 1946–1948, but in a broader sense by the 1960s, had become connected to a general disaffection with the course of Japan's internal politics and Japanese involvement, as logistic support for the U.S. military, in the Korean

(1950–1953) and Vietnam wars (1961–1973). By the mid-1950s the full import of the 'reverse course policy', and the correlation between the rise of an increasingly affluent consumer society coupled with the exploitation of Cold War politics, began to be realized. This corresponded with the rise to prominence of a generation of Japanese filmmakers too young to have participated in the war but old enough to be conscious of its effects. Within this context, some idealistic young filmmakers attempted to challenge what they saw as the exploitative and often corrupt foundations of what was to become known as Japan's 'economic miracle'. However, prior to the emergence of this generation, in films of the post-defeat decade, the underlying ethos was the desire for a renewal of society based on the promises of 'democracy' offered by the occupation reforms. Framed within the political-industrial context outlined above, this chapter, through an analysis of films produced in the post-defeat era, aims to isolate both the thematic and stylistic trends that contributed to the determination of dominant social discourses of war, defeat and occupation.

## The Question of War Culpability and the Tōhō Studio Strikes

One of the immediate planks of the Occupation Forces' policy was the removal from public life of people deemed to have been active in support of the war. Under the terms of this policy, the various organizations representative of the film industry—the screenplay writers' group, the critics' association and the newly formed All Japan Film Employees Association (*Zen Nippon Eiga Jūgyōin Kumiai Dōmei*)[1]—were assigned the task of compiling a list of such people. By October 1947 thirty-one people involved in the industry during the war period were placed on the banned persons list (Satō 1995 vol. ii: 186). These were all people active at executive levels in the industry between 7 July 1937 and 8 December 1941. They were charged with 'incitement to war' (*sensō chōhatsu hanzaisha*), based on the fact that between the outbreak of the war in China and the end of the Pacific War in 1945 they were, in their capacity as managers of film companies or government officials, responsible for national film policy. Kido Shirō (1894–1977), head of Shōchiku; Mori Iwao of Tōhō, Kawakita Nagamasa (1903–1981), who had been responsible for the film industry in China and formerly ran the foreign film distribution company Tōwa; and Nagata Masaichi (1906–1985), head of Daiei and onetime head of Nikkatsu, were all included on the list. Nagata Masaichi later successfully protested his innocence and was reinstated. The others were all reinstated by the time of the outbreak of the Korean War in 1950, apart from Kido Shirō, who was reinstated the following year. Both Kido Shirō, and Mori Iwao returned to influential positions in Shōchiku and Tōhō, respectively.

Directors and screenplay writers were not excluded from working in public life as it was argued that as employees they had little control over their work. At the very least, it was argued that within a complex hierarchical studio system, it was difficult to prove to what extent they could be held accountable for the content of the films they were involved in producing. Therefore, filmmakers active during the war period were called upon to engage in a process of 'self-reflection' (*jiko hansei*). A more cynical view was that the Occupation Forces needed the cooperation of personnel from the film industry for the dissemination of their own propaganda and were therefore lenient. However, as an undercurrent, this question of artistic control and the political and social responsibilities of individual filmmakers working within the mainstream industry is crucial to an understanding of the developments in the film industry in the postwar period.

In relation to the question of individual responsibility, Onuma Yasuaki (1993), in his book on the Tokyo War Crimes Trial and war responsibility, lays out the main legal arguments pertaining to the role of the individual in civil society that were to influence public debate in the post-defeat period. He explains that the trial raised the question of the individual's moral responsibility of 'conscientious refusal' versus the individual's social duty to follow the directives of his/her government representatives. In the following quotation, Onuma elaborates on the principle upon which the trials (both Nuremberg and Tokyo) were based and which ultimately became established in International Law, that is, the 'duty of an individual to disobey illegal orders' (*ihanna meirei e no fufukujū no kannen*). In his article 'The Tokyo Trial: Between Law and Politics' published in English Onuma states:

> In today's world, all countries, even the most dictatorial, subscribe in principle to democratic forms of government. Thus, on a formal level the leaders of a country derive their authority from the will of the people. Therefore, it is necessary that the people not co-operate in illegal acts in order to establish grounds for arraigning government leaders—and not the people—for such acts. One cannot escape responsibility for co-operating in wars of aggression or genocide by arguing that one was acting under orders. This means a repudiation of the idea that, as one member of the state, the individual is completely subsumed in the state. (Onuma 1986: 50)

This view, first published in the charters for Nuremberg and the Tokyo Trials[2], totally rejects the Neo-Confucian worldview of the individual's fixed relationship to society and the universe. Herman Ooms has argued that it was in the seventeenth century that Japanese scholars first constructed an 'anthropocosmic' worldview, placing humans in harmony with the universe.[3] In effect, this worldview refused 'to recognize man as a source of initiative other than for action confirming [the] general order' (Ooms 1989: 95). Scholars such as Yamazaki Ansai (1618–1682) merged Neo-Confucian teachings and Shintō mythology into an innate Confucian ethic that became the ideological mainstay of the Tokugawa hegemony, being re-appropriated by nationalist scholars such as Kita Ikki (1883–1937) in the 1930s and 1940s.[4]

In the early post-defeat period, the various studio-based unions that formed part of the All Japan Film and Theatre Workers' Union, apart from concerns related to rising inflation, falling wages and unemployment, were also concerned in the light of the discourses surrounding war culpability with the 'democratization' of the industry (*kigyō no minshuka*) and with questions of individual accountability. In part, this is attributable to the timing of events; the unions were being founded at the very time lists of those culpable for the war were being called for by occupation officials. Iwasaki Akira (1958a) cites two conferences sponsored by the Free Filmmakers' Group (*Jiyū Eiga Shūdan*) held in June 1946 and July 1947 that focused on the question of how to re-build and reform the Japanese film industry. Topics raised at these conferences were: what is meant by a democratic film, film production and the producer system, how should filmmakers respond to this call for self-reflection, and how to establish filmmaker autonomy. Iwasaki argues that out of these conferences and related discourses throughout the industry, a new consciousness emerged amongst many filmmakers with regard to their sociopolitical role as part of the mass communication industry. Many felt that the 'dictatorship' of the prewar and wartime studio system had to be challenged. Filmmakers began to perceive their respective roles as stars, as technicians, and as directors with the studio as mutually reinforcing and socially responsible.

Of the mainstream studio unions, the union centred around the Tōhō Studios was perhaps the most radical; in amongst their eighteen-point demands was number five, which called for union involvement in both management and planning (*kigyō kikaku no sanka*). Just prior to the submission of these demands, the two unions associated with the newsreel film companies, Nichiei and Asahi, had won concessions on labour participation in management. However, as far as the Tōhō management was concerned, this was unacceptable and until this item was removed they would defer their decision on the other seventeen items. In March the talks broke down, and on 20 March 1946 the first strike was called. After fifteen days an agreement was reached on improved wages and on labour representation in management decision making and policy.

There followed two other strikes in October/November 1946 and April 1948 supported by the unions of various other companies under the auspices of the All Japan Film and Theatre Workers' Union. During the second strike, there was a split in the Tōhō Studios as ten of the top actors and actresses objected to the 'politicization' of the union and Shin-Tōhō was formed as a breakaway company.[5] Iwasaki (1958a) attributes this split to a divergence of interests between the big stars and directors and the main membership of the union. He also makes the point that the government of Yoshida Shigeru (1878–1967) played up the strike for propaganda reasons, turning it into a 'political strike,' which, it was argued, was brought about by Communist hard-liners.

Under the liberal regime of the Tōhō Studios, the films produced between the second and third strikes received critical acclaim, taking six of the top places in the *Kinema Junpō* film lists for 1947.[6] However, in profitability terms, the company had lost seventy-five million yen in the same year. Watanabe Tetsuzo (1885–1980), an expert on industrial labour relations, was brought in to take control of the company, his aims in his own words were to 'defeat the two kinds of reds at Toho: communists and red budgets' (quoted in Hirano 1992: 224). His attempts to regain control of the company, along with the attempted dismissal of 1,200 employees in April 1948, led to the third and final strike. With this strike the unions were defeated. After a court ruling against the union, they ended their occupation of the studios as the police, with support from the American military, surrounded the studios.[7] This incident became known as the 'Tōhō Red purge'[8] and set the tone of the struggles that were to dominate Japanese 'intellectual' filmmakers up until the 1970s and the decline of the industry.

**The Post-Defeat Decade**

In light of these public discourses, two broad but often interrelated themes emerged in mainstream films produced in the newly politicized post-defeat, post-Tōhō strike era: 'victimized innocence' and a re-emergence of romance. In both cases, these narrative themes represented a shift in nuance, the restoration of the individual as the central element in the narrative rather than, as had been the case in the 'national policy' films of the post-1939 Film Law period, the institution to which the individual was affiliated. A callow concept of 'humanism', derived from Western philosophy and transliterated in the *katakana* script as *hyūmanisumu*, to emphasize its sense of foreignness, became the 'buzzword' used by Japanese film critics and historians to describe this human-centred worldview. However, as the previous chapters have illustrated, this did not represent as radical a change as at first might have appeared, as post-defeat films often built upon and experimented with stylistic forms developed in the 1930s and adapted in the 1940s to the exigencies of 'total war'. As the analysis of 'national policy' films in chapter three has demonstrated, by framing the hero within the wider context of the war, individualism, as expressed through the Hollywood-derived 'goal-orientated hero', was co-opted to the narrative needs of a hyper-masculinist ideology underpinning total mobilization. In the early 1940s, individualism per se was not therefore derided as long as it was directed towards the goals of the nation-state. Similarly, in the immediate post-defeat period, many of these same narrative conventions and stylistic forms, employed since the silent era, were adopted and adapted to meet the needs of the newly emerging post-defeat 'democracy'.

One of the principal characteristics that defined the adaptation of both narrative themes and stylistic trends at this time was a subtle shift in emphasis from action to the development of the characters' psychological depth. Psychological motivation had never been absent in 'national policy' films, however it had been directed towards common goals framed within an ethos of the 'family state'. In contrast, in films produced in the post-defeat decade, characters' inner struggles are between, on the one hand, their desires articulated in the 'human' sense of wanting to live and, on the other hand, the demands of the militarist ideology that required individuals to sacrifice themselves for the greater good. However, this theme was not fully articulated until the end of the occupation in 1952 when filmmakers were again granted a degree of autonomy, free from the overt political censorship of the occupation agencies. Prior to that, an alternative view of 'humanism', in keeping with rigid SCAP directives and exemplified in the early *gendaigeki* films of Kurosawa Akira (1910–1998), was evident, (*No Regrets for Our Youth/Waga seishun ni kuinashi* [1946], *Drunken Angel/ Yoidore tenshi* [1948], *The Quiet Duel/Shizukanaru kettō* [1949] and *Stray*

*Dog/Nora inu* [1949]). In these films, set for the most part in the post-
defeat period, the individuals are cast as autonomous beings capable of
self-determination with the underlying assumption that through their
choices, in a democratic society, they can alter society.

Stylistically these films drew upon and developed the realistic modes
of filmmaking evident in the 1930s' 'social realist' films by, on the one
hand, giving the *mise-en-scène* a diegetic function, which is clearly linked
to location shooting, and on the other hand, an often loose documentary-
style plot linearity. (Films directed by Kurosawa Akira are one of the exceptions as, although they employ many realist stylistic devices, his films
adopted a tight linear plot structure.) Within this loose 'slice-of-life' plot
structure, by emphasizing how characters react to the environments in
which they are placed, the *mise-en-scène* functions as a distinct spatio-
temporal co-ordinate beyond that of mere setting. Unlike classical Hollywood films in which place is generally subordinate to the story, in post-
defeat Japanese films the actualities of time and place are often of equal
importance to the plot. Throughout Japanese film history, location shooting of, in particular, *gendaigeki* films has been the norm. Unlike Hollywood and some other national cinemas, Japanese studios, until the late
1950s and the emergence of the Tōei and Daiei stylized *jidaigeki* films, did
not have the space, facilities or finances to rely entirely on studio filming.
In this sense, it can be argued that Japanese *gendaigeki* films have always
had a strong tendency to realism. What did change over time was the
spacio-temporal coordinates in which the action is framed. It is these
changes that provide one of the novelty elements, ensuring that films made
within the 'social realist' style remain fresh and responsive to the concerns
of contemporary audiences. In the 1930s films directed by Ozu Yasujirō
(1903–1963) and scripted by the James Maki collaborative, the emphasis
was placed on urban Tokyo as the site of the emergence of the 'modern
girl' and the 'modern boy'. The challenges they represented to social concepts of patriarchal authority, and the concomitant disintegration of the
traditional family, were all played out in Tokyo's developing urban sprawl.
These were all themes Ozu returned to in the early 1950s, his most famous
film being *Tokyo Story* (*Tōkyō monogatari* [1953]). Similarly, in the 1936
film directed by Mizoguchi Kenji (1898–1956), *Osaka Elegy* (*Naniwa erejii*), as the title suggests, Osaka has a diegetic significance for the connota-
tive meanings associated with this major merchant-centred city. Equally,
'national policy' films were often set within documentary-style travelogue
footage of the colonies (*Suchow Nights/Soshū no yoru* [1942] and *Sayon's*

*Bell/Sayon no kane* [1943]). On the home front, films were shot on location in and around the various military academies (*The War at Sea from Hawaii to Malaya/Hawai Marei okikaisen* [1942], *Navy/Kaigun* [1943] and *Army/Rikugun* [1944]) and in factories and airfields (*The Most Beautiful/Ichiban utsukushiku* [1944] and *The Bases Where the Maidens Are* aka *Girls of the Air Base/Otome no iru kichi* [1945]). In the immediate postwar period the *mise-en-scène* became the chaotic post-defeat remnants of bombed-out urban centres. Within this *mise-en-scène* we are given intimate psychological portrayals of how contemporary social situations affected personal relations between individuals.

In the early post-defeat films directed by Kurosawa Akira, the environment often becomes a hostile force against which the characters are pitted. The 'sump', around which much of the action of *Drunken Angel* takes place, is a recurring motif of the social and moral decay drawing morally weak characters (the gangster Matsunaga/Mifune Toshirō 1920–1997) to their destruction. Diseases rampant in post-defeat Japanese society— tuberculosis[9] in *Drunken Angel,* syphilis in *The Quiet Duel* and cancer in *Living/Ikiru*—are all recurring themes, as is crime[10] in *Stray Dog/Nora inu.* The shots in the long montage sequence (eight minutes) filmed in and around the entertainment/market district of Tokyo's Ueno Station in *Stray Dog*, as the hero Murakami (Mifune Toshirō) searches for contacts in the black-market sale of guns, has become the iconic post-defeat landscape against which films made in the 1960s and 1970s set in a similar temporal frame are defined (such as *The Gates of Flesh/Nikutai no mon* [1964] directed by Suzuki Seijun 1923—and *The War Without Morality/Jingi naki tatakai* series directed by Fukasaku Kinji 1930–2003). The *Stray Dog* montage sequence, and the constant visual signifiers denoting the oppressive weather throughout the first half of the film, provide the visual counterpoint for the discussion below between Murakami and his senior colleague in the police force, Satō (Shimura Takashi 1905–1982), regarding the role of the environment as a cause of crime.

> **Satō:** As you can see my house isn't that great, but Yusa's place is terrible. It's not fit for human habitation; it is in filthy places like that, that maggots breed.
>
> **Murakami:** There are no bad people in the world, only bad environments, or so it is said. But when you think of Yusa, he is pitiable.
>
> **Satō:** You mustn't . . . Thinking in that way is taboo for the likes of us. When all we do is chase around after criminals, it is easy to come

under that misapprehension. We must not forget the sufferings of the
many lambs for the sake of one wolf. [Looking up at the many cita-
tions hanging on the wall, Satō continues.] Out of that lot, half were
executed. If I didn't believe that it protected the happiness of the
majority, for us police officers there would be no salvation . . . Leave
the psychological analysis of the criminal to the novelists . . . We
simply detest fellows like him . . . bad fellows are bad.

**Murakami:** I still can't think in that way. When I was away at the war,
many times I saw fellows, human beings, become beasts over the
merest trifle.

**Satō:** Is it the difference in our ages or the difference in the times?
What do you call it? Apre . . . Apre . . .

**Murakami:** *Après-guerre.*

**Satō:** Yes, that's it, fellows from the postwar generation. Probably you
and Yusa . . . You understand Yusa's feelings too well.

**Murakami:** You are probably right. When I was demobilized I had my
rucksack stolen on the train. [Here Murakami is likening his experiences to those of Yusa, who also had his rucksack stolen.]

**Satō:** Ah!

**Murakami:** I felt an absurd sense of spitefulness (*muchana dokudokus-
hii*) and I could have easily turned to stealing. But I realized I was
at a dangerous turning point, and I took the opposite course and applied for my current job.

**Satō:** There are two kinds of *après-guerre*, those like you and those
like Yusa. You are the real thing and fellows like Yusa are beasts.[11]

The film's juxtapositioning of the two characters, Murakami the detective
and Yusa (Kimura Isao 1923–1981) the criminal, within the same experiential reality, clearly raises ethical questions about the innate ability of an
individual to make choices between good and bad. This same strategy was
employed in the earlier film *Drunken Angel* where Mifune Toshirō, the
yakuza stricken with TB, ultimately succumbs to and is destroyed by a
combination of the disease and the black-market environment, while a
young high school girl effectively defeats the disease.

The 'fated generation' theme, by far the more dominant as occupation
censorship restrictions relaxed, is exemplified in films set in the war period, directed by Imai Tadashi (1912–1992), Kinoshita Keisuke (1912–
1998), Ieki Miyoji (1911–1976) and Kobayashi Masaki (1916–1996),
amongst others. In these films the historical trauma of defeat finds expres-

sion in a compulsive re-enactment of disempowerment in the symbolic terms of emasculation. The individual, while central to the narrative, is thrown into a situation in which he can only react to sociopolitical events beyond his control. In stylistic terms, these films differed from 'national policy' films in the level of subjective reality they depicted. The complex manipulation of time through flashbacks exploring personal histories and the use of subjective voice-over monologues are two of the defining features of this narrational mode, as characters' psychological motivations and reactions to circumstances became central plot devices.

*Until the Day We Meet Again* aka *Till We Meet Again* (*Mata au hi made*), directed by Imai Tadashi and released in 1950 to great acclaim[12], opens *in medias res* as the hero Saburō (Okada Eiji 1920–1995) is obstructed by a series of events from meeting Keiko (Kuga Yoshiko 1931–), his fiancée. His voice-over monologue in the opening sequence establishes the scene, and in particular the war, as the contextual element that will determine the characters' fates. An air-raid siren reinforces this point on the soundtrack, being the trigger that evokes the following thoughts: 'Oh, the war! The war has been hanging over our heads now for eight long years. This long, long war is like a devil toying with life and death . . . Amongst this we continue our struggle to live. Ah, when we first met, at that time too, the black shadow, the shadow of death was descending on us . . .' (Here Saburō is referring to the imminent air-raid siren.)

The visuals shift to searchlights in the night sky as pedestrians run to the shelters. In the air-raid shelter the key light focuses our attention first on Saburō and then on the object of his gaze, Keiko. A series of reverse-cut shots visually reinforces his position as subject, the author of the memory, and Keiko as the object of his interest. She only notices him when the impact of a bomb exploding nearby throws them together and he places his hand over hers as he shields her body. The film proceeds from this first meeting through a long flashback primarily from Saburō's point of view tracing the development of their relationship.

These opening sequences link the war as the central defining other against which the fated love of the two protagonists unfolds. Parental opposition is minimal. Keiko's mother, at first apprehensive, gives her consent. Saburō suffers the recriminations of his elder brother, Jirō, an army officer, however he dies in an accident in the first half of the film. During his death scene the two brothers are reconciled as Jirō comes to see the folly of the military ethos and tells Saburō 'to be sure to have two shares of happiness, his [Jirō's] share too'. The actualities of the war thus provide

the primary opposition to the romance, ensuring it never reaches the consummation, symbolized through the 'kiss', central to the narrative closure
of the classical Hollywood mode and insisted upon by the SCAP authorities. Instead, narrative closure is focused on the deaths of the two protagonists, and the dramatic shot of the protagonists' first kiss through a
windowpane foreshadows the barriers that will thwart their love. In the
final sequence, an intertitle flashes onto the screen, 'Autumn 1945'; this is
followed by the voice-over narration of Okada Eiji as he enunciates the
content of a letter he sent to Keiko from the war. This letter is ostensibly
being read by Keiko's mother; it is a letter Keiko never received.

If during the occupation period fated love often provided the narrative
vehicle that defined the traumas of the war generation, in the immediate
post-occupation period, representations of the young student 'volunteers'
of the Special Attack Forces of kamikaze pilots took on a similar iconic
significance as the fated generation in the 1953 film *Beyond the Clouds*
(*Kumo nagaruru hateni*), directed by Ieki Miyoji. Shin-Tōhō followed two
years later with a production based on the 'human torpedoes', directed by
Matsubayashi Shūe (1920–), *The Human Torpedoes* (*Ningen gyorai
kaiten*) (1955). By closely following the stylistic and narrative patterns of
the earlier film, these two films formed the basis of a genre that continued
into the 1970s. Thematically, these early kamikaze films, while concerned
with an exposition of the dynamics of power at work within the texture of
group relations, subordinate the greater discourses of war responsibility
onto narratives centring on the individual's sense of self-identity and his
relationship with the group. As such, thematically, these films focus on the
affinities between men in a homosocial subtext, reaching a climax just before the deaths of the heroes. While ostensibly adopting a pacifist stance,
the visual images reaffirm the centrality of a code of brotherhood (*sen'y-
ūai*) as both a mechanism for control and a site of pleasure. Therefore, at
one level, it is possible to argue that these films conform to the general
formula of most war films, both Western and Japanese, that is, that in the
extremes of a war setting men are allowed to express an intensity of emotion prohibited in civil society; on another level, they expose the negative
aspects of this bonding which, in the case of the kamikaze, demands the
death of the individual as a solipsistic act of group identity.

Both *Beyond the Clouds* and *The Human Torpedoes* are set in the last
desperate stages of the war and cover the time when the young pilots and
submarine operatives, respectively, await their departure on their final missions. Staying within the conventions developed by Imai Tadashi in *Until*

*the Day we Meet Again*, the emphasis in these kamikaze films is on character development through their inner psychological struggles between the
desire to live and the ideological dictates of the 'family-state' that demand
their deaths. In cinematic terms, the protagonists are given a psychological
depth through flashbacks, flash-forwards into their imaginations and voice-
over monologues.

The loose plotlines are built around the period of time before their final
departure, which is prolonged due to bad weather and mechanical problems. Thus tension is maintained as missions are aborted and comrades
die during training exercises, forcing the protagonists to face the reality of
their own impending deaths. In contrast, it is through dialogue, flashbacks
depicting the time when they volunteered for the Special Attack Forces,
and flash-forwards into the lives they might have led had there not been a
war, that the spectator is made aware of their scepticism of wartime propaganda. As one young pilot in *Beyond the Clouds*, mimicking the voice of
a senior officer, declaims during a drunken evening, 'Students of Japan,
the fate of the historic Imperial Navy rests on your innocent shoulders.
Pilots of the Imperial Navy rouse yourselves . . .' After pausing and reverting to his normal voice, he concludes, 'It's all a lot of bunkum ( . . . *tena
koto wa detarame de aru*)', at which point the others all laugh. In another
scene an orderly looks at the sleeping Matsui and muses, 'Is this the face
of a living god?' While in *Beyond the Clouds*, a scepticism is often expressed subtly through humour as in the example above, which plays on
the promise that all dead military personnel would become gods housed in
the Yasukuni Shrine in Tokyo, in the later film, *The Human Torpedoes*, this
scepticism is discussed openly amongst the submarine operatives.

Despite the general assumption that all kamikaze died during their mission, many in fact returned. This was particularly the case with the submarine operatives who were sent out as part of the general armoury of the
mother submarine and during the voyage kept on constant alert. If, as was
sometimes the case, they were not required, they returned to the base with
their mother submarine. In the following two dialogues taken from *The
Human Torpedoes*, this situation of the return of two submarine operatives
becomes the context in which to question the use of 'human bullets' and
the wartime propaganda surrounding their image. Tamai (Kimura Isao) is
rebuffed in the following dialogue when he greets the young Kitamura
who returned with his ship.

**Tamai:** Kitamura, it is great that you came back.
**Kitamura:** No, I have soiled the good name of the Cadet Corps.

**Tamai:** Do you really think so?

**Kitamura:** Yes.

**Tamai:** But your single death won't affect the outcome of the war.

**Kitamura:** If we all hit our targets, Japan is certain to win.

**Tamai:** I would like to think so.

**Kitamura:** Ensign Tamai, although you are an officer, you don't have the martial spirit (*gunjin seishin*).

**Tamai:** You are probably right. But I am not speaking to you now as an officer, but as a brother—a helpless brother . . . I have changed, and you will probably change too. But if you are allowed to live, don't take lightly the feelings of those who secretly prayed for you. If your mother were here, what would she say.

In a later scene, a young recruit confronts the more senior Murasei (Utsui Ken 1931–) who has also returned due to a fault in his submarine.

**Matsumoto:** Your return was a great shame, as now I have been taken out of the formation.

**Murasei:** Do you really want to die so much?

**Matsumoto:** Yes, I want to die for the Emperor and have my spirit enshrined at the Yasukuni Shrine as a guardian of our country.

**Murasei:** Yes, I see. How old are you?

**Matsumoto:** Eighteen . . . Ensign Murasei, let me go ahead of you.

**Murasei:** Fool! Tonight, write a letter to your parents, and live at least until you reach my age.

In scenes such as these, the films question discourses of sacrifice established in the 'national policy' films. This then leaves the question: If the pilots and submarine operatives of the Special Attack Forces did not offer their lives as a gesture of patriotism, then what was the motivation for their sacrifice? The answer lies partly in an analysis of the actor Kimura Isao's star persona as weak romantic hero (*nimaime*) and the characters he portrays and their relationships with other members of the group.

In both films, Kimura Isao plays the part of the young pilot/submarine operative who, through a superficial wound in *Beyond the Clouds* and because of the unexpected return of Murasei and Kitamura in *The Human Torpedoes*, entertains the vague hope that he might just survive. In each of the films the characters he portrays are a narrative device through which the inner fears of the other kamikaze are articulated. In *The Human Torpe-*

*does* it is Tamai/Kimura Isao who voices the fears the others also share but dare not speak of, 'But, on that first night when we fifteen first arrived at this post, didn't we promise to speak honestly to each other? Am I the only one who hates this? Am I the only coward? Please, everyone, let me hear your honest feelings . . .' Similarly in *Beyond the Clouds* Fukami/Kimura Isao, in a conversation with his friend, Ōtaki, expresses a similar sentiment. 'At the time I broke my arm, I thought just maybe I might survive. From that moment on I began to lose confidence. I shan't deny that I love Michiko, but that is unconnected to my fears. Ōtaki, honestly, don't you want to live? That's what I want to ask'.

It is only in the final scenes when he rejects the hope of life, allegorized through the romance subplots of both films, and rejoins the male group that his character is fully redeemed. In this sense, both films represent a 'rite of passage' to manhood and self-definition through death. Both characters played by Kimura Isao must make this break with their lovers, which within the war-retro genre represents the symbolic break with their feminine natures. In both films this emphasis on the characters' psychological motivations opens up what would have been deemed flaws in the protagonist's characters during the war period; thus the characters portrayed by Kimura Isao provide the counterpoint against which the idealized images of the heroic protagonists are measured and maintained.

In *Beyond the Clouds*, Ōtaki, played by Tsuruta Kōji (1924–1987), represents the 'ideal' of the stoic male who, as first son, was destined to inherit the patriarchal authority of the father. This is made clear in a flashback depicting him in the centre of the family. In one poignant scene he is shown as an adult sleeping between his parents. However, despite his apparently stoic exterior, on the night before his mission on a wooded hillside he pours forth all the anxieties that had built up within him during the past few days. This moving scene of inner turmoil, viewed in secret by Fukami/Kimura Isao, who at this point mediates the spectators' gaze, is the spur that sends Fukami to his senior officers to request permission to go on the coming mission with his squadron. It is the realization that the seemingly more perfect Ōtaki is also torn by human emotion that gives the more flawed Fukami the courage to die with him. After his doubts, and while Fukami is with the officers, Ōtaki swims naked in the lake at the foot of the hill as if to cleanse himself of this weakness. In the denouement, Fukami reaches maturity and is reintegrated into the group. His impending death is distanced from wartime ideologies of sacrifice and visually linked instead to a homosocial ethic, which the film presents as being the force that binds the male group. It is through the use of cinematic devices such as extreme close-ups, lighting and camera movement that the intensity of the relationship between Fukami and Ōtaki and the other members of the group is conveyed to the spectator.[13]

In *The Human Torpedoes* Kimura Isao's alter ego, Asakura, is played by Okada Eiji, whose star persona as the hapless young student, out of step with the militarized society, became established in *Until the Day We Meet Again*.[14] In *The Human Torpedoes*, he is again cast as a student of Western philosophy, who on his final night chooses to read Kant's *Critique of Pure Reason* rather than attend the farewell party. As the film progresses, it becomes apparent that in exploring Western political philosophy, he believes in an individualistic ethos based on moral 'humanism'. Thus, using Kantian moral ethics as his theoretical base, Asakura/Okada Eiji is seeking to define an alternative morality valuing human life that exists independently of everyday sociopolitical relations. Okada Eiji, through his star persona, developed in these roles as the personification of Western philosophy, openly criticizes the military institutions and the utilitarian principles (the sacrifice of the few for the greater good) used to legitimate the formation and existence of the Special Attack Forces. On the other hand, Kimura Isao, who in early films of the occupation period was often cast as the de-mobbed soldier turned criminal (*Stray Dog* and *The Tearstained Doll/Nakinureta ningyō* [1951]), became the flawed counterpoint against which these more heroic 'ideal' types could be measured. His role in the 1954 Kurosawa Akira *jidaigeki* production *Seven Samurai* (*Shichinin no samurai*) opened up his star persona as the young, inexperienced, and so flawed samurai (he sleeps with one of the village girls), that allowed him to articulate thoughts and fears his more perfect heroic counterparts could not.

These films, in endeavouring to portray the deaths of the kamukaze as heroic, recast their sacrifice in order to orientate the spectator towards the future. In *Beyond the Clouds*, this is achieved through Ōtaki's opening and closing letters to his parents. It is these letters, read in voice-over, that provide the frame within which the narrative is set. In the opening shots, as the camera tracks along the line of dozing airmen lying in the sun, it stops at Ōtaki, who has a gentle smile on his lips. The peacefulness of this image is contrasted with his voice-over narration as ironically he tells his parents, 'I am well and don't expect to die until it is time to die.'

*The Human Torpedoes*, like *Until the Day We Meet Again*, begins *in medias res* and is framed within a voice-over monologue sequence that both addresses the audience directly and locates the action of the film as Asakura's memory. This self-reflexive address to the audience clearly situates the spectator in the present (i.e., 1955) in relation to the events portrayed. The opening narration is set over a scene of waves before cutting to the submerged wreck of a torpedo. 'The vast Pacific Ocean: at times the waves are high, at times the stage of world history. Already, ten years have passed since the final stages of the fighting and the ocean is filled with the new movements of the remains of history. The heroes of the human torpedoes even now sleep in the coral reefs deep in the sea. Their indignation and lamentations locked in their hearts; their long silence continues. The letters painted on the fuselage, No. 2 Ensign Asakura, clearly remains. Their sufferings must be recounted by someone at some time'.

The voice-over monologues of the characters played by Okada Eiji, Saburō in *Until the Day We Meet Again* and Asakura in *The Human Torpedoes*, are not neutral as their thoughts and emotions carry moral judgements on the war. Through these thoughts, they articulate the silent position of the 'fated generation' with which contemporary audiences in the 1950s could identify and that increasingly became confused with an 'antiwar' imperative. The 'outer-directedness' of these characters' first-person narratives define the spectators' relationship to the world the characters inhabit, controlling the spectators' emotions and sympathies. The characters in both films look back on a series of events that have led to the present situation. This retrospective approach clearly foregrounds their consciousness as they, and by extension the spectators, attempt to create some meaning out of the maelstrom of events from the recent past. Unlike the use of flashback and voice-of-god narration in the opening sequences of *Stray Dog*, which frames the theft of Murakami's gun within an omniscient newsreel-style narration, the combination of subjective voice-over monologues and flashbacks in *Until the Day We Meet Again* and *The Human Torpedoes* carries the implicit assumption that we, the spectators, have privileged access to the protagonists' subjectivity. Therefore, these characters mediate the audience's position through a shared past. In this way the subjectivity constructed out of the stylistic conventions employed in these films provided the contemporary (1950s) spectators with a collective vision within which to inscribe their own emotions and experiences of the war in iconic patterns of memory.

Within the loose plotlines of these films, coincidence and fate are the causal elements that forward the flow of the narrative. The characters, the war generation, are mere victims of the times in which they live, buffeted by the machinations of history made more poignant by the audience's knowledge of the historical reality of Japan's defeat and therefore the futility of the heroes' sacrifices. In the Japanese lexicon this became known as the 'victimization complex' (*higaisha ishiki*) and was exemplified in films set in the war recounting the experiences of children, for example, the 1952 independent production directed by Shindō Kaneto (1912–), *Children of the Bomb* aka *Children of the Atom Bomb* (*Genbako no ko*), Imai Tadashi's 1953 production *Memorial to the Lilies* aka *Tower of Lilies* (*Himeyuri no tō*), and the 1954 Shōchiku production directed by Kinoshita Keisuke, *Twenty-four Eyes* (*Nijūshi no hitomi*).

### The Documentary 'Slice-of-Life' Narrative Mode

*Children of the Bomb*, while drawing on many of the stylistic conventions of subjectivity established in films such as *Until the Day We Meet Again*, was instrumental in adapting them to a docudrama 'slice-of-life' narrative mode that has remained an important format for the recounting of events related to the war, post-defeat reconstruction, and to the 'subject-as-victim' theme. The camera, as apparent recorder of events, lingers on the destruction caused by the atomic bomb in Hiroshima, while the teacher, Miss Ishikawa (Otowa Nobuko 1924–1994), guides the spectator through the streets and amongst her former pupils, the innocent, living with the consequences of the bomb. Two years later, Kinoshita Keisuke would adopt this exact same narrative format in his film *Twenty-four Eyes*, which chronicles the lives of a group of twelve children growing up on an island in the Inland Sea who all began school in 1928. The children are representative of the war generation, and the film traces their lives, and in some cases their deaths, through the mediations of their primary school teacher (Takamine Hideko 1924–), who takes up her first post with this class on the island in 1928. As a 'modern girl', educated in Tokyo, she is a product of the so-called period of 'Taishō democracy,' symbolized by her Western clothes and bicycle. Framed within this historical context of 'liberalism', she is the first-person subject of the narrative, the nexus through which we see and understand the events of the war and through whom the collective memory of the film is defined.

In both films the establishment of place is central to the events recorded. In *Children of the Bomb*, the teacher sets out during the summer holidays from her adopted home, also an island in the Inland Sea, on the ferry bound for Hiroshima. As the ferry nears Hiroshima her reflexive voice-over address to the audience is linked to a roving camera recording the sights as the ferry nears its destination.

> Everyone (*minasama*), this is Hiroshima.
> These are the remains of Hiroshima after the atomic bomb.
> The beautiful river of Hiroshima, today, as on that day, flows beautifully.
> The beautiful Hiroshima sky, today, as on that day, stretches out beautifully before us.
> The children in Hiroshima on that day have grown quickly and have become so big.
> Upon the scorched earth of that day, this beautiful city is being reconstructed.

When the boat docks, she visits the site of her former home where her parents died. This triggers a flashback sequence of the events of the morning of 6 August 1945 leading up to the seconds before the bomb was dropped. There follows a montage sequence that mixes documentary footage of the 'mushroom' cloud with shots of individuals suffering the immediate effects of the bomb. These sequences have become established in 'iconic memory' through their repetition in subsequent films and television dramas depicting the same events (for example, the 1970s yakuza series *War Without Morality/Jingi naki tatakai* and *Black Rain/Kuroi ame* [1989] directed by Imamura Shōhei 1926–). After these establishing sequences, the film proceeds through Miss Ishikawa's investigations to recount the fate of three of the surviving children she taught in primary school and an old man, who had worked for her parents, and his grandson.

Just as the opening travelogue-style shots of the island in *Children of the Bomb* establish the island from which Ishikawa *sensei* (teacher) sets forth as an idyll, in contrast to the destruction of Hiroshima, so too do the opening sequences of *Twenty-four Eyes* establish the island setting as a utopia against which the tragedy of war is defined. The problems the students face are clearly situated in the external world, as in the second half of the film, after graduating from middle school, some of the pupils leave the island to find work. Later, and linked to the progression of the war through intertitles establishing first the Manchurian Incident and later the China Incident, adolescent boys leave the safety of the island to go to war and the young girls from poor families reluctantly leave to find employment in businesses or to train as geisha. The island is thus separated off, a utopian metonymic vision of an essential 'Japaneseness' into which the cruel realities of an alien otherworld intrude.

Just as the flashback sequences and subjective voice-over monologues, linked to the star persona of Okada Eiji in *Until the Day We Meet Again* and *The Human Torpedoes*, define the spectators' relationship to the world the characters inhabit, so too do the teachers in *Children of the Bomb* and *Twenty-four Eyes*. They simultaneously mediate the spectators' point of view while they testify to the truth of the events recorded and the image of the teacher as a socially respected profession after the severe criticism that accompanied post-defeat recriminations. The teachers both define our understanding of the events depicted and provide the narrative continuity that links the various episodes that make up the 'slice-of-life' micro-plots that form around the experiences of the children. This format was also used to great effect in subsequent films, for example, in the 1952 Shōchiku production *No Consultations Today* aka *The Doctor's Day Off* (*Honjitsu kyūshin*), directed by Shibuya Minoru (1907–1980), and the later Nikkatsu 1955 production *Diary of a Policeman* (*Keisatsu nikki*.)[15] Both films chronicle the problems of everyday people in a post-defeat landscape through the mediated gaze of respected figures of the community.

In *No Consultations Today*, the roving camera again establishes the 'place' of the action in the opening sequence, as the old doctor (Yanagi Eijirō 1895–1984) confirms the time frame as he recounts in voice-over the following: 'It was eighteen years ago that I started the practice here. Naturally during the war the hospital was burnt down, but after the war, with my nephew as director, we rebuilt the hospital. It was exactly one year ago and tomorrow is the anniversary. Tomorrow, on the anniversary, we shall put out the sign "No Consultations Today". I intend to sleep in until noon and rest . . .' The reality of this post-defeat urban landscape is reinforced as the first of several patients, who will disrupt the doctor's day off, appears. The de-mobbed mentally damaged son of the doctor's house-keeper attempts to hold a parade in the bombsite near the hospital, becoming embroiled in a brawl with some passing men. Through the course of the film, the doctor mediates between the worlds of the various patients and people connected to the hospital, guiding the spectators' understanding of their problems. He also provides the narrative continuity, being the link that connects the various episodes that make up the film. The sympathetic attitude that the doctor adopts to the various problems people in the local community face is supported cinematically. When the de-mobbed soldier imagines the bugle and the sounds of the parade ground, the sound track makes this real to the spectator. In each case, the patients with whom the doctor comes into contact are representative of character types and social problems common to the post-defeat decade of social and economic upheaval. However, the film, through the overriding humanity of the doctor and various people associated with him, overcomes the social problems raised by the film. This position is cinematically reinforced through stylistic devices such as the use of flashbacks and voice-over narration.

In one instance, a young girl arriving by train from Osaka, while looking for her friend's apartment, is robbed and raped. The film structures the scene of the robbery and rape as a flashback with the voice-over of the sympathetic policeman explaining the circumstances to the doctor, guiding the spectators' interpretation of the events. In this way the potential moral ambiguity that often surrounds women in such circumstances is overruled by the authoritative voices of the policeman and doctor. As a result of this mediation, by the end of the film, the victim is re-inscribed into the community with a boyfriend whom it is assumed she will marry. Equally, the mentally disturbed ex-soldier's antics relegate wartime memories to the absurd, a device used in many subsequent films reflecting the deranged memories of an insane world. Later Kurosawa Akira would subvert this device in *Record of a Living Being* aka *I Live in Fear/What the Birds Knew (Ikimono no kiroku)* released in 1955, bringing it to bear not on memory but as a critique of the present (1955). This film raises the question, Who is really mad? The old man confined to a mental institution because he fears nuclear destruction, or his family, representative of normal people who are politically acquiescent and live with the threat of the 'bomb'?

## The 'Script of Femininity', Romance and Women Re-contained

As argued in the previous chapter, under the terms of sexual equality inscribed in the new postwar Constitution, the myth of heterosexual romance became one of the narrative vehicles through which dominant constructions of sexuality are defined and the ideals of patriarchal society upheld. The rule that women should wait while men actively pursue 'act[s] to position women as passive objects to be chosen (or rejected) and men as agentic subjects with a right to dictate whether sexual relationships succeed or fail' (Ussher 1997: 437). While this can be said to apply quite clearly to Western social ideals, in Japanese narrative fiction, the distinction between the active, stoic hero and the more passive romantic hero of the *nimaime* tradition complicates the simple dichotomy between active male and passive female. The romantic hero often becomes equally enmeshed and powerless against the social forces that overwhelm the female protagonists.

In cinematic terms, in the immediate postwar period the re-inscription of women into passive roles of containment within narratives of heterosexual romance was not only evident within film plotlines but also built into the very structure of films. In *Until the Day We Meet Again*, structured in a flashback format, Keiko does not have an existence beyond Saburō's memories of her. Apart from a few short scenes with her mother, it is only during the final parallel sequences, which cut between Saburō detained and Keiko waiting at the station just before her death, that she too engages in several brief voice-over monologues. In the example of the kamikaze films, women exist in a purely symbolic role as poignant reminders of what the pilots and submarine officers must give up, thus reinforcing the sense of the sacrifice these young officers are making. Alternatively, women serve in these films as symbols of the officers' own feminine natures, the rejection of which, in the solipsistic terms of desirable masculinity, signifies the protagonists' arrival at true manhood. Even in the case of films produced post-1952 by the Shōchiku Studios, whose policy since the mid-1920s was to target female audiences and that had, in many ways, successfully incorporated women as active agents into an ethos of 'total mobilization', women were re-contained through romance within traditional roles of passivity and sacrifice.

One of the most successful cinematic structures for this re-containment developed by the Shōchiku Studios became known as the *surechigai* film. Quite literally, this term refers to people passing nearby but not actually seeing each other. This structure has endless possibilities for prolonging the denouement in romance scenarios and has been used by Shōchiku to great effect in the three-part *The Love-Troth Tree* aka *The Compassionate Buddha Tree* (*Aizen katsura*) of 1938 and the hugely popular postwar three-part romance *What Is Your Name?* (*Kimi no na wa*) released between 1953 and 1954. The *surechigai* structure owes much to its serial origins; in the case of *The Love-Troth Tree* the story was first serialized in a women's magazine, and in the case of *What Is Your Name?*, it was first broadcast to record-breaking ratings (forty-nine percent) as an NHK Radio serial.

The open-ended serial structure of the narrative and the omnipotent audience position structured around scenes of 'near misses' automatically places the protagonists in a vulnerable and weak position as it reinforces the point that they are not active but reactive agents in the causal chain of events. The Hollywood-style 'happily-ever-after' ending of the union of the couple in the final instalment occurs due to the forbearance and patience of the main protagonists and is not based on their actively pursuing their union. In fact, the opposite is the case, as they try to conform to social 'morality' and avoid each other, thus further contributing to prolongation of the denouement and providing a pretext for travel to exotic locations throughout Japan. In the latter example, the prolongation of the romance theme of the earlier hit *The Love-Troth Tree* became further complicated by the linking of the romance to war and the 'victimization complex'.

Although in many ways sharing similar thematic and structural characteristics with *Until the Day We Meet Again*, the film *What Is Your Name?* differs in relation to the part played by the war in the romance of the two main protagonists, Atomiya Haruki (Sada Keiji 1926–1964) and Machiko (Kishi Keiko 1932–). In *Until the Day We Meet Again*, it is clearly the war which is the main obstruction to the romance, hence the protagonists, the 'fated generation', are victims of the times. However, in *What Is Your Name?*, it is Machiko's failure to conform to the codes of the myth of romance in choosing material security above love, when she makes the fateful error to marry Hamaguchi Katsunori rather than wait for the man she loves, that sets the tragic chain of events in motion. Drawing on the iconography of the popular 1940 Hollywood production *Waterloo Bridge* (Mervyn Le Roy), the couple meet during an air raid on Sukiyabashi (bridge) on 24 May 1945 and promise that if they are still alive, to meet again on the bridge in six months' time. However, Machiko, obeying her uncle, returns to Sado Island for a meeting with a prospective marriage partner, Hamaguchi Katsunori, on the very day—24 November 1945— that she had promised to meet Atomiya. This is the point at which the film opens *in medias res*, as Machiko recounts the events to Aya (Awashima Chikage 1924–), an acquaintance from Sado who is also travelling on the ferry. Throughout the six hours of the film as the two lovers repeatedly meet only to be driven apart until the final scene when Hamaguchi, Machiko's husband, agrees to divorce her, Machiko remains the faithful wife and dutiful daughter to her mother-in-law, despite the cruelty she suffers at their hands. The film thus places romantic love within traditional concepts of desirable femininity based on passivity and forbearance (see figure 13). The ending reinforces the view that through suffering and patience a woman finds true happiness (*shiawase*). The character of Machiko becomes the site where the newly inscribed terms of women's autonomy before the law, stipulated in the postwar Constitution, is deflected from the political onto the right of women to choose a marriage partner. Machiko is caught between the traditional female role as subservient to the male household head, in this case her uncle, and modern concepts of the nuclear family based on the conjugal relationship between a man and woman founded on mutual consent. The film ultimately supports the myth of romance whereby women, in a 'democratic' worldview that espouses freedom of choice in marriage, are still primarily dependent on the men in their lives (fathers, brothers and uncles) to secure their happiness by creating the appropriate circumstances in which they are able to express their preference. By the 1960s this ideal of a woman reaching fulfilment through passivity and suffering was being questioned, not only by radical directors such as Ōshima Nagisa but even in conservative productions directed by Ozu Yasujirō.

The 1962 Ozu film, *An Autumn Afternoon* (*Sanma no aji*), utilizes the breakdown of this system as the catalyst in the overall disintegration of the traditional family. The first son of a widower lives in an apartment with his wife and relies on his younger sister, Michiko (Iwashita Shima 1941–), to maintain the main household. Due to this unorthodox but increasingly common situation, both father and brother, too caught up with their own lives, fail to fulfil their responsibilities to Michiko, who is attracted to a friend of her brother's. Unlike Machiko in *What Is Your Name?*, and despite her passivity and forbearance, through the failure of her father and brother to live up to their traditional roles, she does not marry the man she loves but goes ahead with a marriage proposal put forward by her boss. The film thus reflects the changing social roles of the company as replacement *ie* (family) in the age of the 'economic miracle'.

While women were contained within the 'scripts of femininity' defined in the romance film of the post-defeat period, the persona of the child star Misora Hibari (1937–1989) came to symbolize a fluidity of subjectivity that gave her a freedom of expression and action denied her more mature peers. In keeping with the image of youthful purity, in the sense that children and youth cannot be held accountable for the atrocities of a war foisted upon them by their parents' generation, the child star/singer Misora Hibari shot to fame in 1949 with the release of her song and the film of the same title, *The Sad Whistle* (*Kanashiki kuchibue*), directed by Ieki Miyoji. This was followed by a string of films in which she starred alongside famous male leads of the day, Okada Eiji and Tsuruta Koji amongst others, in films such as *Tokyo Kid/Tōkyō kiddo* (1950), *The Tearstained Doll*

(1951) and *Crossing That Hill* (*Ano oka koete*) (1951). However, unlike *Twenty-four Eyes*, which through images of 'victimized innocence' offered the war generation a vicarious exculpation from a foreign-imposed sense of guilt, Misora Hibari's star persona became the embodiment of both the sufferings and hopes of the post-defeat period. This was connected to both her child status, as symbol of the first postwar generation (she was born in 1937 and age twelve when she made *The Sad Whistle*), and the fact that although a child, her appearance and manner were that of an adult's. In fact, when she first began to perform in public at the age of nine, the media were harsh in their appraisal of her, arguing that she was part of a hoax, a deformed adult playing the part of a child. As a child star with the voice, appearance and sensibility of an adult, she became the post-defeat embodiment of both 'victimized innocence' and the hopes for the future offered by American-style 'democratic' reforms. As the line from the chorus of her hit song *Tokyo Kid* goes, 'the Tokyo kid carries her dreams in her right pocket, and her chewing gum in her left pocket' (see figure 12). By the end of the film *Tokyo Kid*, she is reconciled with her estranged wealthy father and depicted boarding a plane at Hanada Airport bound for the USA. The 'Tokyo kid', the modern version of the 'Edo-ko' (the child of Edo, Edo being the old name for Tokyo in the Tokugawa period), has clearly been co-opted into the American dream.

Japanese interpretations of Misora Hibari's attraction to adult audiences have tended to focus on the 'escapist' thesis popular in early media studies theory. Drawing on research carried out by Japanese social psychologists, the editors of the *Weekly Asahi Magazine History of the Shōwa Period* (*Shūkan Asahi no Shōwashi* 1989) argue that the great appeal of Misora Hibari lay in an escapist sensibility prevalent in Japanese society in the immediate postwar period. This sensibility they link to three factors, first, the desire for a 'spatial escape' (*kūkanteki tōhi*). This manifested itself in a romanticization of the foreign. The titles of many of Misora Hibari's songs from this period—'The Longed For Voyage to Hawaii' (*'Akogare no Hawai Funji'*) and 'San Francisco China Town' (*'Sanfranshisko no chaina taun'*)—add veracity to this position as do many of her films, which include her going to and/or dreaming of America and/or Hawaii—*Tokyo Kid*. Second, the desire for a 'temporal escape' (*jikanteki tōhi*); this, the editors argue, was evident in the resurgence of interest in kabuki and other traditional theatrical forms as well as a revival in period novels. Finally, an escape from one's generation (*nenreiteki tōhi*), which manifested itself in a romanticization of the world of children, or as described by social-psychologists, to a 'tendency to infantilism' (*shōniteki keikō*). In support of this claim, the editors of the *Weekly Asahi Magazine History of the Shōwa Period* also cite the growing popularity of *manga* (comics) and *pachinko* (a pinball game) with adults at this time. Through these pastimes, 'adults sought to merge into the simple world of children. This represented an attempt to escape from the adult world, where in various forms, there were things, which at times they were unable to bear. Amongst adults, alienation and conflict were severe. When they felt excessively repressed, adults sought various means of escape' (*Shūkan Asahi no Shōwashi* 1989 vol. ii: 255).

Certainly Misora Hibari's status as child star was crucial to her persona at this time; however, her role within these early film scenarios as an innocent was not entirely escapist, as she confronts and withstands the sufferings inherent in the chaos of the aftermath of war and defeat. In 1949 her small body with its 'aged' features was a contradiction that reflected a period devoid of childhood in the modern sense. As a child born during the war, these films exploited her role as bearer of the burdens of adulthood. The press reinforced this image, as it was widely reported that in her personal life she was the main support of her family.

Misora Hibari's films were often based on narrative structures employed in adult genres. In particular, many of the early films rely on narrative devices developed in the *surechigai* film. *The Sad Whistle* adapted this structure to the exigencies of post-defeat society where people, separated by the war, search for loved ones. Drawing on the contemporary social problem of street children, many of whom were displaced by war and repatriation or just abandoned, Misora Hibari as a street child, orphaned and separated from her brother, represented the lowest denominator in post-defeat society.[16]

In *The Sad Whistle*, Mitsuko (Misora Hibari) searches for her brother, a former composer (the fictional composer of the title song *The Sad Whistle*). Now a de-mobbed soldier, he too wanders about the docks of Yokohama aimlessly looking for his sister before getting involved in the black market. The convoluted plot is constructed around the two passing at various points in the film but not recognizing each other until the final scene, when the soldier hears Misora Hibari singing his song, *The Sad Whistle*, in a nightclub, and they are reunited. This ending provides not only the satisfaction of the reunion but also the material acknowledgement that they will henceforth achieve fame and wealth together as singer and songwriter. This film set the pattern for subsequent films in which beloved relatives die, and brothers and sisters, fathers and daughters are separated only to be reunited by the film's end.

Implicit within the narratives of these early films and portrayed through the supporting characters is a generational consciousness. Males from the parent generation are often flawed characters. The old violinist father in *The Sad Whistle* is financially dependent on his daughter, as he fails to attract audiences as a busker, and when given the opportunity to audition for an orchestra he fails to get the job. Later, after coming home drunk one evening, he suffers a seizure and goes blind only to knock over a kerosene lamp and burn down their shack. The father in *Tokyo Kid* returns to Japan in search of his wife and daughter after having abandoned them many years before. As he confesses twice in the film, first to Mariko's (Misora Hibari) friends and then later when reunited with Mariko his daughter, he had become involved with gangsters and run away to America where (in keeping with the American dream) he had worked hard and become rich. Unable to return to Japan because of the war, he has now returned in search of his wife and daughter in order to make amends. As melodrama would have it, at the beginning of the film just as he is reunited with his wife, she dies telling Mariko to have nothing to do with him. In *Crossing That Hill*, Mariko's (Misora Hibari) estranged father remarries and enters his wife's family as an adopted son-in-law (*yōshi*). As a result he becomes wealthy, taking over his father-in-law's factory. However, he is swindled out of his fortune and threatened with bankruptcy. Alternatively, the male leads who costar with Misora Hibari are from the modern generation representative of the future and are instrumental in aiding the characters played by Misora Hibari in solving the problems raised by the films.

Reflected within Misora Hibari's star persona at this time is an ambiguity of identity that allows her an often active role in solving the problems faced by the adult characters. Marilyn Ivy contends that in the immediate postwar period 'the struggle for survival created an intensely fragmented and individualized sense of consciousness . . . (Ivy 1993: 245). Both in terms of the contradictions inherent in Misora Hibari's child/adult status and her gender coding—in these early films she is often mistaken for a boy (*The Sad Whistle* and *Tokyo Kid*) and at other times she adopts the 'top hat and tails' costume as she sings in nightclubs (*The Sad Whistle*)—she embodied many of the contradictions inherent in a period of rapid social change. Within these early films, the fluidity of her identity allows her to move freely between generations, becoming the nexus around which new communities and pseudo-families form. Through her sufferings, generations made disparate by accusations of war responsibility, represented by the flawed parent generation and pure fated generation, are again reunited within some sort of communal structure by the end of the films. This fluidity of identity opened up the possibilities for multiple interpretative frameworks at a time when questions of subjectivity, both with regard to traditional understandings of the role of the individual in civil society and definitions of gender, were in a state of flux.

In all the films discussed so far, there is an underlying humanism that transcends the harsh realities of the *mise-en-scène* and provides a basis for social reconstruction. In this way many films of the post-defeat decade direct the spectator towards a particular vision of the future. At its most simplistic, the early films of the child star Misora Hibari—*The Sad Whistle* (1949), *Tokyo Kid* (1950), *The Tearstained Doll* (1951) and *Crossing That Hill* (1951)—re-invent family and communal relationships from within the material context of the prosperity offered by the 'American dream'. Often filmed within the studio set, the 'dream' lacks the conviction that the material reality of the location shooting of the 'social realist'-derived films portrays. Alternatively, the trilogy *What Is Your Name?* offers a vision of a purity of romance that transcends the deeds of a past criminalized through accusations of war guilt and the compromises made to survive the chaos of the immediate post-defeat era. As the editors of the *Weekly Asahi Magazine History of the Shōwa Period* explain, much of the popularity of the radio serial and then the film rests on the fact that, 'Apart from Haruki and Machiko [the principal couple], the characters in the story, due to the war, are all burdened with an unhappy past. The sad circumstances of these characters aroused great sympathy and people centred their compassion on them, but at the same time, the love between Haruki and Machiko, both of whom have no 'personal histories' (*zenreki*), appeared more beautiful than possible in a world such as this' (*Shūkan Asahi no Shōwashi* 1989 vol. ii: 414).

The serial structure of the drama necessitated the incorporation of numerous subplots juxtaposed against the romance of the two principal characters. As the quotation makes clear, these peripheral characters suffer many hardships in the post-defeat era. The de-mobbed general (Ryū Chishū 1904–1993) becomes involved in the black market and is arrested; two young women working as prostitutes on Sukiyabashi become involved with Haruki, who early on in the first film helps to save one of them from suicide; and Haruki's elder sister arriving in Tokyo is tricked by gangsters into prostitution. In each case these characters, by the end of the third film, have been re-inscribed within makeshift communal structures. The de-mobbed general takes the two prostitutes in and offers to raise the illegiti-mate child as his own. Despite the fact that it is clear that the child is the result of the girl's relationship with an American GI, the child is still ac-cepted. Haruki's sister marries a widower with a small child. Having inves-tigated her past, the widower decides that circumstances led her to prostitution and proceeds with the marriage. In each case it is the ideal of the pure romance of Haruki and Machiko that binds these disparate charac-ters together as a caring community of friends. The past is forgiven and romance provides a future ideal.

*Children of the Bomb* similarly re-orientates the spectator to the future through the ideal of marriage. When Ishikawa *sensei* visits Heita, the last of her three pupils, we are introduced to his elder sister, who was injured during the atomic bomb blast and is now lame. As it happens, the very day Ishikawa *sensei* visits is the day the sister is due to leave to go to her future husband's house. The elder brother explains the circumstances of the mar-riage in the following conversation:

> Mr Tanaka, an acquaintance, at the time he was called up promised to marry my sister. But, on that day [6 August], she was injured, her foot was crushed under the building. It was very sad. My sister and I both gave up any thoughts of her marriage. Even if Mr Tanaka did manage to return alive, we thought he wouldn't want to proceed with the marriage. But the year after the end of the war, Mr Tanaka was de-mobbed and the first thing he did was to visit our house and according to his promise he wanted to go ahead with the marriage. I put my hands together in prayer and thanked god for Mr Tanaka. At that moment, I was pleased to be alive. There aren't only bad things in this world. There are still people with warm feelings that one can trust. Mr Tanaka had one condition, he asked that we wait five years. He said that as everything had been burnt and there were no jobs, that in five years' time, he would come for my sister, having re-built the foundations for their life. The five years have passed and the day has come.

*Twenty-four Eyes* reaffirms the cycles of life, explicit in the imagery of the seasons depicted throughout the film, as by the end of the film the teacher, somewhat older, is back in school with a new class of students in their first year of schooling. As she reads the roll call it becomes apparent that some of the children are the offspring of her original 1928 class. The film ends with her riding a bicycle (which the surviving members of the

1928 class had given her at a reunion) along the coastal roads of the island just as in the opening sequences of the film. The intrusions of the war into the utopian island are past and life continues as before. However, it is perhaps the 'tragic heroes' of, for example, the kamikaze war-retro genre who most palpably symbolized the naturalization of history through suffering and a cyclical explanation of the war as a national purgation and renewal. *Beyond the Clouds* contributes to these discourses of renewal, as Ōtaki expresses these sentiments in his letters, urging his parents to believe in Japan's ultimate victory and to live long lives. In *The Human Torpedoes*, this sentiment is expressed by Asakura who, in rationalizing his own death, says that others will come to realize the senselessness of war. Ivan Morris's study implicates the actual kamikaze pilots in this discourse when he argues that they seemed to be aware of Japan's inevitable defeat. As Vice-Admiral Ōnishi Takijirō, who was responsible for the establishment of the first squadrons of Special Attack Forces in the Philippines and Taiwan, is reputed to have said '[E]ven if we are defeated, the noble spirit of the kamikaze attack corps will keep our homeland from ruin' (Morris 1980: 284). Both kamikaze films are excellent examples of a wider conservative, postwar discourse of defeat, which co-opted the image of the kamikaze as symbols of the spirit of postwar regeneration. Surviving kamikaze and the military establishment represented at the Yasukuni Shrine Museum, among others, had a vested interest in contributing to, and encouraging, this hegemonic image, which gave meaning to the young officers' deaths despite the failure of defeat. These images helped to counter the theoretical arguments put forward by such radical intellectuals as Sakaguchi Ango (1906–1955) in his essay 'Discourse on Decadence' (*Darakuron*), which was first published in 1946 and by all accounts widely read. In this essay Sakaguchi puts forward the proposition that with defeat the ideologies associated with militarism and *bushidō* (the code of the samurai) were dispelled. Japanese 'spiritualism' had been unable to defeat American 'materialism'; therefore, out of the ashes of defeat Japan had to find a new truth, which, he argued, should be founded on the physical senses and desires. Hence, Sakaguchi's call for 'decadence' as the only real truth. *Beyond the Clouds* and *The Human Torpedoes* contributed to a conservative counter-discourse by displacing the wider discourses of war responsibility through the depiction of the youthful 'tragic heroes' onto themes of a spiritual regeneration and through the homosocial subtext, a reassertion of the primacy of the male group. As one kamikaze pilot is reported to have rationalized, 'a nation had to suffer and be purified every few generations, so that it could become stronger by having its impurities removed' (quoted in Morris 1980: 314).

Both *Beyond the Clouds* and *The Human Torpedoes* attempt the impossible in a bid to harness this legacy to reconstruction. They attempt the reconciliation of an antiwar imperative through the tragic 'subject-as-victim' theme and an acknowledgement of the heroic sacrifice of the young officers in the Special Attack Forces. This sentiment echoes that expressed in a poem composed by Vice-Admiral Ōnishi (the founder of the Special Attack Forces):

> Refreshingly
> After the violent storm
> The moon rose radiant
>
> (Quoted in Iguchi, Nakajima and Pineau 1958: 187)

Tracing the transhistorical etymology of the 'tragic' in Western literature, Terry Eagleton similarly links the development of the sacrificial victim with expiation of communal guilt: '[The sacrificial victim] acts as a displacement for their sins, and is in that sense metonymic. In burdening it with their guilt, the people at once acknowledge their frailty and disavow it, project it violently outside themselves in the slaying of the sacrificial victim or its expulsion beyond their political frontiers. The victim is thus both themselves and not themselves, both a thing of darkness they acknowledge as their own as well as a convenient object on which to offload and disown their criminality' (Eagleton 2003a: 279). Within the postdefeat Japanese historical context of foreign-imposed 'war guilt,' the propitiatory, 'sacrificial' kamikaze heroes provided a discourse affirming the newly imported values and ideals of the regenerating community. In the historical context of defeat, the narrative of the 'sacrificial hero' of the humanist war-retro film can in general terms be understood as forming part of a process of communal internalization of the values of the nascent American-dominated world order. In giving this redemptive postwar meaning to the deaths of the young officers, the visual subtext of homosocial bonding reconfirms the underlying principles upon which the ideologies of the 'family-state' (*kazoku kokka*) were predicated; this occurs despite the films' apparent challenge to wartime propaganda through dialogue and voice-over monologues. Satō Tadao confirms this reading in his essay on the 'Genealogy of the Antiwar Film' when he states:

After *Beyond the Clouds* many films based on the Special Attack Forces were made, but for the most part they stayed within this format. Film-makers probably intended to emphasize the misery of war due to the portrayal of the enforced death of personable young men out of a sense of comradely love and love of family. However, if we alter the perspective slightly, if these young men are only capable of comradely love and love of family, we can probably say they were incapable of opposing the war. Films made during the war to promote a fighting spirit did not depict the enemy as a monster to stimulate hatred, instead they depicted men rich in comradely love and love of family. (Satō 1989: 133–134)

Satō goes on to suggest that for films to present a truly antiwar stance, they need to effect a 'wider field of vision', for example, the portrayal of the enemy as human beings similar to ourselves. Alternatively and perhaps more poignantly, parody as adopted by Okamoto Kihachi (1924–) in his 1960s' war films would appear to make a far stronger antiwar statement.

## 'The Tragedy of Japan'—Humanism Betrayed

> The winter wind has gone
> and long-awaited spring has arrived
> with double-petalled cherry blossoms.
>
> (Emperor Hirohito on his fifty-first birthday in 1953, a year after
> Japan regained sovereignty, quoted in Dower 1999: 553)

After the occupation officially ended on 28 April 1952, the 'tragedy of Japan', foreshadowed in 1946 in Kamei Fumio's (1908–1987) iconic montage sequence of the emperor changing his clothes from military uniform to a crumpled civilian suit in the suppressed film *The Tragedy of Japan* (*Nihon no higeki*), became increasingly apparent. At the psychosocial level of the individual, this was portrayed through the depiction of the breakdown of the family in the 1953 Shōchiku production, echoing Kamei's title, *A Japanese Tragedy* (*Nihon no higeki*), directed and scripted by Kinoshita Keisuke. More specifically, the 'tragedy of Japan' was articulated through a depiction of the unresolved legacies of the generational divisions of the immediate post-defeat years that the star persona of Misora Hibari came to epitomize and gloss over within the 'happily ever after' fantasies of the 'American dream'. Despite the fact that Japan had officially regained its sovereignty in 1952, due to the Korean War and the politics of the Cold War, the USA maintained a heavy military presence and it became increasingly clear, from the civil unrest, that the fantasy happy endings offered by the 'American dream' were not sufficient to heal the contradictions inherent in defeat, the implications of the 'reverse course' policy, and the corruption associated with reconstruction. Kinoshita, in *A Japanese Tragedy*, utilized the docudrama structure as the macro-political framework that clearly links these generational divisions, allegorized through the micro-narrative of the fissures that result in the dissolution of the Inoue family, to the failures of postwar political institutions. In this way he adapted the docudrama format, used so prodigiously in the era of the 'national policy' films, to a critique of the first eight years of the post-defeat period.

The opening montage sequence constructed out of newsreel footage juxtaposed against newspaper headlines and intertitles refers to the film's inter-textual legacies in the earlier Kamei documentary film of the same title while contextualizing the disintegration of the Inoue family in the historical temporal frame of the defeat and occupation. At the level of the emperor, Kamei's *The Tragedy of Japan* provided the iconic image of the 'permanence-amid-change theme' that encapsulated the Yoshida-led elite's attitude to 'democratic reform'. Kinoshita in this opening sequence traces the political realities of this policy from the emperor through the political organs of 'democracy', the Diet, elections and public demonstrations, finally ending with intertitles placed over newsreel footage of unknown and unnamed individuals suffering the consequences not of war but of reconstruction, these unnamed and inconsequential individuals being the real subject of the film. As Kinoshita explains in the introduction to his screenplay published in 1953, in which he makes an appeal to universal principles of humanity that transcend politics,

> *A Japanese Tragedy* is a familiar tale, of people who, despite their house being burnt down in the war and family members not returning, commit suicide unconscious of the tragedy of their situation. I wanted to portray simple people like that. The war widow [Mochizuki Yūko 1917–1977], not such a splendid mother as those who have appeared up to now in films made in the 'mother' genre (*hahamono*), but I cannot somehow bring myself to despise such simple people. Japanese politicians advocate the building of a civilized nation (*bunka kokka*), but miserable people like this are abundant on the streets. No matter what kind of social structure, no matter what form of government, I think humans must not be left in a state of misery. (Kinoshita 1953: 1)

   The juxtapositioning in the opening shots of two newspaper headlines, the first reporting on the emperor's proclamation to end the war and the second referring to the Tokyo War Crimes Trial, clearly echoes Kamei's documentary by locating the emperor at the apex of events. These two headlines are immediately followed by newsreel footage of the trial: a high-angle medium-long shot of Prosecutor Keenan and a left pan across the court to General Tōjō Hideki (1884–1948) in the dock. The editing further focuses attention on Tōjō by a cut to a medium close-up shot. This is again followed by a newspaper headline announcing the decision of the court to 'exempt' (*menjo*) the emperor from appearing at the trial. A medium close-up shot of the Emperor in his crumpled civilian suit heading for his car on one of his many 'meeting the people' tours and a long shot of him announcing the promulgation of the New Constitution immediately follows this headline. The positioning of these shots raises questions about General Tōjō's role in the trial as guardian of the Imperial institution, and the emperor's post-defeat role as unifier of the nation. A fluttering national flag provides the backdrop to the first intertitle, marking the transition of the subject of the montage sequence from emperor to the people, as the newspaper headlines shift to 'Mother and three children commit suicide'. Crime becomes the next topic as headlines report a 'police raid on a cabaret' and a 'youth burns down a *pachinko* parlour'. The sequence ends with the following intertitles superimposed above images of a flood and finally concluding with violent clashes between demonstrators and riot police. The juxtapositioning of shots, the newspaper headlines and the intertitles clearly directs the spectators' reading of the historical events depicted. The opening intertitle superimposed over the fluttering flag, 'It has been eight years since the war ended and still the government is in confusion', locates the action of the film in the present, 1953, the year of the film's release. The superimposed intertitles then proceed to direct the spectator to a specific interpretation of the chaotic scenes of demonstrations that concluded this sequence.

   Life is insecure.
   Crime is increasing.
   All Japanese have become caught up in this gloomy melting pot.
   This is the scene of Japan today.

The stark title, *A Japanese Tragedy*, accompanied by loud discordant music, immediately follows shots of riot police firing tear gas into a crowd demonstrating in front of the Diet. Following the credit lists, another series of three intertitles introduces the micro-narrative of Haruko (Mochizuki Yūko 1917–1977) and her two children.

> The story of this mother and her children is one such episode [in the tragedy of Japan].
>
> Furthermore, the sprouts of this tragedy that are occurring close around us, and from now on, will more than likely grow thick throughout Japan.

The docudrama framework and the use of flashbacks are all geared to explain the past experiences of the three principal characters from within the specifics of the post-defeat political context. Unlike the flashback sequences in the kamikaze films and *Until the Day We Meet Again*, which used flashbacks to critique the war through an exploration of the consciousness of the main protagonists, in *A Japanese Tragedy* these sequences provide an insight into mitigating circumstances that allow us to feel compassion for these flawed characters. At key points in the micronarratives of Haruko and the two adult children, the docudrama format gives further credence to their subjective memories expressed through the flashbacks. In this way Haruko's decision to turn to prostitution, depicted through flashback, is foreshadowed by documentary footage of American GIs cavorting with Japanese women in the street.

Food is the trigger for the two now adult children's flashbacks to their difficult childhood in the early post-defeat period when their mother left them with an unscrupulous uncle. The misunderstandings between the two generations of the one family are made clear to the spectator through a privileged all-knowing omniscient placement that in effect further supports the protagonists' positions as 'victims of the times', as they are only partially aware of their circumstances *vis-à-vis* the other characters. Seiichi, the son, who in the normal course of events would be expected to look after his mother in her old age, wants to enter the household of a rich doctor as an adopted son. As the biological son of the rich doctor had been killed in the war, Seiichi, a medical student, would inherit the hospital. As an adult, through his interactions with his mother, Seiichi appears a cold and unloving son. The flashbacks into his childhood, when his mother's involvement in the black market caused him embarrassment at school, and his uncle's cruel treatment of him as a child provide a contradictory image of him as the victim. Similarly, we learn through flashbacks that his sister was raped by her cousin. In both cases the children, through misunder-standings and misinformation (from the uncle), come to the conclusion as adults that their mother abandoned them to the cruel machinations of the uncle's family because she enjoyed working at the Atami hot spring resort. Alternatively, the mother's remembrances of her own experiences lead to the contradictory conclusion that she indeed suffered at the hands of many of her male clients and that what sustained her was the knowledge that she was doing it for the children.

Ozu Yasujirō's *Tokyo Story*, released in the same year as *A Japanese Tragedy*, also portrays this generational breakdown but from the wider context of the forces of modernity. In the sense that Japan underwent two periods of rapid 'modernization', the first phase in the early twentieth century and the second as part of postwar reconstruction, films directed by Ozu continued, in the postwar period, to develop themes of the alienation of the individual in the material world of urban society. In these latter post-war films, his criticism of the processes of modernity increasingly became linked to a critique of materialism, both in terms of consumerism as desirable objects—TV sets, refrigerators, golf clubs and train sets—became narrative devices around which minor conflicts develop, and in terms of the conditions of marriage (*Early Summer/Bakushū* [1951], *Good Morning* aka *Too Much Talk/Ohayō* [1959] and *An Autumn Afternoon* [1962]).

In the example of *Early Spring (Sōshun)* (1956), Noriko (Hara Setsuko 1920–) rejects materialism as a basis for marriage when she turns down the proposal of marriage lined up for her by her boss. Going against her family, and thereby exercising her right to choose her own marriage partner, she marries the widowed friend of her deceased brother. As she explains to her sister-in-law, despite the fact that he has a daughter by his first wife, she chooses him because she feels she can trust him. The other marriage proposal had been put to her in purely financial terms; at forty the prospective husband is the director of a company. In this context, the human qualities of trust supersede material concerns as Noriko's choice is a low-level doctor who is assigned to a hospital in Akita, northern Honshu, not the most desirable location for a sophisticated young woman. Similarly in *Tokyo Story,* the generational rift is focused on the materialistic attitude of the children who have become enmeshed in their own lives, built around the struggle to survive in the metropolis. In this sense *Tokyo Story* has its inter-textual roots in *The Only Son (Hitori musuko* [1936]), as does *Good Morning* in *I Was Born But . . . (Umareta wa mita keredo* [1932]). However, in this latter example the two boys go on strike, not due to questions surrounding masculinity and the salaryman as in the 1932 film but due to the pressures of consumerism to compel their father to purchase a TV. While Kinoshita, in *A Japanese Tragedy*, clearly locates these generational divisions in the specifics of a pervasive social and political breakdown, which through the docudrama structure of the film is linked to the failures of democratic reforms, films directed by Ozu link these same divisions to the universal experiential realities of modernity. As the German director Wim Wenders stresses in his tribute to Ozu, *Tokyo-Ga* (1985),

> If in our century something sacred still exists, if there were something like a sacred treasure of cinema, then for me, that would be the work of the Japanese director Yasujirō Ozu . . . With extreme economy of means and reduced to the barest essentials, Ozu's films again and again tell the same simple story of the same simple people in the same city, Tokyo. This chronicle spans nearly forty years and depicts the transformation of life in Japan. Ozu's films deal with the slow deterioration of the Japanese family, and thereby, the deterioration of a national identity. But they do so not by pointing with dismay at what is new, western or American, but by lamenting with unrelenting nostalgia the loss taking place at the same time. As thoroughly Japanese as they are, these films are at the same time universal. In them I can recognize all families in all countries of the world, as well as my parents, my brothers and myself. For me, never before and never since has cinema been so close to its essence and its purpose, to present an image of man in our century. A usable, true and valid image in which he not only recognizes himself, but from which above all else he may learn about himself.

Unlike the characters in Kurosawa Akira films from the early post-defeat period in which people make choices between different courses of action (Murakami and Yusa in *Stray Dog*), in *A Japanese Tragedy* it is the sociopolitical environment that impacts on the characters and turns them into the 'miserable people . . . abundant on the streets' that Kinoshita refers to with such compassion in the introduction to his screenplay. Heroes in Kurosawa Akira's post-occupation *gendaigeki* films, although often 'goal-oriented' and action driven, are also increasingly overwhelmed by their sociopolitical circumstances (*Record of a Living Being* aka *I Live in Fear* [1955]) or destroyed by corporate corruption (*The Bad Sleep Well* aka *The Worse You Are, the Better You Sleep/A Rose in the Mud/Warui yatsu hodo yoku nemuru* [1960]). In stylistic terms they are framed within narrative modes denoting introspection and psychological motivation as the hallmarks of these fated heroes.

## The Late 1950s: Communal Patterns of Interpretation and Memory—The Case of *The Human Condition*

Within early post-defeat Japanese films, romance, often set within the *mise-en-scène* of the Second World War, was used as a motif in which an individual's subjectivity was constructed out of heterosexual desire. Thus romance became one of the vehicles that redressed the overvaluation, during the war period, of the sacrifice of the individual for the greater good of the group, the nation-state. This can be related back to such intellectuals as Sakaguchi Ango, who in his influential essay 'Discourse on Decadence' (*Darakuron*) set out a philosophical dichotomy of the body/*nikutai,* representative of the individual, and the spirit/*seishin*. The 'spirit', during the latter stages of the war period, had become equated with a hyper-militarist ideological position that was needed to maintain a situation of total war. In total war, the individual was called upon to make great sacrifices—that is, to deny his or her own personal desires—for some abstract ideological entity defined as the innate spiritual essence of the 'family-state' (*kazoku kokka*). In the immediate aftermath of the war, as Sakaguchi Ango explains, the ideologies surrounding Japan's spiritual supremacy were exposed. The reality of Japan's defeat by American materialism completely debunked them.

Within the conservative discourses of mainstream cinema, the ideal of heterosexual romance (as opposed to the more carnal sense of desire employed by Sakaguchi and the novelist Tamura Taijirō (1911–1983) in their use of the word 'body,' *nikutai*), became just one of the mainstream narrative manifestations of this worldview in films such as *Until the Day We Meet Again* and *What Is Your Name?* Thus in mainstream post-defeat cinema, the myth of heterosexual romance became established as a thematic device into which two complex discourses relating to individual subjectivity became conflated. Romance provided both a vehicle through which the requisite dominant constructions of sexuality were inscribed in the cultural and economic terms of masculinity and femininity, while simultaneously becoming synonymous with an antiwar imperative that challenged the underlying text inherent in images of a masculinity predicated on a sexual repression that dominated 'national policy' films. Reflected in films of the early 1940s was the conflation of the private and public under the rubric of the 'family-state' (*kazoku kokka*). Romantic love (*ren'ai*) was spurned, as the hapless young girl who is infatuated with Makoto, the hero of *Navy* (1943), experiences. 'If sex is repressed, that is, condemned to prohibition, non-existence, and silence, then the mere fact that one is speaking about it has the *appearance* of a deliberate transgression' (Foucault 1990: 6, emphasis mine). One of the reasons for the popularity of the re-introduction of romance into films, in the immediate postwar period, was related to this sense of transgression.

By the end of the 1950s and the release of Kobayashi Masaki's three-part epic[17] *The Human Condition* (*Ningen no jōken*)[18] released between 1959 and 1961, discourses of humanism, the myth of heterosexual romance and the 'subject-as-victim' had become fixed within the war film genre as communal patterns of interpretation and memory. In mainstream cinema, these patterns of interpretation and co-optation (i.e., the image of the kamikaze) have continued to the present day, and it was these narrative and stylistic conventions that newly emerging directors of the 1960s' avant-garde, such as Ōshima Nagisa and Okamoto Kihachi, challenged.

*The Human Condition*, based on the best-selling six-part novel by Gomikawa Junpei (1916–1995)[19] and perhaps one of the greatest war epics ever made, is a complex film, which from a humanitarian perspective systematically examines and ultimately condemns three of the great 'isms' of the twentieth century—industrialism, militarism and Stalinism—through the conscience of its main protagonist, Kaji (Nakadai Tatsuya 1932–). The title of the film, ambiguous in the use of the English 'condition', carries in the Japanese use of *jōken* not so much the sense of the 'conditions' as circumstances, but more the idea of the 'conditions' as requirements or the terms of humanity. In other words, the Japanese title raises complex questions regarding the terms of human existence. In pursuing this 'humanist' (*hyūmanisto*) agenda, *The Human Condition* utilizes romantic love expressed in heterosexual marriage as a vehicle to criticize the prewar and wartime ideologies of the 'family-state'. Unlike *Until the Day We Meet Again*, which similarly uses fated romance as a mechanism to delineate between the private and public, *The Human Condition* makes a direct link between wartime excesses of violence and sexual repression,.

In *The Human Condition*, two narratives are interwoven around Kaji: his public role as a supervisor of labour in a Manchurian mine, then as a soldier in the last stages of the war and finally, as a prisoner in a Soviet labour camp; and his private role as husband and friend. It is in this latter role, in keeping with established thematic conventions, that he is given a psychological depth through which wartime ideologies are challenged. The first scene in *The Human Condition* visually juxtaposes the two spheres of Kaji's life. In the war situation these are incompatible and will provide the psychological conflict that motivates the narrative for the nine hours of the film. Kaji and Michiko (Aratama Michiyo 1930–2001) are standing in the snow in front of a shop window; behind them an endless column of soldiers is marching past in time to a martial tune. An intertitle informs us that the setting is Manchuria and the year 1943. In the centre of the window is a small reproduction statue of Rodin's *The Kiss*, a poignant intertextual referent to the symbolic significance of the 'kiss' in the post-war economies of heterosexual exchange. In his mind Kaji is trying to reconcile his 'desire' for Michiko, established through a series of reverse-cut shots between Kaji and the statue, and a sense that, because of the war, they will have no future as he could be called up at any time, and like the soldiers behind him, forced to march off to war. Michiko who throughout the film represents in Kaji's mind an ideal of feminine innocence by her blind devotion to him, reinforced by her own admission to a friend that she does not understand the complexities of his work, while looking at the statue asks, 'Don't you want me?' Kaji clearly does, but in this instance, his concern for the future is linked to his superior worldly knowledge and contrasts with Michiko's more narrowly centred understanding of events. This first sequence clearly defines the dichotomies of postwar heterosexual exchange that will underpin the romance between Kaji and his wife in terms of the active and rational Kaji and the acquiescent and emotional Michiko.

Through the iconography of the statue, signifying mutual sexual pleasure, this first scene bases Kaji's and Michiko's love in the postwar terms of the fulfilment of the individual through the expression of heterosexual desire, thus defying the prewar and wartime ethos that sought to limit sex to procreation for the good of the nation. It similarly challenges premodern myths of love as undeclared and unrequited[20] as set out in the *Hagakure* and co-opted into the military ethos in the late 1930s. Later in the film, when asked by a nurse, 'Who is Michiko? Is she your lover or your wife?', Kaji replies that she is both, thus conflating the two previously separate and conflicting female roles into one woman.

The film continues this theme of the physical union between a man and a woman through 'structuring absences' as defined by Richard Dyer (1993: 105), that is, the film's refusal to equate Kaji's and Michiko's relationship with the wartime institution of marriage and procreation for the good of the household (*ie*) as symbolic of the 'family-state'. There is no mention of the involvement of either Kaji's or Michiko's families in the wedding, nor is there any hint of the premarital negotiations (*miai*); theirs is a simple decision as individuals to be together.[21] After the scene in which Kaji is offered the prospect of exemption from military service if he transfers from the head office to the Manchurian mine, he simply asks Michiko if she will go with him. The scene then cuts to their arrival at the mine, where they are shot kissing and embracing in the back of a truck. This, the only frontal shot of them kissing, denotes the cinematic consummation of the marriage. In addition, as their union is childless, their sexual relationship centres on individual desire rather than on procreation.[22] Themes related to the traditional extended family, symbol of the 'family-state', were central to 'national policy' films such as *The War at Sea From Hawaii to Malaya* (1942), *Navy* (1943) and *Army* (1944). Their 'absence' in *The Human Condition* is clearly structured into the narrative and gives the *appearance* of transgression.

Throughout the remainder of the film, the relationship between Kaji and Michiko provides the reference point against which all other male-female relationships are measured and found wanting. According to the film, wartime ideologies distorted men by sublimating a natural sexual desire onto violence. This then results in the abuse of the weak, whether in the male rape, the culmination of months of bullying that leads to the suicide of the soldier, Obara (Tanaka Kunio 1932–), or in the cynical use of 'comfort women' by the manager of the mine to keep his Chinese labourers docile and compliant. In the hyper-masculine world of the army, violence in such circumstances becomes purely functional, to obliterate a fear of weakness associated with the feminine in the perpetrators. This is obvious in the scene in part three of the film when Michiko visits Kaji at the military training camp. The officers are hostile in their attitude to her; she is intruding into a masculine world systematically designed to deny the feminine. Even so she is allowed to spend one night with Kaji. In this scene, the film again reasserts the physical nature of their union when Kaji asks Michiko to stand naked in the soft light from the window. This is the last time they meet and it is this image of Michiko, naked, that Kaji will carry in his mind through the subsequent battles and his wanderings in Manchuria. The next morning during *kendō* practice, Kaji suffers the acrimony of his seniors and is severely beaten.

As a war epic, *The Human Condition* shows not so much a conflict between the Japanese and the enemy but an internal conflict between the Japanese themselves. There is a clear dichotomy between the good characters, Kaji and his few friends who are opposed to the war, and the bad characters, who represent both the inhumanity of the system and the weak-

ness of human beings who succumb to and perpetuate the brutality of that
system. In earlier Japanese films set in Manchuria the camaraderie (*sen'y-
ūai*) between men was the central motivating force in the causal chain of
the events (*The Five Scouts/Gonin no sekkōhei* [1938] and *Mud and Sol-
diers/Tsuchi to heitai* [1939]), a theme transposed in the post-defeat decade into the kamikaze film. *The Human Condition* challenges this
convention by giving prominence to Kaji's relationship with Michiko,
which is portrayed as the only constant and satisfying relationship in the
film other than perhaps the relationship, only hinted at, of an old couple
fleeing Manchuria at the end of the war. They join Kaji's party only to
realize that they cannot keep up and therefore decide to commit suicide
together (*shinjū*). In contrast, Kaji's relationships with men are unsatisfying. In defiance of corrupt authority and in his refusal to compromise
and accept the status quo, Kaji, as the representative of postwar humanist
principles, rejects his place in the social order. He refuses the identity the
brutal socialization methods of the *kenpeitai* (gendarmerie) and the army
seek to impose upon him. Instead his subjectivity is defined in relation to
Michiko and his fundamental humanitarian beliefs. As a result, in the public world, he occupies an isolated position midway between the authority
of the various institutions within which he is expected to operate (the military-industrial complex of the Manchurian mine, the army and finally the
Soviet labour camp) and the physically weaker men he tries to help.

*The Human Condition* depicts situations in which the individual, the
'subject-as-victim', becomes locked into a series of power relations that
often force him to act against his own beliefs; therefore, in such situations,
all become simultaneously victims and perpetrators. The Chinese are exploited by the Japanese military-industrial complex (*zaibatsu*). The Chinese labourers are further betrayed by a Korean labourer and a Chinese
'comfort woman' (comfort women were employed/conscripted by the Japanese army to service Japanese soldiers as prostitutes during the war). Chinese labourers happily take advantage of Chinese 'comfort women', and
Kaji, despite trying to help the Chinese labourers, is not trusted by them
and not only suffers their recriminations but the retributions of his colleagues and torture by the *kenpeitai*. Therefore, within this system all are
implicated within cycles of exploitation. In the army the enemy is incidental; the conflict is the institutionalized internal rivalry between divisions and between veterans and new recruits. As Kaji states, 'The enemy
is not the senior soldiers. It is here, it is the army itself'. In the labour
camp, the conflict is between collaborators, who exploit their position,

and prisoners of war and a few good Soviet guards, who, taking Kaji's former role, try to intervene on behalf of the weak. During Kaji's wanderings in Manchuria, he meets Japanese 'comfort women' who find their new Soviet patrons more agreeable than their former Japanese patrons. They are later contrasted with the Japanese refugee who is raped and then discarded and thrown from a moving Soviet army truck. Similarly, the forced Chinese labourer Kao's relationship with a Chinese 'comfort woman', a relationship based on love and mutual respect, is contrasted with the brutal rape and murder of a fleeing Japanese 'comfort woman' by Chinese militia. As such the film is a critique of war that implicates humanity in general and not the Japanese in particular.

In this sense *The Human Condition*, through this depiction of manifold power relations that reduce everyone in varying degrees to the levels simultaneously of both victim and perpetrator, succeeds both as a pacifist statement and as a critic of societies founded on industrialism, militarism and Stalinism. The very concept of a *Rambo*-like 'goal-orientated hero' who takes on a problem and is victorious is alien to the reality of the worldview depicted in *The Human Condition*. To borrow Foucault's term, the 'technologies' of power at work on the individual are so great that not even the exceptional strength, both physical and moral, of Kaji can withstand them. All that the individual can do is acknowledge his complicity as an unwilling vehicle of these mechanisms and make restitution in death. This then brings us back to Onuma's statement quoted at the beginning of this chapter regarding the duty of the individual to disobey illegal orders under the terms of the Tokyo Trial. 'Most people are ordinary citizens and not heroes. To disobey an illegal order is to call for heroic actions, something one cannot unconditionally demand of people' (Onuma 1993: 52).

Kaji becomes the quintessential 'subject-as-victim' in attempting to live up to the humanist ideals of a society founded on concepts of justice and the rule of law. 'It is not a crime that I am Japanese, but my greatest crime is that I am Japanese'. Within these lines, repeated twice in the film by Kaji, lies the core of the dilemma. The geographical and temporal arbitrariness of birth condemned Kaji, despite his own beliefs in humanism, which were at odds with the current social ethos. Thus his life becomes a contest between two opposing ethos—the only possible solution is his death, as the 'technologies' of power operating upon him are too great for one to withstand.

*The Human Condition* presents a bleak worldview in which the individual 'subject-as-victim' is powerless to alter the circumstances that govern his/her life, and the position of the majority, who often compromise their ideals for the perceived 'greater good', is thereby legitimated. I would argue that it is for this reason that *The Human Condition* was so popular with audiences, particularly the war generation, who were confronted not only with defeat but a foreign-imposed sense of guilt that accompanied the War Crimes Trials. Kurosawa Akira's films from the mid-1950s present a similar bleak worldview (*Record of a Living Being* and *The Bad Sleep Well*) transposed into the post-occupation *mise-en-scène*.

In Japan, the post-defeat decade meant Allied Occupation, political revolution, and economic and social upheaval. Filmmakers Kurosawa Akira, Shindō Kaneto, Shibuya Minoru, Kinoshita Keisuke and Ozu Yasujirō, amongst others, all produced films that were concerned with the moral and ethical foundations of the actualities of life. *Stray Dog* showed how in times of social upheaval and high unemployment a de-mobbed soldier could easily turn to crime and murder. *Drunken Angel* took up the issue of the black market and de-mobbed soldiers falling into the hands of the yakuza. *No Consultations Today* depicted, amongst other things, the vulnerability of single young women coming to the cities in search of work. *Children of the Bomb* documented the lives of children living with the lingering consequences of radiation. Thematically, films produced in the post-defeat decade are therefore products of the existential upheavals of the war and occupation, and on another level, they are also products of the second wave of modernization that came about due to postwar economic reconstruction. Hence many of the same themes and stylistic conventions found in the 1930s 'social realist' films were carried over into the post-defeat decade. Ozu Yasujirō, a specific example, was able to continue making films that transcended the specifics of Japan by focusing on the decline of family and questions of social alienation in the material world of urban modernity.

Both *Beyond the Clouds* and *The Human Torpedoes* followed narrative and stylistic conventions established in the immediate post-defeat period, primarily by giving the heroes a private life and a psychological depth through which wartime propaganda is challenged while at the same time maintaining, through the depiction of the heroic image of the kamikaze, a particular ideal of masculinity. This was in part achieved through the creation of a weak alter ego in the characters portrayed by Kimura Isao, a narrative strategy previously employed by Kurosawa Akira in *Stray Dog* (1949) where Kimura is cast as the criminal Yusa in opposition to Mifune

Toshirō's police detective, Murakami. This device provided a counterpoint against which the more perfect heroes, who are constructed as pure, masculine, ideal types, could be measured. Within this narrative construction moralities are personalized with weakness often being equated with the feminine, a trait which in the kamikaze film must be overcome.

The desire to reclaim the image of the kamikaze in these films should be understood from the social context of a callow humanitarian questioning, 'What do you tell the dead when you lose?' Dower cites the example of Nanbara Shigeru, a Christian educator who became president of Tokyo University. In a speech he made to returning students in November 1945 he opened up a discourse in which war was condemned while the war dead were honoured. Nanbara told his students,

> that the real victors in the war were 'reason and truth' and that the United States and Britain, not Japan, had been the bearers of these great ideals. This was a victory to be celebrated, and both defeat and the supreme sacrifice of those who had died should be seen from this perspective. Out of tragedy a new national life would be born, although not without struggle . . . He concluded dramatically by welcoming back not only those present before him, but also their 'comrades in battle' who had perished. From this time forward, those who had survived the war would be engaged in a new 'war of truth' together with these departed comrades whose images remained in their hearts. (Dower 1999: 488–489)

The contradictions inherent in this desire to condemn war while simultaneously reclaiming the image of the kamikaze was reflected in the ideological confusion that surrounded the reception of these films. In an article published in the film journal *Kinema Junpō* in 1953, the author quotes the reactions of a youth after seeing *Beyond the Clouds*. 'The film depicts the pilots of the kamikaze Special Attack Forces gathered on the front-line before leaving on their missions. These officers struggle with questions of life, death and love before going on to an heroic death' (*Best of Kinema Junpō 1950–1966*: 225). The article goes on to question whether this youth was in fact feeling a sense of 'nostalgia' (*nosutarujia*) for Japan 'as a country of the Gods rather than being conscious of the anti-war elements of the film'. As the above analysis has shown, these films play on the nostalgia for a past that offered a level of male bonding not possible in a society based on competitive individualism. In this sense they can be read as a critique of the materialism of modern postwar society.

While men were portrayed as victims of the wartime regime, romance re-inscribed women within passive feminine role positions in films such as *Until the Day We Meet Again* (1950) and the record-breaking box-office hit *What Is Your Name?* (1953–1954) As the postwar generation sought to redefine the foundations of marriage within the democratic terms of the postwar Constitution, women's political rights were deflected onto a woman's right to choose a marriage partner. However, there is one overriding thematic concern that both unites films produced in the post-defeat decade and links them stylistically, and that is the belief in a fundamental humanism in which no one is to be reduced to an object or a symbol. In stylistic terms, these films—although built upon existing 'social realist' formats— reflect a compelling urge to explore new forms that place the individual in a central position in relation to the social. These attempts to develop new expressive forms to articulate the human situation came at an historical juncture when existing formulations were no longer adequate. However, the extent to which these new forms could depict the truth of war and occupation was limited by many factors, not least the SCAP occupation censorship authorities coupled with the Yoshida-led elite's desire to minimize the effects of change. This was compounded by a popular desire to give some purpose to the sacrifices made by the war dead. It was only from the mid-1950s that the betrayal of ideals of 'democracy', due to the exigencies of the Cold War and its manifestation in the 'reverse course' policy, fully impacted on film content and was portrayed in films such as *A Japanese Tragedy*, the war epic *The Human Condition* and the socially critical films of Kurosawa Akira, *Living*, *Record of a Living Being* and *The Bad Sleep Well*. Within these films the multifarious forces of power at work on the individual are so great that, apart from the old bureaucrat Watanabe in *Living*, the individual does not achieve what he sets out to do but is instead crushed by sociopolitical 'technologies' of power. Even in the case of Watanabe (Shimura Takashi 1905–1982), he does oversee the building of the park for the children, but the film ends on a bleak note, as it is obvious that he was an aberration and that after his death the system will continue unabated.

The screenplay writer and filmmaker Itami Mansaku (1900–1946) predicted this trend as early as August 1946 in his essay entitled 'The Question of War Responsibility' (*Sensō sekininsha no mondai*) in which he questions the acceptability of 'passive resistance' through an analysis of his own actions during the war. In this essay, in prophetic terms, he challenged the notion of 'deception' (*damasareru*) that fed so conveniently into the 'subject-as-victim' theme. Itami is clear in his opposition to the war; however, he makes the point that he did nothing to actively protest against war. This forms part of his argument in support of the call for 'self-reflection,' which was clearly prompted by the growing popular sense that we the people were victims of the war because we were 'deceived' by our leaders and therefore cannot be held accountable for the war. Itami extrapolates:

> The crime of being deceived is not included in the actuality of simply being deceived, it is bad in itself, in that, by being deceived, we lose the ability to criticize, we lose our ability to think, we lose our faith, and like domestic animals we entrust ourselves in blind obedience. Culturally the populace becomes spiritless, insensible, unable to reflect, and unwilling to accept responsibility.
>
> In substance this is equivalent to the period in Japan's history [here he is referring to the Meiji Restoration and drawing an analogy with the occupation] when without the threat of the foreign, we were unable to overthrow feudalism or the closed country policy with our own strength, we were not even able to secure fundamental human rights by our own efforts.
>
> And again, the populace is drawing close to a slave mentality in forgiving the people who supported tyranny and oppression.
>
> No matter in how small a way, this desecrates the dignity of the individual; namely it is an abandonment of the ego and a betrayal of humanity.

He continues:

> 'To have been deceived', is a convenient and effective phrase to indulge in, when I look at the extremely easy attitude of the great number of people who are completely released from responsibility by this phrase, I cannot help feel gloomy and insecure about the future for the Japanese people.
>
> If we become a race that happily says 'I was deceived', then it is likely that in the future we will be deceived many times. Yes, I am sure that even now, at the present time, we have begun to be deceived by yet another lie. (Itami 1961 vol. i: 209–210)

CHAPTER 5

# Cinema and Transgression

Why are criminals bad? (*Hanzaisha naze warui*). (Ōshima 1993: 126)

Our generation is a fatherless generation. (*Bokura no sedai wa, chichi naki sedai nan desu yo.*) (Ōshima 1993: 132)

In the previous chapter I argued that, in the light of public discourses surrounding the War Crimes Trials and SCAP interventions in Japanese society through a policy of 'democratization', two dominant narrative themes emerged in the newly politicized film industry of the era of the post-Tōhō Studio strikes. These thematic trends were centred around, on the one hand, a Kurosawa-styled humanism, which, as with the Western humanist philosophical tradition, designated a secular worldview based on the belief in the individual's capacity for self-cultivation and improvement. Linked to this is the view that each human is an autonomous being capable of self-determination and the assumption that through an individual's choices he/she can alter society and effect the course of history (*No Regrets for Our Youth/Waga seishun ni kuinashi* [1946], *Drunken Angel/Yoidore tenshi* [1948], *Stray Dog/ Nora inu* [1949] and *Living/Ikiru* [1952]). On the other hand, there is the more dominant derivative 'victimization' (*higaisha ishiki*) theme, characterized by the films of, amongst others, Kinoshita Keisuke (1912–1998), Imai Tadashi (1912–1992), Kobayashi Masaki (1916–1996) and Ieki Miyoji (1911–1976). In these films the individual is often depicted as a powerless pawn, caught in the machinations of a geo-historical trajectory that, in its cinematic form, transforms *mise-en-scène* as location into a causal force acting against the individual (*A Japanese Tragedy/Nihon no higeki* [1953], *Twenty-four Eyes/Nijūshi no hitomi* [1954], *The Human Condition/Ningen no jōken* [1959–1961], *Until the Day We Meet Again* aka *Till We Meet Again/Mata au hi made* [1950], *Memorial to the Lilies* aka *Tower of the Lilies/Himeyuri no tō* [1953] and [1982], and *Beyond the Clouds/Kumo nagaruru hateni* [1953]). The avant-garde director Ōshima Nagisa (1932–), in his analysis of the Japanese film industry in the decade following defeat, argues that these trends were part of a rearguard action as the mainstream film industry drifted back into a conservative mould as the 'reverse course' policy took effect in American/Japanese relations. Allied to this was the reinstatement by 1950 of the many former studio controllers dominant during the war period. In his book, *An Experiential Discussion of Postwar Film (Taikenteki sengo eizōron)*[1], Ōshima illustrates this turn of events by drawing on his own experiences at Kyoto University under Professor Takikawa Yukitoki (1891–1962), the left-leaning academic Kurosawa Akira modelled Yukie's father on, in *No Regrets for Our Youth*. Ōshima was deeply impressed as a young fourteen-year-old viewing *No Regrets for Our Youth* with the images of 'shining youth', which so contrasted with the experiential reality of his generation that came of age during the war. In his conclusion he makes the observation that Professor Takikawa Yukitoki, who was reinstated at Kyoto University in 1946, becoming president in 1953, was himself instrumental in opposing the postwar students' movements and thus negated his wartime status as champion of free and open debate. In an earlier article (1958) and in more abstract terms Ōshima deals with this same issue:

> For some years after the war, the struggle against the pre-modern system and for human freedom and human rights was carried on passionately in the midst of a chaotic Japanese society. The film industry, too, retained works with the traditional pre-modern form and content on the one hand, while making films whose content struggled against the traditional on the other. At that time, artists like Kinoshita, Imai, and Kurosawa won the immeasurable support of the young film audience. Immediately after the war, however, the power of the government, in the form of a democracy-promoting institution, once again began to defend openly the pre-modern tendencies of Japanese society. A little later, such a defence occurred in the context of film as well. However, the quest for human freedom and human rights continued. Supported by that quest, artists like Kinoshita, Imai, and Kurosawa continued to fight a splendidly beautiful battle from around 1950 onward . . . However, from the latter half of the 1950s, a decade after the end of the war, the chaos of that time initially receded and things basically stabilized materially. (Ōshima 1992: 31–32, translated by Dawn Lawson)

In thematic terms Ōshima and other radical filmmakers of his generation, such as Yoshida Yoshishige (1933–) and Imamura Shōhei (1926–), sought to carry on the struggle for a political cinema and, in so doing, their struggle exerted an immeasurable influence on both film style and, through the narrative content of their films, they pushed the boundaries of social mores. As Ōshima explains in a joint interview with Yoshida Yoshishige published in *Kinema Junpō* in August 1960, 'For us making a film is an action. It is not the case that we turn something into a film as a product. In the case of film-making, we think of it as a social action (*yononaka hitotsu no kōi*)' (*Best of Kinema Junpō 1950–1966*, 1994: 948). In the same interview he goes on to explain that he felt cinema was a medium through which one could bridge the gap between the masses (*taishū*) and the so-called intellectual class (*interi*) and that this was a major factor in his motivation to work in the industry. Ultimately, these radical directors attempted to create a socially transgressive cinema that, particularly through the positive reception of Ōshima's films on the international 'art house' cinema circuit, impacted on world trends in filmmaking.

### Changing Masculinities in the *Season of the Sun* (*Taiyō no kisetsu*)

In July 1956, Nakahira Kō breezed onto the scene with *Crazed Fruit* . . . In the rip of a woman's skirt and the buzz of a motorboat, sensitive people heard the heralding of a new generation of a new Japanese film. (Ōshima 1992: 26, translated by Dawn Lawson)

In the second half of the 1950s and on into the 1960s, sex and crime increasingly became the transgressive mediums through which dominant social values were challenged. As the analysis in the preceding chapter has demonstrated, in films of the early postwar period romantic love, that is the love between a man and a woman, is reified as the antithesis to war, destruction and death. In these mainstream studio productions, romantic love is denied, or consummation delayed, as a social consequence of war and/or an ideology grounded in a pure masculinity. Within these narratives, individual desire is pitted against the macro-political machinations of the nation at war. As romantic love is either delayed or denied consummation, it retains a reified tragic purity, becoming an expression of the individual subject, which in an allegorical sense came to represent postwar humanism. However, in the films of Japan's newly emergent radical directors from the mid-1950s on into the 1960s and early 1970s, sex and crime increasingly replaced the pure love characteristic of the romance elements in *Until the Day We Meet Again, What Is Your Name? (Kimi no na wa* 1953–1954), *Beyond the Clouds* and *The Human Condition*, becoming the expressive mediums through which a radical individuality is asserted.

These young directors, often critical of the hypocrisy of post-war Japanese governments and the failure of Japanese society to live up to the promises of 'democracy', challenged this humanism as it was depicted in mainstream cinema. Following on from the theoretical positions adopted by Sakaguchi Ango (1906–1955) and others of the post-defeat period, they challenged humanism by exposing the ideological constructedness of reified romantic love by subverting it to carnal desire and taking it through to consummation, perversion, crime and punitive acts of violence. In this way the pure spiritual love of unconsummated romance is defeated through the body by corporeal desire. The locus of the individual is therefore shifted to the materialism of the body and not some abstract ideological essence associated with the spirit. However, as the following analysis will demonstrate, this re-assertion of carnal desire as the essence of subjectivity was often complicated by the libidinal economy of the filmmakers concerned and was perforce a masculine-defined and ultimately misogynistic subjectivity.

Following closely in the wake of Hollywood's Marlon Brando (*A Streetcar Named Desire* [1951] and *The Wild One* [1953]) and James Dean (*Rebel Without a Cause* [1955] and *East of Eden* [1955]), Ishihara Yūjirō (1934–1987), in the hedonistic Nikkatsu films of the 'sun tribe' (*taiyōzoku*) youth culture, became the first star to embody these themes. As a result, the construction of Ishihara Yūjirō's star persona marks an important turning point in the creation of Japanese male film stars in the postwar period. He was the first to establish certain conventions that would successfully be repeated with minor variations throughout the industry in the 1960s and 1970s, the marketing of the male star being one of the dominant marketing strategies of product differentiation adopted by the major studios until their terminal decline in the late 1960s and 1970s.

In *Season of the Sun* (*Taiyō no kisetsu*) (1956) and *Crazed Fruit* aka *Affair At Kamakura/Juvenile Passion/ This Scorching Sea* (*Kurutta kajitsu*) (1956), both based on novels by Yūjirō's elder brother Ishihara Shintarō (1932–), affluent, disaffected youth destroy themselves and others in an *apparent* nihilistic rebellion against the work ethic morality of their parents' culture. However, in reality, two far more complex and threatening discourses affecting the changing status of masculinity in newly emerging affluent, consumerist Japanese society are played out in these dramas. The first is connected to the re-emergence of the independent woman in postwar society (the 'modern girl' of the 1930s representing the first wave).

The second and related issue is the commodification and display of the male body. These issues combined, necessitated both a re-negotiation of the place of women within the political economy of masculine exchange and, relatedly, a re-negotiation of the binary, active/male–passive/female gender dichotomy. In both films, the former is avowed through the narratives only to be disavowed with the death of the heroines at the end of the films, while the latter is resolved through a naturalized male rite of passage.

In *Season of the Sun* the narrative evolves around the shifting positions of male characters as active agents in their pursuit of women and as passive objects of female desire. As the characters are ostensibly high school students, this negotiation of the masculine position within the phallocentric economy of the film is presented as a rite of passage to manhood. The setting of the male group within the framework of a high school boxing club establishes the primacy of male/male relations through homosocial bonding rituals associated with sport (violent competition) and the ritualistic 'girl hunt' (*gāru hanto*), while legitimating the visual display of young muscular male bodies (in the boxing ring and in the showers, etc.). Equally the heroine's intrusion into the boxing club, this bastion of maleness, accentuates her (by the standards of film's sexual politics) perverse role as active desiring subject. She enters the boxing club in pursuit of the male lead, Tatsuya (Nagato Hiroyuki 1934–), thereby inverting the role of male pursuer and female pursued established in an earlier sequence when the boys from the club go out on the town and aggressively chase girls in the 'girl hunt'.

Eiko and her two friends are first constructed as desiring subjects during the inter-high school boxing championships where Tatsuya is competing for his school. Prior to his bout, Tatsuya in the locker room, with other members of his team, symbolically disavows the feminine by punching at a bunch of flowers Eiko had sent him. However during his actual bout, the camera and the sound track both foreground the three girls seated amidst a sea of male supporters in their black school uniforms. The camera and sound track thus highlight the transgressive nature of the scene by visually reinforcing the crossing of established gender boundaries between the active (male) gaze and the passive (feminine) 'to-be-looked-at-ness'. The sound track privileges the girls' calls of encouragement rising shrilly against the background of male cheers, while the camera documents the exchange of looks between Tatsuya, vulnerable and seminaked in the ring, and the three girls seated securely amongst the crowd of spectators. After the fight and after Tatsuya has been fixed up at the hospital, Eiko collects him in the family car and takes him to a nightclub. It is clear from the conversation and Eiko's actions that the terms of relationship have shifted as Tatsuya is now being actively pursued by Eiko.

Just prior to the scene depicting the consummation of their physical relationship, Eiko again actively seeks Tatsuya out at the boatyard. After driving around in Tatsuya's motorboat they go to his family's holiday house. Tatsuya is filmed from a low angle, naked in the shower, water running down his smooth back, accentuating the muscle structure of his upper arms while Eiko, fully clad in a demure dress with a crew neck, sits in his room on the bed. Tatsuya enters the room with just a towel knotted around his waist; his seminakedness is highlighted by his mother, who reprimands him for wandering around the house 'naked' (*hadaka*). Then he appears at the door of his room and a series of reverse-cut shots establishes mutual desire, but when Tatsuya moves towards Eiko, she immediately regains control as the active agent ordering him to punch the sandbag. The camera, from her point of view, holds on Tatsuya in a medium close-up as he punches the bag before cutting back to Eiko in a desiring subject position. The scene ends with Eiko coming up behind Tatsuya and grabbing him in an embrace. He swings round, picking her up in his arms, and takes her to the bed, slamming the sliding door shut. The camera lingers on the sandbag, abandoned but still swinging from the force of Tatsuya's punches, before cutting to a shot of the same room, only now it is dark, signalling a time ellipsis.

After this physical consummation of their relationship, the positions of active subject and desiring object are again reversed as Eiko reverts to a passive female position, waiting for Tatsuya. There follows several meetings and partings designed to display Tatsuya's newfound assertiveness. Symbolically, in this latter half of the film, when not at the beach, Eiko wears a kimono, a shift traditionally associated with marriage. Finally, pregnancy seals her fate. Tatsuya asserts his newfound patriarchal authority by refusing to legitimate her and her unborn baby's social position in marriage, and Eiko is punished through death on the abortionist's table. Her transgression was not becoming pregnant before marriage, but rather by being an active desiring subject she had reduced Tatsuya to a passive desired object; to become a man he had to gain authority in the patriarchal economy of the film. The film thus conflates and solves two problems associated with postwar masculinity: the containment of women within a re-defined 'democratic' sexual economy that re-asserts the primacy of the

male, while simultaneously displacing the homoerotic element implicit in
the display of young male bodies for male spectators onto the desiring
gaze of a heterosexual woman.

Under the conditions of a re-emergent consumerist economy, masculinity increasingly became re-defined in the commodity terms of a narcissistic desire to be channelled into consumption. Ōshima, in *An
Experiential Discussion of Postwar Film*, elaborates on the question of the
commodification of the star in the postwar Japanese film industry and the
relationship of film fans to stars. He argues that, historically, one of the
great appeals of cinema has been the depiction of the human face in close-
up. Following on from scholars such as Susan Sontag[2], he links this to
trends in classical art, in particular to the development of the portrait and
later to the commemorative photograph in that it captures a moment in
time, a sensibility. Like commemorative photographs, the close-up and
more specifically the pinup seal a moment in an image of the actor's star
persona. He continues, '[T]he predilection [of fans] with the star pin-up,
is based on a desire to possess the star, it is the manifestation of the spectator's desire to possess the star in a moment of symbiosis. It is the pin-up
that provides a limited satisfaction of this desire. As the fan possesses the
pin-up, he possesses the star and gains a symbiosis through possession . . .'
Ōshima goes on to explain that this desire to possess the star was structured into the economics of the industry.

> In this sense the situation is perverse. It is not the case that because s/he is
> a star that the pin-up sells, it is because the pin-up sells that s/he becomes
> a star . . .
>     It is not the case that the fan him/herself loves the star in the film, they
> come to love the star in the pin-up. Furthermore, rather than the star being
> the seeming object of love it is closer to a narcissistic love. Therefore, a
> strange phenomenon has occurred whereby one can purchase the pin-up
> before the film is released. When this happens, the situation is reversed and
> the condition of becoming a star is to be photogenic. Someone who is pho-
> togenic is easily turned into private property. (Ōshima 1978:221)

In the *taiyōzoku* films, two strategies are employed in order to disavow
the homoerotic element implicit in the narcissistic commodification of the
masculine image for male spectators. On the one hand as outlined above,
desire is displaced onto female characters, who, in keeping with their new
perceived political/legal independence, become active agents. On another

level, it is disavowed through the male star persona. In the case of Ishihara Yūjirō, his body paradoxically works on two inter-dependant but contradictory levels as both proof of his virility and as that which turns him into the passive object of the spectator's gaze (see figure 14). In order to elide the passivity the display of his seminaked body invites, he affects an 'unaffectedness' that is supported through publicity material, which emphasizes his virility through a 'tough guy' image in articles titled, 'The Appeal of the Tough Guy: A Sketch of Ishihara Yūjirō' (*Tafu gai no miryoku Ishihara Yūjirō no sobyō*).[3] More important, in promoting the image of Ishihara as unaffected, the editors of *Kinema Junpō* in an article published in 1958, 'Has Yūjirō Advanced Japanese Films?' devote much space to Ishihara's acting style, which they describe as 'natural'[4] by making a distinction between acting styles in theatre and film. They quote the director Tasaka Tomotaka (1902–1974), who, having made several films starring Ishihara including *The Pram* aka *The Baby Carriage* (*Ubaguruma*) in 1956 and *The Sunny Hill Path* (*Hi no ataru sakamichi*) in 1958, makes the astute observation that although his style is apparently spontaneous and therefore unaffected, it is nonetheless still a style that Ishihara has cultivated.

'Since former times, when young stars emerged existing theories of acting have been overthrown, but large or small, there were none who caused such a violent change as Yūjirō . . . [His] quality of film acting is different from other young actors. How one theorizes this form of acting is extremely problematic. Some have explained it as non-acting. However, although it does not conform to traditional acting methods, I think it is correct to consider it acting. (Quoted in *Best of Kinema Junpō 1950–1966*, 1994: 728)

Another critic, echoing Ōshima's analysis of the role of the pinup in the fan/star relationship, goes on to describe the effect this acting style has on young audiences: 'Generally between characters on the screen and young spectators there was a psychological distance. However, in films starring Ishihara Yūjirō, a sense of affinity penetrates into the hearts of young spectators sitting in the audience' (*Best of Kinema Junpō 1950–1966*, 1994: 728). This sense of 'affinity' the editors again link to Ishihara's style of acting, a style, they argue, to which young spectators can relate—in other words, an 'unaffectedness' that permits a narcissistic identification that disavows the concomitant passive position of the star as object to be admired. Another complicating element was related to Western, particularly American, influences, as the ideal masculine type offered for display was predicated on the star personas of James Dean (1931–1955) and Marlon Brando (1924–2004).

The granting of political and legal autonomy to women under the terms of the postwar Constitution reverberated most strongly in a woman's right to choose a marriage partner. As a result, the relationship between men and women within the political economy of marriage altered drastically. In the premodern system of 'arranged marriages,' women's place as object of exchange between men was clearly defined. Under the terms of women's newfound political/legal autonomy, a woman's place within the phallocentric economy of 'the sun tribe' (*taiyōzoku*) films is reduced to that of a fetish to be exchanged between men, her active status thus rendered harmless. While *Season of the Sun* both contained women within a misogynistic narrative that emphasized the positive aspects of the bonds of the male group, *Crazed Fruit* depicted a woman's potential to destroy those bonds and the men associated with her. The sultry, *noir*-like heroine of *Crazed Fruit*, played by Kitahara Mie (1933–), soon to become Ishihara Yūjirō's wife, simultaneously exists as the object of exchange between her aged American husband and two Japanese brothers, the sophisticated and cynical *taiyōzoku* youth played by Ishihara Yūjirō and his younger naive brother played by Tsugawa Masahiko (1940–). The plot, drawing on a subplot of sibling rivalry (established in Elia Kazan's *East of Eden* [1955]) of the earlier film *Season of the Sun*, complicates the situation by giving the heroine and the two male leads a psychological depth that depicts the pain involved in the transgression of established gender boundaries. In other words, where in *Season of the Sun* the transgression of gender boundaries was allegorized through geographical place, the heroine's entry into the male world of the boxing club, in *Crazed Fruit* she impacts on her male admirers at a psychological level that ultimately destroys them all. The Westernized Frank (Okada Masumi 1935–), a son of a mixed-blood marriage, provides the 'ideal' counterpoint to the two Japanese brothers, both of whom break the rules of the male group by giving the heroine an intrinsic value beyond that of her sexual exchange value. The depiction of the heroine as *noir*-like ensures that the intrinsic value the two Japanese youths attribute to her is palpably misplaced. She is, after all, a married woman having affairs. The nihilism of the film's renowned final scene, as the younger brother turns his motorboat on the heroine swimming in the sea, killing her, before crashing his boat into his brother's small sailing yacht and killing him, confirms the fundamental rule for the maintenance of the harmony of the male group: that women should not be valued other then as objects of exchange. An earlier scene in the film both illustrates and complicates this point when the mixed-blood youth Frank is accosted at a fairground with his Japanese girlfriend. He is confronted by a group of local Japanese lads who make racist aspersions; to placate them Frank immediately offers to hand over his girlfriend. She naturally walks out on him in a scene that shocks the naive Haruji.

Within these films women are inscribed into new 'democratic' systems of patriarchal exchange as their newfound assertiveness, their right to choose a husband, is crushed at a most brutal level. In *Season of the Sun*, the boyfriend, by refusing to marry his pregnant girlfriend, re-asserts patriarchal authority as he withholds social legitimacy. In *Crazed Fruit* the *noir*-like heroine is devalued as she simultaneously has a sexual relationship with three men. Therefore, the two Japanese brothers' ascription of an intrinsic value to her is mistaken. It is a fatal mistake of youth that will destroy their lives. Haruji survives and has clearly gone through his 'rite of passage' but at the cost of becoming a murderer. Only Frank, as the Westernized youth, is fully conversant with the rules of the sexual economy of masculine exchange in the advanced consumerist culture of the film's *mise-en-scène*.

In these two 1956 *taiyōzoku* films, the main characters' subjectivities are further complicated by the clash of cultures inscribed in the films' consumerist ethos. Japanese youths live the life of the affluent American middle class. Cars, nightclubs, beach houses and boats: leisure is inscribed into the lifestyles of the *taiyōzoku* generation just as the work ethic of postwar reconstruction had been for their parents' generation, a means of self-definition. Consumption of leisure and the cultivation of a seemingly non-Japanese style became the hallmarks of their identity. The instability of their identities is thus extended beyond that of the negotiation of masculinity in adolescence to that of both class and ethnicity. This is alluded to in the Blue Sky nightclub sequence in *Crazed Fruit*, when a waiter, mistaking Frank for a foreigner, apologizes and asks in English what he would like to drink. While the other Japanese youths all order Black and White whiskey or American bourbon, Frank replies by asking if they have any *shōchū*, a working-class drink made from sweet potatoes. As the following analysis will demonstrate, in subsequent films starring Ishihara Yūjirō in the late 1950s and early 1960s, this negotiation of identity and subjectivity remained important.

**The Fatherless Generation**

> Our generation is a fatherless generation. When I look at our fathers' gen-
> eration, who defeated in war did not accept responsibility and who even in
> the post-war period continued with the lies, I feel that we are a generation
> of orphans. (Ōshima 1993: 132)

Ishihara Yūjirō's third film of 1956, *The Pram,* marks the beginnings of a
reclamation and re-inscription of youth politics within mainstream cinema
and society that can in part be attributed to a media moral backlash against
the perceived nihilism of *taiyōzoku* antiheroes. *The Pram* clearly seeks a
moral cause for youthful disaffection and shifts narrative causal motivation from desire back to the myth of romance. This is achieved through
the depiction of a generational clash over sexual mores, not as one would
expect with rebellious youth resisting parental control, but the reverse, an
emphasis on the centrality of monogamy in postwar marriage. It is the
father who, in the postwar age of 'democracy' and the nuclear family,
transgresses by remaining within an outdated premodern morality that allowed him to maintain two families. The film clearly condemns the father
figure (Uno Jūkichi 1914–1988) as both women, his wife (Yamane Hisako
1921–1990) and his mistress (Aratama Michio 1930–2001), drawing on
their new-found freedom and a new ethic closely related to the ideal of
monogamy between marriage partners, abandon him. The wife sets up a
small bar/nightclub in Tokyo and the mistress refuses the father's offer
of financial support and chooses to work and raise their child as a single
mother.

The character Muneo, played by Ishihara Yūjirō, the mistress's
younger brother; and Yumiko (Ashikawa Izumi 1935–), the adolescent
daughter of the main wife and father, as representatives of the new morality, are instrumental in guiding the parent generation, acting as mediators
between the two families. In this sense Ishihara Yūjirō's character, as representative of one extreme side of the generational divide in the *taiyōzoku*
films, is softened. Therefore, like Bandō Tsumasaburō (1901–1953) before
him, we can follow a similar reclamation of Ishihara's image through the
historical trajectory of his star persona as developed by the Nikkatsu Studio. In this sense it is possible to draw a parallel with films from the late
1920s and 1930s as the rebellious hero, alienated by the machinations of
modernity, is inscribed into mainstream society through the myth of romance. In both ages, the responses to rapid sociopolitical changes and

their implications for masculinity were similar, and many films of the late 1920s/1930s and those of the late 1950s/1960s represented a backlash, an attempt at a re-definition or re-assertion of masculinity built upon quasi-traditional concepts. Like the star persona of Bandō Tsumasaburō before him, Ishihara Yūjirō is thus a good example of the shift that occurred in the latter half of the 1950s from a political cinema, as defined by Ōshima above, to the conservative sensibility that was to dominate mainstream Japanese cinema until its decline through the late 1960s and 1970s.

The generational fissures in *Season of the Sun, Crazed Fruit* and *The Pram* are elaborated on in many of Ishihara's subsequent films of the late 1950s. *Season of the Sun* and *Crazed Fruit* toyed with a nihilistic characterization of youth by avoiding historical contextualizations. The two 1956 *taiyōzoku* films present the narratives within a specific temporal frame in which the characters are constrained—there is no memory, there are no flashbacks and no future plans—only the present exists, a narrative device later adopted by Ōshima in three of his early productions (*Town of Love and Hope/Ai to kibō no machi, Cruel Story of Youth* aka *Cruel Tales of Youth/Seishun zankoku monagatari* and *The Sun's Burial/Taiyō no hakaba*). However, in subsequent films starring Ishihara Yūjirō, the past enters the narratives and fills in the voids in our knowledge. In this way rebellious youth is given a legitimating cause. As part of this reclamation process, the intrusion of the past into the narratives provides answers to our questions and allows the spectator to feel sympathy and/or empathy with the characters Ishihara Yūjirō portrays. The answers, the films tell us, lie in the generational change in attitudes towards marriage and morality. The parents' generation represent a prewar, outdated morality that allowed affluent men to maintain more than one household and/or permitted the patronage of geisha, while Ishihara and his generation came to represent the new postwar 'democratic' ideals defined in the myth of romance, monogamy and the expression of individual subjectivity through mutual fulfilment in marriage.

The families depicted within these films are perforce affluent; in this sense Ishihara Yūjirō is allowed to stay within the *taiyōzoku* consumerist ethos of the idle rich. It also affords the fathers the financial position to maintain secondary households, therefore setting up the ethical divisions between the two generations. Within these films the role of the father figure is precarious, as they are the emasculated representatives of the generation who lost the war and were criminalized through war crimes trials. They play the benign postwar *papa* while simultaneously maintaining a visible, but morally redundant, display of economic power by having mistresses and children by women other than their wives. Within the narratives this contradiction is often solved through the mother figure, who accepts her husband's infidelities and sometimes rears the children of such liaisons herself (*The Sunny Hill Path*). In the 1961 comedy *That Fellow and Me* aka *That Guy and I* (*Aitsu to watashi*), directed by Nakahira Kō (1926–1978), this situation is parodied through reversal. The *mama* figure is a successful businesswoman of the postwar age of affluence. She owns a chain of beauty parlours, and her emasculated, physically small husband reared the child while she worked. Not only is he designated a house *papa* but his wife openly has a boyfriend who freely comes and goes from the house; later it becomes clear the Ishihara Yūjirō character is not his child but his wife's child by another man. Within the economies of these films, the younger generation must successfully negotiate a new basis for their own relationships. The characters played by Ishihara Yūjirō must go through a rite of self-discovery both in terms of the negotiation of gender boundaries and also questions of social identity, as these characters often discover that they are the child of an affair. In other words, they are not who they thought they were. The rite of passage these youthful characters go through in the films is linked to self-discovery through an investigation into their families' past. In the parodic terms of the comedy *That Fellow and Me*, the Ishihara Yūjirō character's confusion over gender issues, ostensibly brought about by his parents' transgression of established dichotomies, is played out in a scene of cross-dressing. Ishihara Yūjirō dresses in women's clothes after he is pushed into a swimming pool by a group of college girls. In terms of identity in *The Sunny Hill Path*, the Ishihara Yūjirō character discovers he is the result of a liaison his father had with a geisha and that he has a younger half-brother reared by his biological mother; in the case of *That Fellow and Me*, he discovers that the *papa* who raised him is not his biological father. His mother had had an affair with a man who went to America and made his fortune and has now returned to Japan seeking an heir.

While *Season of the Sun* and *Crazed Fruit* masked the insecurities of masculinity in the mid-1950s within an apparent nihilistic rebellion against the work ethic culture of their parents' generation, Ōshima's early films of the 1960s broadened this theme by locating it within a specific *mise-en-scène* that turned the apparent nihilistic actions of the protagonists into a political rebellion. *Cruel Story of Youth* brought youth politics back to the failures of the parents' generation, focusing on the consequences those failures had for the post-defeat generations. Drawing on many of the motifs associated with the *taiyōzoku* films (students, abortions, sun, sea and motorboats), the film frames the principal characters within a generational consciousness that clearly locates the causes of their tragedies within a political context of materialism allegorized through prostitution. Through these strategies, *Cruel Story of Youth* attacks the myth of romance that shores up the generational fissures raised in *The Pram* and *The Sunny Hill Path* through the re-inscription of youth into the political economy of monogamous marriage. *The Pram* concludes with a shot of the Ishihara Yūjirō character (the baby's uncle) and Yumiko (the baby's half sister) walking along the road with the baby in a pram—a pram they have just won at a baby competition at which they pretended to be the baby's parents. They have just telephoned the now scattered father, mother and mistress to invite them all to a party to celebrate the baby's success in the competition. The film ends with the young couple musing on whether the others will come. The implication, from the positive reactions of the three to the telephone calls, suggests that they will and a new pseudo-family will form around the innocent child and the young couple. *The Sunny Hill Path* and the comedy *That Fellow and Me* also conclude with the expectation of the marriage of the principal couples. *The Sunny Hill Path* concludes with the assumption that the Ishihara Yūjirō character, after marriage, will take over the responsibilities of the first son. The film, follows the plotline of *East of Eden,* having revealed that the elder brother (the biological son of the *mama* character) is morally weak. To further complicate matters, the Ishihara Yūjirō character's half brother (the son of the geisha by a different father) will marry his half sister (the daughter of his biological father and the main *mama*). Thus another complicated pseudo-family structure is formed. In *That Fellow and Me* the house-*papa* figure—who attempts to leave home, feeling redundant now that the children have grown up—is re-inscribed into another pseudo-family structure by the film's close as the Ishihara Yūjirō character and his intended point out that he will soon have grandchildren to look after. *Cruel Story of Youth,* by contrast, ends with the simultaneous deaths of the hero Kiyoshi (Kawazu Yūsuke 1935–) and the heroine Makoto (Kuwano Miyuki 1942–) in a nihilistic love suicide. Kiyoshi is beaten to death by a local gang of pimps with whom he had become entangled, and Makoto in attempting to escape from the sexual advances of an older man jumps from a moving car. Reminiscent of Omocha in *Sisters of Gion* (*Gion no kyōdai*) (1936), Makoto's foot is caught in the door, and she is dragged to her death. The parallel editing and the framing of this concluding scene links the two in a modern-day love suicide. The generational framework within which the film structures their relationship is the social force that determines the failure of their relationship and ultimately causes their deaths.

Unlike the *taiyōzoku* films in which generational conflict is structured within the narrative through absence or glossed over as in an early scene in *Season of the Sun* when the hero, the boxer Tatsuya, punches his father in the stomach as he is exercising in the garden, this conflict is structured as a causal force in the narrative of *Cruel Story of Youth*. It is complex and operates on three distinct levels: the parents' generation represented by Makoto's father; Kiyoshi's lover, an older woman to whom he prostitutes himself; and the men from whom Kiyoshi and Makoto extort money as part of their scam. An alternative conflict centres on the immediate post-defeat generation represented by Makoto's elder sister and her former romantic interest Akimoto, the doctor turned abortionist, and the seemingly nihilistic *taiyōzoku* generation represented by Kiyoshi and Makoto.

The film draws on intertextual referents to the 1956 *taiyōzoku* films, in particular, the centrality of the abortion to the rite of passage to manhood of the main character in *Season of the Sun*. In *Cruel Story of Youth*, the confrontation between the two postwar generations and Kiyoshi's emotional maturation takes place in a conversation over the abortionist's table. Makoto is lying on the table, still unconscious from the anaesthetic used during the operation. In *Season of the Sun*, although not depicted, in the penultimate sequence Tatsuya learns that Eiko has died during the abortion. In opposition to the Tatsuya character of *Season of the Sun*, part of Kiyoshi's rite of passage is his acceptance of Makoto's condition and his realization that his role within their relationship is one of provider and protector. In this way *Cruel Story of Youth* complicates the appropriation of blame. Unlike *Season of the Sun*, the characters in *Cruel Story of Youth* are not reduced to mere representations of the personalized moralities good and evil.

In the scene at Akimoto's surgery, Kiyoshi arrives only to find Makoto's elder sister, Yuki, already there. Dissatisfied with her life and inspired by Makoto, Yuki has come to try to re-kindle the passion of her youth with Akimoto. Until Kiyoshi arrives she is unaware that Makoto is in the next room or that Akimoto has resorted to carrying out backstreet abortions to supplement his income. Kiyoshi goes through to the next room divided by a flimsy wall through which the conversation between Akimoto and Yuki on the other side is clearly audible. The camera stays with Kiyoshi as he tenderly caresses Makoto's hands and face. Yuki and Akimoto continue their conversation, discussing how they tried to change the world through the student movement and how their desire had been channelled into romance that did not even permit the holding of hands. This conversation alludes to the betrayal of the immediate post-defeat generation of humanists whose dreams were shattered by the return to conservatism of the 'Yoshida doctrine'. Ōshima returns to this theme, the betrayal of the student movement, in *Night and Fog in Japan/Nihon no yoru to kiri*, his last film of 1960. However, in *Cruel Story of Youth,* in the surgery, Akimoto concludes that their generation had been defeated, and he goes on to speculate on the fate of Kiyoshi and Makoto:

> **Akimoto:** Your sister and her generation, by contrast, vent their rage against society by fulfilling all their desires. I wonder if they will win. For example, things like having to go through with this abortion will pile up and distort them and their relationship will be destroyed.

Kiyoshi, hearing this, angrily shouts back, 'It won't be destroyed'. After which the camera holds on a close-up of his forehead, his eyes highlighted by the key light. The other two continue their conversation, to which Kiyoshi adds, 'We have no dreams, so we will never end up wretched like you'. At this point he determinedly bites into an apple and continues eating as the camera holds on him. The words of Akimoto, the abortionist, are prophetic, however. After a brief interlude at the sea during which Makoto recovers and Kiyoshi experiences a genuine affection for her not based on desire as she is unable to have sex so soon after the abortion, they are arrested and the mechanisms of power operating on them in the social world are too great for them to overcome.

*Cruel Story of Youth* thus shifts the central motivating conflict of the *taiyōzoku* films from questions of gender boundaries and their transgression back to the generational fissures that arose out of defeat and the betrayal of the promises of 'democracy'. Makoto never challenges Kiyoshi's dominant position. The punishments she suffers are for reasons other than those suffered by the active Eiko in *The Season of the Sun* or the *noir*-like heroine of *Crazed Fruit*. The violence Makoto suffers at the hands of Kiyoshi is an outward manifestation of his general disaffection with the world. As he explains in the following conversation just after he has forced himself on her,

**Makoto:** You don't dislike me now, do you?
**Kiyoshi:** I just got a little angry. It's probably not that I am so angry
   with you.
**Makoto:** Well, what then?
**Kiyoshi:** Anything and everything.

Rape and their extortion racket within this context are manifestations
of male youths' general disaffection and not a vehicle for the containment/
punishment of women as in *Crazed Fruit*. Romance, as in the myth of romance of the post-defeat decade, and the corporeal desire of the two 1956
*taiyōzoku* films are, in *Cruel Story of Youth*, both equated with materialism
through prostitution, a theme to which Ōshima's next film, *The Sun's
Burial*, would return and develop. Kiyoshi is paid by an older woman to
have sex with her, and the older men whom Makoto asks to take her home
in their cars all attempt to exploit her. Even the apparently more sympathetic Horio ultimately exploits her, taking her to a hotel and spending the
night with her. When the two young people attempt to turn this corrupt
situation to their advantage through extortion, they are criminalized and
the agencies of the law return them to the very people who either exploit
them (the woman to whom Kiyoshi prostitutes himself) or who have
proved themselves incapable of protecting them (Makoto's benign father).
The law thus supports the exploitation of the young and powerless while
protecting the position of the exploitative parent generation. Within the
dystopian worldview of the film's *mise-en scène*, the acts of blackmail and
extortion committed by youth are not crimes; they become political acts
of disaffection and defiance. This theme of the exploitation of the powerless and weak through the commodification of their bodies is a central
theme of *The Sun's Burial*—not at the psychological level of a consumerist narcissistic identification with the likes of the Ishihara Yūjirō star
persona, but at the more basic level of the physical: the sale of blood, prostitutes and social identities through the sale of family registers (*koseki*).

   *The Sun's Burial,* although billed as the sequel to *Cruel Story of
Youth*[5], makes a strong statement on gender issues through the main female protagonist Hanako (Honō Kayoko 1941–). Perhaps more important, through its setting in the Osaka slum-district of Kamagasaki (now
known as Airin), it offers a critique of postwar society. The 'cruelty' of
the title of *Cruel Story of Youth* is in *The Sun's Burial mise-en-scène* of
Kamagasaki, the objective cruelty of a rapacious consumer society at its
lowest level. The intermittent tracking shots through the streets, alley-

ways and ruins of this district, where the poor of Osaka eke out their lives as day labourers, ragpickers and criminals, establishes the diegetic function of place as does the shot of industrial chimney stacks, which also provide a self-reflexive reference to the Ozu-style 'social realist' film. Only in this case the film presents no redeeming sense of community, no humanist compassion, because within the film's worldview there is no morality, as the characters have no moral reference except life itself.

## The 1960s: Ōshima Nagisa and the Cinema of Cruelty

> By the gaze that surprised him, by the finger that pointed at him, by the voice that called him a thief, the collectivity doomed him to Evil. They were waiting for him. (Sartre 1964: 31)

> The execution scaffold is waiting for us [Koreans]. (*Shikeidai ga bokura o matte iru*) (Yun 1968: 18)

The 1960s cinema of Ōshima Nagisa offers a vision of the cruel and the unjust through the creation of a counter-aesthetic that challenged the sentimentalism of the humanists. On the narrative level this was achieved through an often open-ended plot structure that fails to proffer moral solutions to the social problems raised in the films. On the stylistic level, many films, often through black comedy and satire, develop what can be described as oxymoronic qualities that both engage with the subject matter and yet maintain a distance or estrangement in its presentation[6]; a quality earlier deployed by Ichikawa Kon (1915–) in his depiction of Japanese society during the period of the 'reverse course' policy leading up to the Korean War in films such as *Mister Pu/Pūsan* (1953) and *A Billionaire/ Okuman chōja* (1954). Both films analyse the psychological realities of 'little people' whose memories of Hiroshima and Nagasaki are still vivid and who, due to government policy, are now forced to live with the threat of the 'bomb'. Okamoto Kihachi (1924–) would further develop this style in the 1960s in his war-retro films.

Many filmmakers who came to prominence in Japan during the late1950s, such as Imamura Shōhei and Yamada Yōji (1931–), present a similar *mise-en-scène*, but they also offer a redeeming ideological sentimentalism derived from the earlier humanist style in the form of compassion. They proffer the possibility of change based on an individual's choices and therefore they offer hope. For example, Haruko (Yoshimura

Jitsuko 1943–), the young heroine of *Pigs and Battleships/Buta to gunkan* (Imamura Shōhei [1961]), walks out of Yokotsuka and in so doing rejects the materialism that the town, synonymous with the American naval base, had come to signify in Japanese popular consciousness. She determinedly walks through a group of young prostitutes waiting at the harbour as a boat full of American sailors make their way to the wharf to begin their leave. Haruko walks onto the station and onto a new life of probable poverty in a factory in Kawasaki, thus rejecting the material affluence on offer in Yokotsuka. The film ends with a high-angle shot of the station as the soundtrack reverberates to a naval tune. In this sense, *Pigs and Battleships* ends with a classic liberal statement advocating self-reliance and perhaps more important, self-worth. The heroine (Baishō Chieko 1941–), in the 1963 film *The Sun of Shitamachi* (*Shitamachi no taiyō*), directed by Yamada Yōji, by choosing to marry a steelworker and stay in Shitamachi, a working-class district in Tokyo, rather than marry a salaryman, similarly rejects the consumerist ideal established in the opening sequences of the film set in a Ginza department store. In this example, the film concludes with a distinct Marxist statement about the positive values of manual work and community.

The settings of these films—Yokotsuka and Shitamachi, respectively—reinforce and play against inter-textual metonymic meanings ascribed to them in Japanese popular culture. Yokotsuka represents all the negative aspects of American materialism and foreign occupation allegorized through prostitution, while Shitamachi represents all the positive associations of working-class culture allegorized through a communal generosity of spirit. Shitamachi provides a positive other against which the nascent middle-class culture of the impersonal 1960s suburban *danchi* (apartment housing) estates are measured and found alienating. Yamada Yōji would exploit and develop this mythic quality of Shitamachi through the characters of *Tora-san: It's Tough Being a Man* (*Otoko wa tsurai yo*), a series of forty-eight films made between 1969 and the death of the lead actor, Atsumi Kiyoshi (1928–1996). Equally, as discussed earlier in films directed by Ozu, in both the pre- and postwar periods, there is an ideological antinomy between Tokyo and the country manifested in the *furusato*. On the other hand, the industrial cityscape of Ōshima's *A Town of Love and Hope* and the working-class district of Kamagasaki on the outskirts of Osaka, the setting for *The Sun's Burial*, have an internal circularity, which brings the protagonists back to the destructive point of theirs, and the film's, beginnings by not permitting the protagonists any such escape. Ōshima, in stating his reasons for choosing Kamagasaki as the *mise-en-scène* for *The Sun's Burial* describes it as,

> a place piled with the seeming burnt-out remains of the post-war black-market. In terms of revolutionary energy, it seemed that by 1960 ordinary labourers no longer existed. It was the student movement that took the lead in the Anpo struggle, the labour unions merely followed on behind. After thinking that the labour unions had lost their revolutionary energy, then suddenly I had the feeling that this probably was the last place that something interesting like this could occur in. That is why I chose Kamagasaki. (Ōshima 1993: 191–192)

This circularity of the cinematic cityscape, John Orr has noted in European and American films of the 1990s, is above all, 'the *fabula* of the cinematic city' (Orr 2003: 286). It would appear that Ōshima's productions pre-empted this diegetic use of the cityscape, as in the final shots of *The Sun's Burial*, after the destruction of the riot, Hanako and the medic survey the ruins and walk off into the slums as the medic mutters 'to work, to work'. They are off to set up another illegal clinic for the purchase of blood through transfusions taken from day labourers for sale to cosmetic companies. Ōshima describes the significance of this final scene:

> The upheaval the agitator, Ozawa Eitarō, wants is a reoccurrence of the past. He asks if World War II won't happen again. The upheaval Honō Kayoko [Hanako] is eagerly waiting for, indeed instigates, is a new type of upheaval something of which she has no experience. In Kamagasaki [and other such places] from time to time violence breaks out and the circumstances in which people are placed are transformed (*henka*), it is a longed-for change (*hendō*). It is a long-awaited sense of being set free from a place. This kind of longing, in certain places amongst certain people exists in the form of an easily ignitable spark. The last scene, shot from a high-angle, as Honō Kayoko and Hamamura Jun [the medic] holding hands turn away from the burnt ruins and run off, is an image of the end of the war and the end of the Anpo struggle. (Ōshima 1993: 194)

The film has come full circle, the words of the medic 'to work, to work' clearly link the film's ending to its opening credit sequence when pimps traverse the docks at knock-off time to entice labourers to sell their blood. One destructive cycle is complete and the next is about to begin.

Many of the characters in Ōshima's films exist on the margins of society. The young boy in Ōshima's debut production for Shōchiku, *A Town of Love and Hope*, lives in the slums and has no father, and his sickly mother (Mochizuki Yūko 1917–1977) works as a shoeshine in front of the station. His little sister appears to be mentally disturbed as she has an obsession with drawing dead animals. Haruko and the people with whom she interacts in *The Sun's Burial* are clinging to the lowest social rung of capitalist Osaka society. The distant castle looms large in the sunsets over the bombed-out skeletal remains of former wartime munitions factories. The people who exist in this society are reduced to selling their bodies, at best as day labourers, at worst as pimps working for the local gangs or through prostitution and the sale of their blood, and ultimately their identities as Japanese citizens through the sale of their family registers (*koseki*). The main character in *Violence at Noon* aka *The Daylight Demon* (*Hakuchū no tōrima*) (1966), Etsukei (Satō Kei 1928–), is a serial killer and a rapist. "R" (Yun Yundō) in *Death by Hanging* (*Kōshikei*) (1968) is a Korean, a social outcast, and the "boy" of the 1969 film *Boy* (*Shōnen*) is the son of a criminal. His father (Watanabe Fumio 1929–) and stepmother (Koyama Akiko 1935–) traverse the length of Japan making their living by an extortion racket that involves the elaborate staging of traffic accidents. The autocratic father uses the stepmother and later the "boy" to stage the accidents. The stepmother or the boy throw themselves against a moving vehicle. At the doctor's surgery the father storms in and threatens the hapless driver with police prosecution. The drivers offer cash settlements in order to avoid prosecution. In each of these films, the protagonists are linked by their status as social outcasts, and in each case it is society's ascription of them as criminals that determines their destiny. As Sartre has argued in his study of Jean Genet, 'Fortunately [for the social majority of good citizens] there exist in our society products of disassimilation, castoffs: abandoned children, "the poor", bourgeois who have lost their status, "lumpen-proletariat", déclassés of all kinds, in short, all the wretched' (Sartre 1964: 31). It is these social outcasts, the 'déclassés', that populate films produced by Ōshima in the 1960s. However, they are not the passive victims of their circumstances. They interact with society and challenge the dominant common sense standards of the majority's moral understanding of good. Without the existence of these characters good could not exist. In Sartre's terms, they are the other against which the majority defines its goodness. This line of argument can be extended through an analysis of Foucault's discussion of the relationship between the 'limit' and 'transgression'. The 'limit' in Foucault's explication can be equated with the self-imposed inhibitions to individual freedom that Sartre refers to when speaking of the relationship of 'Evil' and 'Goodness'. Foucault's statement below applies equally to the symbiotic relationship between Sartre's concepts of 'Good' and 'Evil' in civil society. 'The limit and transgression depend on each other for whatever density of meaning they possess: a limit could not exist if it were absolutely uncrossable and, reciprocally, transgression would be pointless if it merely crossed a limit composed of illusions and shadows' (Foucault 1993: 34). It is precisely this relationship between the social outcast as the necessary other against which civil society measures the 'density' of, and defines, its common sense understandings of the 'good' and the 'limit' that Ōshima's films explore. This theme is analysed in the dual sense that society needs social outcasts and therefore creates them through processes of social ascription and internalization in, for example, *A Town of Love and Hope*, *Cruel Story of Youth*, *Death by Hanging* and *Boy*, and in the sense that the criminal both tests and at times alters the definitions of the 'limit' (*Violence at Noon* [1966] and *In the Realm of the Senses* aka *Empire of the Senses/Ai no koriida* [1976]).

The circularity of the industrial cityscape provides the background against which the young boy Masao comes to consciousness of himself as an individual on the verge of adulthood. *A Town of Love and Hope* thus illustrates the symbiotic relationship between these two complex processes (social ascription and internalization) out of which individual subjectivity emerges in advanced capitalist society. Masao, from a poor single-parent family, sells homing pigeons to supplement the meagre income his sick mother makes as a shoeshine working in front of the station. Kyoko (Tominaga Yuki 1943–), the daughter of an affluent family who runs an electronics factory, buys the birds and thus becomes involved with Masao. At first she tries, through compassion, to offer him financial help. Masao, through pride, rejects this; later he will give her a map giving false directions to his home because he is ashamed of his circumstances, shame being the obverse of pride.

Masao's schoolteacher, through the mediations of Kyoko, asks the factory boss to give Masao and a few other boys due to graduate from the local school the chance to sit the entrance exam to the factory. The company policy has been to hire employees from the country and house them in the company dormitory. Local boys from the suburbs surrounding the factory were considered unreliable. Masao goes through the medical examinations and sits the entrance exam. However, a check into his background reveals that he has been knowingly selling homing pigeons, which return to his home within a few days, and this act constitutes fraud. The company duly rejects him. He thus confirms the social prejudices held by the majority of good citizens regarding the unreliability of youths from this background. As Kyoko's brother explains to Masao's teacher when he is trying to justify the company's employment policy, 'In the case of families that are incomplete (*fukanzen*), many warped individuals are formed . . .'

The film thus traverses the turning point in the life course of Masao who, by the end of the film due to his circumstances, comes to define his own subjectivity in the image and likeness of society's ascription of him as unreliable. After the teacher has confronted Masao at home in front of his mother with the pigeon-selling accusation, Masao and his mother have the following conversation:

> **Mother:** It would have been better had I not told you to sell the pigeons. It is my fault, you would have been taken on. It was very bad of me, I am sorry.
> **Masao:** It's all right.
> **Mother:** All the same, we shouldn't. We shouldn't have sold the pigeons.
> **Masao:** No, we had to, there was no other way.
> **Mother:** But because of this they think you are a bad boy.
> **Masao:** That is regrettable.
> (Pause, at which point Masao's mother begins to sob, Masao moves near her and, placing his hands on her shoulders as he looks into her eyes, he says)
> **Masao:** Mother, I am going to sell the birds again.

At this point, through pride, Masao turns the situation around and convinces himself that he chose to sell the pigeons and to confirm this, will do so again, thus negating in his mind his own passivity in the face of society's ascription of him. Instead, the act of fraud is transformed into an assertion of his subjectivity. Through this process, by internalizing his ascribed social identity as defined by Kyoko's brother, he is acquiescent in supporting and maintaining social definitions of 'Good' and 'Evil'. Earlier in the film, as part of his maturation, Masao had attempted to question the ethics of selling the pigeons in a conversation with his mother. Later he came to want to work at the factory in order to fulfil his social role as first son and support his mother and sister by legitimate means. To this end, he was willing to accept Kyoko's and the teacher's help, only his act of selling the pigeons to feed his family was discovered and was labelled fraud. As Sartre says of the adolescent Jean Genet, 'By the gaze that surprised him, by the finger that pointed at him, by the voice that called him a thief, the collectivity doomed him to Evil' (Sartre 1964: 31).

At an impressionable age when the ego and sense of self are being formed, Masao internalizes the negative characteristics that the good majority ascribe to him. The socialization process is completed when, by the end of the film, Kyoko, the daughter of a wealthy family, is also confirmed in her antithetical bourgeois role as she buys the one remaining pigeon back and asks her brother to shoot it. Through this act, she is accepting the majority's definition of good by condemning Masao's act in selling the pigeon. She, who had argued against her brother out of compassion for Masao's circumstances, becomes of one mind with her brother in the act of destroying the pigeon. She too has been through a rite of passage that has confirmed her in her prescribed social role. The teacher, as the mediator between the two positions, comes to the realization not only that there are no moral absolutes, as circumstances often determine behaviour, but also that she too is powerless to alter social roles. As she explains when breaking off her relationship with Kyoko's brother, '[D]epending on the times and the circumstances I would probably sell pigeons . . .' Kyoko's brother as representative of the moral majority cannot compromise and clings to his definition of good. By the end of the film, all the characters are again fragmented, separated off within their ascribed social positions with their beliefs/prejudices confirmed. Masao and Kyoko are condemned to their respective roles as mutually supporting representatives of 'Evil' and 'Good' while the teacher must confront her failure, her inability as a mediator to transcend the two positions and facilitate the creation of a more equitable society. The majority create the 'Evil' (in Sartre's terms) through a symbiotic relationship of ascription and internalization without which good and evil would have no meaning.

The depiction of the formation of individual subjectivity at the time of adolescence, in relation to the often conflicting forces of 'free will' and socialization, is a dominant theme in other films directed by Ōshima, for example, *Death by Hanging* and *Boy*. However, in both these later films the critique is extended and linked not only to an unnamed bourgeois ma-

244 A New History of Japanese Cinema

jority of good citizens but also directly to the State and its role in civil society as the only legitimate organ of violence.[7] This critique is focused on the State's dual powers to authorize men to kill in war, and its authority through the criminal justice system to punish individuals up to and including the deprivation of life through the enforcement of the death penalty. Satō, in an article published in 1968 in which he sets out the contextual issues surrounding *Death by Hanging*, argues that the starting point for Ōshima was the question of a 'sense of guilt' (*tsumi no ishiki*), that is, the criminal's consciousness of having transgressed a social limit. This is then juxtaposed with the State's power to authorize certain people to kill without a sense of guilt as in war or the execution of a criminal. The argument continues that if people can kill legitimately in the name of the State without a sense of guilt, then guilt is not an innate human characteristic, but culturally defined and learnt. This is what the Chief Prosecutor demonstrates to the convicted "R" in the final scenes, when "R", refusing to recognize his guilt, attempts to leave the execution chamber. As "R" opens the door a flash of light forces him back.

> **Prosecutor:** Do you know why you stopped? It is the State that allowed you to think you could go. It is also the State that stops you. You said that you couldn't see the State. But you are now looking at the State. You know the State. You have the State inside you. To the extent that the State is inside you, you feel guilt. You have a guilty conscience. You are now thinking that you should be executed.

In this way the film links guilt to cultural concepts of 'justice' (*seigi*) and the necessity of the State to be seen to be 'just' to maintain its authority. One form of securing State legitimacy is through the internalization of communal concepts of 'justice', through shared understandings of crime as a specific act of social transgression. In the case of *Death by Hanging*, this is manifested in the necessity for the representatives of the State, the witnesses at the execution, to bring the criminal, "R" who has lost his memory, to full consciousness of the crime for which he is about to be executed. Through this process the criminal should demonstrate his internalization of communal concepts of 'justice' through an admission of his guilt, something "R" refuses to acknowledge when in the final scene he states,

> **"R":** Now, I think I have probably committed a crime (*tsumi ga aru*). But, I am not guilty (*muzai*). The limit to which I am willing to accept guilt, limits the existence of the State. I am not guilty.

Through this process "R'" goes beyond Masao from *A Town of Love and Hope* and the "boy" in *Boy* and comes to a political understanding of the symbiotic nature of the relationship between socialization and consciousness. In the lines above, "R's" acceptance of his crime and his rejection of his guilt turns his crime and, more important, his refusal to acknowledge guilt into a political act of transgression. As a person of Korean descent living in Japan, the Japanese State has effectively condemned him to a position of statelessness, and he ultimately negates, through his denial, the legitimacy of the Japanese juridical state apparatus over his person.

The depiction of "R's" coming to political consciousness both as a criminal and a dispossessed Korean is framed within the wider social discourse of the Japanese public's support for the death penalty that is foregrounded in the opening and closing sequences of the film. With regard to the death penalty, protestors have long made the case that the execution of criminals does not reduce the incidence of crime. Therefore, public support for the death penalty, seventy-one percent in favour as quoted from a Ministry of Justice survey carried out in 1967, is, as Satō Tadao rightly points out, a public affirmation of the State as just rather than a reflection of the public's belief in the efficacy of the death penalty. This, from the perspective of a just civil society, Satō demonstrates, is dangerous. 'Why, because justice (*seigi*), rather than being something that each individual considers for himself, is entrusted to the state. If the state in the name of justice orders people to commit murder, then there is the possibility that people will take part in wars without any sense of guilt' (Satō 1968: 7–8). This point is made explicit towards the end of the film when the Education Officer sums up the attitude of the officials present to capital punishment. This occurs after a long conversation of those in attendance about their experiences during the war and the fate of war criminals in the post-defeat era.

**Education Officer:** Even though a lot of things have happened here today, now after listening to everyone, there is one thing that I understand. Killing someone by execution is for the sake of the country, and killing someone in a war is for the sake of the country, well, ultimately, execution and war are the same thing. At this time we will go on with our work and discharge our duty [executing criminals], but as individuals we are opposed to war and the death penalty and we pray that the day will quickly come when wars, executions and such like stop. You would all agree with this.

In other words, the State is empowered to authorize killing, during war and through the implementation of the death penalty, by public acquiescence, and *Death by Hanging* is based on the premise that these two mutually reinforcing and dependent positions are predicated on shared concepts of 'justice'.

The film, drawing on a high profile case involving a Korean youth who was arrested in 1958 and executed in 1962 for the murder and molestation of two Japanese high school girls, explores this question of the State's legitimacy to authorize such killings. The theme of "R's" coming to consciousness is developed against this background through his interactions with the various official representatives of civil society, present as witnesses to the execution, and finally, through the intervention of an imaginary Korean woman. The public prosecutor (Komatsu Hōsei 1926–2003) and his assistant and the head of the prison (Satō Kei 1928–) are representatives of the criminal justice system; the doctor (Tōra Rokkō 1930–1993) argues the case from a scientific perspective; the priest from the religious/metaphysical; and the Korean woman (Koyama Akiko 1935–) from the nationalistic. The prison education officer (Watanabe Fumio) and other lesser members present are representative of the good majority.

The film offers a series of staged episodic improvised re-enactments of the crimes the condemned "R" has committed. These are contained within Brechtian intertitles that cue the spectator to the various stages of "R's" coming to consciousness. These staged sequences are framed within a direct address to the film's audience by the voice-of-god narration (Ōshima Nagisa), 'Are you opposed to the abolition of the death penalty or do you support the abolition of the death penalty?' A further intertitle, listing the results of a Ministry of Justice Survey carried out in June 1967, immediately follows.

> Those against the abolition of the death penalty 71%
> Those who approve of the abolition of the death penalty 16%
> The don't knows 13%[8]

The narration continues with the following: 'Ladies and gentlemen, the ladies and gentlemen who make up the seventy-one percent opposed to the abolition of the death penalty, have you ever seen an execution chamber? Have you ever seen an execution carried out?' The narration then describes in detail the layout of the prison and the location, dimensions and architectural features of the execution chamber set within the grounds of the prison confines. This docudrama-style narration is supported through the visuals with aerial shots of a prison compound. As the narrator continues with a description of the inner execution chamber, followed by a description of the procedures leading up to an execution, the camera moves into the execution chamber as we explore the layout. Finally, we are introduced to "R" as he goes through the rituals leading up to and culminating in his execution. In this way, the opening address locates the abstract Ministry of Justice statistics within the immediacy of a documentary-style filming of the act of killing a prisoner that directly confronts pro-death-penalty spectators. However, "R" in the first attempt of execution does not die. At this point the film shifts from the impersonal newsreel docudrama style to the micro-narrative of the drama to be played out in the execution chamber, through an analysis of what constitutes a consciousness of crime at the level of the individual, in other words, guilt.

One of the reasons the original case on which the film was based attracted such interest was due to the letters the accused wrote while in prison. In these letters he attempted to come to some intellectual understanding of his actions. These letters were eventually published in Japanese under the title *Crime, Death and Love* (*Tsumi to shi to ai*). As an articulate boy with a good academic record, he did not fit the public profile of a criminal spawned from an impoverished Korean family. He thus not only challenged popular racist stereotypes but opened up a debate in Japanese society on the nature of guilt and remorse. Satō quotes from one of the published letters:

> I was involved in two incidents, if I had not been arrested, and given the opportunity I would have certainly killed again. Since I was arrested, I have shown no remorse, rather I have behaved cheerfully, this is not in the least affected, it is natural. If you ask why, it is because I feel no remorse for my crimes. I feel no remorse for having killed people. Even after being arrested, if I was to be released into society, I feel I would probably kill again. First, regarding my killing people, I feel no emotion. This disposition, even now at this point in time, has remained unchanged within me. When I consider the act of killing someone rationally, not emotionally, I am the same now as before. I feel I have the same disposition and could easily kill again. (Quoted in Satō 1968: 6)

It is this state, the state of no conscious sense of guilt, that the film explores through the re-enactment of the crimes by the officials in the execu-

tion chamber in their bid to restore "R's" memory in order to execute him
again.

After an initial attempt at execution and after his body has been left
hanging for the requisite time, the doctor detects a heartbeat and pro-
nounces "R" physically alive. He is alive, but after resuscitation it is obvious that he has lost his memory; "R" is therefore not conscious of who he
is, where he is or why he is there. This opens up the drama to the exploration of the various social and political definitions of consciousness: the
legal, the scientific, the religious/metaphysical and finally, through the intervention of the Korean woman, the nationalistic. After the failed hanging
attempt, the Japanese officials stage a re-enactment of the crime (the rape
of a Japanese high school girl) to ensure "R" is conscious of the crime for
which he is about to be re-executed. However, during the course of this re-
enactment, the Japanese officials are taken over by their own impulses and
their actions become seemingly unconscious. As the Education Officer,
overzealous in his assumed role as the criminal, murders a high school
girl, his imagination and reality become blurred. The fact that this murder
is filmed outside the execution chamber on the roof of the school and that
upon returning to the prison at first only the prison Education Officer and
"R" can see the girl not only unites them, but further blurs the distinction
between the imagination and reality. Gradually the others do come to see
her. However, they each see her in different clothes, thus confirming her
place within their separate imaginings. In this way, through the re-enactment of "R's" crime, the differences between "R" and his Japanese exe-
cutioners, that is the criminal and the 'good' seventy-one percent majority
of the Japanese population that supports the death penalty, also becomes
blurred.

Unlike the young boys, Masao in *Town of Love and Hope* and "boy"
in *Boy*, and the Korean "R" in *Death by Hanging*, by the end of *Cruel
Story of Youth*, the university student Kiyoshi succumbs to the demands of
society. Having tested the limit he attempts to revert to the majority good
position. On the other hand, Makoto presents a stronger and more defiant
character. As she leaves the police station with her sister and father, she
states that her apparent repentance had been a lie to ensure her release.
She refuses to acknowledge that their extortion racket was wrong. She immediately leaves them to find Kiyoshi. The two young lovers attempt to
escape in a taxi from Kiyoshi's ex-lover, the older woman to whom he
prostituted himself, only to find that they have no money. The older
woman, after following in her car, pays the driver, after which Kiyoshi

says they are beaten and should separate. He loses the resolve he expressed at the abortionist's clinic not to be beaten. This is the weakness that seals their fate. Kiyoshi was willing to compromise, he had tested the limit but was ultimately unable to cross it. It is his weakness in the face of society that destroys the two, just as it had done for the immediate postwar generation represented by Yuki, Makoto's sister, and her first love Akimoto, and the war generation who acquiesced in their own deaths. Kiyoshi dies because his past, in the form of a malicious group of pimps, catches up with him. Makoto, dejected, dies attempting to escape from the advances of a middle-class man (he has a car) representative of the good majority. The film's ending mirrors the final lines of Sartre's 1943 play *No Exit*, 'Hell is other people'. The film thus links the three generations through the failures of individuals to make choices in Sartre's existentialist sense of 'freedom of will'.

In contrast, in *Death by Hanging*, "R's" position as a social outcast is explored through his heritage as a Korean national resident in Japan and is expressed in the dialogue with the Korean woman. The Japanese officials' re-enactment of his life at home with his family clearly reflects racist stereotypes held by many Japanese in the 1960s. In one scene the woman challenges the right of the Japanese to punish "R" and in so doing turns "R's" crimes into political acts by placing them within the context of Japanese Imperialism.

> **Korean Woman:** As a Korean, "R" was not born in Japan out of choice. No Korean would be born here out of choice. "R's" father was forcibly brought here . . .
>
> You, as Japanese, do you really understand our feelings as Koreans living in Japan? "R's" crime was a violation caused by the Japanese State, by Japanese Imperialism! The Japanese State does not have the right (*kenri*) to punish "R"! . . .

At this stage in his development "R" has difficulty coming to terms with her ideal of a Korean youth. At first, she denounces him as a common criminal as he is not the Korean "R"; having been raised in Japan, he has internalized Japanese social ideologies and has lost his Korean sensibility (*chōsenjin no kokoro o ushinatta!*). However, later remembering his anonymous telephone calls to the newspaper after each incident, she rationalizes his crimes as political acts of defiance (*chōsen*) in the following dialogue:

**Korean Woman:** In the name of the State, Japanese people have shed the blood of countless Koreans. But we who have no state, as individuals have no other way than with these hands to shed the blood of Japanese people. That is a crime! It is a warped way. But through these kinds of crimes the collective pride and sadness of the Korean people is expressed. "R", you are a person who has committed this kind of crime.

But at this stage "R" still does not understand his position as a Korean, and the woman rants 'Execute him, "R" is not "R". He has lost his sense of ethnicity, his sense of being a Korean. 'This is the voice of Japanese Imperialism . . .'

The opening and closing sequences of *Boy* also frame the film's micro-narrative of the emotional development and maturation of the "boy" within the immediacy of his family, in a similar State-centred meta-discourse. In the opening credit sequences, the Japanese flag features as a background. The first shot holds on the name of Ōshima's independent production company, Sōzōsha, in sharp focus against the blurred flag. As the name disappears, the flag, with a black rather than a red centre, comes into focus, however, it is clear that it is a reproduction from the war period. Upon it all the members of a platoon had written their names in red including the Koreans, whose names appear in the Korean *hangul* script. This is a symbolic gesture of inclusion as, during the war, it was illegal for Koreans to use their own language. Their names were forcibly transliterated into a Japanese rendering of the Chinese ideograms. Hence the flag is a symbolic reproduction that links the war to both the ruthless patriarchal authority of the "boy's" father (a veteran who carries both physical and psychological scars), while extending the definition of war 'victim' beyond that of the 'humanists' to include Japan's former imperial subjects. Through this credit sequence, the war and the exploitative patriarchal authority of the State are established as the historical contexts against which the drama of the socialization of the "boy" is portrayed through a neo-realist-style account of his life with the family. In the final sequences after the arrest of the family, the voice-of-god narration gives an official news-style report of the account of the family's background and activities. As the film's temporal frame remains in the continuous present, this clinical, matter-of-fact historical information provides none of the subjective and, therefore, legitimating force for the boy's or his family's misdemeanours that was so important in our understanding of the flawed characters of, for example, Kinoshita's *A Japanese Tragedy*. It is a cold legal account that jars against the film's intervening rendering of the "boy's" coming to consciousness.

The symbolic nature of the authoritarian power relationship between the "boy" and his father (Watanabe Fumio) is conveyed through his father's continual use of *bōya* when talking to him rather than his name, Toshio. *Bōya* is an impersonal referent that simply means "boy". It is only in the final narrational report that we learn that his real name is Toshio. Like "R" he is a symbolic construct, a nameless representative of the 'déclassé'. Like Masao before him, *Boy* presents a series of events that both inscribes and confirms within the "boy's" mind his place within the family and the social order. Towards the end of the film, after his parents have temporarily separated in order to avoid detection by the police, he and his stepmother (Koyama Akiko) successfully carry out an extortion by themselves. The stepmother automatically reverts to the victim role as she throws herself against a moving vehicle and the "boy" slips easily into his father's role as the indignant male aggressively demanding compensation. At this point the "boy" is confirmed in his future role. His parents recognize this change in his status as they squabble over with whom he will go when they finally want to separate.

The centrality of power as opposed to affection as a structuring device within the family's relationships is plainly apparent as the stepmother and the "boy" side against the father, the weak and suppressed forming an alliance against the autocrat. During this progression from innocent child to confirmed criminal, the "boy" attempts to run away to his grandparents, but lacking the full train fare spends the night alone on a beach trying, through his imagination, to re-create a sense of the normal rituals of family life. In contrast, on another occasion during one of his exploratory wanderings around a new town, he follows a schoolboy into an alley where the schoolboy is set upon by two much larger schoolboys. After this incident the bullied schoolboy immediately turns on the "boy" and throws his prized yellow baseball cap into a muddy puddle and stands on it. These and other experiences confirm in the "boy's" mind the reality of extortion and the role of power as the ruling imperative of social life.

Ōshima, in numerous writings, has asserted that an opposition to the 'victimization' (*higaisha ishiki*) theme as it was manifested in the post-defeat period, both in terms of narrative and stylistic interpretation, drove much of his work. He opposed the compassion of the humanists that legitimated the failures of the powerless through psychological explorations of their past experiences as in, for example, *A Japanese Tragedy*. Within this discourse of compassion, the powerless individual is transcribed into the flawed individual and the wider context of the State becomes at best a *mise-en-scène* against which the individual struggles. As such, Ōshima discounted the use of subjective flashbacks[9] and many other stylistic devices of filming synonymous with the psychological development of characters enshrined in the Shōchiku house-style as defined by Kido Shirō (1894–1977), whose writings on this subject have been lovingly collected in an edited edition by the director Yamada Yōji.[10]

Ōshima states in *Ōshima Nagisa 1960* that he wanted, in *Cruel Story of Youth*, to break with the Shōchiku ideal of the Japanese family. Hence Makoto's family is comprised of the two daughters and a father. There are no shots of people sitting in *tatami* mat rooms talking. The conversations that do take place are outside the home or restricted to Kiyoshi's lodgings and the abortionist's clinic. Ōshima's use of the telephoto lens when shooting close-ups of people blurs the background and, in his words, 'puts the face into abstraction'. This was a reaction to the preponderance of the use of the medium close-ups in Shōchiku films. Furthermore, he often cuts off protagonists' foreheads in extreme close-up shots in the wide screen format of the newly introduced CinemaScope (*Cruel Story of Youth* and *Violence at Noon*). As he explains:

> The basic composition of Shōchiku Ōfuna cameramen is under no circumstances to cut off the face. The whole face should be in the frame. It must be shot as the face of a human being and not as an object. It is considered good to harmonize the face with something in the background. I wanted to take close-ups of people's faces in the abstract. I wanted to capture the total situation, but not in any way to explain that situation. Up until that time, Japanese films always explained things. This person was born into this type of family, therefore he committed this type of crime, that kind of thing: I hated it. . . . When CinemaScope came in, everyone hesitated about using close-ups. But for me, conversely, because the frame was wide I had to take the plunge and shoot in close-up. Well, because it is CinemaScope, it is possible to shoot two people together in close-up. (Ōshima 1993: 156)

Through his resistance to established styles, Ōshima was instrumental in creating a counter-aesthetic that was set in motion by, amongst others, the *taiyōzoku* films he admired directed by Nakahira Kō. In these films, epitomised by the youthful *taiyōzoku* antiheroes, the male characters represent a raw physicality that needs no moral justifications for its actions. Their existence is presented in a timeless present with no past and no future. In an article Ōshima wrote for the film journal *Film Art* (*Eiga Geijutsu*) in 1966, he contrasts the notion of *kakushinhan,* that is, a crime committed out of a conscious political, moral or religious belief, to the criminal's impulsive desire to commit crime. He continues,

> Recently, I have wanted to portray demonic criminals [here Ōshima uses the Chinese ideogram *ma*, which is in the Japanese title of *Violence at Noon* released in the same year and clearly refers to Eitsukei the serial killer/rapist] who only reach consciousness through an impulse inside them of wanting to commit a crime, they are people who do not know why they want to commit crimes. (Quoted in Ōshima 1993: 28)

In this sense, as he argues in *Ōshima Nagisa 1960*, the criminal who commits a crime within the terms of the concept *kakushinhan* (a conscious moral, political or religious act) has a clearly defined sense of self. On the other hand, many criminals commit crimes unaware of why they do so, as in the case of "R", who only comes to a political understanding of the significance of his crimes after a long and tortuous process, as did the French writer Jean Genet. It is no mere coincidence that the title for Ōshima's 1969 film *Dairy of a Shinjuku Thief* (*Shinjuku dorobō nikki*) mirrors Jean Genet's *The Thief's Journal.* The important point is that not only is the perpetrator conscious of and unrepentant for his crime, but that the impulse stems from some socially derived ascription of him as a criminal rather than a purely intellectual reaction to his environment. In these circumstances, the crime becomes an instinctual act of transgression that automatically challenges the limit, as does the young boy, Masao, who knowingly sells homing pigeons in *A Town of Love and Hope*. This is also one of the main points raised in *Death by Hanging*, which is not only about the Korean "R" coming to consciousness as a criminal and a member of the second-class minority Korean population but perhaps, more important about the Japanese who are trying to execute him.

While the humanists elicited compassion for the predicament of the powerless through the victimization theme, Ōshima evoked cruelty as a thematic device to critique the symbiotic relationship of the outcast to moral society. In this way the cruelty of the moral majority of society— that needs the outcast and therefore creates and subsequently destroys him to provide the standard against which the good is maintained—is laid bare. This is one of the main differences between Ōshima's cruel films and, for example, Kurosawa Akira's (1910–1998) *The Bad Sleep Well* aka *The*

*Worse You Are, the Better You Sleep/A Rose in the Mud (Warui yatsu hodo yoku nemuru)* (1960), *High and Low* aka *Heaven and Hell (Tengoku to jigoku)* (1963) and the 'black' films produced by the Daiei Studios in the early 1960s centred on the actor Tamiya Jirō (1935–1978). These 'black' films share a common theme: an examination of morality in an age of rampant materialism. In each case, the heroes, in a corrupt world, are tempted to descend to the levels of their adversaries in exacting revenge or to further their ambitions, and in each case the hero does, in fact, appear to succumb but is redeemed through romance. Romance, in the context of these 'black' films, becomes the emotional force that breaks through the barriers of materialism, restoring the humanity of the protagonist. Only in the case of *The Bad Sleep Well*, the hero's redemption comes too late, as he has already gone beyond the limits of the acceptable and he must perforce, by the end of the film, die at the hands of his rival. However, in the majority of 'black' films the heroes, their humanity restored, escape their environments and, rejecting their ambitions, become new men facing new beginnings.

There is also the question of tragedy intrinsic to the humanist films discussed in the preceding chapter, which is linked to sentimentalism and compassion. However, Ōshima's characters are neither heroic nor tragic; they are, by society's standards, damaged characters who often, having accepted society's ascription of them as a criminal, reaffirm it through criminal acts. Other than perhaps the "boy" in *Boy*, we are not permitted to feel compassion for them as their weakness is exposed, but more important, in the course of that exposure a parallel exposition of the multifarious forces of power that work upon the individual is also laid bare.

Films such as *Pigs and Battleships* and *The Sun of Shitamachi*, produced within the studio system (Nikkatsu and Shōchiku, respectively), play against each other and reinforce the symbolic meanings of the geographical centres of their *mise-en-scène*, whereas Ōshima's third film, *The Sun's Burial*, depicts social dislocation as spatial. People live beside one another, connect and then separate, and no sense of community forms. Films starring Ishihara Yūjirō, critics argue, are the opposite. They describe these films as 'international' (*kokuseki fumei eiga*) in that the location has little diegetic function. Despite this quality, Izawa Jun, writing in *Kinema Junpō* in 1958, states that Ishihara's films contain an element of Japanese sentimentalism, which made them popular (*Best of Kinema Junpō 1950–1966*, 1994: 716). However, this element of a seemingly Japanese sentimentality, when analysed, has its roots not in some Japanese sense of nostalgic communal past but in Hollywood melodramas, such as Elia Kazan's 1955 *East of Eden*, upon which the sibling rivalry theme of *The Sunny Hill Path* was based.[11]

While the *taiyōzoku* films took up issues relating to youth from the individual male perspective of the psychosocial through the re-assertion of patriarchal authority in a new age, Ōshima's films presented social conflict at the wider level of youth politics through the development of the 'cruel' film. Nineteen sixty, one of Ōshima's most productive years, marked a crucial time in the student movement known as the 'Anpo struggle'. The Anpo movement, in accordance with Clause 9 of the postwar Constitution, attempted to stop the extension and revision of the Japan–U.S. security treaty. So violent were the protests that President Eisenhower's planned visit to Japan to ratify the treaty revisions was cancelled and Prime Minister Kishi was forced to travel to the U.S. to sign the ratified treaty at the end of 1960. Nineteen sixty thus marked the culmination of many struggles that had occurred throughout the 1950s, during which the conservative Yoshida-led elite was pitted against left-leaning opponents. Although *Cruel Story of Youth* did not specifically focus on the Anpo demonstration, other than as a temporal marker through the inclusion of newsreel footage of the Korean student protests against the government of Rhee Syngman (1875–1965), President of the Republic of Korea from 1948–1960, and the use of actual footage taken at the 1960 May Day demonstration in Tokyo, in symbolic terms, the timing of its release coincided with what many saw as the defeat of the student movement. In fact, Ōshima recounts that he had been specifically instructed not to make a film about politics but about 'youth' (*seishun*). However, Ōshima later reasoned, 'If I had been permitted to portray [politics], I probably would not have done so. I think that is the nature of expression. When something is suppressed one has to express it; if it is permissible to express it, then I feel there is probably no need to express it' (Ōshima 1993: 121). *Cruel Story of Youth* was released on 3 June 1960 and on the 15 June, a female student member of the All Japanese Student Union, *Zengakuren*, was killed in a violent clash with riot police outside the Diet. The ending of *Cruel Story of Youth* captured a sensibility of the age and the defeat of youth politics, which was confirmed in July when Prime Minister Kishi resigned and Prime Minister Ikeda took over and promptly announced his 'income doubling' policy (*shotoku baizō*). This marked the end of resistance. Materialism had again triumphed as the people were to be bought off as a concession to the contin-

ued heavy American military presence. *Night and Fog in Japan*, released
on 9 October 1960 and withdrawn on 12 October, the same day as Asa-
numa Inejirō (1898–1960), a socialist politician, was assassinated by a
right-wing extremist, is a postmortem of the failure and defeat of the left
in the 1950s. Framed within a generational debate between student communists of the early 1950s and disillusioned student activists in the contemporary 1960 Anpo movement, the film described as a 'filmed
ideological treatise' (*shisō ronbun*) was based on a 'one-scene-one-shot'
editing pace. Sweeping camera movements between characters and the inclusion of flashbacks all contributed to an antithetical style at odds with
Shōchiku's Ōfuna-*cho* (style). *Night and Fog* thus became the catalyst that
forced Ōshima out of the studio system and prefigured a stylistic shift that
fluctuated between a documentary-like toying with reality and a theatrical
distancing of the subject. These stylistic innovations were central to many
of the independent films produced and/or distributed under the auspices of
the Art Theatre Guild.

In his writings Ōshima states that he was influenced by the lack of sentimentalism employed in the depiction of post-defeat Italian society by the
neo-realists (*Rome, Open City* [1946] and *Paisàn* [1946], both directed by
Roberto Rossellini 1906–1977 and *Bicycle Thieves* [1948], directed by
Vittorio de Sica 1902–1974). In his mind, the Italian neo-realist style became associated with 'resistance'. Within this context 'resistance (*rejisu-
tansu*) had the simple meaning of ultimately withstanding limitless cruelty
(*muzan*)'. Ōshima goes on to explain that, during the occupation the idea
of 'resistance' also became linked to a popular anti-American sentiment
(Ōshima 1978: 133). Italian neo-realist films remained popular in Japan
until 1950 when *Until the Day We Meet Again* and *Listen to the Roar of
the Ocean* (*Kike wadatsumi no koe* aka *Nihon senbotsu gakusei no shuki:
kike wadatsumi no koe*) were released in March and June, respectively.
As Ōshima explains, the antiwar sentiment in these films is conspicuously
presented as 'a protest that was filled with the sadness of youth destroyed
by the war. War was portrayed like a natural disaster that descended from
heaven. It was not presented as a consequence of the evil of actual organizations and people' (Ōshima 1978: 134). It was against this background
that the often iconoclastic director Okamoto Kihachi made his satirical
1960s' war-retro films. Through 'black comedy' and parody, these genre
conventions, so firmly established during the previous decade, are derided
in films such as *Desperado Outpost* (*Dokuritsu gurentai*) series (1959–
1965) and *Human Bullet* (*Nikudan*) (1968) amongst others. In the 1970s

Fukasaku Kinji (1930–2003) would similarly challenge the war-retro conventions through his docudrama style in *Beneath the Battle Flag* (*Gunki hatameku moto ni*) (1972).

## The Decline of the Major Studios, the Avant-garde and the Politics of Porn

If romantic love of the early postwar mainstream studio productions offered one avenue of ensuring the primacy of the heterosexual politics of exchange, with the rise to prominence of the political directors from the mid-1950s on, romance as an expression of individual subjectivity increasingly came under attack. However, one of the important changes to come out of the postwar mainstream cinema's depiction of romance, and the more radical Tamura Taijirō-style novel, was the inclusion of a female desiring subject position, which had been totally denied in films produced in the post-1939 Film Law period.

Despite the attack on romance by directors such as Ōshima Nagisa, Imamura Shōhei (*Insect Woman/Nippon konchūki* [1963]), Teshigahara Hiroshi (1927–) (*Woman of the Dunes/Suna no onna* [1964]) and Suzuki Seijun (1923–) (*Gates of Flesh/Nikutai no mon* [1964] and *Story of a Prostitute* aka *Joy Girls/Shunpu-den* [1965]), the corporeal individuality expressed through carnal desire was still framed within a political economy of masculine desire. Hence the recurrence of the same misogynistic themes and anxieties that were once played out in romance in terms of the containment of women's sexuality within the institution of marriage and the constraints of child rearing. As has been argued above, from the mid-1950s and the *taiyō-zoku* films on, these same misogynistic themes and anxieties where allayed through physical violence, rape, coerced abortion and the often violent death of the heroine. Despite the attempts at a political cinema that was to free the individual through corporeal desire, the libidinal economy of the filmmakers ensured that, through the narrative devices employed, the authorial voice of masculine desire, channelled through heterosexual relations, remained dominant. This was further complicated by economic considerations, as the major studios lost their monopolistic grip on the industry as independent companies were formed around the production of both low-budget soft-core pornographic 'pink' films and 'art house' films, these latter being distributed through the Art Theatre Guild network of small cinemas. In the 1960s, Nikkatsu, in its attempts to lure back declining audiences, re-appropriated a female subject position in its soft-core pornographic genres. Two examples from the mid-1960s are Suzuki Seijun's two films based on novels by Tamura Taijirō (1911–1983), *Gates of Flesh* and *Story of a Prostitute*.

In the Nikkatsu re-make of Tamura Taijirō's 1946 novel *The Gates of Flesh*, set in the immediate post-defeat period, masculine desire is channelled through the sadomasochistic rites that maintain the social order and the social hierarchy within the female group. Women who can no longer rely on marriage as a means of support must find a place within the post-war economic market in which to survive. Within the political economy of masculine discourse, female marketability is defined in terms of the body. The internal rule that no one should have sex without payment, enforced by the SM punishment rite, is based on the economic imperative of survival, as it underpins their existence as prostitutes and binds the group together. The film thus shifts Tamura Taijirō's philosophical positioning of the body, as the site of individuality, to the economics of heterosexual capitalist exchange. Tamura, writing in 1948, explains his position:

> All the established ideals have been deemed unworthy. The only things we can now place our trust in are our physical desires, our instincts; in short, we can only trust those things we have experienced ourselves through our own bodies. The only things that really exist are those desires that fill our bodies—the desire to eat when hungry, to sleep when tired, the desire to be physically close to another. (Quoted in English in Slaymaker 2002: 92)

The girls in the main group (Ishii Tomiko 1935–, Matsuo Kayo 1943– and Tominaga Misao 1933–1975), reaching maturity during the final years of the war, are primeval in their reliance on their instincts for their survival. The disruptions to normal life caused by the war have stunted their emotional growth. They represent the lowest denominator in the social hierarchy, and it is for this reason that Ibuki Shinichirō (Shishido Jō 1933–), the de-mobbed male interloper, despises them. Just like Omachi, the kimono-clad war widow driven to prostitution, Ibuki represents a generation that has experienced civil society. Despite his total rejection of the wartime ideological position and his avowal of the *nikutai* philosophical position 'to live for food and love', in his memory, Ibuki still has some residues of a former life, as does Omachi. In the case of Omachi, it is her desire to return to married life, a hope that one of her clients offers her. In this way, the exclusive female group is depicted as the other against which civil society, founded on patriarchal principles, is measured and found desirable.

Within this display of primeval society, the independence of women, legalized and legitimized by occupation reforms, is constrained and offered as voyeuristic titillation through the commodification of the women's bodies. However, in the postwar chaos it is the women themselves who apparently act as the agents of their economic exchange and not the usual 'pimps' (*chinpira*). As one of the prostitutes explains, it is like the wholesale fish seller—we cut out the middleman and sell direct to the public. Equally, it is the women themselves who maintain their power hierarchy through masculine fetishistic fantasies of S/M rituals. However, the imagery of the S/M theme remains the same as in much mainstream Japanese soft-core pornography, as the man is still in control. The camera takes Ibuki's point of view and positions him as the controlling gaze through which audience desire is channelled, and in the final scenes he intervenes to halt the punishment. Furthermore, he is posited as the cause of the action as Maya's (Nogawa Yumiko 1944–) voice-over narration so clearly states: 'With Ibuki the central figure, someone will break our rule. This became a serious problem in our lives. We had to show others and ourselves how horrible punishment is'. Maya's first sexual awakening during the flogging sequence, depicted through subjective super-impositions, also serves to locate her desire in the feminine terms of masochism, as does her jealousy at seeing Ibuki's attraction to the emotionally more mature Omachi, whom Ibuki describes as 'a real woman'. Through these narrative strategies, independent women are thus contained and re-inscribed into hegemonic discourses of feminine masochistic desire and jealousy through the controlling gaze of the dominant male protagonist who is given a privileged position within the female group.

In the sequel, *Story of a Prostitute*, set during the war in northern China, the dichotomy between the 'body'/*nikutai* and the 'spirit'/*seishin* is played out between Harumi (Nogawa Yumiko), the willing 'comfort woman' serving the army, and the military institution represented by the adjutant (Tamagawa Isao 1922–). Mikami (Kawachi Tamio 1938–), the adjutant's hapless orderly, is torn between these conflicting personalized moralities, which eventually destroy him. Harumi, as the embodiment of desire, is the hysterical female whose sexuality has not been contained within the institution of marriage. Her potential sexual autonomy as a prostitute is therefore threatening and dangerous.

Some Japanese filmmakers, in the context of postwar reconstruction, sought to re-define individual subjectivity in terms of the primeval body devoid of culture; however, this postwar re-evaluation of the 'decadent' body as the essence of individual subjectivity remained grounded in a masculine bias. As the examples outlined above indicate, they sought the locus of the individual in desire expressed in the sexualized woman, the prostitute. In cinematic representations, these developments cannot be divorced from the changes taking place within the Japanese film industry in the 1960s; in particular, the influences of a burgeoning independent 'pink' film market. In films such as *Cruel Story of Youth* and *The Sun's Burial,* by shifting the emphasis from the misogynistic re-assertion of masculinity to an effective social emasculation of the protagonists through a *mise-en-scène* of poverty and generational conflict, Ōshima effectively turned this discourse from the psychosocial re-containment of female characters to the political. He would take this further in the 1970s in his hard-core rendition of the story of Abe Sada, *In the Realm of the Senses* (*Ai no koriida*), where crime would again form the transgressive complement to sexuality.[12] However, in this case his adherence to pornographic conventions, formalized by the 1970s in the Nikkatsu *romanporuno* genre, would make the subversion of dominant masculine and feminine positions more problematic.

Ōshima states quite explicitly that *In the Realm of the Senses* was produced as a direct challenge to both the censorship laws in Japan at the time and the restrictive practices of the Japanese film industry. He saw both these conservative forces stifling the artistic potential of Japanese directors at a time when directors in European countries, in particular France post-1968, were exploring new modes of expression in an atmosphere in which censorship of hard-core had been lifted. As Ōshima explains, 'In the world, restrictions on sexual expression in Japan are matchless. Excellent films by directors such as Wakamatsu Kōji [1936–] and Kumashiro Tatsumi [1927–1995] are not accepted sufficiently in the film world because of, for example, the need to hide pubic hair and the restrictions on sexual expression. I thought I would utilize a joint production to investigate to the limits the possibilities of sexual expression' (Ōshima 1979: 173).

In the legal sense Ōshima challenged not only the infamous Japanese obscenity law, No. 175, but also, and perhaps more important, the symbolic structures of Japanese patriarchal authority. By depicting the male organ, Ōshima risked disrupting the correlation between the penis and its symbolic meaning as phallus. In terms of the film industry, Ōshima also saw the method of making *In the Realm of the Senses* as ushering in a new system of filmmaking. By seeking foreign backing, importing film stock, shooting the film in Japan using Japanese actors and technicians and sending the undeveloped film abroad for processing and editing, Ōshima saw this as a potential revolutionary system of filmmaking that would free directors from the rigidities of the industry and the constraints of censorship laws at one stroke.

Locating the concept of 'obscenity' (*waisetsu*) firmly within the cultural, Ōshima argues in his preface to the screenplay of *In the Realm of the Senses* that pornography exists in the imagination. '*In the Realm of the Senses* became the perfect pornographic film in Japan because it cannot be seen there. Its existence is pornographic—regardless of its content. Once it is seen, *In the Realm of the Senses* may no longer be a pornographic film . . .' (Ōshima 1992: 253). He continues, 'I daresay that internalized taboos make for the experience of "obscenity". Children, on the other hand, don't feel that anything they see is "obscene"' (Ōshima 1992: 261). It was these culturally specific 'internalized taboos' that the film's content, filmed as hard-core, attempted to challenge in order to bring Japanese censorship laws into line with international standards, or, as Satō Tadao states, '[T]he film represents a refusal to recognize any barriers between love and sex' (Satō 1996 vol. iii: 172), impediments (*surichigai*) to the 'love' between a couple being the dominant causal agent in the mainstream romance film.

Peter Lehman points out that *In the Realm of the Senses* does not conform to conventions established in Western hard-core pornography as identified by Linda Williams in her seminal study *Hard Core*. There are no 'money shots' in the conventional sense, the hero suffers a postmortem castration, and perhaps most important, the flaccid penis is visible. As Lehman explains:

> In one scene Ōshima emphasizes a different view of the penis than that commonly found in hard-core. We see several close-up shots of the unerect penis of an old man who is first taunted in the street by women and a child after a child exposes him and who tries to have sex with one of the women [Sada] but, due to impotence, fails. In addition to being "impressive", penises in hard-core are always erect or become so in moments . . . The close-up of the old man's flaccid penis after the woman has tried to arouse him is far removed from the spectacle of the phallicly powerful penis that dominates hard-core. (Lehman 1993: 177–179)

However, despite the film's transgressive credentials, *In the Realm of the Senses* is still a film supportive of a phallocentric worldview. Although

Sada (Matsuda Eiko 1952–) is clearly positioned, as her Nikkatsu counterparts are, as an active desiring subject, her desire is structured to over-
value the penis as the sole source of her pleasure. In much the same way,
Ibuki in *Gates of Flesh* and the adjutant in *Story of a Prostitute* metaphorically represent the phallus as the site of female desire/pleasure. In *In the
Realm of the Senses* this point is made even more explicit when, just before the scene with the old man described by Lehman above, we are first
introduced to Sada as she rejects the lesbian advances of a female colleague, who then takes her to watch Kichi (Fuji Tatsuya 1941–) and his
wife engaged in sex. As the structuring of this sequence of nine reverse-
cut shots clearly locates Sada and her female companion as the active voyeurs who mediate the spectators' gaze, and Kichi as the object of their
gaze, it is worth considering in some detail.

1. Medium close-up of the first geisha's face partly obscured as she
   looks from the courtyard veranda through the small vertical opening
   of the dark wooden sliding door.
2. Cut to interior shot of Kichi's wife dressing him in his *fundoshi*
   (loincloth-style) underwear. He is standing impassively and she is
   positioned kneeling in front of him. The camera then cuts to a medium close-up low-angle shot of Kichi's upper naked torso and
   face, thus clearly identifying him and not his wife as the object of
   the woman's interest.
3. Cut-back to a medium close-up shot of the first geisha's face, her
   eyes tilted upward, thus linking the angle of the previous shot back
   to the direction of her gaze.
4. Cut to interior. Medium close-up of Kichi's wife still positioned
   screen left kneeling in front of Kichi, her face pressing in against
   his lower stomach as she attempts to tie his *fundoshi* at his back. As
   she adjusts the fabric around his upper left thigh, the camera pans
   down as she lowers her head to the level of his penis (which is not
   in view). She then, clearly aroused by her proximity to his penis,
   instigates sexual activity by slipping her hand under the still untied
   frontal flap of his *fundoshi*.
5. Cut-back to the door, only now Sada is also positioned as viewing
   subject. She occupies the primary viewing position, formerly occu-
   pied by her companion, who is now positioned slightly above Sada,
   her head turned away from the camera as she explains, 'Each morn-

ing it is like this. Afterwards he goes to the market.' Following this dialogue she turns again to observe the interior action.

6. Cut to medium close-up of Kichi and his wife as Kichi stimulates her with his hand. She falls backwards to the floor, as he bears down on her, they both disappear out of the bottom of the frame.
7. Cut-back to the two women's faces watching.
8. Cut to a medium close-up of the couple copulating on the floor. The camera pans quickly left along the line of their bodies coming to rest on Kichi's buttocks as he thrusts, at which point his wife lowers her right leg to the floor to allow the camera an unimpeded view of the movement of Kichi's penis in and out of the vagina. This shot both confirms the penis as the focus of the watching women's interest and establishes the 'hard-core' nature of the film.
9. Cut-back to the two women. The camera is centred on a reaction shot of Sada as her head moves in small rhythmical movements in time with Kichi's thrusting motion. In this shot Sada is positioned in the centre left of the screen, and her companion's face is partially obscured. Sada is thus defined as the central protagonist within the frame.

The camera then cuts to an exterior high-angle daytime shot of a group of geisha crossing a bridge. Sada is amongst them, signifying a time ellipsis. This next sequence involving the old man again focuses spectator's attention on Sada's interest in the penis through a reverse-cut shot sequence. As some children expose him, there follows a cut to a close-up of Sada's face actively looking; this is then followed by a medium close-up from Sada's point of view of his exposed flaccid penis. Her interested gaze is given greater poignancy when contrasted with the reaction of the other women, who recoil in mock horror. There then follows a series of shots built around Kichi's observations of, and his growing desire for, Sada, beginning with his first encounter with her as she threatens a senior geisha/ prostitute with a knife and culminating in a series of furtive attempts at consummation in the confines of his establishment. Within Japanese pornographic conventions, established in 'pink' films in the early 1960s and refined by the Nikkatsu Studio in the *romanporuno* genre of the early 1970s, Sada's behaviour and position as desiring subject and Kichi's position as desired object is not unusual. In fact, Ōshima's 1976 version is a close remake of the 1975 Nikkatsu *romanporuno* version *A Woman Called Abe Sada* aka *The True Story of Abe Sada* (*Jitsuroku Abe Sada*) (1975) directed by Tanaka Noboru (1937–), which also clearly locates the relationship between the two in terms of Sada desiring subject, and Kichi desired object.[13]

What is different between Western and Japanese pornography conventions of the 1970s is the locus of male pleasure. Ōshima clearly locates this pleasure in the woman's active desiring position within the film. If we take Ōshima at his word, men want women to desire them. As he explains, when he states that, with regard to the castration scene in *In the Realm of the Senses*, 'I would like for that film and that incident not to be viewed in terms of a general kind of symbolism about castration, because the importance of it is that the incident actually took place and entered popular consciousness. *But once again, I think that is how men would want a woman to feel, and they don't think of that act in terms of pain or something like that*' (quoted in Lehman 1993: 58, emphasis in the original). When understood from within the context of arranged marriages that traditionally emphasized the parent/child relationship over and above that of the husband/wife couple, this could also be taken as a plea for a greater emotional bonding between partners. Just as in Western pornography, the Japanese positioning of female desire is clearly from within a male-centric vision, it is just a different vision.[14] As Williams's assessment of the S/M theme of the film reinforces,

> Sada's goal is to effect an impossible merger with/engulfment of her lover through mutually agreed upon strategies that cannot be reduced to fixed positions of domination or submission. This, I think, is the meaning of the final castration: it is not so much an emasculation (in the sense of what Kichi loses) as a fantastic and utterly perverse image of what the mythic sadomasochistic couple, 'Sada/Kichi together', gains. And this gain does not at all subvert the power of the phallus; rather, it moves it around, manipulating its dominance between the two poles of the couple. (Williams 1991: 222).

By the act of castration, Sada is acknowledging her 'lack' and fully accepting her deficiency and dependence on men. This is confirmed by the voice-over narration that concludes the film, stating the circumstances of Sada's arrest and adding that she had hidden in her clothing the severed genitals of her dead lover, and that she had a strange look of happiness on her face at the time of her arrest. It also accounts for why the actual Abe Sada received a relatively light prison sentence of six years and not the death penalty as so many of her 'feminist' compatriots did at this time.[15] In short, *In the Realm of the Senses* constructs its female protagonist as an active subject in the narrative and not a totally passive object of desire. However, although the film is focussed on active female pleasure, it defines that pleasure from a phallocentric ideological position, a position that, taken further in the 1980s and early 1990s, enveloped nascent feminist tendencies within a masculinist ethos in films produced by the Tōei Studios and exemplified in the work of the director Gosha Hideo (1929–1992).

When taken from both within the context of Japanese 'obscenity' laws and Japanese pornography conventions of the time, Sada's position, as active desiring agent, and Kichi's, as desired object, provides no conflict. As the film is ostensibly constructed around Sada's own desire, she confirms the sense of female 'lack' and the desirability and impossibility of possession, thereby privileging the phallus and confirming its possession as central to the hierarchy of social power. In this way the film reinforces the rationale for the system of opposites inherent in a phallocentric ideological position. What I would suggest did upset the censors' sensibilities was the display of Kichi's average-size penis and the numerous shots of it in its flaccid state. As Linda Williams reminds us, 'The phallus is fundamentally not real and not possessed by anyone. In psychoanalytic theory, it is the illusion of the power of generation the control of meaning, the belief in an integral unity of self that no one actually attains but everyone desires. A penis, in contrast, is an organ that men really have' (Williams 1991: 266–267). The scenes depicting Kichi's average organ in a flaccid state became transgressive in that they opened up fissures between the reality of the physical organ and its symbolic function within patriarchal society. In this sense, if we elaborate on and extend Sakaguchi Ango's position and apply it to *In the Realm of the Senses*, the ideology is exposed and some sort of humanity is inadvertently discovered in the naked carnal bodies of Sada and Kichi.

Japanese censorship laws have constantly permitted the most grotesque caricatures of oversized penises to be displayed in everything from *manga* and *anime*, to woodblock prints and *sake* cups decorated with copulating couples, but, until very recently, placed a total ban on the depiction of even pubic hair. In this sense, *In the Realm of the Senses* posed a direct challenge to censorship laws that upheld, not public decency as purported, but rather the symbolic phallus through prohibitions on the disclosure of the naked organ.

Some Japanese filmmakers, philosophers, intellectuals and artists, in
the context of postwar re-industrialization, sought to re-define individual
subjectivity in terms of the primeval 'body' devoid of culture and, perhaps
more important, the hyper-masculinist ideology that had been necessary
to sustain 'total war'. They sought the locus of the individual in desire
expressed in the sexualized woman. However, despite the political use of
the 'body' (*tai*) to counter the wartime over-determination of the 'spirit'
in the ideologies of the 'body politic' (*kokutai*)[16], this postwar re-evaluation of the decadent 'body' as the essence of individual subjectivity in
avant-garde cinema was both constrained by the libidinal economy of the
filmmakers and co-opted and in many ways perverted by both the emergence of independent, exploitative 'pink' films and the major studios that
sought to temporarily sustain a declining industry through the production
of 'erotic' films. As such, a clear masculinist bias was inscribed into these
once radical themes, which were clearly exploited as a means of attracting
male audiences. In these works, the body again represents the emotional,
the nonrational and the hysterical: all aspects associated with the feminine.
Such films sustained the very dichotomies of gender that underpinned the
'body politic' as the 'family state' (*kazoku kokka*) of the war period, thus
contributing to the ever extending multifarious centres of power so central
to Foucault's explications of the role of sexuality and the perverse in industrial society.

In Japan, the 1960s represented a period of high economic growth and a
return to the international arena through the Tokyo Olympic Games of
1964. Television, which had begun transmission in 1953, continued to
make inroads into film audiences in the 1960s. In 1959, at the time of the
Crown Prince Akihito's wedding, NHK subscriptions rose to 3,460,000
and by 1962 had reached the ten-million mark, which translated into
48.5% of households owning a television (Usui 1998: 24). Shōchiku, with
its emphasis on women's films and 'home dramas', suffered badly as married women, often confined to the far flung conurbation's of the apartment
housing estates (*danchi*) of the newly forming middle-class salarymen,
stayed at home with the television. Young unmarried women, the ubiquitous office ladies, remained an important audience group, but they tended
to patronize theatres (Roadshow) specializing in foreign, Hollywood
and European romance films. As a result, by 1958 Shōchiku, which had
been the top-grossing studio in 1951, was pushed into third place by
Daiei. By 1961 the first of the major companies, Shin-Tōhō, collapsed.[17]

A decade later the Daiei Studios would also cease operations, and Nikkatsu would be reduced to the production of 'soft-core' pornography. However, as Matsushima Toshiyuki (2000) argues, it was not only television that impinged on box-office receipts but new forms of leisure and consumption commensurate with a society based on high economic growth.

During the 1950s the major studios had consolidated their positions through a vertical integrated system of production, distribution and exhibition, forcing any independent filmmakers to distribute films through the major studios. This had encouraged a certain conformity of production standards as the big studios invested in big-budget productions built around star personas that ensured large audiences. By the 1960s the decline of the studio system and the increase in independent production companies forced the major studios to experiment with new production styles to attract new and diverse audiences. This was reflected in a trend in film content away from melodrama towards action and 'soft-core' pornographic genres targeted primarily at male audiences.

In the 1950s Nikkatsu had successfully exploited the fashion for American culture. As a principal distributor of Hollywood films after the war, the company, under the leadership of Horiki Yūsaku, resumed production in 1954. In the latter years of the 1950s, they successfully attracted a youth market through the promotion of Ishihara Yūjirō and the *taiyōzoku* films, becoming the top-grossing company by the end of the 1950s. Ishihara remained the top star from 1957 to 1962, after which his star persona was softened and he was turned into the quintessential sensitive 'tough guy'. The Tōei Studios, which had successfully re-established the *jidaigeki* genre in the late 1950s, went on to found the *ninkyō* yakuza genre in the 1960s, taking over from Ishihara Yūjirō in the popularity ratings through the promotion of stars such as Tsuruta Kōji (1924–1987) and Takakura Ken (1931–). In other areas, new genres also began to spring up, in particular the 'pink' film and 'art house' films (*āto shiatā*). It was against this background that Shōchiku promoted young assistant directors, such as Ōshima Nagisa and Yoshida Yoshishige, to full directorial status under the slogan 'the new Ōfuna-style' (*shin Ōfuna-chō*). Ōshima's debut film *A Town of Love and Hope* was the first film to be launched under the company's new policy. The company then tried to link this 'new style' to the French film movement of the late 1950s known as the *nouvelle vague*, a label with which Ōshima was never happy. Shōchiku's attempts to cash in on the sensationalism that surrounded the *taiyōzoku* youth subculture were

268 A New History of Japanese Cinema

clearly instrumental in Ōshima's early rise to prominence, and in terms of their impact on film content, these industrial considerations cannot be overemphasized.

As box-office takings continued to dwindle in the 1960s and on into the 1970s, the major studios sought ever new sensational grounds to attract back audiences. However, despite this decline in audiences, the number of domestic films produced remained high, due to an increase in low-budget independent productions. The 'pink' film, by 1965, accounted for forty percent of domestic production (Satō 1996 vol. iii: 75) and the establishment of an 'art house' cinema circuit around the distribution company, the Art Theatre Guild, also contributed to the increase in independent productions. The Art Theatre Guild, more commonly known as ATG, began operations in 1962 as an independent distribution agency specializing in foreign films. However, by the late 1960s, ATG increasingly distributed independent Japanese productions rejected by the major studio chains. Ōshima's 1967 low-budget film produced by his own company Sōzōsha, *Manual of Ninja Martial Arts (Ninja bugeichō)*, was one of ATG's first domestic successes, attracting audiences to their main Shinjuku cinema. The success of *Manual of Ninja Arts*, a film comprised of non-animated *manga*-style drawings strung together in montage sequences with music and voice-over narration, was indicative of the major changes taking place within the domestic market, signalling the collapse of the studio star system. Quality and not budget or star persona became a criterion in the equation for a film's success. With this and other successes, ATG was able to assist with production costs, and many outstanding films of the 1960s were produced and/or distributed under this system. These included Imamura Shōhei's *A Man Vanishes (Ningen jōhatsu)* (1967), Okamoto Kihachi's *Human Bullet (Nikudan)* (1968), Hani Susumu's (1928–) *The Inferno of First Love (Hatsukoi: jigokuhen)* (1968), Ōshima Nagisa's *Death by Hanging* (1968) and *Boy* (1969), and Shinoda Masahiro's (1931–) *Double Suicide (Shinjū tenno amishima)* (1969).

By 1970 the major studios had cut their production to half that of 1958. Nikkatsu and Shōchiku both increasingly failed to keep pace with youth trends during the 1960s. The generational conflicts of the *taiyōzoku* films spilled over into the industry itself as the abrupt departure of Ōshima from Shōchiku after the withdrawal of his last film of 1960, *Night and Fog in Japan*, and the dismissal of the director Suzuki Seijun from Nikkatsu in 1968, clearly illustrate. Suzuki Seijun, who was fired from Nikkatsu by Horiki Yūsaku after the release of *Branded to Kill (Koroshi no rakuin)*, was taken up by the predominantly university student fans of the 'new wave' at the Cinema Club (*Shinekurabu*). The Cinema Club, which was run by Kawakita Kazuko, the daughter of Kawakita Nagamasa (1903–1981), who had set up the Tōwa Film Importation Company in 1928, was a forum for film research, and in 1968 the Club attempted to hold a retrospective of Suzuki Seijun's works. Horiki Yūsaku, born in the Meiji era and generally purported to have been out of touch with the youth market of the 1960s, attempted to stop the release of Suzuki's films. Suzuki Seijun's cause was taken up by the fans of the Cinema Club circle and various prominent filmmakers of the time, including Ōshima Nagisa. Demonstrations were held in central Tokyo and the incident became inextricably linked to the youth movement and the Anpo sentiments of the period. Ultimately, the matter was settled in court in Suzuki Seijun's favour. It is against this background that Nikkatsu intensified its forays into soft-core pornography, leading to the exclusive production of *romanporuno* films from 1971 until 1988, when the video market effectively encouraged a shift in the site of pornography consumption from the small cinemas to the home. These industry-related factors impacted on narrative content; as fewer women went to the cinema, men became the principal target audience of the major studios.

In 1956 a Westernized ideal type, in the star persona of Ishihara Yūjirō, mobilized a new narcissistic but fierce heterosexual masculinity that challenged sexual politics of the mid-1950s and formed the basis of a new postwar social conception of masculinity that would become the foundation of subsequent male star personas. Ishihara's body overcame the contradictions inherent in man's new passive consumerist role as object 'to-be-looked-at' through both narcissism and the relegation of women to objects of sexual exchange between men. In the late 1950s his body paradoxically worked on two interdependent and contradictory levels, as both proof of his virility and that which turns him into the passive object of the spectator's gaze, hence the emphasis in the publicity material on his 'tough guy' status and the long discussions about his 'natural' style of acting. With Ishihara's physical decline into middle age this role was taken over by stars of the Tōei Studios new action genre of the 1960s, the *ninkyō* yakuza genre, Takakura Ken, and the Daiei Studio's 'last samurai', Ichikawa Raizō (1931–1969). The following chapter develops these links between genre and gender.

## CHAPTER 6

# Genres and Gender

The modern self is the product of sacrifice or internal renunciation, as we relinquish our sensuous unity with nature in a way which is both the root of civilization and the cause of irreparable self-damage. (Eagleton 2003a: 275)

Stars articulate what it is to be a human being in contemporary society; that is, they express the particular notion we hold of the person, of the 'individual'. They do so complexly, variously—they are not straightforward affirmations of individualism. On the contrary, they articulate both the promise and the difficulty that the notion of individuality presents for all of us who live by it. (Dyer 2004: 7)

The previous chapter explored the often violent reactions of young innovative filmmakers of the late 1950s and 1960s who rebelled against not only the constraints of the studio system but also conservative sociopolitical structures that were epitomised in the leadership of the major studios throughout the 1950s, many of whom were re-instated former managers banned under the immediate post-defeat aura of 'democratic' accountability. Contained within these youthful filmmakers' rebellion was an implicit critique of Japanese society, which they saw as returning to the same political expediencies and compromises that had led Japan into imperialist policies and wars of aggression in the 1930s. This chapter focuses on the other side of this equation, the postwar studio system, and attempts a preliminary exploration of the complex relationship between masculine identity—in its idealized form of the 'star persona'—and society at the historical juncture when female audiences for domestic productions were in decline. This will be followed by an analysis of the invention of an aggressive yet conservative femininity evident in the mid-1980s and epitomized by films produced at the Tōei Studios. As will become clear, these films had their origins in the *ninkyō* yakuza films of the 1960s.

As has been considered in the previous chapter, television and changes in patterns of consumption and lifestyle in the 1960s had a detrimental impact on the major studios. As box-office takings dwindled, the industry perceived a clear gender division in audiences between the two competing technologies of television and cinema. Television became associated with the domestic and the female, as genres such as the home drama and later the *jidaigeki* (as opposed to the 'historical spectacular') changed mediums. Alternatively, the major studios increasingly sought to attract predominantly male audiences with 'soft-core' pornography (Nikkatsu); the development of new action genres built around the star persona of male actors such as Takakura Ken (1931–) and Tsuruta Kōji (1924–1987) in the *ninkyō* yakuza films of the Tōei Studios; the violent, eroticised samurai heroes played by Ichikawa Raizō (1931–1969) of the Daiei Studios; and later, in the 1970s and 1980s after the decline of the *ninkyō* film, Takakura Ken in the Tōei Studio's war/military genre.

Film companies operating under a studio system are concerned with profit, therefore at its simplest level the rationalization of film content through the repetition of proven formulas, such as genres, film series and the re-makes, becomes attractive both in the terms of capital risk reduction and product differentiation. Central to these marketing strategies is the star as studio asset through the creation of persona, genres and cycles of films as star vehicles. However, as Steve Neale (1987) points out, for genres to be popular a dynamic has to be maintained between the formulaic demands of the genre, that is, the need to conform to some extent to spectator expectations, and the inclusion of elements of novelty that ensure continued interest. Obviously the maintenance of a similar dynamic, between repetition and similarity versus variation and change, is also crucial to the film series and the re-make. Bearing in mind Neale's further point, 'that profitability—and popularity—was and is always relative' (2000: 225), and the as yet formative stage of audience research, I still adhere to the position that, due to the close links between studio genres and star persona, the study of genre is fruitful in shedding light on cultural imaginings of masculinity and femininity, particularly in an age when studios defined target audiences in terms of gender.

Historically genre studies, by focusing on the production of taxonomies of characteristics that are then used to define a corpus of films, has rightly been criticized as reductive (Neale 2000). Therefore, in the case of this study, the focus on genre and gender will emphasize the role of genre and the series as industry-based criteria of studio product differentiation that, combined with the star system, resulted in the development and perpetuation of specific cinematic images of masculinity and femininity. Furthermore, by going beyond the two broad genre classifications of *jidaigeki* (period drama) and *gendaigeki* (contemporary drama) traditionally employed by Japanese filmmakers and scholars, this chapter will explore the development of in-house studio-derived images of masculinity and femininity that emanated from studio-specific genres, series and cycles of films in the early postwar oligopolistic period of the major studios' hegemony. This is not to argue that the Japanese film industry in any way lacked diversity. Quite the contrary, as was argued in the previous chapter, particularly from the 1960s and the decline of the major studios' hegemony, the independent sector burgeoned, albeit primarily in sexploitation films. However, it was also at this juncture, 1961, when a dedicated 'art house' cinema circuit was formed around the independent company Art Theatre Guild (ATG). Furthermore, the decline in in-house production of the major studios inadvertently supported the rise of independents as the major distributors needed films to screen in their vast national cinema chains. Thus, for example, Ōshima Nagisa's (1932–) two films, *The Pleasures of the Flesh* (*Etsuraku*) (1965) and *Violence at Noon* aka *The Daylight Demon* (*Hakuchū no tōrima*) (1966), although produced by Ōshima's own company Sōzōsha, were distributed by Shōchiku long after Ōshima had left the company after the ignominious withdrawal of *Night and Fog in Japan* (*Nihon no yoru to kiri*) in 1960. Even in the 1950s at the height of the major studios' hegemony, their oligopolistic practices having been re-affirmed and re-enforced by the occupation reforms, the sheer number of films produced ensured a certain level of diversity. However, the standardizing influences of the major studios in terms of the development and perpetuation of star-genre formulations, series, re-makes and cycles of films often provided the benchmark against which innovation emerged. This occurred both through the development of film series and cycles within and amongst the studios themselves and as a set of criteria that revisionist filmmakers challenged.

### The Post-Occupation Revival of the *Jidaigeki* Genre: the Tōei and Daiei Studios

The Tōei Studios, founded in 1947 and formally established in 1951 through a merger of Tōyoko Eiga, Ōizumi Eiga and the film distribution company Tokyo Eiga Haikyū, became known colloquially as the 'production factory of the popular' (*tsūzoku no seizō kōjō*). Founded on a system of the mass production of 'programme pictures' supported by a rigid star system, the company, drawing on the talents of prewar and wartime stars, revived many *jidaigeki* classics banned by the occupation forces during the post-defeat era. Developing long-running series around such popular prewar *jidaigeki* favourites as *Tange Sazen, Tōyama no Kinsan, Mito Kōmon* and Mondonosuke of *The Shōgun's Retainer, a Man of Leisure* series (*Hatamoto taikutsu otoko*), the company had considerable success until the early 1960s when these heroes were increasingly taken up by television. At this point, the cinematic genre underwent a period of change as the format shifted to what became known as the cruel-*jidaigeki* (*zankoku jidaigeki*) presaged by the release of Kurosawa Akira's (1910–1998) *Yojimbo the Bodyguard* (*Yōjinbō*) in 1960 and *Sanjuro* (*Tsubaki Sanjūrō*) in 1962.

Founded by a group of Japanese filmmakers who had worked in Manchuria for the Man'ei Studios, Tōei gathered together many of the former *jidaigeki* stars who had fallen on hard times during the post-defeat years of exclusion; these included Kataoka Chiezō (1903–1983), Ichikawa Utaemon (1907–1999) and Ōtomo Ryūtarō (1912–1985). The studio also nurtured new rising stars into the *jidaigeki* traditions, including Nakamura/ Yorozuya Kin'nosuke (1932–1997), Ōgawa Hashizō (1929–1984) and the singer/actress Misora Hibari (1937–1989). As a strategy to compete with the newly developing technology of television, Tōei established the *jidaigeki* film as spectacle, through both the introduction of technological innovations such as the 'wide-screen' format, Tōei Technicolor[1], and experimentation with innovative narrative content, for example, the introduction of the musical-*jidaigeki* constructed around stars such as Misora Hibari and Eri Chiemi (1937–1982). The spectacularization of the genre and the centrality of the star system to the personnel structure of the Tōei Studios, combined with the fact that the narrative content of the films themselves was often well known to audiences—either as re-makes or as long-running formulaic series—had important implications for the way masculinity was encoded in terms of character development and star persona.

In addressing these structural issues connected with star persona and the 'super samurai' hero, who within these films came to represent the mythic embodiment of social justice, I am indebted to Umberto Eco and his essay 'The Myth of Superman'. In this essay, Eco puts forward the view that the episodic structure of the American comic book hero *Superman* narrative, as a set scheme where a series of events are repeated 'in such a way that each event takes up again from a sort of virtual beginning, ignoring where a preceding event left off' (Eco 1984: 117), breaks with the concept of time as progression. He schematizes this structure as follows: A provokes B, B provokes C, C provokes D and D provokes A. In other words, due to this break in temporal unity, the characters in the *Superman* narrative do not age (*Superman* first appeared in 1938). The same can be said of many of the *jidaigeki* heroes of the serial format, many of whom it should be noted are officials of the Edo system of public justice, for example, Mondonosuke of *The Shōgun's Retainer, a Man of Leisure* series (Ichikawa Utaemon/Tōei)[2], *Tōyama no Kin-san* (Kataoka Chiezō/Tōei)[3], *Mito Kōmon* (Kataoka Chiezō/Tōei)[4] and *The Case Notes of Zenigata Heiji/Zenigata Heiji torimono hikae*) (Hasegawa Kazuo 1908–1984/ Daiei)[5], to name just a few. In this respect, these heroes have reached mythic status through iteration and temporal omnipotence. As Eco explains, referring to the heroic figures of classical Nordic mythology and the figures of Messianic religions, '[T]he story followed a line of development already established, and it filled in the character's features in a gradual, but definitive manner' (Eco 1984: 108). The *Superman* series and, I would suggest, the *jidaigeki* detective series of the 1950s Tōei/Daiei-style, follow the same narrative trajectory in that the formulaic structure of the plot ensures both the viewer's familiarity with the story and the timelessness of the hero, similarly so the re-make.

Despite the detective-style narrative structure of many of these *jidaigeki* series, the pleasure for the audience of these productions lies less in hypothesis building in the whodunit sense but in the performative aspect of how an actor manages a specific role, in particular, how he handles the sword-fight (*satsujin*) scenes. The lack of blood during these choreographed scenes supports this hypothesis as violence is distanced from any sense of the real. On the contrary, the narrative orchestration of violent scenes ensures that they function as performative 'numbers', simultaneously interrupting the linear flow of the plot as the male actor displays his physical prowess, while serving as dramatic climaxes that advance the plot towards narrative closure.

In short, in the 1950s' Tōei and Daiei series, the episodic structure ensures that each film stands alone. There is little sense of temporal progression, in other words, each episode of the *jidaigeki* series forms a separate and discrete unit. Notions of character development and psychological depth are sacrificed to a denial of the processes of aging and death, thereby elevating the heroes, who already display extraordinary prowess in swordsmanship and judgement, with everlasting life and, by extension, the omnipotence of the social values of justice they have come to embody. As such, these characters outlive the actors who play them. However, these samurai heroes are not entirely beyond the reach of the viewers' self-identification in that most of the heroes, like Superman, live double lives as officials of the Tokugawa government (*bakufu*) and as commoners (*chōnin*). It is in this latter role as commoners that heroes such as Kin*san* and Mito Kōmon are endeared to their audiences; in this way their human qualities are revealed to the spectator. In their commoner role, they are shown to have a sense of humour, to be sensitive to the needs of others and to enjoy the same pleasures as the rest of society. Hashimoto Osamu (1989) in his analysis of *The Shōgun's Retainer, a Man of Leisure* series argues that the character Mondonosuke (Ichikawa Utaemon) appealed to male audiences as a role model, and he goes so far as to refer to him as a 'textbook for life' (*jinsei no kyōkasho*). This, Hashimoto argues, is made explicit in the title of the series, which includes the word *taikutsu*. *Taikutsu* is normally translated into English as 'boredom', however, within the context of this series it carries few of the negative connotations associated with the English translation, but rather it means 'freedom from care'. Saotome Mondonosuke has all the comforts of family life provided by those within his immediate group, but as he has no actual wife, he bears none of the burdens of family life. Hence he is a man of leisure, free to follow his interests.

Tsutsui goes further by arguing that the *jidaigeki* genre provides a 'lifestyle model' for Japanese people in times of rapid social and economic change by providing, through nostalgic images, the essences of a past 'Japaneseness'. In the following quotation he emphasizes the centrality of the star persona as a role model.

> [J]idaigeki films have offered a lifestyle model for many years. From the first *jidaigeki* films in which the hero is a samurai seeking truth, to even the *matatabimono* (wanderers) and *chōnin* (townspeople) heroes, *jidaigeki* films have offered distinctive and splendid models for life. In these films is conveyed the sense that people should live in this way. Even in the case of women, actresses such as Yamada Isuzu and Mizutani Yaeko, offer a distinctive image of womanhood. The quasi-*jidaigeki* of the *ninkyō* films starring Takakura Ken and Tsurota Kōji continued to offer this distinctive image of people through the ethos 'help the weak and frustrate the strong. (Tsutsui 2000: 158–159).

While Tōei established a reputation for the popular through its many *jidaigeki* revivals, the Daiei Studios are generally attributed with producing films of a higher cultural standing. Founded during the war in 1942 as a direct result of the government policy that effectively nationalized the film industry, the company's long association with such acclaimed writers as Kikuchi Kan[6] (1888–1948) and Kawaguchi Matsutarō[7] (1899–1985) ensured its reputation. This reputation was further enhanced in the postwar period due to the company's success in securing prizes at foreign film festivals, beginning with Kurosawa Akira's *Rashōmon*, which in 1951 won the special prize for foreign films at the Oscars and Golden Lion at the Venice Film Festival. This was followed by Mizoguchi Kenji's (1898–1956) success in three consecutive years also at Venice.[8]

### *Daibosatsu tōge* (*The Great Bodhisattva Pass*) and the Demonic

I want to perish together with my sword. *Ken to tomo ni horobiru.* (Ichikawa Raizō as Shingo in *Destiny's Son* [1962] [*Kiru*]

One does not live today for tomorrow. *Ashita no tame ni kyô ikiru no de wa nai.* (Ichikawa Raizō as Nemuri Kyōshirō in the series of the same name [1963–1969])

A man on the road to death will die at his own convenience. *Shinu yatsu wa katte ni shinu.* (Ichikawa Raizō as Tsukue Ryūnosuke in *The Great Bodhisattva Pass* trilogy [1960–1961])

Within Japan's modern history there have been two periods of rapid socio-economic change, the first coming in the post-Meiji Restoration (1868) period of economic industrialization and cultural modernization; and the second in the postwar period of reconstruction, the so-called 'economic miracle' of the Korean, and Vietnam wars period. In both instances rapid economic change and restructuring brought in their wake social dislocation and a weakening of traditional Neo-Confucian-derived social structures. The analysis in chapter one of the 'social realist' *gendaigeki* films highlighted the contradictions in the individualizing ethos of modernity and the stresses and strains this placed on the family during the 1930s, a factor compounded by the economic recession.

   In the period dramas (*jidaigeki*) of the wandering yakuza/*rōnin* (*matatabimono*) genre productions of the 1920s and early 1930s, similar themes of displacement and alienation were often played out on the body of the dispossessed *rōnin*, as his refusal or inability to conform to the new civil order condemned him to a solitary existence on the margins of society. As anachronisms, the bodies of these *rōnin* are thus beaten and bound, as in the 1925 production *The Serpent* (*Orochi*), or mutilated, as in the one-armed, one-eyed Tange Sazen. As we saw in chapter two, these heroes often act out their narratives of isolation in the historical time frame of the declining years of the Tokugawa hegemony, known as the *bakumatsu* period. This period is marked, within *jidaigeki* film discourse, by a transition from the dominance of premodern social organizations to the emergence of a civil society based on state-ism and the law.

Alternatively, in the postwar, post-occupation period, the bodies of the so-called nihilistic heroes of the *ninkyō* yakuza films and those of the cruel-*jidaigeki* films of the late 1960s also became the site upon which emotions of alienation are played out, only this time it is against a background of affluence and with one essential difference: out of 'hubristic' defiance comes a vain individualizing self-affirmation. The difference between the *jidaigeki* produced during these two historical periods can best be grasped by an understanding of the subtle linguistic shift in the meaning of 'nihilism' (*kyomu*), frequently employed by Japanese film critics and historians when describing these films. The 'nihilism' of the 1925 *The Serpent*-style film is grounded in the heroes' alienation from the community through the failure of moral concepts of justice. Heizaburō is arbitrarily expelled from the Confucian Classics School and his domain. His unjust expulsion sets off a chain of misfortunes leading to his ultimate incarceration. The nihilism of the 1960s' *jidaigeki* films is, by contrast, founded on a transgressive refusal to adhere to the norms of a corrupt society. This is particularly the case in those films based on the novels written in the 1950s by Shibata Renzaburō (1917–1978), such as the popular *Nemuri Kyōshirō* series of twelve films produced by the Daiei Studios between 1963 and the death of the star Ichikawa Raizō in 1969, and the *ninkyō* yakuza films produced by Tōei and epitomized through the star persona of Takakura Ken. The conscious transgression of these norms by the hero sets off a chain of events that similarly leads the hero to either a form of heroic isolationism, as in the case of Nemuri Kyōshirō, or to a search for an authentic identity in a prison community, as in the *Abashiri Prison* films of the *ninkyō* yakuza genre starring Takakura Ken.

In both genres the heroes, Ichikawa Raizō of the *Nemuri Kyōshirō* series and Takakura Ken of the *ninkyō* yakuza genre films, are frequently described in the literature as nihilistic in the philosophical sense of people who reject the existing social order and moral restraints. Nemuri Kyōshirō fights against the two evils 'money and desire', which the series, and the myriad of other films based on Shibata novels starring Ichikawa Raizō produced in the 1960s by Daiei portray as being at the centre of corruption. As Nemuri Kyōshirō expounds in the fifth film of the series released in 1965, *Nemuri Kyōshirō: the Sword Inflamed with Emotion* (*Nemuri Kyōshirō: enjō ken*), 'Money, money, money, everyone in this world is in an intimidating eddy of avarice . . . Yet on the surface all appears peaceful.' This observation is followed by a montage sequence of shots of a bustling street scene that visually reinforces this sentiment: beggars are contrasted with wealthy noblemen, an errand boy struggles under a load of merchandise as his master strides on ahead and a group of bedraggled *rōnin* saunter along a crowded street. Similarly, within the narratives of the Tōei *ninkyō* yakuza film series, 'money and greed' are also posited as being at the heart of the social breakdown of relationships between individuals. Out of this postwar linking of nihilism to specific geo-historical configurations of *mise-en-scène*, through the hero's rejection of the society founded on utilitarian principles, the individual emerges pure and untainted. Nihilism as a term adopted into the Japanese lexicon and transliterated from the English as *nihirizumu* thus carries positive meanings of the heroic in that the material world is rejected in favour of some higher abstract spiritual system of values symbolized by the heroes' martial skills and confused with star persona.

In broad terms, there is a subtle historical shift in emphasis in that in the earlier 1920s' films of *The Serpent*-mould the hero is not only unjustly excluded by society but is physically forced into some form of submission or symbolic castration. In these latter, postwar films it is the hero who ultimately chooses to reject a corrupt society, and out of that rejection he defines himself as an autonomous and moral individual. This is well illustrated through a comparison of the 1966 Daiei Studios version of *The Great Slaughter and the Serpent* (*Daisatsujin Orochi*), starring Ichikawa Raizō and directed by Tanaka Tokuzō (1925–), and the 1925 version discussed in chapter two. In the 1966 version, the hero agrees, out of loyalty to his clan, to accept responsibility for a dishonourable attack on a rival samurai perpetrated by the son of a senior clansman. The hero agrees on the understanding that this is purely a political measure and that in twelve months he will be re-instated and free to marry the girl he loves. However, due to the death of the senior clansman and the political machinations of his rivals, he is not re-instated as promised and is instead condemned to continue his wanderings as a dispossessed *rōnin*. In the final sequences, unlike his 1925 counterpart played by Bandō Tsumasaburō (1901–1953), the hero is not led beaten and bound through the jeering crowd to prison but fights off the magistrate's officials (*yakunin*), his rivals from his own clan and the aggrieved opposing clansmen. In the concluding shots, he is left standing amongst the carnage. As the woman he loves runs to him and crouches at his feet, the camera tracks back and the film concludes with this simple affirmation of 'justice'. His rivals have been destroyed and the wronged hero survives.

The genealogy of the themes that came to dominate action genres targeted at male audiences in the 1960s is clearly traceable to the latter half of the 1950s and the Tōei and Daiei studios' revival of the *jidaigeki* genre after its initial banning by the occupation authorities. Despite the many revivals of benign romance themes of the Nikkatsu-style 1930s' *jidaigeki*, other films were produced in the 1950s and early 1960s that resurrected the dispossessed *rōnin* of the late 1920s in re-makes based on popular serialized novels of the Taishō and early Shōwa periods. For example, between 1955 and 1957 the Tōhō Studios produced a three-part re-make of the conservative *kōdan*-derived tale set in the early 1600s, *Miyamoto Musashi,* based on the novel by Yoshikawa Eiji (1892–1962) and directed by Inagaki Hiroshi (1905–1980). Tōei followed suit with a five-part version directed by Uchida Tomu between 1961 and 1965, having earlier released a three-part version of Nakazato Kaizan's (1885–1944) epic novel *The Great Bodhisattva Pass* (*Daibosatsu tōge*) also directed by Uchida Tomu (1898–1970) between 1957 and 1959. This was followed by the Daiei Studios' three-part version starring Ichikawa Raizō released between 1960–1961 (see figures 8, 9, and 15).

In order to trace the genealogy of the postwar hero of the *ninkyō* yakuza and cruel-*jidaigeki* films of the 1960s, it is helpful to reach an understanding of the post-occupation revival of the antihero, Tsukue Ryūnosuke, of *The Great Bodhisattva Pass*. For the purposes of the current discussion I draw on the version directed by Uchida Tomu at the Tōei Studios between 1957 and 1959, starring Kataoka Chiezō, and as comparison, I refer to Inagaki Hiroshi's 1954–1956 version of the more ideologically conservative *Miyamoto Musashi*, starring Mifune Toshirō (1920–1997).

*The Great Bodhisattva Pass* deals with many of the same issues as *Miyamoto Musashi.* However, while the character of Miyamoto Musashi undergoes a rite of passage from a raw youth existing in a state of nature to play a positive role in civil society through a physical and spiritual transformation, Tsukue Ryūnosuke, an unparalleled swordsman, follows the reverse course to damnation. Both films are set in periods of civil unrest. *Miyamoto Musashi* opens in 1600 just before the battle of Sekigahara, which was to divide the country into two opposing groups until Tokugawa Ieyasu (1542–1616) consolidated his victory in the Winter and Summer battles of Osaka in 1614 and 1615, respectively. *The Great Bodhisattva Pass* is set in the last years of the Tokugawa hegemony, the *bakumatsu* period, when the forces loyal to the shōgun, the *Shinsengumi*, fought against the modernists seeking to restore political power to the emperor. While Miyamoto Musashi travels the land seeking knowledge and enlightenment, Tsukue Ryūnosuke traverses the land indiscriminately killing. Located within violent periods of civil strife, both characters are symbolic of the clash of the premodern and modern civil order. Ryūnosuke is a relic from an age, like the *Shinsengumi* he joins, that will soon cease to exist while Miyamoto Musashi, with the aid of Takuan the Buddhist monk, undergoes a lengthy period of training that allows him to maintain a legitimate position in the new order.

Both Miyamoto Musashi and Tsukue Ryūnosuke are contrasted with characters who represent their symbolic other. Miyamoto's youthful but flawed friend Matahachi (Mikuni Rentarō 1923–) succumbs to all the temptations Miyamoto will resist throughout the trilogy. Ryūnosuke's sworn enemy, Utsuki Hyōma (Nakamura/Yorozuya Kin'nosuke), the younger brother of a rival swordsman whom Ryūnosuke kills in the first part of the trilogy, is more in tune with the modern age, becoming involved with a new breed of samurai entrepreneur interested in Western technology and science. Utsuki Hyōma goes through a rite of passage, providing the contrasting personalized morality of the virtuous as against the demonic of Ryūnosuke.

In the final sequences leading up to Ryūnosuke's presumed death, having undergone the ceremonial cutting of his fringe symbolic of his transition to manhood at a nearby Buddhist temple, Utsuki Hyōma returns to the Great Bodhisattva Pass and there meets a former servant of the Tsukue household who is rearing Ryūnosuke's son Ikutarō. At this point Utsuki Hyōma, confronted by the child of his sworn enemy, is torn between feeling an affection for the child as he is also the son of his brother's dead wife, Ohama (Hasegawa Yumiko 1926–), and a hatred of the child fathered by Ryūnosuke; Ohama fled with Ryūnosuke after being seduced by him and after he killed her husband in an inter-school sword contest in part one of the trilogy. In the penultimate moment of the final part of the trilogy at the Great Bodhisattva Pass, Utsuki Hyōma, at the prompting of this servant and his female companion, Omatsu, chooses the path of compassion and embraces the innocent child while musing on the loneliness Ryūnosuke must suffer being unable to embrace his young son. The rains begin to fall and as the river swells its banks, Ryūnosuke, disturbed at having found Ohama's grave, sees hallucinations in which she shows him the severed heads of the people he has killed. Distraught, he stumbles blind in the rain, calling for his son Ikutarō, finally being swept away in the raging river. Utsuki Hyōma, standing on the bank, is unable to intervene and thus saved from extracting his revenge. Within this ending, as with *Miyamoto Musashi*, an accommodation is reached between a powerful masculinity predicated on action and the restraint of civil society predicated on Buddhist morality, which advocates compassion. As with Miyamoto Musashi, Utsuki Hyōma's great skill as a swordsman is tempered by Buddhist compassion. However, the important difference is *The Great Bodhisattva Pass*'s failure to end with a climactic *tachimawari* showdown between two sworn enemies; this ending is iconoclastic in that it breaks the cycles of revenge characteristic of *Miyamoto Musashi* and many *jidaigeki* films. Justice, within the film's discourse, depicted in Ryūnosuke's death and damnation, is taken out of the human sphere as his conscience and nature combine to destroy him. Throughout the trilogy Ryūnosuke suffers bad dreams, hallucinations and by the end of part one is blinded by a bomb blast in an attack made by Utsuki Hyōma and the Imperialist forces on a *Shinsengumi* hideout. Ryūnosuke's physical ailments thus externalize his inner torments. As a master swordsman, he remains undefeated despite his blindness, but as a remnant from a bygone age he lacks the moral principles of Buddhist teaching that would curb the indiscriminate and cruel violence of his sword.

Within the more conservative discourse of *Sanshiro Sugata* (*Sugata Sanshirō* [1943]) and *Miyamoto Musashi*, Buddhism tempers the violence of *judō/bushidō* through compassion and self-abnegation through 'transience' (*mujō*). Hubris is the antithesis of these discourses. Miyamoto Musashi takes the path from hubris to self-knowledge through a variety of learning experiences during his travels including a brief spell as a peasant cultivating the soil. Tsukue Ryūnosuke follows a different path: existing in a world that no longer equates hubris with honour, he is fated to wander dispossessed to damnation. The opening credit title sequence foretells Ryūnosuke's path, as the credits are superimposed over an illustration of the Buddhist world order that scrolls down from *nirvana* to the flames of hell. By the film's end, the cycle of revenge is broken as Ryūnosuke's enemy, despite Utsuku Hyōma's dutiful display of filial piety towards his dead brother, is unable to kill Ryūnosuke, who is swept away by nature in a flood to perdition.

The Buddhist implications of the story line are reinforced in the film versions by the serial structure of the original novel (thirty-two volumes), which highlights the theme of the interconnectedness of all human life. It is in the nature of long-running serials for the development of subplots to be created around peripheral characters. Nakazato Kaizan created a world order perfectly suited to the serial format as, without their being aware of the fact, all the subsidiary characters are interconnected as Ryūnosuke's senseless act of killing the old pilgrim at the Great Bodhisattva Pass in the opening sequence reverberates throughout their lives. In these opening sequences the granddaughter of the old pilgrim, Omatsu, returns with a flask of water to find her grandfather has been cut down. At that moment the thief, Shichbei (Tsukigata Ryūnosuke 1902–1970), is passing after having just robbed the Tsukue house. Shichbei, out of compassion, then takes Omatsu to Edo where, towards the end of the first part of the trilogy, she inadvertently meets Utsuki Hyōma, who has come to Edo to study swordsmanship in order to avenge his brother's death at the hands of Ryūnosuke. It is not until the latter part of the story that these characters realize it was Ryūnosuke's act of killing that connects them. There are many such 'coincidences' that lock the characters into communal relations throughout the trilogy. This Buddhist worldview, so amenable to the serial structure, provides a metaphorical structure through which to interpret the interdependence of human relationships within modern civil society.

Both narratives, *Miyamoto Musashi* and *The Great Bodhisattva Pass*, work on two levels: at the political, the individual must adapt to the restraints of civil society or perish, and second, Buddhism is re-invented as a moral system for the twentieth century within Eric Hobsbawm's conception of the 'invention of tradition', or in this example, its re-invention.[9] However, the endings of the two films differ in the ideological construction of the heroic that they present. Tsukue Ryūnosuke, a character born from the imagination of Nakazato Kaizan in the early 1920s, challenged traditional conceptions of the heroic in the *kōdan* storytelling tradition that developed into the popular print fiction of the Taishō and early Shōwa periods. Unlike Miyamoto Musashi, whose image was taken up by the militarists of the prewar years, the image of the samurai of the Ryūnosuke-style could not be adapted to the utilitarian dictates of civil society. To paraphrase a Japanese literary critic, Ishii, writing on 'men burdened by nihilism', the inevitable nihilism (*kyomu*) of Ryūnosuke's unmotivated killings emerged out of the mists of an oppressive state and an economy in recession. Ryūnosuke 'pushed into the background the brave image of the heroic of general popular culture' (Ishii 1994: 106). Tsutsui Kiyotada argues that the figure of the exiled Ryūnosuke wandering in a spiritual darkness (*mumyō no yami*) embodies both an ancient Japanese consciousness of 'transience' (*mujōkan*) and the sufferings of modern humanity. The sufferings of modern humanity are, Tsutsui suggests, evident

> in the gloomy and depressing lives of Ryūnosuke, Ohama and their child in Edo. In these scenes the pathos is expressed of people who have left their country home for the city, and in the midst of harsh competition have been excluded. These are the people who are inevitably spawned from Japan's modern competitive society. This image overlaps with the socialists with whom Nakazato Kaizan associated. (Tsutsui 2000: 143).

As a socialist and a pacifist Nakazato Kaizan was, according to Ishii's account (1994), greatly affected by the events that became known as the High Treason Incident of 1910 (*Taigyaku Jiken*), which took place just three years before the publication of the first episode of *The Great Bodhisattva Pass*. In 1910 a group of left-leaning intellectuals were charged with conspiring to assassinate the Emperor Meiji and in 1911, after a court case held in closed session, twelve of the group were executed. During the course of the investigation hundreds of left-leaning activists and sympathizers were arrested. Within historical accounts, this incident signalled the beginning of what became known as the 'winter years' (*fuyu no jidai*) of the socialist movement. Ishii argues that it was against this background that Nakazato created Tsukue Ryūnosuke. He goes on to argue that the 'nihilism' (*kyomu*) displayed by the postwar character Nemuri Kyōshirō and the heroes of the cruel-*jidaigeki* films of the 1960s, although firmly rooted in the postwar period of the 'economic miracle', can be traced back to Tsukue Ryūnosuke.

Furthermore, in terms of psychosocial discourses, the legacy of the dispossessed *rōnin* can be seen to have transcended the purely popular and to have been incorporated into mainstream academic debate, as close readings of the film historian Satō's account of the centrality of 'pride' in Japanese popular culture and the historical account of samurai culture given by the Berkeley scholar Ikegami Eiko reveals. Satō (1976) stresses the centrality of *iji* (pride) as a concept for understanding the popularity, and causal motivation, of the hero in Japanese popular culture. He defines 'pride', as does the historian Ikegami (1995) in her sociohistorical account of samurai culture, in terms of honour (*meiyo*). However, contained within these concepts is one of the principal contradictions of the modern condition, described most aptly by Terry Eagleton in the Western context in the epigraph that opens this chapter.

Ikegami, within the context of the Japanese 'honour culture' of the samurai class, echoes the centrality of this contradiction to discourses of samurai self-esteem and dignity—that is, the maintenance of a balance between individual volition and the underlying utilitarian principles upon which civil society is founded. She argues that during the early years of the Tokugawa hegemony, the demilitarization of classes other than the samurai had built into it the contradiction of modernity, as only those who were permitted to carry swords 'deserved the title of honorable men'. 'The pacification of Japan through the collective monopoly of violence by the samurai class virtually destroyed the medieval tradition of self-determinism, which included various forms of horizontal alliance . . .' (Ikegami 1995: 155). This process, Ikegami argues, brought the Tokugawa samurai into a difficult 'cultural dilemma', the solution to which is aptly summed up in the title of her study as *The Taming of the Samurai* and reverberates in both the narratives of Kurosawa Akira's *Sanshiro Sugata* and the many versions of *Miyamoto Musashi*, to name but two examples.

In the psychosocial context of postwar Japan, Satō continues the argument: 'Human beings are living creatures who have an impulse to prove their righteousness'. He also stresses the often conflicting role of the social within the context of the individualizing force 'hubris' (*ijippari*) (Satō 1976: 45). It is this 'hubris' which Satō argues is a motivating force in the causal chain of much Japanese popular culture and which Ikegami sees as being central to samurai 'honour culture'. In answering the question why, despite a logical understanding of the negative meanings attached to 'hubris', Japanese people have such a deep affection for doomed heroes who display an uncompromising degree of 'hubris', he argues that it is an emphatic response to an almost universal experience of childhood.

> A young child at the time he first distinguishes between good and bad becomes confused, when by mistake or caprice, he is unfairly corrected by an adult or an older child. At such a time, the child learns obstinacy and hubris. Why hubris? As the child cannot explain the situation logically, he has two possible reactions, the expression of hubris or doing exactly what

he is told and thereby losing his sense of his own subjectivity. Put another
way, it is at this juncture that the ego is awakened. (Satō 1976: 50)

Translated into the adult world, Satō's explication can be interpreted as an
expression of the contradiction between the often arbitrary mechanisms of
social restraint and cultural expectations of masculinity that evolve around
domination and power. Or to follow Eagleton's (2003a) argument, the
'tragic' is formed out of contradictions inherent in modern life where 'determination and free agency are subtly interwoven'.

Historically, in Japanese mainstream cinema one of the dominant constructions of an idealized masculinity has been encoded within a discourse
of the taming of manhood that is seen to exist in a state of nature. Kurosawa Akira's *Sanshiro Sugata* and the many versions of *Miyamoto Musashi* provide two conservative examples of powerful men whose raw
strength is contained within the arts of *judō* and *bushidō*, respectively.
Thus through the inclusion of a spiritualist element, by linking the art of
the sword or the art of *judō* to Buddhism, these films offer an accommodation between determination and free agency that does not undermine the
ideological construction of a powerful masculinity. In these two examples,
both heroes overcome the contradiction inherent in a society founded on a
utilitarian system of restraint, the subordination of individual desires and
free agency for the greater communal good, through an understanding of
the more esoteric aspects of Buddhism. However, the obverse hero, the
doomed hero of the 1960s, who attains a final level of self-affirmation
through death or incarceration remains, in the postwar age, the more dominant and by definition attractive.

Hayden White reminds us, 'Just as there can be no explanation in history without a story, so too there can be no story without a plot by which
to make of it a story of a particular kind' (White 1985: 62). In general
terms, *jidaigeki* films give a material presence to philosophical questions
of vengeance and justice. Set in periods of sociopolitical transition, acts of
private vengeance are played out against the background of the establishment of institutional forms of public vengeance: justice. One very obvious
and conservative illustration are the many film versions of *The Story of the
Forty-seven Loyal Retainers* (*Chūshingura*).

In historical discourse, the dilemma posed by Ōishi Kuranosuke and
the forty-six *rōnin* has been framed within the analysis made by the Confucian scholar Ogyū Sorai (1666–1728) who sought, on behalf of the Tokugawa government (*bakufu*), a compromise solution to the problem posed

by the act of private vengeance, the killing of Kira Kōzuke-no-suke, carried out by the forty-seven *rōnin*. Ogyū Sorai reportedly posed the question in the following terms: 'If a private principle predominates over a public principle, how can the law of the world stand?' (quoted in Ikegami 1995: 233). In order to uphold the ideal of the law and due to the demands of political expediency (the forty-seven *rōnin* had by this time gained great public support), Ogyū's compromise solution was to permit the forty-seven the privilege of committing ritual self-immolation (*seppuku*) rather than being executed as traitors. This assessment and solution to the problem posed by the actions of the forty-seven *rōnin* has been posited in both popular and academic discourse as a compromise between the old ideologies of political legitimacy and the newly emerging rule of law. As René Girard, within the modern context of the contemporary Western penal system, explains, the rule of law 'operates according to principles of justice that are in no real conflict with the concept of revenge. The same principle is at work in all systems of violent retribution. Either the principle is just, and justice is therefore inherent in the idea of vengeance, or there is no justice to be found anywhere'. Girard continues, 'There is no difference of principle between private and public vengeance; but on the social level, the difference is enormous. Under the public system, an act of vengeance is no longer avenged; the process is terminated, the danger of escalation averted' (Girard 1979: 16). And it is this limiting of the act of reprisal to a single act and thereby breaking the potential for the premodern/feudal cycle of vengeance to become established that informs the narrative motivation for many *jidaigeki* film cycles and series.

Thematically *jidaigeki* films have changed little over the years, remaining centred on justice in one manifestation or another. What did change in the 1960s was the depiction of violence and the *mise-en-scène* in which the characters found themselves. A realistic display of blood and the use of black-and-white filming became the outward defining hallmarks of this subgenre. In terms of the narrative, increasingly the main protagonists fight an isolated battle against a corrupt and ultimately overpowering bureaucratic society. While Tōyama no Kin*san* and Zenigata Heiji et al, as superheroes can intervene and, through a vision of powerful masculinity, overcome the machinations of evil merchants and corrupt officials, the protagonists of the cruel-*jidaigeki* films are doomed to failure by the sheer magnitude of the corruption of society. Under this rubric we can list *Harakiri* (*Seppuku*) (1962) and *Samurai Rebellion* (*Jōi uchi hairyō zuma shimatsu*) (1967), both directed by Kobayashi Masaki (1916–1996), and

*Samurai Assassins* (*Samurai*) (1965) and *The Great Bodhisattva Pass aka Sword of Doom* (*Daibosatsu tōge*) (1966), both directed by Okamoto Kihachi (1924–) for Tōhō.[10]

## The Cruel-*jidaigeki* Films and the 1960s

Nineteen sixty and the release by Tōhō of Kurosawa Akira's *Yojimbo the Bodyguard* (*Yōjinbō*), followed two years later by the release of the sequel *Sanjuro* (*Tsubaki Sanjūrō*), is generally cited within Japanese historiography as a period that ushered in major changes in the postwar *jidaigeki* genre.[11] In the case of the Tōei Studios, Tsutsui (2000) marks the release in 1963 of *The Thirteen Assassins* (*Jūsannin no shikaku*), directed by Kudō Eiiji (1929–2000), as the point when Tōei moved its focus of production from *jidaigeki* to the *ninkyō* yakuza genre. However, as Yamane Sadao explains, the early 1960s was a period of transition between the two genres. It was in 1965 when Tōei opened the April holiday season with a *ninkyō* yakuza double bill that marked the studio's real transition to the new genre (Shundō and Yamane 1999: 74).[12] Daiei successfully adapted the *jidaigeki* genre to the times in two long-running series: the erotic *rōnin* hero Nemuri Kyōshirō of the series of the same name, which continued until 1969 and the untimely death of the star, Ichikawa Raizō, at age thirty-eight from cancer, and the ever-popular blind wandering (*tabigarasu*)[13] swordsman, Zatōichi, starring Katsu Shintarō (1931–1997).[14]

In stylistic terms, the most obvious break with the *jidaigeki* conventions established by Tōei, and to a lesser extent by Daiei, in the 1950s was a transition to realism marked by a reversion to black-and-white filming, an emphasis on depth of field, a realistic display of blood in the action scenes, and the inclusion of docudrama-style voice-over narration. Linked to these changes in the depiction of violence was speed of action, which became increasingly important as the now aging *jidaigeki* stars of the pre-war period had to relinquish their positions to younger more agile stars such as Mifune Toshirō, Nakadai Tatsuya (1932–) and Tanba Tetsurō (1922–). These changes directly challenged the sensibility of nostalgia central to the genre of the 1950s as scruffy *rōnin* sporting 'designer stubble' roam aimlessly around windswept, dusty streets. Gone are the flat kabukiesque studio-built sets filmed in wide screen that Hashimoto Osamu (1989) likens to *ukiyoe* prints of the floating world that emphasize the parallel lines between the sky and the earth. In their place are the architectural structures—walls, courtyards, labyrinths of internal corridors and external alleyways—that trap and confine the characters within their internecine battles. Gone too are the clean pristine kimono and newly laid *tatami* mat rooms of the idealized Edo time-space configurations of the Tōei *mise-en-scène*. These cruel-*jidaigeki* films aestheticized violence beyond the Tōei-style conventions of a choreographed performative language of good versus evil, shifting the focus to the corporeal consequences of violence, cruelty and death.

Allied to the inclusion of blood and realistic sound effects, as swords are plunged into bodies, was a reconsideration of the value of violence in the genre. Within these films moral distinctions between characters become increasingly blurred. The hero (Mifune Toshirō) of *Yojimbo* intervenes in the town politics, not out of any altruistic sense of restoring justice for the commoners but because the situation 'seems interesting' (*omoshirosō*). The final confrontation between Sanjūrō (Mifune Toshirō) and his adversary (Nakadai Tatsuya) in *Sanjuro* is not a contest between good versus evil but a quarrel between two equals. Both men are *rōnin* existing on the margins of society, neither belongs to either group, they are both representatives of the 'unsheathed swords' so aptly described by the magistrate's wife (Irie Takako 1911–). Both are anachronisms as neither can adjust to an age of bureaucratic institutions when swords should be kept in their sheaths. Similarly, the *rōnin* Niiro (Mifune Toshirō) of *Samurai Assassins* becomes involved in the assassination plot against the Elder Statesman Ii for one simple reason, he wants to find a job. The same is true of the hapless protagonist who joins the *Shinsengumi* in *Cruel Story of the Bakumatsu Period* (*Bakumatsu zankoku monogatari*) (1964) directed by Katō Tai (1916–1985).

In some films the graphic depiction of blood becomes part of a sensation-driven spectacle to achieve profits, as in the Tōei production *Cruel Story of the Bakumatsu Period*. However, in other films, such as those directed by Kobayashi Masaki, *Harakiri* and *Samurai Rebellion*, the plots are character-driven and violence becomes a physical manifestation of the harm inflicted on individuals who resist the machinations of bureaucratic organizations. In these films the ethic of *bushidō* (the moral code of the samurai) is deconstructed as an outdated ideology of oppression in a society centred on material rather than humane principles. In *Samurai Rebellion* it is the lustful lord who insists the Sasahara household take in his concubine as wife to the heir of the family when he is no longer interested in her, only to demand her back when the need arises. The film thus poses a question of loyalty from within a humanist ethical view. Should the father of the household, Isaburō (Mifune Toshirō), be loyal to his son, Yogorō (Ehara Tatsuyoshi 1937–), and his wife, Ichi (Tsukasa Yōko 1934–), the former concubine, whom he has come to love, or should he be loyal to a corrupt lord and return the young wife to the castle upon demand? The opening medium close-up shots of the suit of samurai armour in *Harakiri* raise similar ethical questions. The armour is symbolic of the Ii household's ancestors and the traditions of *bushidō* that the film's humanist position challenges. The fact that Tsugumo Hanshirō (Nakadai Tatsuya) picks up this armour and hurls it at his opponents in the final moments of his protracted solitary battle with members of the Ii clan towards the end of the film is symbolic of his attack on the ideology of *bushidō*. The restoration of the armour to its original pedestal after Tsugumo's death is equally symbolic of the *bushidō* ideology's ability to withstand such attacks by individuals.

In terms of narrative, many of the cruel-*jidaigeki* films are based on actual historical incidents that interweave a private, personal narrative around the experiences of an individual *rōnin*. The final scenes are then framed within a discourse, either as voice-over narration or conversation, explaining that the actions of the principal character have been expunged from history—hence the spectators' ignorance of these facts. The narrator explains that either the history books have been falsified or the accounts deliberately destroyed. In the case of *Samurai Assassins*, the main character, Niiro Tsuchiyo, is caught in an Oedipal web that leads to the assassination of his father, Ii Naosuke, an elder statesman (*tairō*) of the shogunate and virtual ruler of Japan from 1858, until his assassination in front of the Sakura Gate (Sakuradamon) entrance to Edo Castle in March 1860. In the final scene Niiro, ignorant of the fact that Councillor Ii is his biological father and that his fellow assassins, having suspected him of being a spy, had attempted to have him killed the night before, runs through the snow waving his sword impaled upon which is the decapitated head of Ii Naosuke. Niiro jubilantly shouts that he will now achieve his goal, which was to find employment as a legitimate samurai.

> **Narrator:** However, the leader of the assassination group, Hoshino, had the night before deleted all trace of Niiro's connection from the records. Accordingly, the name Niiro Tsuchiyo does not exist amongst the names of his comrades.

**Niiro:** 'Look! This head will bring me two hundred *koku*[15], no three hundred *koku* would be cheap. Today a most distinguished deed, the head of Elder Statesman Ii, is in the hands of the Banshū *rōnin*, Niiro Tsuchiyo.

**Narrator:** On 3 March 1860, during the Peach Festival unusually the snow fell in Edo, at Sakuradamon these events took place.

Niiro's aim in joining the assassination plot set up by members of the Mito and Chōshū clans was not political. He was not concerned with the rights and wrongs of the foreign treaty negotiations that Councillor Ii was involved in; his only concern was as a *rōnin* to find employment. These endings thereby deny these 'tragic heroes' the hubristic defiance central to the *Nemuri Kyōshirō* series and the *ninkyō* yakuza films of the same period. Niiro is simply an ignorant unemployed man manipulated by fate. Even Tsugumo Hanshirō of *Harakiri*, who attempts to pit a humanist worldview against the ideology of *bushidō*, is denied the self-affirmation of the morally just. As the subsequent conversation between the Chief Retainer of the Ii household, Benosuke (Mikuni Rentarō 1923–), and his officials inform us, any account of this incident is to be removed from the clan records and the warriors who died at the hands of Tsugumo are to be recorded as having died from illness. Tsugumo's own death was to be recorded as *seppuku*. In *Samurai Rebellion* as Isaburō, although mortally wounded, attempts to crawl to the spot where Yogoro and Ichi's child has been left, he cries out that they will not be able to go to Edo and that no one will ever know the fate of the child's mother and father. The film concludes with a close-up of Isaburō's face lying dead amongst the bamboo and cuts to a shot of the nurse holding Tomi, the baby, in her arms.

It is clear that some Japanese film critics and historians resented the changes that took place in the genre in the 1960s (Hashimoto 1989, Tsutsui 2000). They argue that due to the success of Kurosawa's *Yojimbo* in the West, the studios were tempted to emulate this style of filmmaking in order to achieve international success. In the late 1950s Tōhō opened a cinema, the Toho La Brea, in Los Angeles, which was followed by the purchase of cinemas in São Paulo, New York, Rio and Honolulu. As the first manager of the La Brea Cinema, Ōhira Kazuto explains, 'After the San Francisco Peace Agreement, Tōhō planned to expand their business all over the world, including America. The La Brea was the first part of the plan . . . The purpose of La Brea, which was in a white neighbourhood, was to directly invite American audiences to come and see Japanese films.

Of course, we were planning to distribute our films to the entire nation, but thanks to La Brea, our films came to the attention of the directors and producers in Hollywood' (quoted in Galbraith 2002). According to Galbraith's account, Kurosawa's *Throne of Blood* (*Kumonosujō*) (1957) ran for five weeks in America. This success was followed by *Yojimbo* and helped establish an American audience for Japanese films. Other films from this subgenre also had success at international film festivals, for example *Harakiri* won the Special Jury Prize at Cannes in 1963; *Bushido: Samurai Saga* (*Bushidō zankoku monogatari*), directed by Imai Tadashi (1912–1992), also won a prize at Berlin in 1963 and *Samurai Rebellion* received a prize at Venice in 1967. Tsutsui (2000) also reminds us that both Kurosawa's *Seven Samurai* (*Shichinin no samurai*) (1954) and *Yojimbo* were re-made in Hollywood as *The Magnificent Seven* (1960) and *A Fistful of Dollars* (1965), respectively.

Some Japanese critics and historians argue that this desire to please foreign audiences led to a bastardization of the genre. Hashimoto, framing his argument within traditional discourses of 'Japaneseness' (*nihonjinron*) popular in academic circles in the 1970s and 1980s, goes so far as to speculate why foreigners were so keen on the gory display of blood in these cruel films while rejecting the classics of Japanese *jidaigeki* such as *The Loyal Forty-seven Retainers* and the then contemporary *ninkyō* yakuza genre films. First, he suggests that the tempo is different. *The Loyal Forty-seven Retainers* and the *ninkyō* yakuza films are about 'endurance and mortification' (*gaman, kuyashisa*). These themes, he argues, slow the pace down and are different from the themes in Western films. Second, he takes up the issue of aesthetics and the display of 'blood'. 'To westerners, who are a meat-eating race . . . blood is not considered impure (*kegare*), we can understand this because wine is offered as the blood of Christ. Granting this, as for Japanese people blood is a taboo (*tabū*)' (Hashimoto 1989: 209). He then goes on to talk about Japanese attitudes to blood from the context of the native *Shintō* religion. Tsutsui (2000), on the other hand, by linking the dissatisfaction many Japanese people felt regarding the changes to the genre to the question of nostalgia, makes a far stronger case. During periods of rapid sociopolitical change that threatened Japanese national identity—post-Meiji modernization and the post-defeat occupation periods—the *jidaigeki* films have functioned as one of the few popular forums for the re-processing of history as a vehicle for the redefinition of what constitutes Japanese national identity in an age of increasing convergence. Therefore, as a genre *jidaigeki* films are seen as a means to stabilize an exclusive identity through the establishment of clear boundaries both in the geographical and temporal terms of Edo.

During the 1960s Tōei shifted the moral values of the 1950s-style *jidaigeki* films to the modern age in the *ninkyō* yakuza genre. The 'textbook' nostalgic vision of Japan, engendered by the 1950s-style Tōei *jidaigeki* films, was increasingly absorbed into the newly emerging television *jidaigeki* format as home entertainment. A popular guide to television *jidaigeki* published in 1996 confirms the continued 'nostalgic' appeal to Japanese audiences of these dramas in terms very similar to those employed by Tsutsui (2000) when talking about the Tōei-produced *jidaigeki* films of the 1950s.

> There is a saying that the Meiji Restoration represents the 'dawn of Japan'. This surely has the meaning that the dark period ends and a bright period begins. However, when the dawn breaks, people have to work. Furthermore, work after the Meiji Restoration continued until today with the following slogans: 'wealthy nation strong army', 'out of Asia into Europe', 'treaty revision', 'annexation of Korea', 'all eight corners of the world under one roof', 'postwar reconstruction', 'economic growth' and 'the bursting of the bubble economy'. Is it unreasonable to once again yearn for the repose of night? This is perhaps the secret of the popularity of the *jidaigeki*, particularly those set in the Edo period. (Takizawa 1996: 11).

The cruel-*jidaigeki* films' appeal to realism was concomitant with a shift to historical themes drawn from the latter half of the nineteenth century that challenged the idealized image of the harmonious and 'just' Japan of the Edo period. The morality tales constructed around fictional and/or quasi-historical figures from the height of the Edo period and derived from the *kōdan* tradition were replaced by internecine struggles that emerged in Japan in the *bakumatsu* period. These struggles, sparked by the threat of foreign intervention in Japan's internal affairs precipitated by the arrival of Commodore Matthew Perry and his 'black ships' in 1853, were polarized in films of the 1960s into the pro-shogunate factions, the Imperialist factions and those who sought a union between the court in Kyoto and the shogunate in Edo. Some of the key historical figures around whom these plots are woven are Kondō Isami (1834–1868), the leader of the pro-shogunate faction in Kyoto known as the *Shinsengumi* (*The Great Bodhisattva Pass* and *Cruel Story of the Bakumatsu Period*); Takechi Zuizan/Hanpeita (1829–1865), a samurai from Tosa who supported the pro-

Imperial faction; Sakomoto Ryōma (1836–1867), a samurai also from Tosa who initially joined with Takechi's pro-Imperialist faction, but left to take up the life of a *rōnin* (*Tenchu/Hitokiri* [1969], directed by Gosho Hideo 1902–1982); and Ii Naosuke (*Samurai Assassins*). While the cruel-*jidaigeki* films focused on these internecine struggles often devoid of 'morally' positive characters, the 'good versus evil' dichotomy of the *kōdan*-derived Tōei *jidaigeki* films of the 1950s was transferred to the *ninkyō* yakuza genre. This superficial shift is marked by a transference to the historical *mise-en-scènes* of the Taishō and early Shōwa periods, and in the related *Abashiri Prison* film series, the contemporary (1960s) setting of Hokkaido. These configurations of historical settings were much cheaper to replicate in a rapidly re-constructing Japan where bitumen roads and the ubiquitous TV antennae made location filming for *jidaigeki* productions increasingly difficult and expensive. *Ninkyō*, the term used to describe these films of the 1960s and to distinguish them from the 'true account' (*jitsuroku*) films that followed in the 1970s, is usually translated as 'chivalrous'. However, in more specific terms it relates to political conceptions of an 'authentic' masculinity epitomized by the star personas of, for example, Takakura Ken and Tsuruta Kōji. Like the masculinity of Tōyama no Kin*san* and Mito Kōmon, it is defined primarily in terms of the defence of the weak against the injustices of the powerful.

**Fantasies of Rebellion**

In an article written for the journal *Scenario* (*Shinario*) in 1966 after the release of the fourth film in the *Abashiri Prison* film series (*Abashiri bangaichi*)[16] titled '*Abashiri Prison* Series: an Elegy to the Drifter', Tayama speculates on the reasons for the great popularity of these films in terms of a fantasy of rebellion. Set in the harsh climate of the northern island of the Japanese archipelago Hokkaido, this series of fourteen films, produced between 1964–1971, the majority directed by Ishii Teruo (1924–), follows the fortunes of a group of prisoners who share the same cell in the infamous prison at Abashiri.[17] Tayama considers the relevance of this narrative to Japanese audiences in the 1960s in terms of the tensions and contradictions inherent in conformity and individuality.

> The majority of the audience would probably not perceive of themselves as *nagaremono*. Most belong to the group who live their lives working en-

meshed in the system. Although the standard is low, it offers a degree of stability. However, where is the interest in an unsatisfying stability? . . . Seemingly sinking in the stagnant mire of today's reality these fellows, while enduring the pressures of work, live a tedious life. In their hearts they reject this stability and ambition, it is only natural that they yearn for the hero who returns to Abashiri after freely wandering. (Tayama 1966: 135)

Tayama later shifts the discussion to a related discourse of rebellion, that of alienation. According to this argument, the ambiguities of the Abashiri hero's characterization opens up potential sites for spectators to affiliate their own sense of alienation with the hero's omnipresent sense of loneliness articulated in the theme song sung intermittently by Takakura Ken in a 'gravelly' voice: 'Far, far away by the Okhotsk Sea through the deep red of the brier roses I look at the sea and weep. This place is called Abashiri *bangaichi*'. Tayama gives the example of men who fail to make the grade in a competitive commercial system and who are forced to leave their families behind and are shunted from branch office to branch office across the country. He continues, 'Amongst the audience are factory workers, men that look like yakuza and middle-aged women, all of whom in one way or another have been alienated by the system. It is certain that they can all sympathize with the loneliness of the Abashiri hero' (Tayama 1966: 135). Indeed the Japanese title of the films, which includes the term *bangaichi*, supports this reading. *Bangaichi* literally means 'land that has no address' (*banchi no nai tochi*), which in geographical terms can be applied to the country around Abashiri, a remote part of Hokkaido. However, *bangai* also carries the metaphorical sense of the 'social outsider' in phrases such as '*kare wa bangai da*'. The use of the word in promotional trailers for the series gives a further indication of its metaphorical use in the context of the films, e.g. '*bangaichi no otoko wa doko e iku*' (where will the outsider go?), and '*bangaichi otoko kokyō Nagasaki ni tatsu*' (the outsider will make a stand in his hometown Nagasaki).

In contrast, Shundō Kōji (1916–), the principal producer of *ninkyō* films at Tōei in the 1960s, offers an alternative studio-centred, more conservative explanation that focuses on the moral code of the *ninkyō* films to explain why these series became so enormously popular with audiences in the 1960s. He argues that these films were based on 'dreams and romance', or 'to put it another way, the purity of men who, without calculating their self-interest, risk their lives, and thereby touch people's hearts' (quoted in Shundō and Yamane 1999: 88–89). Both explanations allude to the underlying fantasy the series offers to resolve: the search for an authentic identity and a sense of social connectedness played out in the melodramatic modes of alienation and rebellion. However, where these films differ from those starring the youthful Ishihara Yūjirō, as discussed in the previous chapter, is that this quest is shifted from the domestic sphere of the family melodrama to the breakdown of the relationship between men in the exclusive male world of the action yakuza genre. The origins of this search for an authentic identity are similarly displaced onto a loss of the patriarchal figure (either a biological father or the corrupt entrepreneurial 'father' figure, the *oyabun*) and the 'son', the *kobun*. This loss of the father figure is further correlated with a loss of place, which accentuates the sense of the loneliness of the 'drifter'. Within these scenarios the entrepreneurial father figure, being a morally weak but scheming bully concerned only with material gain, complicates the formation of a positive masculine subjectivity in the 'son' and thus provides much of the dramatic action. The resolution to the dilemma posed by these films is a fleeting homosocial bonding with men of equal standing, which in many instances is consummated in death, as an hubristic expression of individuality, or separation through the return to the prison environment.

Within these films the *oyabun/kobun* relationship refers to a quasi-familial patriarchal relationship between senior and junior men founded on Neo-Confucian precepts popularly known as *jingi* (the moral code of the yakuza), that is, a rigid hierarchical relationship based on seniority. Used predominantly in the Tokugawa period, *jingi*, according to popular conception, was adopted by manual labourers before being taken up by yakuza in the postwar period as part of their attempts to legitimize their social position through historical continuity (Kasahara 1973a: 138). The *oyabun/ kobun* structure of relationships in these postwar yakuza films is ultimately replaced by the lateral *kyōdaibun*, or sibling/brother relationship, which although fleeting, becomes the more emotionally satisfying. *Jingi*, in this context, refers to the mutual code of obligations or morality that binds men in these relationships, that is, the *oyabun/kobun* relationship as well as that of *kyōdaibun*. Up to the end of the Second World War and including the 1950s' Tōei-style *jidaigeki*, narratives centred on the loyal relationship between vassals and their lords, for example, *The Loyal Forty-seven Retainers*, or on the ethic of helping the weak against the powerful, Tōyama no Kin*san* et al. The group, or the 'super samurai', fights against a common external foe in the name of justice. In the postwar period from the 1960s on, as we have seen in the example of the cruel-*jidaigeki* films, this narrative pattern shifts as enemies are multiplied and exist both within the organization or group to which the hero is affiliated and in the external world. As such, there is a clear breakdown in the vertical ties formerly founded on loyalty in favour of lateral ties based on a voluntary homosocial bonding. Broadly speaking, the analysis in this section will follow an historical trajectory by focusing on two highly popular series of films, the *Abashiri Prison* films and the War *Without Morality* (*Jingi naki tatakai*)[18] series, which stars Sugawara Bunta (1933–) and reflects the stylistic shift in the genre that occurred in the 1970s to the 'true record' (*jitsuroku*) yakuza films. This series of nine films, made between 1973 and 1979, is purportedly based on historical 'facts' and follows the internecine struggles of Hiroshima-based gangs in the postwar period. I shall also make reference to three other series central to the genre: *Tales of Japanese Chivalry* (*Nihon kyōkaku-den*), *Remnants of Chivalry in the Shōwa Era* (*Shōwa zankyō-den*) and the *Scarlet Peony Rose Gambler* (*Hibotan bakuto*).[19] Finally, this chapter will conclude with a discussion of the role of women in these films and a consideration of the legacies of the *ninkyō* and *jitsuroku* yakuza films in productions of the 1990s directed by/starring Beat Kitano/ Takeshi (1948–).

Central to the *Abashiri* series narrative is the relationship between Tachibana Shinichi (Takakura Ken) and Akuta, known within prison circles as Onitora ('devil tiger') (Arashi Kanjūrō 1903–1980).[20] The first film in the series sets up the basis for this principal relationship through a complex interweaving of time frames that parallel the present (1965) and Tachibana's childhood through the extensive use of flashbacks. This complex temporal structure juxtaposes Tachibana's rejection of his stepfather and his adoption of the more perfect father figure, Akuta, as simultaneous actions. The film links the loss of the father figure to both the loss of place and the loss of sense of social connectedness as Tachibana's biological father is absent (presumably he did not return from the war) and his cruel stepfather forces him out of the family home. This absence of a positive father figure in Tachibana's childhood carries two contradictory meanings; first is the clichéd but poignant connection between a deprived childhood minus a positive father figure and Tachibana's alienation from mainstream society culminating in his entry into the criminal world.[21] The second is in a sense liberating, as Tachibana is free to choose a man as his surrogate father who is worthy of his loyalty. The relationship between the two men is cemented in an exchange of glances held in medium close-up between the two as Tachibana leaves the prison on the back of a truck and looks back at Akuta, who is shovelling snow by the roadside. This poignant scene of 'nonverbal' communication is overlaid with Tachibana's voice-over narration as he muses, 'Akuta*san*, thanks to you I didn't get mixed up in the attempted jailbreak. For my sake you took a great risk.' This scene set in the early morning follows immediately after Akuta had intervened in an escape attempt the night before that would have prevented Tachibana's release from prison. This scene represents Tachibana's first experience of the father as protector, an experience linked to the exclusive male world of the shared prison cell.

As the series progresses and as Tachibana matures under the influence of the strong father figure of Akuta, he takes on an increasingly patriarchal role with the other younger alienated men with whom he comes into contact. In the 1967 episode *Abashiri Prison: The Evil Challenge* (*Abashiri bangaichi aku e no chōsen*) the above scenario is repeated as a youth, Takeshi, rejects his cruel stepfather and adopts Tachibana as his mentor. In one scene, Akuta ties a piece of string around the thumbs of Tachibana and Takeshi as symbols of their union. In each case the relationship between the elder and younger man is established without words (voice-over narration of inner thoughts is instrumental to this process), through close-up reverse-cut shots, which carry poignant connotations of *ishin denshin*, the immediate communication of truth between two people who share an intimate knowledge.[22] These scenes of bonding are contrasted through flashbacks with violent scenes from Tachibana's and Takeshi's youth.

Within the genre's discourses food is symbolic of the father's role as provider and it is the denial of food by the stepfather figures that sparks the revolt from the sons in the *Abashiri* series. Within the patriarchal discourse of the films, which rigidly delineates gender roles, the stepfathers clearly transgress in failing as providers. In the first film in the series in the prison, the shackles and the guards provide potent images of unjust social restraints against which Tachibana and his friends struggle. These images are linked to the failure of the father figures as Tachibana, bound with his hands tied behind his back, sits in solitary confinement, remembering his childhood conveyed through flashback sequences. In the first such sequence, Tachibana in voice-over narration, interspersed between the on-screen dialogue, explains the images as a woman walks along a country road several paces ahead of a young boy and a small lame girl who clearly cannot keep pace. 'It didn't matter how often I called, Mother didn't respond. She was somehow different, as if she was frightened of something, as if something had made her angry. I was too young to understand at the time, but Mother, who was physically weak, had remarried into this poor house so that we kids could eat.' As the aging groom takes his new bride off to another room one of the guest throws two rice balls to the two children. The young Tachibana rejects them and, taking his sister's hand, they call out through the door to their mother, saying, 'Let's go home, Mother'. As the young Tachibana cautiously opens the door a man's voice shouts out, 'Shut up, you brats'. Simultaneously a porcelain cup, thrown from the interior of the room, misses the children and shatters against an iron kettle hanging over the fireplace. The noise of its shattering overlaps with the crash of the iron door of the food hatch as the guard, having left Tachibana's food, slams it shut, triggering the end of the flash-back and a return to the present. Tachibana, his arms still tied behind his back, kicks the food bowl away in disgust.

In this melodramatic tradition, rebellion ostensibly becomes the vehicle through which the hero separates himself from the established social order. Rebellion thus marks the point of departure on the hero's quest for an authentic identity, which will lead him to an alternative society and sense of connectedness based on homosocial bonds. However, the structure of personnel in these groups as depicted in the films is highly conservative and mirrors academic treatises popular at the time on the nature of Japanese corporate structures. As the social anthropologist Nakane Chie (1972) argues, in a situational-based framework of interpersonal relations, the vertical, i.e., hierarchical ordering of the group dominates over and above horizontal ties between people who share the same attributes. This, she argues, is a characteristic ideal of Japanese group relations and is evident in the structure of social relations in the family, village and more recently the company.

The opening sequences of the first film in the *Abashiri* series, where Tachibana and his group of new prisoners are brought to the jail, are parodies of the often painful initiation of new company recruits. Order is established only towards the latter half of the film, with the emergence of the strong patriarchal figure of Akuta. The rigid structure of the hierarchical relations between the *oyabun/kobun* and those of the legitimate company are reflected linguistically in the chart below and in the plotline of the eighth film of the *Tales of Japanese Chivalry* series, *Severing Relations* (*Nihon Kyōkaku-den: zetsuenjō*), becomes an issue. This episode set in the contemporary era, late 1960s, deals with the changing social status of ya-kuza organizations and a concurrent shift in public discourse that occurred at this time as yakuza organizations became increasingly perceived as predatory 'violent gangs' (*bōryokudan*) rather than noble defenders of the weak. In light of this hostile public opinion, the traditional Hamada-*gumi* decides, under the leadership of its *oyabun* (Takakura Ken), to become a legitimate company (*katagi ni naru*). In one scene there is some discussion about the necessary changes in language usage within the organization as the *oyabun* becomes the *shachō* and his wife is to be referred to as *okusan*, literally 'wife', and no longer as *onēsan* 'elder sister', and so on down the scale.

| **Yakuza** | **Company** |
|---|---|
| *Kumichō/oyabun* | *Buchō/shachō* |
| (leader of a yakuza organization) | (section or company head) |
| *Aniki* | *Senpai* |
| (familiar term for a senior) | (term of address to a senior colleague) |
| *Omae/kimi* | *-kun* |
| (terms of address to a subordinate) | (a prefix attached to the name of a subordinate) |

The functioning of this hierarchical system is played out in two early scenes in the first film of the *Abashiri* series that revolve around cigarette butts. In the first instance, just after Tachibana and the new prisoners arrive and while out on a work detail, Otsuki (Tanaka Kunie 1932–) manages to retrieve a cigarette butt discarded by a passerby. During their break, Yoda (Abe Tōru 1917–1993), claiming the rights of the *senpai*, proceeds to smoke the butt by himself as the others look on. The scene immediately cuts to a long shot of the prison and the following intertitle appears: 'Two years later'. Again the previous scenario is re-enacted, only this time Tachibana and his friends have moved up the scale and, according to rank, share the cigarette butt. In this example the cigarette butts represent continuity, but more important as markers of time, they are symbolic of the integration of the new recruits into the group.

Despite the fact that through the fantasy of rebellion these films call for a radical realignment of an authentic masculine identity that permits a degree of connectedness with other men, the fact that these unions carry homoerotic overtones means they must perforce be fleeting. Therefore, what these films offer is a generally conservative vision of masculinity constrained within existing hierarchical structures, as a comparison of the following statements demonstrates. The first, from a Japanese film studies text devoted to the yakuza genre, links these hierarchical structures to quasi-familial relations.

> The regulation of yakuza society, which binds men in quasi-blood relation-ships of parent/child and brother, is based on '*giri*', which means that one must bear the burdens of past favours to the point of exacting revenge out of obligation. A yakuza is bound by the law, which demands that if your *oyabun* refers to a black object as white you must also call it white. To break this law is to be called a 'heretic' (*gedō*). (Shiba and Aoyama 1998: 25)

The second statement, made by the social anthropologist Nakane, from the perspective of mainstream society, focuses on the significance of hierarchy as structuring principle in 'legitimate' organizations. This, she argues, dis-courages individual members from forming lateral relations. 'Relative rankings . . . are centred on the ego and everyone is placed in a relative locus within the firmly established vertical system. Such a system works against the formation of distinct strata within a group, which, even if it consists of homogenous members in terms of qualifications, tends to be organized according to hierarchical order' (Nakane 1972: 28).

The iconoclastic Nikkatsu studio director Suzuki Seijun (1923–) paro-died this conservative subtext of the *ninkyō* yakuza films in productions such as the 1966 *Tokyo Drifter* (*Tōkyō no nagaremono*). By linking the complete breakdown of *oyabun/kobun* relationships to the specific geo-historical *mise-en-scène* of Tokyo in the post-1964 era, Suzuki's film, in contradistinction to the nostalgia of the *ninkyō* films, explores the inher-ent weakness of this structure by exposing the inherent potential for abuse of power. The *mise-en-scène* of the action of the film is confirmed in its title, *Tokyo Drifter*, and the series of establishing shots in the opening credit sequence. These include iconic shots of Tokyo Station with the 'bullet trains' (*shinkansen*) arriving and departing, a motorway junction and the Olympic Stadium, all of which serve to locate the action of the drama within the contemporary context of Tokyo post-1964. In terms of popular discourse, 1964 and the Olympic Games marks the psychological cutoff point when Japan was reinstated within the world community, the postwar austerity period formally ended and the years of the 'economic miracle' were well under way. However, it also signifies a period of politi-cal scandals, corruption and continued student unrest, and it is this theme of corporate corruption that is parodied in *Tokyo Drifter* as the hero, Tetsuo (Watari Tetsuya 1941–), becomes expendable. Finally, betrayed by his *oyabun* who, devoid of the ethic of *jingi*, is willing to sacrifice Tetsuo for profit, Tetsuo becomes the contemporary, archetypal *nagaremono*. *Tokyo Drifter* thus pre-empts the move away from a nostalgic view of the yakuza as some remnant for an idealized past, or the all-male world of the prison presented in the *ninkyō* series of the 1960s, to the socially critical *jitsuroku* 'true account' series of the 1970s.

## Form and Narrative in the *Jitsuroku* 'True Account' Yakuza Film

The *Abashiri* series, along with the other two main *ninkyō* series starring Takakura Ken, *Tales of Japanese Chivalry* and *Remnants of Chivalry in the Shōwa Era*, present male homosocial bonding as a traditional virtue and principal site of male connectedness that the modern age of industrial capitalism was increasingly eroding. Within the vertical structure of social relations presented in these films, and echoed in academic discourse by Japanese scholars such as Nakane, the *oyabun/kobun* relationship is central. However, the 1970s *War Without Morality* series[23] takes an antithetical position by presenting masculinity beset in a 'post-moral' (*jingi naki*) world. The depiction of this decline in the patriarchy in the 1970s was accompanied by a stylistic shift away from the 'nostalgia' of the *ninkyō* films to 'realism'. These radical stylistic changes to the genre earned the films much critical acclaim as the first and the third films from the series were ranked in second and eighth places, respectively, in the *Kinema Junpō* top-ten lists in 1973, and in 1974 the fourth film was ranked in seventh place.[24] Furthermore, all the screenplays from the first series were published in the journal *Scenario* (*Shinario*) replete with commentary by the screenplay writer Kasahara Kazuo (1927–2002). Ōshima Nagisa also published a lengthy critique of the series in *Kinema Junpō* in 1975 in which he correctly argues that these films, although stylistically breaking with Tōei genre conventions, in fact, are still conservative in their portrayal of the dynamics of the male group.

The structure of loyalty depicted in *jitsuroku* yakuza films of the 1970s moved entirely from the vertical to the horizontal or lateral, as all successful *oyabun* came to be depicted as scheming entrepreneurs. The archetypal bad *oyabun* of the *War Without Morality* series, Yamamori (Kaneko Nobuo 1923–1995), who by the fourth film reaches the ultimate heights of yakuza authority in Hiroshima, is portrayed as a weak man who resorts to tears and tantrums as a means of imposing his will. As Sakai (Matsukata Hiroki 1942–) says as he resigns from the Yamamori gang in the first film of the series, 'Yamamori was like a portable shrine (*mikoshi*), which he had been burdened with all these years'. Yamamori is therefore suitably depicted throughout the series counting money, powdering his nose with a gold compact and in later films surrounded by young mistresses who affectionately refer to him as 'papa'.

This theme of the breakdown between father figures and sons is even more explicit in the second film of the series, *War Without Morality: Mortal Combat in Hiroshima* (*Jingi naki tatakai: Hiroshima shitōhen*), which centres on the betrayal of a young man, Yamanaka (Kitaōji Kin'ya 1943–), by his *oyabun*. As a young man leaving prison in the early postwar period, Yamanaka is set upon by a group of yakuza only to be saved by the intervention of Muraoka, an *oyabun* from a rival gang. After rescuing the young Yamanaka, Muraoka proceeds to manipulate him until, towards the end of the film, Yamanaka—cornered by the police—realises the truth and shoots himself in despair.

The *War Without Morality* series draws heavily on narrative conventions established in the 1960s *Abashiri* series, particularly in the inclusion of the prison as a setting in a corrupt world where male bonding can still occur. In both series the prison environment represents an authentic setting outside mainstream society where men can form relationships that transcend the material concerns of legitimate society. The establishment of these relationships is facilitated by the clear lines of demarcation between the guards as the antagonistic 'them', representatives of legitimate society, and the 'us' of the alienated outsider, the prisoners. In mainstream society as portrayed in *War Without Morality*, these lines are becoming increasingly blurred, and the subsequent disorientation of the principal characters provides much of the dramatic action. This theme, which forms the basis for ensuing conflicts throughout the series, is established in the early sequences in the first film, when Hirono (Sugawara Bunta 1933–) finds himself caught up in a riot over the poor quality and meagre rations of food given to prisoners. He is placed in a cell with the instigator of the riot, a young yakuza, Wakasugi (Umemiya Tatsuo 1938–) who, as becomes apparent in the course of the film, adheres to the code of *jingi*. In this early sequence, Wakasugi informs Hirono that he intends to cut his stomach (*hara o kiru*). This is not, as within the traditional 'tragic hero' discourse of Japanese cinema, an act of atonement or an act of self-sacrifice but a ploy to force his *oyabun* to pay the requisite bail/bribe to secure his release. Wakasugi asks Hirono to call the guards when he attempts suicide and to perform the *coup de grâce* for him if for some reason his plan fails and he is left to die in pain. As a repayment for his help, Wakasugi promises to raise the necessary bribe money to secure Hirono's release. To seal the pact and in lieu of the fact that they do not have any *sake*, Wakasugi makes a cut in both their arms and they drink each other's blood. Thus Hirono is inducted into the world of the yakuza by a man who still honours the homosocial code of *jingi*. Wakasugi's plan succeeds and both men are released. However, upon release both men find themselves in different gangs allied to scheming entrepreneurial *oyabun* who are attempting to rig the local elections. As both *oyabuns'* interests come into conflict, so are the loyalties of Hirono and Wakasugi tested. Wakasugi, choosing to remain loyal to Hirono by eventually severing relations with his *oyabun*, is betrayed to the police and shot in the arrest attempt.

In this example, as in subsequent subplots throughout the series, the hero, Hirono, is bonded to a man of similar age and status rather than to his *oyabun*. The relationship is perforce fleeting, both because of its homoerotic undertones and, as the academic Nakane argues, in a hierarchical structure lateral relationships are impossible to maintain. In the second film of the series, Hirono similarly bonds with the young Yamanaka while in prison. Again, a riot is the cause of Yamanaka's punishment in solitary confinement and again, in a scene reminiscent of Takakura Ken's confinement in the first film of the *Abashiri* series, food is the catalyst that, in this case, bonds the two characters. And again Yamanaka dies in the film's concluding sequences.

In both the *Abashiri* and *War Without Morality* series, the repression experienced by the yakuza at the hands of the guards is representative of the social forces that restrict spontaneous male freedom. However, in the *Abashiri* series where these scenes serve to lighten the dramatic tension as Tachibana and his group often get the better of the guards, in *War Without Morality* these scenes form part of the sadistic power play of the guards, who represent legitimate authority at its most arbitrary. This is particularly evident in scenes that depict intimate body searches and therefore increase the sense of powerlessness of the yakuza victims involved.

The myriad of micro-narratives interwoven around and between individuals throughout the series are contained within the meta-narratives of defeat, the Occupation, the Korean and Vietnam wars and the Anpo demonstrations. These are all alluded to in the opening title sequences with shots of the atomic bomb mushroom over Hiroshima, the devastated post-war landscape and the Hiroshima Dome. The Hiroshima Dome was the Prefecture Industry Promotion Hall and is located just one hundred and sixty meters from the epicentre of the atomic blast. This building has been preserved in its original post–August 1945 state as a memorial. The Hiroshima Dome, which in popular consciousness is symbolic not only of defeat but also of social discourses of victimization perpetuated by, amongst other things, the genre of films known as the *hibakusha* cinema[25], punctuates all the films of the series. These shots often follow a funeral of a young yakuza whose death was caused by the machinations of a corrupt *oyabun*. These deaths, forming the conclusion to a structural subplot of the series—a 'rite of passage' of a young 'hood'—are therefore visually linked to the war and victimization. The penultimate sequence, Yamanaka's death scene in the second film of the series, set this precedent, which was followed in the third film with the death of a hotheaded youth whom Hirono had taken in at the request of his teacher. As the funeral party leave the crematorium, the rival gang attempt to assassinate Hirono, and in the mêlée the bones of the dead youth are smashed on the road as their car speeds off. Hirono picks up the bones, still burning embers from the crematorium, and painfully crushes them in his hand. As he looks up, the camera, as if from his point of view, tilts up to a view of the Hiroshima Dome to the accompaniment of the sobs of the boy's mother on the sound track followed by a shot of her as she collapses in the street. Although there is no geographical connection between the two places, the crematorium and the Dome, the editing clearly links the two in Hirono's and the audience's thoughts. Hirono and various other yakuza with whom he comes into contact are all either de-mobbed soldiers or, as in the case of Yamanaka, the hero of the second film, too young to actually be sent to war, they were reservists trained in kamikaze tactics of self-sacrifice. As Yamanaka says towards the end of the second film, 'This is my *zerosen*', referring to his pistol as his suicide plane and thus predicting his own solitary death.

Like *Tokyo Drifter*, the *War Without Morality* series gives the socio-historical background of the action a very specific diegetic function. This is all the more poignant when viewed from the intertextual context of the nostalgia of the preceding *ninkyō* films. However, while *Tokyo Drifter* depicts a highly stylized *mise-en-scène*, the employment in the *War Without Morality* series of docudrama techniques of filming emphasizes the sense of reality the films project. Drawing on conventions established in war-retro films, the series makes ample use of cinematic devices such as iconic newsreel footage and stills, newspaper headlines, voice-of-god narration and captions over freeze-frames giving details regarding each character's gang affiliations, date of death or length of prison sentence.

The voice-of-god narration in the opening sequences of each film, specifying the historical background to the events depicted, connects the struggles of the various gangs and right-wing politicians to the disorder and chaos of the early-occupation period. The opening narration to the first film in the series links the black-and-white stills of the market to defeat in the Pacific War. This sequence follows immediately after still shots of the atomic mushroom cloud exploding over Hiroshima to the accompaniment of discordant music on the sound track. By only referring to the Pacific, and not the war in China, this opening sequence introduces the principal contextual theme of the series, which is a critique of the intimate connections between Japan's postwar economic recovery and American foreign policy. Visually this is reinforced within the micro-narrative of Hirono's personal experience, as immediately following the credit sequence Hirono intervenes to save a Japanese girl from being raped by three American GIs.

> **Narrator:** 1945, Japan was defeated in the Pacific War. The great violence of war has disappeared, but a new violence is raging in the country devoid of discipline. The hot-blooded young men back from the battlefields, although confronting this lawlessness, they had nothing to rely on but their own violence . . .

The second film in the series, *War Without Morality: Life and Death Struggle in Hiroshima* (*Jingi naki tatakai: Hiroshima shitō-hen*), begins in much the same vein:

> **Narrator:** We return to 1950. In June 1950 the Korean War breaks out and Japan, which has become a munitions dump for the American military, with a growing sense of the good times, is taking the first steps towards prosperity. But on the other hand, the poverty and confusion of the populous, who are oppressed by a labour movement that is dependant on the strong authority of the American military occupation, steadfastly continues.

In subsequent films references are made to the student Anpo demonstrations, the Vietnam War, and by the fourth film in the series, to the Tokyo Olympics of 1964 and Prime Minister Ikeda's 'income doubling' policy.

However, iconic imagery of the Hiroshima Dome, the thriving black markets of the post-defeat decade, and shots of the Hiroshima ghetto where the victims of the atomic bomb eke out their livings, always bring these later films in the series back to their origins in defeat and occupation. Highlighting the implicit critique made by the films of rapacious economic materialism of this 'post-moral' age, the violence of the internecine struggles is given a visceral quality as the hand-held camera is situated in the middle of the action, resulting in distorted camera angles and the occasional splats of blood that hit the camera lens as someone is stabbed. Driven by postwar anti-American discourses, the films clearly associate the 'post-moral' age of capital with American foreign policy in Asia.

Publicity material and articles written by the screenplay writer Kasahara Kazuo emphasize the fact that the films were based on the prison memoirs of Minō Kōzō, a former Hiroshima *oyabun,* and collated by Iiboshi Kōichi (1927–1999). Much is made of the fact that pressure was put on Minō by other yakuza not to reveal this information. These discourses of the 'factual' nature of the films have even been incorporated into recent Western discussions of the series (Schilling 2003).[26] However, as is clear from an analysis of the publicity literature, this was part of a promotional drive to differentiate these 'true account' *jitsuroku* films from the former *ninkyō* films. In fact, the so-called links between 'real' yakuza and the Tōei-produced yakuza films has long been employed in promotional material for the *ninkyō* films of the 1960s, the *jisturoku* films of the 1970s and in the 1980s the *Gangster Women* series (*Gokudō no onna tachi*). As in *War Without Morality,* much is made of the fact that these films are based on the 'best-seller' *Gangster Wives* (*Gokudō no tsumatachi*) by the 'non-fiction' writer Ieda Shōko (1958–).[27] Similarly, the principal producer of the main *ninkyō* yakuza series at Tōei in the 1960s, Shundō Kōji, gives historical legitimacy to the *ninkyō* films in a book co-written with Yamada Sadao when he emphasises his connections with real yakuza during the war years when he worked for a munitions company in Kobe. Referring to one particular *oyabun* of his acquaintance he states, 'That man was truly chivalrous (*kyōkaku*). This impression of *oyabun* Ōno remains vivid' (Shundō and Yamane 1999: 19). Later, when speaking about the film that is generally accredited as being the first film of the *ninkyō* genre, Shundō has this to say: 'When *The Theatre of Life: Hishakaku* (*Jinsei gekijō Hishakaku*) was a big hit, I felt my blood stir. In other words, because I had read the original novels by Ozaki Shirō [1898–1964] many times, I knew that [the main characters] Hishakaku and Kiratsune were authentic yakuza

. . . Underlying my thinking was the fact that since I was young I had come into contact with real yakuza. I felt strongly that I wanted to make films about these yakuza' (Shundō and Yamane 1999: 67).

In an article written for the film journal *Scenario* (*Shinario*) in 1974, Kasahara Kazuo recounts his various meetings with Hiroshima yakuza as part of the research he carried out for the films. He states, '[W]e could not say that the films were a true record in the publicity material', however in another section of the same article he writes, '[T]he films are close to a true record' (*jitsuroku ni chikai*). The sense that the films are factual is further in evidence when in the same article he states that the Yamanaka narrative was based on an actual Hiroshima yakuza, Yamakami Koichi. Kasahara continues, 'I intended to write an elegy to Yamanaka, a youth trained in the military tradition, but too young to have actually gone to war. He offers his *oyabun* the loyalty he once offered the state. He uses his twenty-four-calibre pistol, a substitute *zerosen*, freely, as he assassinates people while whistling a military tune' (Kasahara 1974: 111). Having stated earlier that he himself had been a reservist too young actually to be sent to the war but nonetheless trained to defend the home islands, Kasahara concludes that through the films, '[I]n reality I had wanted to expel the vestiges of that time which remained within me' (Kasahara 1974: 111), further authenticating the narrative as a true reflection on a past reality.

Satō Tadao (1974), writing in an article on the series, argues that the appeal of the *War Without Morality* series lay in its depiction of the transformation of yakuza organizations from groups involved primarily in gambling enterprises to the modern-day organizations that form part of the quasi-legitimate world of Japanese political and economic life. He argues that in the early postwar period right-wing politicians employed yakuza to disrupt demonstrations and to act as strikebreakers. This alliance between right-wing politicians and the yakuza, based on a mutual dislike of any form of communism or socialism, became the vehicle through which yakuza organizations gained a place within legitimate society. It is this transformation that the *War Without Morality* series documents, therefore, '[I]t is possible to write the history of modern Japan by documenting the rise and fall of yakuza organizations . . . The majority of young men who climbed up through yakuza organizations came from the lowest and most discriminated against social classes' (Kasahara 1974: 112).

While the earlier Takakura Ken-style of yakuza fought against the entrepreneurial, self-interested *oyabun,* the yakuza organizations depicted in the *War Without Morality* world have become the mainstay of that same 'post-moral' society. The heroes of this series, like the Takakura Ken model, exist on the margins of mainstream society; however, they take on a pathetic pathos because, unlike Takakura Ken, they are denied any form of hubristic self-assertion, as their deaths are portrayed as mean and degrading. In the final shot of the second film in the series, the narrator, commenting over shots of a broken grave set in a graveyard flanked by gas tanks and industrial chimneys, sums up the pathos of death in this series, when he states, 'Yamanaka, as a typical Hiroshima yakuza, has had his name passed down to today, however, now no one visits his grave. And the Hiroshima yakuza wars continue to expand'. The principal characters' struggles are solitary against monolithic organizations, which collude with legitimate authority to destroy them. Within the 1960s' genre conventions, through the hero's death or his confinement in prison (known colloquially as *jigoku chū*/time in hell), the values of *jingi* are upheld and the hero achieves some short moment of connectedness. From the 1970s and the institution of realist yakuza films, spearheaded by the *War Without Morality* series, the hero often dies a solitary death, and the system that caused his death remains unaltered and if anything continues stronger than before. The values of *jingi*, as the title clearly states, *jingi naki*, are absent in this 'post-moral' age of the 'post-tragic' (to borrow Eagleton's [2003b] term).

### Death and the Hero

> [*Ninkyō* yakuza] films portray all that has been lost in the modern age. (A statement made by a designer working on the *Tales of Japanese Chivalry* series quoted in Shiba and Aoyama 1998: 42)

In Japan of the 1960s, the contradictions inherent in a situation of high economic growth formed the basis of the tragic in mainstream cinematic genres. The ambiguity of the tragic, embodied in the persona of the principal stars of the *ninkyō* yakuza films of the 1960s—Takakura Ken, Tsurota Kōji and Fuji Junko (1945–)—opened these films up to multiple positions of identification that ensured their huge public following. In his article Tayama (1966) focuses on the appropriation of these films by middle-class salarymen. He places emphasis on the fact that the conditions of work in an advanced industrial society reduce most men to a state of dependency. This is in some sense compensated for in the family through the role of household head as provider. However, this is a double-edged sword as the family also represents a constraint to male freedom. In short, high economic growth offered in the same instant greater levels of material security but at a cost of self-abnegation as security and welfare were built upon acquiescence; and concurrently urban society spawned increasing feelings of alienation. Furthermore, in a society in which women were entering the workforce, this source of masculine esteem continued to be further undermined.

Shiba and Aoyama, following this line of argument, also stress the appeal of these films to radical students in the 1960s.

> At that time, even while economic prosperity was being extolled, it was an age when the various contradictions, inherent in a controlled society symbolized by the students' sociopolitical opposition, were being exposed. The *Remnants of Chivalry in the Shōwa Era* series which was based on the theme of 'chivalry and affection between men' (*ninkyō purasu otoko no aijō*) received tremendous support from students and people who felt alienated. (Shiba and Aoyama 1998: 51)

They go on to explain how verses from the theme songs of these films were appropriated by students in the songs they sang at demonstrations and how the term *bangaichi* from the *Abashiri Prison* series was adopted by students to name a square in Shinjuku where protests were held. These crossovers, and at times the antithetical appropriations of the hero/star persona were possible because of the ambiguities of the defining plotline of the strong defending the weak regardless of personal cost. Suzuki Seijun, in his films in this genre, dispelled this potential ambiguity by linking the plotline to very specific sociohistorical time frames, for example, *Tokyo Drifter*—Tokyo in the post-Olympic era. By filling in the historical detail and linking the films to the realities of corporate corruption evident in the media of the day, his films lost their sense of ambiguity, becoming subversive. While continuing to appeal to student activists they alienated the more conservative middle-class salaryman, including the head of production at Nikkatsu, Horiki Yūsaku.

Although the *ninkyō* yakuza films were initially targeted at male audiences, as increased television ownership and changes in lifestyle precipitated a decrease in female audiences for domestic productions, this did not entirely exclude women from the potential range of spectators for the genre. Tayama hints at this, in his reference to middle-aged women in the

310 A New History of Japanese Cinema

audience at the screening of the fourth film in the *Abashiri* series, when he speculates that they could also identify with the loneliness of the hero. The inclusion of the actress Fuji Junko into the *ninkyō* yakuza tradition in the late 1960s, as Oryū in the series *The Scarlet Peony Rose Gambler*, further opened up the genre to a female viewing position by specifically addressing issues of patriarchal loyalty as they applied to women (see figure 16).

Describing Katō Tai's concept for two of the films from the series that he directed[28], Shiba and Aoyama draw attention to the fluidity of cultural conceptions of masculinity depicted in these films in the following statement: 'Katō's concept was, that even if you escaped from the status quo to the world of the outlaw (*autolō*), there were still laws (*okite*) that regulated outlaw life. And as this world was a complete male world, Oryū of the scarlet peony rose could not exist unless she became a man' (Shiba and Aoyama 1998: 53). A theme born out in the first film in the series directed by Yamashita Kōsaku (1930–1998) in which Oryū, after the assassination of her father, a Kyushu *oyabun*, states that from now on until she can avenge her father she is no longer a woman. The tattoo of the scarlet peony rose on her body bears testimony to her stoic intent.

Traditionally in Japanese society the masculine/feminine division of social roles is encoded in the topographical terms *soto* and *uchi*. *Soto* refers to the outside public world, the domain of men and the masculine, while *uchi* refers to the inside, the private world symbolized by the home, the family unit and by extension the feminine. These gendered dichotomies of place are further reinforced through their linguistic adaptation into the use of '*uchi*' as a personal pronoun used by women, and the husband's familiar reference to his wife as '*kanai*', which can be translated literally through the colloquial English expression of 'her indoors'. Equally, one of the main forms of address to a married woman, by someone other than a close family relative, is '*okusan*', which is an alternative reading of the Chinese ideogram for '*uchi*', but with the polite '*san*' attached. Despite the acknowledgement of the complementary nature of this division, these concepts have traditionally combined to keep women in a secondary position to that of men. However, within the quasi-familial world of the yakuza organizations presented in films, women are permitted a degree of authority in the outside masculine world. In this sense, these films offer a complex linking of masculinity to questions of endurance and power that, to a limited extent, permit women to transcend the biological divisions of male and female and enter the public world of the yakuza, while still remaining firmly within acceptable standards of the feminine. The later series *Gangster Women*, which began in 1986, demonstrates this point, as the *onēsan* as de facto head of the yakuza organization must bear the burdens of 'obligation' (*giri*) in much the same way as defined in the classic line uttered by male *ninkyō* stars in numerous films: 'When forced to weigh the balance between duty (*giri*) and love/human emotions (*ninjō*), duty weighs most heavily in a man's world'.

Rather than overtly linking these conflicts to gender, the images and narratives of this later film series, which are centred on strong female protagonists, link them to the role of the female as support for men within an organization. The Japanese title of the film series alludes to this interpretation, focusing attention on the relationship of the women to the organization as the Chinese ideogram used to write '*onna*', woman, is usually pronounced as '*tsuma*', or wife (the *furigana* given above the Chinese character directs the spectator to this alternative reading). This is a semantic device that emphasizes the fact that the main characters are affiliated to the 'organization', the *kumi*, and that this affiliative group membership has priority over their roles as wife to one man.

In the subtext these women are operating within a conservative ethic of 'co-operative unity'. This ethic carries with it the expectation that when a woman marries she cuts off her emotional ties with her natal home and transfers her loyalty to her husband's house. Within the organization these female characters are invariably referred to as *onēsan*. This term of address, which literally means 'elder sister', locates them within the organizational hierarchy. The loyalty of these women is therefore directed to the organization to which they belong, and they only remain loyal to their husbands as members of that organization as long as the husband is fulfilling his role. If he transgresses, as he invariably does, then it becomes the duty of the *onēsan* to fill the void to the extent that, should the situation warrant it, ties of loyalty to the man are no longer binding. This point is well illustrated in the final scene of the eighth film in the series *Gangster Women: The Scarlet Fetters*, when *Onēsan*, Iwashita Shima (1941–), after killing a large number of the rival gang members including the *oyabun* with a machine gun, meets her dysfunctional ex-husband and shoots him. After the husband has been filmed in medium close-up, slow-motion falling to the ground, the camera holds on a close-up of *Onēsan*'s face as she softly mutters 'darling' (*anata*). This close-up hints at *Onēsan*'s inner conflict between her love for the man, as her former husband, and her duty, both to the organization, which her husband had failed, and finally to her obligation to avenge the murder of her father, the Sendai *oyabun*.

Following the narrative convention of yakuza films, a crisis of the patriarchy, the husband/*oyabun* in the *Gangster Women* series, is always in some way inadequate, either through his absence (he is in prison or dead), or he is a weak man. His wife, the heroine of the series, is left to take responsibility, forming the crux of the female dilemma: her conflict between 'obligation' (*giri*) and 'affection' (*ninjō*) for a blood-related family member of a lover. In the series the development of the 'affection' aspect is expanded upon through the relationships the heroine has with, for example, her younger sister (*Gangster Women* [1986]), a son (*Gangster Women: The Final Battle* [1990]), a daughter (*Gangster Women: The Dangerous Gamble* [1996]), a lover (*Gangster Women II* [1987] and *Gangster Women: Resolve!* [1993]) and a young 'hood' whom she comes to care for as a surrogate mother (*Gangster Women: The Scarlet Fetters* [1995]). These relationships are then brought into conflict with her obligations to her affiliative family, represented by the yakuza organization. The first film in the series illustrates this basic pattern as two plots are interwoven around the two themes, drawing *Onēsan* (Iwashita Shima) into situations of conflicting loyalties. Her husband (Satō Kei 1928–) is in prison when the senior *oyabun* unexpectedly dies. His death sparks off a succession struggle within the wider amalgamated *kumi* structure. *Onēsan* enters the fray in a valiant attempt to protect the interests of her husband's faction. Meanwhile she is negotiating a marriage for her younger sister (Katase Rin 1957–) to a Tokyo University graduate, to ensure that her younger sister makes a respectable marriage outside yakuza circles. However, unbeknownst to her, the younger sister has already been seduced by a yakuza from a rival organization while on holiday in Hawaii. In this way both sisters end up affiliated with opposing factions and relations between the two must be severed, as both are expected to remain loyal to their organizations. Unlike the male-centred *ninkyō* yakuza films starring Takakura Ken, where the main male protagonists are permitted fleeting moments of connectedness with other men, the narrative ascription of a feminine '*jingi*' in the *Gangster Women* series stays within traditionally conservative conventions, as connectedness is defined through her heterosexual links to the organization. The motives behind the often violent actions of these leading female characters thus provides the key to their social acceptability. In each example, *The Scarlet Peony Rose* series and the later *Gangster Women* series, due to external circumstances beyond their control, the heroines find themselves in the position of guardians of the family institutions. The important point is that, unlike many of the other characters with whom they come into contact, they are driven not by personal ambition but act out of an altruistic sense of loyalty to the organization.

Following on from conventions established in films starring the youthful Ishihara Yūjirō (1934–1987), the male body in *ninkyō* yakuza films is frequently offered as object of display. The torso of Takakura Ken in particular has been objectified in both the *Remnants of Chivalry in the Shōwa Era* and in the *Tales of Japanese Chivalry* series. In both series in the final sequences, he is generally found stripped to the waist; either he has removed his upper kimono to allow freedom of movement with the sword, or his kimono has been slashed open in an early encounter in the scene (see figure 17). His tattoo is central to his identity as it simultaneously signifies stoicism and identifies him as someone who exists outside mainstream society.[29] It is also one of the conventions in the genre that invites the spectators' gaze. The homoerotic undertones of this display for the predominantly male audience are displaced through several mechanisms, the admiration of the tattoo itself, through wounds sustained in the fighting and through the heterosexual gaze of a female protagonist as in the tenth episode of the *Tales of Japanese Chivalry* series. In this film *The Rising Dragon* (1970), the heroine (Fuji Junko 1945–) sublimates her love for the Takakura Ken character by carving the rising dragon tattoo on his body. Similarly, in the second film in the *Gangster Women* series, it is the heroine's gaze (Toake Yukiyo 1942–) that channels the audiences' look as we are shown part of the tattoo of Ryoji, a young yakuza. However, unlike the earlier 1960s' films, this admiration of the tattoo carries overt sexual connotations as a few scenes later *Onēsan* seduces him.

Oryū and the *onēsan* characters in the *Gangster Women* series take a traditional Japanese femininity and re-articulate it into a kind of power that is respected by other characters in the films. However, like the Nikkatsu *romanporuno* heroines and Ōshima's Abe Sada, their apparent autonomy is structured within a conservative masculine voice. Conventional concepts of looking are reproduced in the films, often through the secondary characters portrayed by Katase Rin, who appears in all ten films of the first series and is renowned for her large breasts. In the second film of the series, acting as a model, she is displayed in triplicate while modelling for a men's magazine. She is in a bubble bath being photographed, while simultaneously she is being viewed through a telephoto lens from a nearby rooftop and all this is relayed to the audience whose source of voyeuristic pleasure vacillates between the two male characters in control of the cameras.

In the first series of *Gangster Women*, Iwashita Shima, who starred in eight out of the ten films, came to represent the archetypal Japanese woman. Through the tragedy of this role, torn between legitimate womanly feelings for blood relatives and lovers that must ultimately be denied and her stoicism when pitted against interminable odds, she has achieved a symbolic status not unlike that of Takukura Ken and Tsurota Kōji before her. The iconic *mise-en-scène* in which she is filmed, in front of the gang's Buddhist altar (*butsudan*), preparing ceremonial Japanese green tea, or walking under blossoming cherry trees in elegant kimono and immaculate coiffeur, all serve to connect her and the values she has come to embody throughout the 1990s with a very specific construction of Japanese femininity (see figure 18). I would argue that Iwashita Shima's appeal to an essential Japanese femininity in these films transcends the audience gender dichotomies of the yakuza genre and in part accounts for the enormous popularity of the series.

Within the *ninkyō* tradition, the loneliness of the main characters, either male or female, is that of the individual locked into a hierarchical system of relations that does not permit any lateral ties. As such, any unions—connectedness—must perforce be fleeting. In the male world, this is related to the homoerotic overtones of the encounter, or as in *jidaigeki* films, it is antagonistic because of the implications of competitive individualism inherent in the genre.[30] In the female world of the *Gangster Women* series, where the heterosexual imperative remains dominant, the heroine must reject romance and/or affection for blood-related family members for the good of the organization[31] and, in so doing, she stays firmly within conservative definitions of the feminine, regardless of the violence she may employ.

From within a scenario in which the homosocial moral code of brotherhood (*jingi*) is brought into confrontation with what is presented as an unjust restraint to male freedom, the hero of the *ninkyō* school displays his individuality through a hubristic refusal to compromise. Thus the fantasy of rebellion offered in these films appealed to the oppressed students of the National Federation of Students (*Zengakuren*) and, in terms of the acquiescent salaryman, this fantasy helped close the gap between the ideological image of a powerful masculinity and the experiential reality of most men's lives. Simultaneously the hero's ultimate failure alerts the spectator to the need to adjust his/her own values to the realities of his/

her social existence. In contrast, as the analysis in the preceding chapter demonstrates, in the world of the independent political cinema, Ōshima Nagisa exposed these contradictions through the portrayal of the criminal, the outsider who, either consciously or unconsciously, disrupts the social order.

As is evident from the previous chapter, the films of the 1950s centring on the alienated star persona of Ishihara Yūjirō were also engaged in a search for a new postwar authentic masculine identity. However, in these films this quest is played out in variations of the *East of Eden* (Elia Kazan [1955]) James Dean-style sibling rivalry theme of the domestic drama. In *East of Eden*, the James Dean character, Cal's search for his authentic self leads to a search for his mother, who had abandoned her two sons when they were very young, leaving them to be raised by their religious father. Similarly, in films starring the youthful Ishihara Yūjirō, the loss of the father and/or generational divisions between father and son provide much of the dramatic conflict. Unsure of his identity, the rebellious star persona of Ishihara Yūjirō lacks a sense of social connectedness. Like James Dean, his search for connectedness often leads him to an investigation of his family heritage. However, in the case of these characters, they find their biological mother, father or siblings were not who they had supposed them to be. Ultimately the films' endings secure a movement towards assimilation, not through the acceptance of the former premodern-derived family structure but rather through the re-configuration of a variant, postwar 'democratic' structure. In short, the star persona of Ishihara Yūjirō in the 1950s facilitated a bridging of the conceptual gap between a changing 'democratic' nuclear family and the earlier Neo-Confucian-derived extended family structure. Okamoto Hiroshi, writing in *Kinema Junpō* in 1958, describes Ishihara's position as follows: 'The great gap brought about by defeat in war stopped all communication between the parents' generation and the children's generation. It seemed that neither the war generation nor the generation in their teens was willing to fill in this deep gulf. Mutual anxiety and distrust kept them apart. At this time moral education and Ishihara Yūjirō appeared and bridged the gap' (*Best of Kinema Junpō* 1994: 724). In keeping with the ideological demands of narrative closure in the domestic melodrama, the characters portrayed by Ishihara Yūjirō in the latter half of the 1950s are affiliated within a re-configured monogamous moral family order, which simultaneously comes into being as the pre-

modern Japanese family structure, which permitted wealthy men a degree
of sexual promiscuity, is castigated.

In contrast, for the heroes of the *ninkyō* yakuza genre, their death or
incarceration at the end of the films, in the performative language of violence, becomes the ritualized vehicle of a fatalistic but nonetheless heroic
expression of an authentic self that marks their connectedness to other men
of similar standing. The closure of films, such as the third film in the *Remnants of Chivalry in the Shōwa Era: The Lone Wolf* (*Shōwa zankyōden:
ippiki ōkami*) (1966), directed by Saeki Kiyoshi (1914–2002), exemplifies
this point. In the penultimate scene, Takakura Ken, on his way to the rival
gang's headquarters, sword in hand, is joined by Ikebe Ryū (1918–), who
asks to be allowed to accompany him in the full knowledge that he will
probably die in the attempt. The two walk slowly together without speaking as the theme song from the series, 'rasped' out by Takakura Ken, is
played on the sound track. The song ends at the precise point they reach
the rival gang's headquarters. The long slow walk, strung out to emphasize
the diegetic significance of the song, represents a fleeting moment of connectedness that disappears in the carnage of the following scene. The film
historian Satō Tadao describes the significance of these scenes in the terms
of the *michiyuki*, the scene in a kabuki play where the two star-crossed
lovers walk to the place where they will carry out their suicide pact. 'The
scenes in which the hero and his brother (*kyōdaibun*) walk in silence to
their deaths are enacted according to a prescribed mode; these scenes represent a continuation of the '*michiyuki*' in the double suicide plays (*shinjū*)
of the kabuki theatre. These scenes are a revival of the traditional aesthetic,
which depicts the beauty of the incomparable purity of the love and trust
of two people who are resolved to die' (Satō 1996 vol. iii: 52). Due to
the overt homosocial nature of the bonding between the two main male
protagonists, their scene of connectedness must perforce be fleeting and
end in death and separation. Ikebe Ryū dies in the mêlée that follows while
Takakura Ken, wounded and naked to the waist, is led off by the police.
Earlier in the film the woman (Fuji Junko), with whom both men had been
involved, was accidentally killed in the cross fighting. The inevitability of
the female character's involvement with both men simultaneously works
to shore up the heterosexual credentials of the main male characters while
reinforcing the homosocial subtext, a theme Fukasaku Kinji would re-
employ in 1975 in *Yakuza Graveyard* (*Jingi no hakaba kuchinashi no
hana*). The tragic pathos of the connectedness of these final scenes in
*ninkyō* films is reflected in their unsustainability. In a society founded on

heterosexual unions, these narrative closures contrast with the assimilation of Ishihara Yūjirō into a new, and by the films' standards, authentic monogamous heterosexual family structure. The homosocial is relegated to the mists of nostalgic prewar historical periods or to the exclusive male worlds of the prison and the war film.[32]

With the change in the aesthetic of the yakuza genre that occurred in the 1970s towards the realist style of the innovator Fukasaku Kinji '*jitsuroku*' film series, the *ninkyō* ethic of the 1960s films again shifted genre. After the great success of the three-part epic *War and Humanity* (*Sensō to ningen*), based on the six-part novel by Gomikawa Junpei (1916–1995) and released by Nikkatsu between 1970 and 1973, epics based on the war or military themes became increasingly popular throughout the 1970s and 1980s. The great majority were produced by the Tōei and Tōhō studios. Former stars of the *ninkyō* genre increasingly took on roles as military leaders in films such as the three-hour epic *Mount Hakkōda* (*Hakkōdasan*), released by Tōhō 1977. Based on an ill-fated military training incident that occurred in 1913, where many young Japanese soldiers died on the snow-covered slopes of Mount Hakkōda in the northernmost part of Honshu, the film stars Takakura Ken and Kitaōji Kin'ya. *Disturbance* (*Dōran*), a three-hour epic released in 1980 by Tōei, was based on the 26 February 1936 Incident when a group of young army officers staged a military *coup d'état* in Tokyo. This film also features Takakura Ken as the disaffected officer protecting the interests of the hapless soldiers under his command. Both films were directed by Moritani Shirō (1931–1984). Furthermore, as accomplished yakuza genre screenplay writers, such as Kasahara Kazuo[33], turned to producing screenplays for war epics, these films increasingly became imbued with many of the same conventions of the *ninkyō* yakuza genre. Military epics scripted by Kasahara include *The Battle for Nihyakusankōchi* (*Nihyakusankōchi*) (1980), based on a battle during the Russo-Japanese War, in which Japan took heavy casualties, and *The Great Japanese Empire* (*Dainihon Teikoku*) (1982), both directed by Masuda Toshio (1927–), and *226*, yet another film based on the 26 February Incident released by Shōchiku in 1989 and directed by Gosha Hideo.

Many of these films based on military and war themes, having their origins in the humanist approach to war-retro films of the late 1950s and the *ninkyō* tradition, contributed to a postwar discourse of the cultural reclamation of Japan's military leaders. In part, this reclamation represented a backlash against both the criminalization of Japan during the Tokyo War Crimes Trial in the early postwar period, and increasingly since the 1980s, a response to the hypocrisy of American foreign policy. This theme is clearly evident in the 1990s as the historical events of World War Two portrayed in many war-retro films are framed within newsreel footage of more recent wars, for example, in the 1994 tele-movie re-make of *I Want to Be Reborn as a Shellfish* (*Watashi wa kai ni naritai*)[34], or juxtaposed with parallel narratives of Western imperialistic aggression—the British in India—as in *A Time of Pride and Destiny* (*Puraido unmei no toki*), or political events such as the destruction of the Berlin Wall in *Spy Sorge* (2003). In tracing this discourse, it is useful to consider the portrayal of General Tōjō Hideki (1884–1948) in various films produced by the conservative Shin-Tōhō Studios in the late 1950s, through to his screen image in Tōei productions of the 1980s and 1990s.[35]

In Western historical accounts, it has been put forward that General MacArthur bowed to political 'expediency' (Beasley 1990) in deciding not to indict the emperor on charges of war crimes. Minear states that there was a report to the effect that during the Tokyo Trial, 'at one point in his testimony [before the tribunal] . . . Tōjō commented that no Japanese ever opposed the Imperial will. In consternation at the ramifications of that statement, Chief Prosecutor Keenan requested the Imperial Household to exert its influence on Tōjō to change his testimony' (Minear 1971: 113–114). Onuma Yasuaki (1993: 35) would appear to concur with this view when he states that Keenan, in his cross-examination of Tōjō, structured the questions to ensure that Tōjō's replies would exonerate the emperor. However, films such as the 1959 *The Great East Asian War and the International Tribunal* (*Daitōa sensō to kokusai saiban*) (Shin-Tōhō), the 1982 *The Great Japanese Empire* (Tōei) and the more recent 1998 *A Time of Pride and Destiny* (Tōei) distance Tōjō's narrative away from American policy, implying instead that Tōjō and his advisors agreed that Tōjō should take full responsibility for the war and thereby offer himself up as the victim of the court and 'victors' justice', thus saving the emperor and the Japanese nation-state. In *The Great East Asian War and the International Tribunal*, this is implicit in Tōjō's statement at the time of his arrest when he says, 'I am the person most responsible for the war, but I not a war criminal', a statement he re-affirms later in the film during the trial scene. It is this distinction the film centres on: Tōjō's acceptance of full responsibility for Japan's involvement in the war but his refusal, and by implication Japan's refusal, to accept the guilt being imposed upon him by the victors. Tōjō's status as the 'tragic hero', making the ultimate sacrifice for the emperor and country, is reinforced by the casting of Arashi Kanjūrō as Tōjō. His star persona carries strong intertextual connotations, as Arashi had taken the lead in the swashbuckling *chanbara* series as the masked avenger *Kurama Tengu*[36], not to mention as a benevolent *oyabun* in many of the principal *ninkyō* yakuza series. In the same year as *The Great East Asian War and the International Tribunal* was released, and in keeping with his star persona, Arashi went on to star as the Emperor Meiji in *The Great Emperor Meiji and General Nogi* (*Meiji taitei to Nogi shōgun*) (Shin-Tōhō).

The construction of Tōjō's character in these films as a 'tragic hero' is dependent on the allegoric meanings the films associate with his death. *Seppuku*, within the 'tragic hero' tradition, is encoded as a sincere demonstration of the acceptance of responsibility for one's actions. Satō (1976) has argued that this conception became institutionalized in the tale of *The Forty-seven Loyal Rōnin* (*Chūshingura*) in its manifold manifestations in Japanese popular culture. Tōjō's case is therefore problematic because unlike General Anami, heroically portrayed by Mifune Toshirō in the 1967 Tōhō production *Japan's Longest Day* (*Nihon no ichiban nagai hi*), directed by Okamoto Kihachi, he did not die by his own hand. In *The Great Japanese Empire*, this impediment to the film's ascription of Tōjō's status as heroic is overcome in a crucial scene between the Minister of War, General Shimomura Sadamu, and Tōjō. In this scene occurring immediately following documentary footage of General MacArthur's arrival in Japan on 30 August 1945, General Shimomura asks Tōjō what his intentions are:

**Tōjō:** I feel a great responsibility to the Emperor and the people. Death is the only means by which I can apologize.

**Shimomura:** I fully understand your feelings. However, would you not consider changing your mind? The Occupation Forces are likely to hold an International Tribunal in order to establish responsibility for the war. If they proceed, you are the only person who could answer the charges. If you are not here, the trial will have an extremely adverse affect on the country. As a soldier, I fully appreciate the pain of living with dishonour, but please won't you stop thinking of taking your life and stand up in court. General Tōjō, it is clear that the Allied Powers intend to put the responsibility for the war onto the Emperor and to thereby destroy the foundation of our country's polity (*kokutai*). Will you take the witness stand and tell the court of the Emperor's truly pacifist sentiments? There is no other way to save His Majesty. For the sake of His Majesty, for the sake of Japan's future, please bear this shame . . .

In the context of this dialogue, Tōjō's impending death takes on two interconnected meanings: by his death the emperor will be saved and simultaneously, because of the emperor's symbolic significance, his death is
linked to Japan's future. Within this discourse, Tōjō's failed attempt at suicide just prior to his arrest becomes a public statement of his sincerity and
his true desire to make restitution through *seppuku*. The above quotation
and the attempted *seppuku* thus coalesce to bring Tōjō's character into
conformity with the earlier conceptions of the heroic as defined in the *kamikaze* films of the humanist style. This point is made even more explicit
in one of the most recent portrayals of Tōjō by the actor Tsugawa Masahiko (1940–) in *A Time of Pride and Destiny* (1998). This film juxtaposes
the Tokyo Tribunal and India's struggle for independence against British
colonial rule through the musings of Justice Radhabinod Pal (1886–1967),
the Indian representative at the Tribunal and the main dissenting justice at
the verdict. In this film Tōjō has the following conversation while in Su-
gamo Prison with the Japanese lawyer, Kiyose, appointed to defend him.
In this conversation Tōjō brings together in one scene the many strands of
postwar discourse that began in the 1950s on the nature of Japan's role in
the Second World War with the first tentative attempts at salvaging some
sense of national worth through the legacies of the kamikaze. Tōjō begins
with comments on the testimonies of the former Manchurian Emperor
Puyi (P'u-i), who had been put in place by the Kantō (Kwantung/Guan-
dong) Army in 1932, and an American priest who had purportedly been
in Nanking at the time of the entry of the Japanese soldiers into the city.

> **Tōjō:** This is a serious situation. It is not evidence, it is hearsay, it is an
> exaggeration, it is nothing but pure fabrication. What are you de-
> fence lawyers doing?
>
> **Kiyose:** We are doing our best, but the directives from the Chief
> Justice . . .
>
> **Tōjō:** The directives are not the problem! The strategy and the inten-
> tions of the Allied Powers at this tribunal are clear. The enemy in-
> tends to judge us on the same grounds as the German Nazis.
> However, wherever you look, in our country there are no examples
> of the mass indiscriminate massacre of people like the Jews. That's
> why they seized upon those testimonies. Our country, as an expres-
> sion of its will, has never given orders for indiscriminate massacres!
>
> **Kiyose:** Yes, I understand.

**Tōjō:** If you understand, then do something. If we don't take measures here and now, the problem will affect Japan in the future. Japan and the Japanese people will be perceived as the most evil of nations. That would be an inexcusable legacy for future generations.

**Kiyose:** But we were defeated—that is why they are doing this. If we hadn't been defeated, they couldn't do this.

**Tōjō:** When you say such things, it is painful.

**Kyose:** Forgive me.

**Tōjō:** It is regrettable, but there is nothing for it except to pit ourselves against our enemies' intrigues with all our remaining strength. We didn't have sufficient resources and we were defeated, but if nothing else I want to defend the honour of our country. Kiyose, can anyone really believe that we would indiscriminately have killed Chinese men who were not soldiers, not to mention women and children? We are talking about our Imperial soldiers, I can't believe it.

**Kiyose:** But the court will only give you one opportunity.

**Tōjō:** Yes. Alone, and limited to one engagement. Don't you think that this resembles something, Kiyose? (Pause) The Special Attack Forces, the kamikaze Special Attack Forces. If they who have hero-ically fallen before me can pardon me, although belated, I have the resolve to die in battle.

Cinematically, in war-retro films of this genre, the deaths of General Tōjō, General Anami and various other military leaders are stylistically linked to Japan's postwar reconstruction through lighting motifs and the juxtapositioning of shots to signify historical closure and rebirth. In *The Great East Asian War and the International Tribunal*, after Tōjō's death scene, characterized by dark lighting symbolic of trial and executions scenes generally, the camera cuts to a shot of the sky and a flock of birds in full flight. This is followed by a series of shots of modern Tokyo includ-ing the Imperial Palace as the voice-over narration enjoins the Japanese people never to allow the nation to go to war again. The film ends with a shot of Mount Fuji over which the title 'The End' is superimposed. In *Ja-pan's Longest Day*, prior to his death General Anami (Mifune Toshirō) tells one of his aids that, from this point on, Japan's history will change and that if all Japanese, whatever their position, work hard Japan can be rebuilt. 'Not only that, but the people who survive must ensure that Japan never faces such a wretched day again'. After his protracted *seppuku* scene, the camera cuts to a shot of the morning sun resembling the Japanese national flag. *The Great Japanese Empire* concludes with a similar shot of the sun filtered through the palm trees. This shot follows immediately after the execution of Tōjō and another minor war criminal. *A Time of Pride and Destiny* ends with India's independence. A former Japanese soldier is depicted riding across the scorching open Indian landscape in the back of a truck with former Indian independence fighters.

The visual codes of lighting and the juxtapositioning of images in these scenes form coherent syntagmatic units of meaning complementing the dialogue. They re-inscribe former wartime iconography, such as the rising sun, Mount Fuji and the Imperial Palace, into postwar popular culture, inflecting these icons with new meanings that encourage the view that the war and the trials were a caesura and that Tōjō, Anami and the other 'war criminals' sacrificed themselves and thereby made restitution for the excesses of the war. Furthermore, the framing of these narratives and/or their juxtapositioning with subsequent wars such as the Korean, Vietnam and Gulf wars and/or Western imperialist misadventures (the British in India) raises the poignant question regarding Japan's war culpability: Were Japan's actions on the mainland and her role in the Pacific War any different from American and British interventions in the internal politics of foreign countries? Was, in fact, Justice Pal's dissenting judgement the only truly just appraisal of Japan's role in the war?

Films that take their themes from historical events, as well as academic histories, resonate with the values and concerns of the times in which they are produced (Carr 1990, White 1985). Therefore, they should be considered on two levels: first, through their appeals to historicity, they should be analysed as texts that purport to comment on times past; and second, and perhaps more important, as cultural artefacts that contribute to the cultural discourses of the times in which they are produced. It is this second aspect that has been the dominant concern of the above analysis, and it is my contention that war-retro films produced by the mainstream studios starring influential actors such as Takakura Ken, Arashi Kanjūrō and Tsugawa Masahiko cast historical figures within the *ninkyō* ideological aesthetic of the 'tragic hero', who altruistically defends the weak against the machinations of the powerful. Genealogically, this theme of sacrifice can be traced back to the early 1950s humanist war-retro films that gave death this allegorical meaning in the kamikaze films discussed in chapter four. In this way the allegorical meaning of the deaths of the youthful members of the Special Attack Forces is distanced from overt wartime propaganda; instead it is re-articulated as a purification in which the old was expunged so that the new could come into being. Visually this theme is conveyed through motifs of light and darkness symbolizing historical closure and rebirth and through images of falling cherry blossoms. From the late 1950s on, the images of Japan's military leaders, in particular General Tōjō, similarly emerged as 'tragic heroes', who sacrificed themselves for Japan's future.

Where Ōshima's films critique society through the exposition of cruelty as a social mechanism of control, in the 1950s Tōei-style *jidaigeki* genre, the 1960s *ninkyō* yakuza genre and war/military films, through cathartic appeals to sympathy and compassion, are conservative, offering in place of a critique a 'fruitless rebellion' as a

> way of squaring up to death which [as Eagleton argues] the modern age has much admired. There is a gloomy existential allure about the idea of going down fighting, which is the final refutation of utilitarianism. Utilitarianism calculates the consequences, whereas this kind of snarling, last-ditch self-affirmation damns them, preferring the aesthetic beauty of an act performed entirely for its own sake, a mutinous expression of value which will get you precisely nowhere. (Eagleton 2003a: 103)

And which ultimately re-affirms the existing social order. Satō perhaps most aptly sums up the essence of these sentiments that coalesced in war-retro films from the 1970s on in his discussion of the 1974 war-retro film *The Air Squadron at the Final Battle* (*A'kessen kūkōtai*) starring the quintessential *ninkyō* actor Tsuruta Kōji in the title role as Vice Admiral Ōnishi Takijirō (1891–1945), principal instigator of the Special Attack Forces:

> *The Air Squadron of the Final Battle* is an epic aviation war film centred on Vice Admiral Ōnishi in his capacity as commander of the navy's wing of the airforce in the final stages of the Pacific War. In this film Vice Admiral Ōnishi appears as a man who, in the final stages of the war, is fully aware of the impending defeat. Nonetheless, in the face of defeat he does not consider minimizing casualties, but continues to dispatch the young pilots one after another. His reason being that, if Japan is to be defeated, and if it is not defeated thoroughly, the country could not be regenerated. If the Japanese are defeated doing their very best, even in defeat, they will still retain the sense of pride in having done one's best. If that sense of pride is lost, then the people of Japan will die spiritually. (Satō vol. iii 1996: 145)

Pleasure in viewing films framed within these generic contexts is not based on hypothesizing outcomes. The formulaic structure of genre and the film cycle, the audience's knowledge of the outcome of the war, all ensures a certain predetermination of narrative outcomes.[37] Pleasure, in these contexts, is based on the 'performative' question[38], at once intimately linked to the star system: How does the individual contend with his fate? Although doomed to a predetermined destiny, his resistance becomes a form of self-affirmation enhanced by the aestheticization of the violence that marks his last splendid defeat. In other words, how does the hero play out his own self-abnegation and turn ruin—the refusal to compromise in a corrupt world—into a 'moral' victory? 'If you have to go out, you might as well do so with a grandiloquently rebellious gesture, demonstrating your patrician contempt for the forces which have brought you to nothing, and thus wresting value from the jaws of ruin. The very way you square up to death reveals an energy which negates it' (Eagleton 2003a: 104).

If we accept the depiction of violence in cinema, in the terms set out by René Girard in *Violence and the Sacred* (1979), that is, as a performative language that upholds conventions codified by a given social order, then we can argue that changes in the depiction of violence can mount both a cultural and representational challenge. As this chapter has argued, since the mid-1950s it is possible to identify several historical shifts in the representations of violence in Japanese films. The 1960s marked a stylistic shift to realism in the cruel-*jidaigeki* films through the depiction of blood, a trend also incorporated into the 1970s Tōei 'true account' (*jitsuroku*) ya-kuza films. In this sense many cruel-*jidaigeki* films challenged the conventions, both ideological and stylistic, of the 1950s Tōei-style *jidaigeki* in much the same way as Ōshima challenges the conservatism of the Shōch-iku Studios by subverting the studio house-style.

The 1960s cruel-*jidaigeki* and 1970s-style 'true account' yakuza films are defined by an exaggeration of the formulaic images of aggression. The displays of severed limbs and spurts of blood shifted the intrinsic meanings of the Tōei Studio's stylized violence away from its metaphorical good versus evil connotations onto a corporeal level. This display of the effects of violence on the body focused attention on the mechanisms of power that work upon the individual through rituals of socialization. In films such as *Harakiri*, the powerful body of the individual (Nakadai Tat-suya) is emasculated through the self-inflicted rite of *seppuku*. Within this context, unlike the hubristic self-assertion of the Takakura Ken star persona, *seppuku* takes on an anti-establishment tenor as it exposes *seppuku* as a masochistic expression of conformity to the tyranny of an outdated masculine code of honour. It is perhaps for this reason, their challenge to the myths of *bushidō*, rather than the more spurious reason, that these films were made to appeal to foreign audiences, that Japanese film critics and historians did not like the changes to *jidaigeki* conventions that occurred in the 1960s.

This trend continued into the 1990s as yakuza films became increasingly characterized by ritualized pathological violent reciprocity between characters played out in 'virtual worlds' in sado/masochistic narratives of power—killer and killed—in, for example, the films of Miike Takashi (1960–), such as *Ichi the Killer* (*Koroshiya ichi* [2001]). The star persona of the actor/director Kitano Beat/Takeshi[39], as developed in films such as *Violent Cop* (*Sono otoko, kyōbō ni tsuki* [1989]) and *Sonatine* (1993), can be analysed as a transitional site where traditionally defined images of the heroic and masculinity, as per the *ninkyō* star Takakura Ken, are re-negotiated within the *mise-en-scène* of the dystopic post-1970s action/yakuza genre.

*Violent Cop* and *Sonatine*, despite differing narrative content, are based on a similar dual story-line structure. In *Violent Cop*, Kitano Beat/Takeshi plays Azuma, a policeman who fights corruption in the police force and the drug barons in society. On one level the film portrays the disintegration of the work-group ethic through corruption, self-interest and the profit motive, while on the other it maintains the conventional detective story line of a policeman fighting crime. In *Sonatine*, the narrative has a similar dual structure. First, the Beat/Takeshi character is brought into conflict with his *oyabun*, who is conspiring with Takahashi, another yakuza from the same organization, to kill him and take over his 'patch'. Second, the plot revolves around the conventional theme of yakuza films, that is, intergang warfare. In both films, Kitano Beat/Takeshi exists on the margins of society as an anachronism in today's individualistic and profit-orientated society.

Azuma's rejection of modern consumer-derived definitions of masculinity is best illustrated through his ambiguous relationship with cars, perhaps the ultimate icon of masculine consumer culture. In *Violent Cop*, while chasing a suspect in his car, Azuma continually confuses the switches for the windscreen wipers and the indicators. In *Sonatine*, while driving his girlfriend home, he runs the car off the road and into a ditch. In *Kikujirō* (1999) he steals a taxi and, unable to drive, wrecks the car, ultimately abandoning it by the roadside as he and the young boy continue their journey on foot. As Fredric Jameson explains, '[T]he new model car is essentially an image for other people to have of us, and we consume, less the thing itself, than its abstract idea, open to all the libidinal investments ingeniously arrayed for us by advertising' (Jameson 1992: 12). In the comedy *Everyone's Doing It* (*Minna yatteruka!* [1994]), Jameson's point is made explicit in a lengthy sequence when a young man (Dankan 1959–) tries to negotiate the ideal of 'car sex' as promised in the advertising campaigns and the reality of his own experience. Only in *Hanabi* (1997) does the star persona of Kitano Beat/Takeshi successfully negotiate the skills of driving, but when we consider the type of car, a family wagon, it is in keeping with the ambience of the caring side of his image that the film highlights. In all these sequences, he is seemingly rejecting contemporary definitions of masculinity mediated through consumption and advertising. Alternatively, his star persona grounds masculinity in action predicated on violence, which is tempered by appeals to the traditional as, like Takakura Ken before him, he is often linked to local festivals (*matsuri*) and the older working-class districts of Tokyo around Shitamachi and Asakusa.

The star persona of Kitano Beat/Takeshi is predicated on a spontaneous masculinity that draws on iconic meanings of stoicism and masochism institutionalized in the 1960s *ninkyō* yakuza films. His use of violence, which in the late 1980s and early 1990s was often seen as extreme, along with films by American directors such as Quentin Tarantino and Oliver Stone, can be defined as part of the 'new violence'. However, the violence he employs in his dealings with opponents is justified by the 'post-moral' age of the violent *mise-en-scène* in which he is placed.

Within the discourses of the 'new violence' of the 1990s, good versus evil is displaced onto the dominator and the dominated.[40] The homosocial ethic of brotherhood of the *ninkyō* tradition mutates into the violent homosexual penetration of the powerless by the powerful. These narrative trends are clearly evident in films starring and/or directed by Kitano Beat/Takeshi and explicit in the films of Miike Takashi. In the *ninkyō* films, masochism becomes an expression of stoicism (*gaman*) symbolized through the pain of submitting to the tattoo artist's knife, and the sado/masochistic rituals of power play are subscribed within a moral context of the powerful defending the weak. However, the increasing drift towards greater visceral appeals through the spectacularization of violence encouraged in the digital age has further shifted the emphasis away from violence as a performative language of morality or justice to the display of phallic power as the end point, as in the *oeuvre* of Miike Takashi. *Battle Royale* (2001) and *Battle Royale II* (2003), both directed by Fukasaku Kinji, take us into the video survival game of win or lose, as the only winner is the student who can survive by killing off his/her classmates.

# REFLECTIONS

## Cross-Cultural Perspectives or Do Japanese Films Exist?

> The dynamism of modernity derives from the *separation of time and space* and their recombination in forms which permit the precise time-space 'zoning' of social life; the *disembedding* of social systems (a phenomenon which connects closely with the factors involved in time-space separation); and the *reflexive ordering and reordering* of social relations in light of continual inputs of knowledge affecting the actions of individuals and groups. (Giddens 1990: 16–17)

> Modernism, or so it imagined, was old enough to remember a time when there were firm foundations to human existence, and was still reeling from the shock of their being kicked rudely away. This is one reason why so much modernism is of a tragic temper . . . It refuses to turn its gaze from the intolerableness of things, even if there is no transcendent consolation at hand. After a while, however, you can ease the strain of this by portraying a world in which there is indeed no salvation . . . This is the post-tragic realm of post-modernism. (Eagleton 2003b: 57–58)

As Anthony Giddens contends in the above quotation, one of the major consequences of modernity was a time-space distanciation, that is, the separation of time and space and their re-ordering into mechanisms for the regulation of human life essential to industrial society (timetables, the regimentation and disciplinary controls of the factory, military, penal and medical systems[1], and the re-ordering of physical space through cartography). Through the privileging functions of lenses both fragmenting and highlighting, and through the formal processes of editing, cinema is the material manifestation of the ephemerality of the 'time-space separation' of modernity par excellence, and as Jean-Louis Comolli astutely understood, it had to be invented. As a precursor to cinema, the train had already established the convention of people sitting in a seat watching moving images through a frame and by 'eliminating the traditional barriers to space and distance forged a new bodily intimacy with time, space and motion' (Charney and Schwartz 1995: 6). By 1904 and the Russo-Japanese War, this connection had been made manifest as some cinemas screening 'topicals' from the war were

designed as replica railway carriages, taking spectators on a virtual journey through the battlefields. Building on the new technologies' appeals to
visceral pleasures, Yoshizawa Shōten, one of the first film companies to
capitalize on the Russo-Japanese War, had by 1910 built Japan's first
amusement park, the Asakuza Luna Park (*Runa Pāku*).

However, cinema does not only appeal to the visceral but shapes tem-
porally fragmented and spatially disjointed often nonmaterial events into
some form of epistemological or ontological meaning. In particular, due to
the adoption by mainstream cinemas of the classical system of 'continuity
editing', constituted on the premise of verisimilitude purporting to re-present 'reality', and based on formal techniques such as the 180-degree principle, the viewer is positioned as subject within the narrative structure so
that 'the viewer always knows *where he or she is* with respect to the story
action. The space of the scene, cleanly and unambiguously unfolded, does
not jar or disorient, because such disorientation, it is felt, will distract the
viewer from the material at hand: the narrative chain of causes and effects'
(emphasis in the original Bordwell and Thompson 1980: 166).

Understood in this context, 'continuity editing' is ideological in that it
visually re-orders time and space within narrative configurations that have
a coherent sense of order. Furthermore, as 'continuity editing' locates the
viewing subject within a pre-prescribed and advantageous position, it fa-
cilitates a *particular* understanding. The technology of cinema is therefore
itself, perhaps more than any other sense-making mechanism of the modern period, an allegory of modernity, being characterized by spacio-temporal dislocation, the mechanical re-ordering of time, and an emphasis on
the visceral sensations and the spectacular. As Miriam Bratu Hansen argues, with regard to Hollywood cinema, it 'provided, to mass audiences
both at home and abroad, a sensory-reflexive horizon for the experience
of modernization and modernity' (Hansen 2000a: 10).[2]

Due to the cause-and-effect rationale, and by placing the viewer in the
always knowing position of '*where he or she is* with respect to the story
action', cinema offered spectators a 'global vernacular' through which,
however transitory, to negotiate the contradictions between the experiential realities of modern life (alienation, chaos, physical danger and powerlessness) and the ideological imperatives of progress and order. However,
as the Japanese example demonstrates, this 'vernacular' had to be learnt.
Its adoption and adaptation as a relevant articulation of an experience of
modernity came at the juncture when the premodern Neo-Confucian-derived 'reality' was no longer adequate, jarring against the experiential real-

ity of people's lives. The photograph, the technology of cinema and the development of the 'star system'[3] were just a few of the mechanisms that successfully re-framed the individual within the sociopolitical worldview of modernity. The *benshi/katsuben* as 'photo-interpreters', trade journals and film enthusiasts such as Kaeriyama Norimasa acted as intermediaries facilitating the learning of, and the adaptation of, the 'global vernacular' of cinema to the Japanese experience.

In the early part of this century, Shōchiku, through the adoption and adaptation of Western filmmaking practices, developed a behaviourist style of filmmaking that radically broke with former theatrical traditions and yet was responsive to the demands of the local film-going population. Linked to this style was a distinctive worldview that had grown out of the Japanese experience of 'modernity'. Shōchiku cinema of the 1930s, in popular films such as *Marching On/Shingun* (1930) and *The Love-Troth Tree/Aizen Katsura* (1938), re-affirmed the ideological imperative of the inherent rationality associated with Fordism and Taylorism[4], which is in practice the 'adaptation of a means to an end', in other words, a mental protocol based upon a 'cause-and-effect' relationship aimed at achieving a specific goal. In the case of *Marching On*, based on a popular American novel by James Boyd published in 1927, the hero's aim is social mobility through career and marriage. In *The Love-Troth Tree*, for the heroine, it is autonomy through career and free choice in marriage.

Contradicting this utopian view of the promises of modernity are the 'social realist' and derivative films of the 1930s, in which the *mise-en-scène* as place is central to the diegesis. Rather than a simple clash of personalized moralities as a narrative strategy permitting the exploration of psychological realism, in films directed by Ozu Yasujirō (1903–1963) and scripted by the James Maki collaboration, the *mise-en-scène* is an historical force against which the protagonists must also struggle. Thus the mutability of the *mise-en-scène* and not human agency becomes the source of tragedy. The violence or suffering the protagonists experience is divorced from their beings as either moral or flawed characters. They are merely human and they therefore offer a vicarious parallel to our own lives.

This emphasis on the mutability of the *mise-en-scène*, as a recognition of the inability of human agency to impact upon the world except within historically contingent parameters, became the thematic mainstay of the films of the postwar 'humanist' style. As Kaji, the truly 'tragic hero' of the postwar epic *The Human Condition/Ningen no jōken* (1959–1961) demonstrates, even the strongest, most heroic, and most morally virtuous are doomed to failure when the sociopolitical parameters of human agency are at their most restrictive as in times of war. The sociohistorical parameters of constraint, in films from the 'social realist' style to *The Human Condition*, to the *kamikaze* films and to the cruel *zankoku*-samurai films of the 1960s, are the forces against which the individual struggles and inevitably fails.

In the yakuza films of the 'post-moral' (*jingi naki*) 1970s and beyond, a similar pattern emerges as the corrupt machinations of *oyabun* are increasingly linked to a dystopic *mise-en-scène*, providing the diegetic opposition against which the protagonists struggle, both legitimating and masking a spectacularization of the extremities of violence that is central to the genre and spectator pleasure. While the Takakura Ken (1931–) style of yakuza fought against the entrepreneurial, self-interested *oyabun*, the yakuza organizations, depicted in the world of the 'true account' *jitsuroku* yakuza films of the 'post-moral' era of the *War Without Morality/Jingi naki tatakai* series (1973–1976), are fast becoming monolithic organizations of entrepreneurial capitalism. The protagonists of these films, like Takakura Ken, exist on the margins of society; however, they take on a pathetic pathos because, unlike Takakura Ken, they are often damaged individuals. As such, not only are their deaths or defeats in vain, but they are denied the hubristic expression of contempt that came to imbue the star persona of Takakura Ken as he rejects the corruption of the dominant organizations that control society. The star persona of Kitano Beat/Takeshi (1948–), as developed in films such as *Violent Cop* (*Sono otoko kyōbō ni tsuki* [1989]) and *Sonatine* (1993), exists as a site where the transition between the 'heroic' and the 'antiheroic' of the more recent 1990s-style protagonists of the Tōei Studios direct to video, *V-Cinema*, derived style is negotiated. The films produced by the director Miike Takashi (1960–) are good examples of this latter thematic trend. Set for the most part in the dystopic imagination of one of Tokyo's entertainment areas, Shinjuku's Kabukichō, or an alternative post-*Blade Runner* (Ridley Scott, 1982) Asian cityscape, Miike rejects the heroic fantasies of moral endings, depicting instead the social outcasts' and the delinquents' delight in violence. No one is saved and no apparent heroes exist; all are damaged individuals existing as global drifters lacking any geographical or emotional sense of connectedness. Violence and sex provide an alternative libidinal economy through which these characters negotiate their lives in alien cityscapes. The sadistic homosexual character, Kiyohiro, Kitano Beat/Takeshi's alter ego in *Violent Cop*, has become the mainstay.

In various ways the generation of Japan's postwar avant-garde of the 1960s and 1970s challenged the sociopolitical basis of Japan's postwar economic prosperity through a stylistic assault on realism, and thematically, through an attack on social mores. Imamura Shōhei (1926–) confused the boundaries between fiction and documentary in films such as *The Insect Woman/Nippon konchūki* (1963) and *A Man Vanishes/Ningen jōhatsu* (1967). The former film links Japan's postwar history to prostitution, while the latter film exposes the artifice of mainstream cinemas' appeals to verisimilitude, as film sets are dismantled on screen and self-reflexive shots of cameras expose filmmakers in the process of filming. Fukasaku Kinji (1930–2003) shifted the aesthetic of documentary realism into the yakuza genre in the *War Without Morality* series that links postwar economic recovery and corruption to American policy in Japan in the post-defeat period. In *Beneath the Battle Flag* (*Gunki hatameku moto ni* 1972), an exposé of military practices, he used a similar documentary style. Based on a screenplay by Shindō Kaneto (1912–), inspired by an autobiographical account of the final stages of the war in New Guinea by Okuzaki Kenzō (*The Emperor's Naked Army Marches On/Yukiyukite shingun*), the film follows a woman in her quest to learn the truth about her husband's death before a firing squad.[5] Teshigahara Hiroshi (1927–) also employed a *cinéma-vérité* style in his anti-Vietnam War film *Summer Soldiers* (*Samā sorujā* [1972]). Okamoto Kihachi's (1924–) stylized hybridization of Hollywood cowboy films conventions in war-retro films, filmed in black and white, wide-screen, set in Manchuria just before defeat, challenged mainstream representations of the heroic and the victim through parody and black comedy in the *Desperado Outpost* (*Dokuritsu gurentai*) series produced by Tōhō between 1959–1965. And as the analysis in chapter five demonstrates, Ōshima Nagisa (1932–) used crime and sex as thematic mediums to challenge social mores while experimenting with multiple stylistic registers.

The avant-garde rebelled against the homogenizing and restrictive practices of Japan's corporations epitomized in the monopoly practices of the major studios, and the hypocrisy of the U.S. role in Asia, which lay at the heart of the Anpo student movement. They sought an alternative democratic and liberating space where, released from the constraints of a hierarchical studio system and conservative social mores, freedom of expression would flourish. However, despite the considerable success of productions distributed and/or produced under the auspices of the Art Theatre Guild, just as in Europe this radical project ultimately foundered on the promises of consumerist affluence offered by advanced capitalism. In terms of film style, the avant-garde's attack on social mores through an assault on realism came at a time when reality itself was embracing the nonrealist position essential to the advanced capitalist service economy. As Terry Eagleton explains, by the 1960s and 1970s 'Reality itself had now embraced the non-realist, as capitalist society became increasingly dependent in its everyday operations on myth and fantasy, fictional wealth, exoticism and hyperbole, rhetoric, virtual reality and sheer appearance' (Eagleton 2003b: 67).

While Japan's avant-garde filmmakers belonged to the post-defeat, Anpo generation of student activists, the current generation, born into the 'post-moral' (*jingi naki*) sensibility of advanced consumer capitalism where heterogeneity and difference are privileged as liberating, have fewer limits to transgress and *apparently* little to rebel against. However, a film such as *Battle Royale II: Requiem* (*Requiemu* [2003]), inspired by 9/11 and the last film to be directed by Fukasaku Kinji, attempts to negotiate some point of humanist recuperation out of the allegorical post-moral 'survival game' of the film's *mise-en-scène*. In this final chapter, I want to stay within an intellectual paradigmatic tradition founded on the post-defeat generational divisions that dominated the avant-garde's approach to political filmmaking in the 1960s and early 1970s. In concluding, I shall turn to a consideration of the cult director Miike Takashi, born in 1960, as his works are indicative of a 'post-moral', postmodernist, generational consciousness. In particular I shall focus on his *Triad Society* trilogy (*Kuro shakai*), and Kitano Beat/Taheshi's *Violent Cop* (1989) as a film which (for Western audiences) marked the shift from the tragic to the 'post-tragic' in Japanese cinema and the two *Battle Royale* films both directed by Fukasaku Kinji, one of the final authorial voices from the dying avant-garde. These films, all drawing on similar thematic concerns and employing the vast array of visual registers possible in the digital age, are symbolic of an allegorical shift from the modern to the 'post-tragic' realm of the 'post-moral' of postmodernism. As with Kitano Beat/Takeshi, Miike Takashi's films and *BRI* and *BRII* have achieved an international following and, I shall argue, are symptomatic of certain trends in cinema and filmmaking that are, like the global media-entertainment networks themselves, transcending national boundaries.

Miike Takashi's films depict the 'post-moral' decrepit landscapes of the pornographic and violent and are indicative of what Eagleton (2003b) describes as the portrayal of 'a world in which there is indeed no salvation.

This is the post-tragic realm of postmodernism'. Where the postmodern Asian cinema cityscape of *Blade Runner*[6], took us into a futuristic postindustrial landscape of decay, Miike Takashi's Shinjuku and Taipei are the ethical equivalent of dystrophic zones of criminality on the fringes of service sector capitalist affluence. The capitalist exchange of labour in the service sector is played out on the physically abused body, most predominantly the body of the prostitute, the pornographic model and the sale of body parts. In the hybrid 'city speak' that is a mix of Japanese, Chinese and English used by the characters in Iwai Shunji's (1963–) film *Swallowtail* (*Suwarōtairu* [1996]), these bodies exist in a fictionalized Tokyo known as Yen Town. In Miike Takashi's films, the bodies of men, women and children are all represented within this new international déclassé. There is no sexual discrimination and there are no racial distinctions as, reflecting the shifting patterns of migratory labour, Westerners, Chinese, Japanese, Brazilians, black Africans and offspring of 'mixed-blood' relationships are all equally in search of the mighty Yen. In this sense the images of the postmodern city generated in these films are egalitarian, however, not in a Marxist sense of everyone being equal to fulfil their potential but in the capitalist sense of flexible labour with everyone being equally open to exploitation and abuse. In this worldview, the only distinction is, quite literally, between those who do the 'fucking' and those who get 'fucked' and the only guiding principle is the accumulation of capital. As the Taipei policeman explains to the 'mixed-blood' Japanese/Chinese detective Kiriya Tatsuhito (Shiina Kippei 1964–) investigating the illegal sale of children's organs through a Taiwanese hospital in *Shinjuku Triad Society* (*Shinjuku kuro shakai: chaina mafuia sensō* [1995]),

**Taiwanese policeman:** (Medium close-up of a child's stomach as the policeman lifts the child's shirt to reveal a raw scar.) He's had his organs removed. Selling kidneys for transplants. A family can be saved from just one of two kidneys. It seems that it is mostly Japanese who are buying.

**Kiriya:** What are the police doing?

**Taiwanese policeman:** Nothing. There are people who need organs. There are those who want to sell them. What can we say when both sides benefit?

All the characters are alienated, both emotionally and geographically, as migratory labourers eke out an existence in Shinjuku and the Japanese yakuza, Yuji (Aikawa Shō 1961–), is exiled in Taipei in the second part of the *Triad Society Trilogy, Rainy Dog* (*Gokudō kuro shakai: reiniidoggu* 1997). Yuji's alienated persona is reflected on the two registers on the sound track as he thinks his thoughts in voice-over in Japanese, while using Chinese in his dealings with others. These are the new breed of global 'drifters' in search of the promises of Western-style consumer capitalism.

In *BRI* and *BRII*, human relations in advanced capitalist society are portrayed through the allegory of the computer, 'reality TV' generated 'survival game' sponsored by commercial enterprise. There are no rules and only winning counts. As the teacher Kitano Beat/Takeshi, in *BRI*, states, 'Life is a game', and as Riki (Takeuchi Riki 1964–), the teacher in the sequel *BRII* elaborates, 'There is only a winning group and a losing group. Which group will you join?' Like military conscription, the students have no real choice. However, unlike the characters in Miike's cityscapes who, by and large, submit to the contingencies of their situation, many of the adolescents in the two *Battle Royale* films attempt to find some site for resistance and in the case of Shūya (Fujiwara Tatsuya 1982–) and Takuma (Oshinari Shūgo 1981-) survive. The 'survival game', like Miike's dystopic cityscapes, provides the 'post-moral' social force against which humanity and the limits of human agency are played out and tested.

In the two *Battle Royale* films it is clear that the adolescents are victims of a society created by corrupt politicians and an acquiescent majority. In *BRII* this theme emanates from the war-retro genre where youth (as conscripts) are sent to fight battles not of their own making. The two adolescents, the principal survivors of the *Battle Royale*, Shūya and Takuma (of *BRII*), still retain some vestiges of hope for the future and it is this that distinguishes them from the adults in the two films and the protagonists in Miike's films. And it is this belief in a future that transcends the material concerns of contemporary corporate society that confirms their place within the genealogy of the alienated *ninkyō* heroic tradition as individuals seeking a basis for a social connectedness. Set in the mountainous regions that border Afghanistan and Pakistan, the final scenes of *BRII* tell us that this youthful hope in the future is only possible in countries outside the American *imperium*.

In the first two films in Miike's *Triad Society* trilogy and the two *Battle Royale* films, the characters are damaged individuals. However, where the dystopic cityscapes of the *mise-en-scène* of Miike's films overwhelm these characters, drawing them ever deeper into Foucaultian power-based cycles of exploitation and violence, the two boys in *Battle Royale* reject the society that abandoned them as children. Not unlike the heroes of the animation classic *Akira* (Ōtomo Katsuhiro, 1988), the very fact that they were separated off from mainstream society as children, told through flashback sequences, gave them the opportunity to develop their humanity. Shūya, whose mother died when he was a small child, his emasculated father committing suicide soon after, grows up in an institution. It is here in the institution, outside the 'normal' now dysfunctional family, that he forms a close bond with Nobu. Nobu's death (he is killed in the opening sequences of *BRI*), provides the emotional *raison d'être* for Shūya's rebellion and his rationale for saving Noriko, the girl Nobu loved. These emotional attachments of the boys in the war situation of the 'survival game' turns on the same homosocial bonding of the *ninkyō* yakuza genre, alternatively known as the comradely love (*sen'yūai*) of war-retro films, similarly providing the justification for violence under the cloak of humanity. Equally, by the second film, Shūya has found a sense of 'connectedness' fighting with the 'terrorists'. In contrast, *The Triad Society* trilogy offers a bleak view of the symbiotic nature of 'legitimate' and underworld organizations and the regenerative power of this system of economic relations to withstand disruptions. While *Shinjuku Triad Society* depicts the police as mediators who maintain stability between the two mutually dependant financial concerns of 'legitimate' society and those of the underground represented by the triad/yakuza organizations, *Rainy Dog* depicts the cyclical nature of violence as it is passed from father to son. The third and final part of the trilogy, *Ley Lines* (*Nihon kuro shakai: reirainzu* [1999]), like many of Ōshima's films (*Death by Hanging/Kōsikei* [1968] and *Boy/Shōnen* [1969]), documents the creation and destruction of stateless youth by the 'good' majority.

The theme of economic disruption in the capitalist marketplace, in *Shinjuku Triad Society*, is allegorized through the personal relationship between the main protagonists, the Shinjuku police detective Kiriya Tatsuhito, and his alter ego Wang (Taguchi Tomorō 1957–), the leader of an underground triad/yakuza organization. Borrowing thematically from *Violent Cop*, where the police detective Azuma (Kitano Beat/Takeshi) was committed to a bitter and personal struggle against his alter ego, Kiyohiro the drug pusher and 'hit man', *Shinjuku Triad Society* complicates the relationship further by developing this theme along racial lines not unlike that of Fukasaku Kinji in *Yakuza Graveyard* (*Yakuza hakaba: kuchinashi no hana*) (1976). In *Shinjuku Triad Society*, Kiriya is the son of a mixed-blood parentage (Japanese/Chinese) and Wang a native of Taiwan. As his alter ego Kiriya has much in common with Wang, they are both the victims

of racial discrimination, they are both extremely violent, and as the opening and closing voice-over address to the audience in Chinese by the 'rent
boy' makes clear, they are both homosexual and shared the same lover.

The opening establishing montage sequence that cuts between a crime
scene (a murder by decapitation), a disco, and shots of Wang's village just
outside Taipei, immediately conflates the two geographical (Japan/Taiwan)
and temporal (present/memory) worlds of Kiriya and Wang, while simultaneously establishing their representational relationship to the political
economy. Wang, it turns out, was responsible for this murder, which is the
first disruptive act that unbalances the economy, while a brief reverse-cut
shot of acknowledgement in the disco latrines between the 'rent boy', in
the act of servicing a client, and Kiriya establishes the personal motive for
the antagonism that will develop between Kiriya and Wang. Thus this
opening montage sequence visually establishes the confluence of the political and libidinal economies that drive society and the narrative of the film.
In the penultimate sequences, these two worlds collapse into each other as
shared memories. Just before Kiriya kills Wang, Wang sits softly singing
a nursery rhyme that Kiriya overheard a father singing to his children
when he visited the village in Taiwan where Wang was born. In this earlier
scene, Kiriya recognizes the tune and sings gently along with the father.
Also during this visit, Kiriya sees a small child squatting in a courtyard.
This same image flashes through the opening montage sequence and will
flash through Wang's visual field just before Kiriya arrives to kill him.

The conclusion brings the film back to the mediating role of the police
in a capitalist economy as Kiriya, again confronted by a senior policeman
who asks knowingly if he was responsible for Wang's death, tells him that
he will soon get a promotion. Kiriya, by killing Wang, has restored the
balance between the competing economic factions. In the concluding sequence, Kiriya merges into a daylight street scene of suited salarymen
with his voice-over narration of a telephone conversation with his father,
telling him of his impending promotion. In the 'post-moral' age of advanced capitalism, the end justifies the means. The penultimate and concluding sequences in *Violent Cop*, after the deaths of Kiyohiro and Azuma,
can be read as a similar indictment of society in the 'post-tragic' sense
referred to by Eagleton in the epigram that opens this section. In the penultimate scene, the *oyabun*'s successor, surveying the bodies of Kiyohiro
and Azuma, states that 'They were both mad' as he flicks off the light,
turning the scene into near darkness. This is followed by a concluding
scene shot in full daylight as Kikuchi, Azuma's junior, is seen crossing the

same bridge Azuma had crossed on his way to work in the opening sequences of the film. A short scene follows, concluding the film, as Kikuchi, accepting protection money from the new *oyabun*, wryly states, 'I am no fool'. In this way, in both films, through the contrast in lighting the two complementary and coexisting worlds of 'legitimate' society and the underground world of yakuza society are delineated. The darkness of Wang's world as the 'black society' (*kuro shakai*) of the Japanese title of *Shinjuku Triad Society* and the empty warehouse were Kiyohiro and Azuma meet their nemesis in *Violent Cop* are contrasted with the brightness of the daylight world. Only unscrupulous characters like Kiriya and Kikuchi cross the boundaries and survive. In this postmodernist, 'postmoral' vision of society, murder, rape and torture are acceptable when the effective functioning of the market economy is put in jeopardy.

Where, in *Shinjuku Triad Society*, the visual registers of 'darkness' and 'light' signify the two mutually reinforcing and coexistent economic worlds, the conflicting realities presented in *BRII* fluctuate through a pastiche of different technological windows. The dystopic reality of the 'survival game' is played out in digitally computerized war-games' imagery, while Afghanistan, the utopian world of the outsiders, to which Shūya and the few survivors escape, is filmed as a technicolour pastoral scene. The character of Shūya is positioned in the post-9/11 era of President Bush's 'war on terror' as a terrorist leader appealing to the world through a frontal address opening sequence of a disjointed, crackling and grainy hand-held camera broadcast. The punctuating shots of tower blocks collapsing mark the 9/11 trauma in much the same way as the inclusion of shots of the Hiroshima Dome throughout the *War Without Morality* series brought the themes of the films back to their origins in the trauma of the post-defeat era. Fukasaku Kinji's son, quoted in the film journal *Kinema Junpō*, makes this connection clear when he states that the 9/11 attack on the Twin Towers made a strong impression on his father, which became linked to his own feelings of resentment against America. For Fukasaku Kinji, '[M]ore than the public controversy about the rights and wrongs of the justifications for retaliation, he talked about it on a more personal level. It was the question of the hatred he had felt for America when he was young. And at this time I think this question once again boiled up' (quoted in Nakayama 2003:34). According to his son, the themes of *BRII*, 'terror', 'war' and 'Nanahara Shūya' grew out of his father's response to the 9/11 incident. And it was due to this personal response that he obtained permission from the author of the original novel *Battle Royale*, Takami Kōshun, to develop the character of Nanahara Shūya in the sequel.

The film concludes with the escape of Shūya, Takuma and a small band of their followers to the daylight spring of a pastoral scene in Afghanistan. Shūya alludes to the re-generative forces of youth when he observes that even in a country ravaged by war for twenty years, the spring still comes. The survivors set off into the future in two groups in Toyota four-wheel-drive vehicles, avowing their sense of 'connectedness' (*nakama*). Shūya and Noriko, accompanied by several small children, and Takuma and another female survivor, representing the re-configured family group, will be the progenitors of the next generation. The conclusion is a utopian escapism as it leaves unchanged the political system that instituted the BR Law. The film is proposing that the humanist myth of 'connectedness' can redeem youth from the moral void of the postmodernist 'post-tragic' techno-survival-game landscape of contemporary global politics. In both Miike Takashi's films and the two *Battle Royale* films, the impact of competitive social relations are played out on the body. Both groups of films register power in terms of violence and death. In Miike's films it is the sexualized body of the prostitute; in the two *Battle Royale* films it is the death tally given at various points in the films. In Miike's films there is no redemptive human-ism because his films form part of a postmodernist sensibility that, to draw on Eagleton, portrays 'a world in which there is indeed no salvation, but on the other hand nothing to be saved'.

Influenced by the theoretical arguments of Giddens (1990), Comolli (1986), Gombrich (1998, 1996), Williams (1977) and Foucault (1992 a, 1992 b, 1991), I began this study by proposing a methodology based on the 'politics of cinema'—that is, an approach that attempts to reach an understanding of the relationship between filmmaking practice, the con-texts of the economic and sociopolitical, and their connections to narrative themes in cinema. In order to avoid a reductionist analysis (that is, the reduction of content to ideology), and in view of the often nonlinear and nondiachronic nature of 'history' as it impacts on human experience (as opposed to an academic exercise), I chose a thematic approach that at-tempted to link the concept of cinema as social practice (a system of com-munication that is both constituted by, and constituting of the sociopolitical circumstances of its production and reception) with some of the central discourses of the twentieth century—modernism, nationalism, resistance and gender. In attempting to map out an intellectual paradigm through which to understand these relationships, I suggested a division between film form (the technology and techniques of its use) and content (narrative). In brief, I argued that the form of cinema, a Western technological invention, and the content, often derived from ancient storytelling traditions, formed a dialectic out of which some sort of accommodation was reached between the foreign and the familiar.

But what about the present increasingly dominated by multinational entertainment conglomerations and an aesthetic driven in part by changing technologies? Just as cinema was at the heart of the modernist project so too is it central to the postmodernist aesthetic, both in terms of the experiences of film consumption and of content. With fragmenting windows of consumption the centrality of the collective/communal cinema-going experience of the modern age has been supplanted by the fragmented and individualizing experiences of the small screens of pay-per-view, Internet and computer, or the multichoice options of the 'megaplex', thus constituting in the physical experiences of film consumption the fragmenting, mutable and porous qualities of experience so central to the postmodernist self. In terms of content, the digital age of computer graphics has taken us further than even the most sophisticated special effects from the 'reality' of a pro-filmic model in the physical world. The films considered in this chapter form part of a trend that renders human experience and history through allegories of the multiplicity of windows of the newly emerging entertainment media. Complex sociopolitical issues of alienation, racism, migratory labour, juvenile delinquency and 9/11 are interpreted through visual registers that are in themselves a visceral assault on the senses. These images represent a disruption to the narrative flow of cause and effect and continuity editing of the modern period; through fissure, disjunction, and disruption, they disorientate the logic of the Cartesian moral order, offering in its place a utilitarian system of relativity. For instance, the two 'hit men' in *Dead or Alive II* (Miike Takashi 2000), through utilitarian mathematical rationalism, calculate how many children they can save in third world countries with one assassination contract.

While the fast-developing technologies of cinema and the visual appear individualizing and fragmentary, the film industry is fast being subsumed within transnational multimedia organizations, part of whose strategy is the absorption of the former 'local' of the nation of the modern era into a hybridized global aesthetic accessible to all. Consider, for example, *The Last Samurai* (Edward Zwick 2003), a Warner Brothers production filmed on the slopes of Mt Taranaki in New Zealand, about an American who comes to embody the spirit of the samurai in martial arts scenes that bear a greater resemblance to choreographed Hong Kong *kung fu* sequences than Japanese *jidaigeki*.

The transnationalization of film production raises key issues for contemporary film studies: Do such things as 'national cinemas' exist, and if so where, and indeed is it possible and/or necessary to locate the 'local' within the seemingly overwhelming co-opting forces of the postmodern 'global' hegemony? These questions arise out of many factors: the promotion of 'national cinemas' as a marketing strategy in the 'art house' cinema circuit as a 'high' culture alternative to the perceived 'mass' of Hollywood cinema; the role of film festivals as markets for the sale of films; the fact that now very few so-called Hollywood films are actually made in the U.S.; and on a textual level, the increasing hybrid nature of film content; and as a concomitant to all the above, an increased interest in 'world cinema' in academia.

In their book *Japan Movies Now* (*Nihon eiga sangyō saizensen: Japan movies now*), Murakami Yoshiaki and Ogawa Norifumi optimistically cite 1997 as the beginnings of a 'Japanese film renaissance', which they consider has its roots in the globalizing trends within the international film industry. In particular they cite an increase in film attendance figures in Japan starting in 1997, which they argue is symptomatic of a revival of the Japanese industry.[7] They assert that the increase in the number of screens in Japan during the 1990s had a direct bearing on increased attendance. However, this increase in screens is attributable to the aggressive expansion by American film exhibition companies (Warner Mycal, AMC and UCI) into the Japanese market in the 1990s.[8] Japan was targeted as an 'underscreened' country, as a comparison of the figures for the number of screens per head of population, cited by Murakami and Ogawa, clearly demonstrates: Japan: one screen per 63,000 people (1998), USA: one screen per 8,649 (1997), and the UK: one screen per 33,996 (1996) (Murakami and Ogawa 2000: 38). The building of new and the conversion of existing cinemas into multiscreen 'cinema complexes' by American companies is seen by Murakami and Ogawa as the catalyst that finally broke the system of studio-based 'block-booking' and forced the few surviving major Japanese studios into a policy of restructuring.[9] Film production financing is no longer centred on the studios but is made up of consortia built around multiple window outlets and related product marketing with pre-sales strategies central to risk reduction. Strategies that developed from the international success in animation in the late 1980s and videogames are being consolidated within the mainstream film industry. Following Hollywood practices, Japanese consortia are increasingly funding the production of films in Asia employing local directors, cast and staff (*The First Emperor* [1998] China).

Taking the lead from Murakami and Ogawa, I would suggest that one of the strategies in confronting the changing relationship of cinema and nation should be sought in the nature of the multinational entertainment organizations themselves, as they are increasingly becoming the vehicle through which nations negotiate their participation in the global economy. Sony and its leading role in the international entertainment arena is one such example. As new technology-driven entertainment 'windows' (DVD, Internet, pay-per-view) enter the public domain and the new economy of the entertainment/knowledge-based corporations overtake manufacturing sectors of the economy, theories that transcend theoretical categories of the local/global debates of modernism are increasingly necessary. Hence, in the contemporary age when transnational entertainment conglomerations are operating on a scale unprecedented in history, I argue the need to break out of the narrow confines of the minutiae of postmodernist academic analysis and return to overviews of the major discourses of history and theories of capital. It is only through a contextual understanding of the broad sweep of history and culture that we can begin to comprehend the semantic significance of individual films as part of the lexicon of cinema, as a communicative mechanism.

# NOTES

## Introduction

1. '*Romanporuno*' as a term had been coined by Japanese film reviewers and critics writing in the 1960s to make a distinction between '*pinku*' films deemed to have some artistic merit and those to be classified purely as low-level 'soft-core' pornography. When in the early 1970s Nikkatsu decided to change its production policy towards the production of erotic films, they co-opted the term '*roman poruno*' to define their studio-based genre, and to distinguish this term from earlier usage they joined the two words together to form the one word, '*romanporuno*' (see Matsushima 2000).

2. 'The decisive operation in these histories seems inevitably to be the selection and review of the greatest possible number of technical, stylistic and formal innovations, each of which is presented (and researched) as the initiator of a succession of aesthetic developments (the "progress" of a "language"). And the culmination of the process is the cinema practiced at the time that the given historian writes, when it is discovered in its final and *perfected* form' (Comolli 1986: 425).

3. This slogan was first coined by Sakuma Shōzan (1811–1864), a Tokugawa official who had studied Dutch and Western gunnery. The disintegration of China and its defeat in the Opium War by Britain in 1842 had convinced him of Japan's need to adopt Western technology. He was assassinated by an anti-foreign fanatic in 1864. However, as Beasley demonstrates, his followers carried forward his ideas into the Meiji period (Beasley 1990: 25).

4. In 1873 Japan's total population was estimated at 35 million, and by 1925 it had increased to 60 million. By 1920 the population of central Tokyo was 2.2 million with an additional 1.2 million living in the surrounding areas (Beasley 1990: 121–122).

5. The Kinetograph camera and Kinetoscope viewing box were demonstrated and patented in the United States in 1891. Film was pulled through the camera and the Kinetoscope by holes punched into either side of the Eastman film. Films lasted for approximately twenty seconds and featured dancers, acrobats and famous vaudeville acts. In 1894 the first Kinetoscope parlour was opened in New York.

6. In Tokyo in 1903 on average a person went to a vaudeville theatre 2.23 times a year compared with the cinema at 1.53. By 1912 the average for cinema had increased to 5.5 and vaudeville had declined to 1.53 (Satō 1995 vol. i: 112–113).

7. I am aware of the fact that David Bordwell (1997) in his study of film style has found 'empirical inaccuracies and conceptual shortcomings' in Comolli's analysis of depth of field and codes of 'realism'; as he explains, 'However, we conceive

of linear perspective, we can go on to ask what *alternative* system of representation the camera could have produced. It is one thing to say that orthodox cinema reproduces only one conception of reality; it is something else to show that there are other realities to which cinema, or other media, could give access' (Bordwell 1997: 162). However, I would suggest that Comolli's main premise, that the development of technology, in this case photography and cinema, grew out of the particular 'realist' vision of Western science and philosophy, is in fact correct. As I argue in the main body of the introduction, the Japanese did produce other media, the screen and hanging scroll, that depicted an alternative 'realist' perspective commensurate with an Eastern-derived worldview. Equally Screech's study of the 'Western scientific gaze' argues that an Enlightenment-derived way of seeing the world 'impinged on Japan for the first time during the later eighteenth century' (Screech 1996: 2). Furthermore, Screech notes that the importation of devices that structured ways of seeing—looking glasses and microscopes—'melted into a rhetoric of precision that was then applied to precisely non-scientific matters—above all . . . to interpersonal human relations' (Screech 1996: 5).

8. 'A . . . passion for archaeological fidelity in rendering period accessories became a staple of Hollywood epics. Biblical, Greek, Roman, medieval, Tudor, Stuart, Georgian and Victorian costume and furnishings became the distinguishing features and hallmark of the 'real' historical epic, sometimes requiring considerable research, as for the chariot race in *Ben Hur.* Eisenstein's enthusiasm for authentic recreation of period furnishings, costume and armour was perhaps even greater . . .' (Smith 2000: 54). Mizoguchi is similarly renowned for his research on the Genroku period (1688–1704) and the demands he made on set designers and carpenters for authenticity in his epic *The Loyal Forty-seven Ronin (Genroku Chūshingura* [1941–1942]).

9. Ōbora Gengo later went on to become a director.

10. It is interesting to note that this conception of the division between the heavenly and earthly continued in the title of various versions of *The Loyal Forty-seven Retainers (Chūshingura*), which bear the subtitles *Chi no maki* and *Ten no maki.* Also in the latest Shōchiku (1994) production of *Chūshinguragaiden Yotsuyakaidan,* the cloud effect is retained in the filming style of the ghost story segments.

11. For a detailed analysis of style and perception in world art see Margaret Hagen, *Varieties of Realism: Geometries of Representational Art* and with specific reference to Japan see Timon Screech, *The Western Scientific Gaze and Popular Imagery in Later Edo Japan* (Cambridge University Press, 1996).

12. As with many aspects of cinema studies, one can only generalize as there are always exceptions to the rule. Kinugasa's 1926 film *A Page of Madness* aka *A Page Out of Order (Kurutta ichipeiji)* clearly draws on German Expressionist modes of representation and not those of Hollywood.

13. The Nikkatsu negative film library was burnt to the ground in the early postwar period, destroying most of their prewar films.

14. Okajima Hisashi, archivist at the Japan National Film Centre, estimates that only forty-one percent of Japanese films made in the prewar period are still extant (quoted in Bordwell 1995: 29).

## Chapter One

1. It is important to make a clear distinction between the two terms 'modernity' and 'modernism'. In the following discussion I am basing my usage on the definitions set out in *The Penguin Dictionary of Philosophy* (ed.) Thomas Mautner as follows: 'Modernity: a certain historical period to which a 'modern' character is ascribed. The period is variously specified. At the core of this conception is the nineteenth- and twentieth-century world of the nation-states, political democracy, capitalism, urbanization, mass literacy, mass media, mass culture, rationality, anti-traditionalism, secularization, faith in science, large-scale industrial enterprise, individualism, enlightenment ideals and a public ideology in which liberal, progressive, humanitarian ideals are prominent . . . Modernism: a doctrine, or a certain style of thought, or certain style in the arts . . .'(Mautner 2000: 359). In his introductory chapter to *All That Is Solid Melts into Air: The Experience of Modernity*, Marshall Berman divides the history of modernism into three phases: 1500–1789, 1790–1900 and 1900 onwards. These three phases of early, classical and late modernism have been generally accepted in relation to Western societies (Berman 1993: 16–17).

2. In his article, Peter Osborne focuses on three 'ideas' of modernity, 'as a *category of historical periodization,* a *quality of social experience,* and an (incomplete) *project*' (Osborne 1992) [italics in the original].

3. These films were all directed by Ushihara Kyohiko (1897–1985) and starred Suzuki Denmei (1900–1985) and Tanaka Kinuyo (1909–1977).

4. In the Meiji period this process of individuation was tempered by moral restraints as 'rising in the world' (*risshin shusse*), although applauded and encouraged, was only legitimate in terms of what one contributed to the State or in terms of bringing 'honour and wealth to the "family of [one's] ancestors"' (Dore 1963: 195).

5. In 1924 the Shōchiku Kamata Studios lost several of their top stars to their rivals Teikinema and Nikkatsu (Kido 1956: 29).

6. This transition can be seen clearly in the change in film credit titles as Shōchiku films of this period open with the Shōchiku symbol of Mount Fuji with the title, for example, an Ushihara Kyohiko production. The star productions opened with a title to the effect that this was a Kataoka Chiezō film, etc.

7. Kido Shirō of the Shōchiku Studios is sometimes referred to as the other 'father of Japanese cinema' (see Kobayashi 1999).

8. Between 1909 and 1926 Onoe Matsunosuke is reported to have appeared in more than one thousand films.

9. David Bordwell (1988) has calculated that of Ozu's fifty-four films, forty-nine are set in Tokyo and five have Tokyo in their titles.

10. *I Was Born But . . .* (*Umarete wa mitakeredo* [1932]), *Passing Fancy* (*Dekigokoro* [1933]) and *Story of Floating Weeds* (*Ukikusa monogatari* [1934]) all were awarded top *Kinema Junpō* awards for their respective years.

11. Marilyn Ivy contends that *furusato* as a concept is a modern invention that only 'attained force in the wake of large-scale changes in rural Japan, in particular, the exodus of people in search of work in the cities in the early twentieth century

and, more recently, in the post-war period. Concern with the *furusato* indicates a fundamental alienation, a severance from "home"' (Ivy 1995: 105).

12. The hunger strike of the two brothers in *I Was Born But . . .* will again be taken up in the 1959 film *Ohayō* (*Good Morning* aka *Too Much Talk*). In this latter case the two brothers refuse to talk in protest at their father's refusal to purchase a television set.

13. Satō (2000) argues that Ozu's characteristic style was firmly established by 1932 and *I Was Born But . . .* That is, his insistence on the placement of the camera at a low angle, the family as a central theme, and the inclusion of 'harmony shots'—the younger of the two brothers imitating exactly his brother's actions, etc. This technique was used in both Japan and Hollywood in the silent era for comic effect but Ozu continued to use it in the age of 'talkies'. Unison shots were not only used for comic effect but also to show a unity of thought and affection, as in the fishing sequences in *The Story of Floating Weeds* (1934) and *There Was a Father* (1942).

14. The suffixes *ko* and *e* commonly denote female first names.

15. As Sharon Nolte and Sally Ann Hastings point out, '[B]y 1890 women had become the backbone of the developing Japanese industrial economy. Female workers outnumbered males in light industry, especially in textiles, where a work force that was 60 to 90 percent female produced 40 percent of the gross national product and 60 percent of the foreign exchange during the late nineteenth century' (Nolte and Hastings 1991: 153).

16. Suzuki Kazutoshi quotes Kido: 'We shall receive half of all Japanese film audiences' (*Nihon eiga (no kankyaku) no hanbun wa itadaku*). By this Suzuki explains Kido meant that half the Japanese population is female and Shōchiku would target them (Suzuki 1984: 110).

17. The original novel upon which the film versions were based was written by Ozaki Kōyō (1868–1903) between 1897 and 1902.

18. The system of alternative attendance by feudal lords (*daimyō*) in Edo.

19. *The Mother He Never Knew* was re-released on video with *benshi* voice-over narration as part of a series of six classic films by the Matsuda Film Library.

20. Although the world depicted in these films bears similarities to Hollywood productions of the same period, the depiction of the individuals' responses to these hardships is completely different. The Japanese hero either succumbs to, or is defeated by, the society. Alan O'Shea makes the following comments regarding the films produced by Charlie Chaplin (in particular *Modern Times* [1936]:, '[T]he world of Chaplin is characterised by rapidly changing conditions, by repression and brutality, by corruption and hypocrisy, by insecurity and want and by dark despair; but also by the little man's spirit and resilience and an unquenchable aspiration for freedom, love, security, equality, communality, abundance and playfulness' (O'Shea 1996: 7–8).

21. In analysing dominant narrative and stylistic trends, it is helpful to draw on Bordwell's exposition of the Russian Formalists' theoretical divisions of narration into three concepts of *fabula, syuzhet* and style set out in *Narration in the Fiction Film* (1990). *Fabula* refers to the story, '[m]ore specifically, the *fabula* embodies the action as a chronological, cause-and-effect chain of events occurring within a

given duration and a spatial field . . . *Syuzhet* (usually translated as "plot") is the actual arrangement and presentation of the *fabula* in the film' (Bordwell 1990: 49–50). It is from the information given in the *syuzhet* that the spectator makes inferences, hypothesizes and ultimately constructs the *fabula*. Style, within this context, is clearly allied to the *syuzhet*, as it refers to 'the films' systematic use of cinematic signifiers'. In other words, it is an integral component of a film's ability to express the *fabula*. This theory of narration allows us to isolate the various components of narrative and to historicize their use both in terms of theme and style. It is also useful because it acknowledges the role of the spectator in actively piecing together the components of the *syuzhet* and allying these to a given film's stylistic, both extrinsic (in terms of genre, star persona, etc.) and intrinsic, norms to create meaning.

22. Onoe Matsunosuke, who moved to Nikkatsu and had by 1923 become a major star, was the idol of the 'runny-nose brats'. He was affectionately known as '*medama no* [eyeball] *Matchan*' because it was thought at the time that he had unusually large eyes, and in the best kabuki tradition, glaring at one's opponent was an instrumental part of a climactic fight scene.

23. Around 1909 the 'nine-foot line', which effectively cut actors off just below the waist, was introduced by Vitagraph; prior to that, cameras had been placed at twelve to sixteen feet from the actors (Thompson and Bordwell 1994: 46).

24. Between 1905 and 1912 American studios experimented with three-dimensional sets and the use of artificial lighting to create a sense of depth of field (Thompson and Bordwell 1994: 47).

25. It should be noted that Japanese film historians have tended to limit their definitions of 'social realist' films, or to use Satō's (2000: 272) term, 'critical realist' films (*hihanteki rearizumu*), to subject matter. For example, the inclusion of characters from the lower middle classes, in particular, salarymen, alternatively in the case of Mizoguchi, his use of dialects in his sound films. My principal argument is that both types of films often relied on the same basic narratives, and indeed are indicative of social change, but that this extended beyond mere plot to include stylistic questions.

26. An 'adopted son-in-law' is a man who marries into his wife's family taking her family name and registering his children in his wife's family name. He also succeeds to the wife's family property. This is common practice in Japan when couples only have female children.

27. Naturally, one is speaking in relative rather than absolutist terms. However, a clear trajectory of expressive modes can be traced in form, for example, Kinugasa Teinosuke's flirtatious experimentation with German Expressionism in *A Page of Madness* and the minimalist style of films directed by Ozu Yasujirō.

## Chapter Two

1. Young (1999) notes a sharp rise in landlord/tenant disputes from 256 in 1918, 1,532 in 1924, to 2,478 in 1930, rising to a peak of 6,804 in 1936.

2. The relatively low military death toll of 2,530 between September 1931 and July 1933 ensured that, of the general populace, the majority were not overtly affected through the loss of male relatives as a result of the conflict on the continent. In fact Satō Tadao makes the point that people felt a certain relief with the economic prosperity that accompanied the military buildup in China. Louise Young, in her study *Japan's Total Empire* (1998), argues that previously marginalized groups, 'workers and women', embraced the war effort as a means of gaining political recognition. She summarizes her position as follows: 'In the context of the Manchurian Incident war fever, these icons of Taishō democracy seemed to reverse course, turning their movements to support militarism and empire. Like the conversion of the mass media, the volte-face of the labor movement and its affiliated left-wing parties is usually explained as the consequence of government repression. While a step-up in political surveillance, censorship, and arrests certainly placed new limits on the strategies of the social movement, the swell of imperial jingoism that followed the Manchurian Incident also opened up new possibilities for mobilizing organizational support through appeals to patriotism and defence of the empire. Viewed in this light, the support of labor and women for militarism is less a reversal than a continuation of efforts to secure social and political power by whatever means offered them' (Young 1998: 162).

3. Other *jidaigeki* stars of the 1930s were Ichikawa Utaemon (1907–1999), Ōkōchi Denjirō (1898–1962), Hayashi Chōjirō (1908–1984) (later known as Hasegawa Kazuo), Bandō Kōtarō (1911–*), Tsukigata Ryūnosuke (1902–1970) and Ramon Mitsusaburō (1901–*) (Satō 1995 vol. i : 336).

4. Gellner argues quite forcefully that the development of the media as a technological medium of transmission is crucial to the development of popular nationalism. Like universal education, the media encourage the development of a cultural homogeneity through shared idioms and concepts. 'S/he who cannot comprehend the medium through which the message is transmitted is clearly excluded from the "moral and economic community"'. Gellner concludes, 'It matters precious little what has been fed into them: it is the media themselves, the pervasiveness and importance of abstract, centralized, standardized, one to many communication, which itself automatically engenders the core idea of nationalism, quite irrespective of what in particular is being put into the specific messages transmitted. The most important and persistent message is generated by the medium itself, by the role which such media have acquired in modern life' (Gellner 1999: 127). Despite this, an understanding of the message helps us determine (a) what kind of nationalism is coming into being or being perpetuated; and perhaps more important, (b) how the individual relates in private or psychological terms to the concept of the nation in their experiential lives. For the media (as well as the education system) was crucial in shoring up the contradictions inherent in the disintegration of the previously complex structures of local agrarian societies of the premodern age and the establishment of anonymous and impersonal urban societies of the modern industrial period. In other words the 'message' is related to the ideologies upon which a culturally specific nationalism rests at any given point in history.

5. Nakazato Kaizan (1885–1944) was author of the multivolume novel *Daibosatsu Tōge (The Great Bodhisattva Pass)*, serialized between 1913–1941.

6. Osaragi Jirō (1897–1973) was the author of the *Kurama Tengu* series of novels written between 1924 and 1959; he was also the author of *Bijozakura*.

7. Hayashi Fubō (1900–1935) wrote the *Tange Sazen* series of novels titled *Shinpan Ōoka seidan* published between 1927 and 1928.

8. Hasegawa Shin (1884–1963) is considered to be the originator of the *matatabimono* genre. His play *Banba Chūtarō mabuta no haha* has been repeatedly filmed in both the pre- and postwar periods.

9. The *shinkokugeki* theatre movement was founded by Sawada Shōjirō (1892–1929) in 1917 with the aim of developing a contemporary indigenous theatre.

10. Saigō Takamori (1827–1877) was a leader who, during the overthrow of the Tokugawa shogunate, supported the Imperial faction. However, later he changed sides and finally committed ritual immolation (*seppuku*).

11. In the early phase of Japanese industrialization, the introduction of universal education in 1872 and conscription in 1873, combined with the standardization of the language, facilitated the dissemination of the dominant culture to the lower levels of society. The state's mobilization of the population through these institutions, combined with the needs of industry for a mobile flexible labour force, led to a degree of cultural homogenization and even social equality. This equality was, theoretically, institutionalized in the Five Articles of the Charter Oath (*Go-kajō no seimon*) of April 1868 which, among other things, stipulated that 'high and low would be of one heart in carrying out national policy', that 'merchants and peasants would achieve their ambitions' and that the 'uncivilized customs of the past would be abandoned' (Lehmann 1982: 185). The Charter Oath encouraged the subsequent use of phrases such as *shimin byōdō* (the equality of all citizens) and *ikkun banmin* (one ruler, many subjects). Both slogans emphasized the abolition of the Confucian class structure and promoted the equality of all subjects within the *kokutai*.

12. The literal title of this film is *The New Publication of the Trials of Magistrate Ōoka*. Ōoka Tadasuke (1677–1751) was the *machi bugyō* (magistrate) of Edo between 1717 and 1736 and was renowned for his just decisions. Many elaborated tales based on his cases were collected under the title *Ōoka seidan*. Subsequent films centred on the character Tange Sazen are simply titled *Tange Sazen*.

13. The first film in the *Kurama Tengu* series to star Arashi Kanjūrō (1903–1980) was made in 1927, and he went on to star in thirty-five sequels; in all, sixty films were made in the series between 1925 and 1965.

14. In the prewar period a total of twenty-nine films were made based on novels by the popular writer Sasaki Mitsuzō (1896–1934) *The Case Notes of Kondō (Muttsuri) Umon* (*Umon torimonochō*). Yamanaka Sadao wrote the screenplays for the first two films in the series (1929 and 1930). The series ran concurrently with the *Kurama Tengu* series with Arashi Kanjurō (1903–1980) taking the lead in both series. In the postwar period the series was again revived by Tōei, first with Arashi Kanjurō and later with Ōtomo Ryūtarō (1912–1985) in the main role.

15. 'Essentially I had different aspirations and opinions to the other young authors who aspired to write screenplays at this time. Anyhow, at this time audiences who patronized *jidaigeki* (*kyūgeki*) were from the socially lower classes. If I pressed them into viewing films of a higher artistic merit, they would probably

stop coming. Therefore, in the first instance it was necessary to gradually induct audiences into the peculiar delights of *jidaigeki*. Somehow, it had to be moderately entertaining to capture the public. It was here that I adopted a similar doctrine of *hanpo shugi* developed by the founder of the *shinkokugeki* theatre movement, Sawada Shōjirō. In *jidaigeki* films I incorporated elements of detection and a sense of resistance, neither of which had ever been used before, and I incorporated a sense of realism into the action scenes' (quoted in Satō 1995 vol. i: 23–24).

16. This technique of extreme close-up was also used in the 1927 film based on the novel by Mikami Otokichi, *Hyakuman-ryō hibun* (*The Million-Ryō Secret*) and also the 1928 episode of the *Kurama Tengu*.

17. There is some confusion regarding the name of this *rōnin*. In the film he is known as Akagaki Genzō, however history texts documenting the *Chūshingura* incident list him as Akabana Genzō.

18. 'Kanadehon Chūshingura (*The Treasury of Loyal Retainers*) Written by Takeda Izumo (1691–1756), Miyoshi Shoraku (1696–1775), and Namiki Senryo (1695–1751). First staged as a puppet play in 1748, but very shortly after adapted for the kabuki stage. It superseded a number of earlier plays on the same theme, the earliest of which appeared in 1706, only three years after the occurrence of the incident on which the play is based' (A.S. Halford, and G.M. Halford 1983: 138).

19. The Japan Amateur Sports Association (Dai Nihon Taiiku Kyōkai) was founded in 1911, and Japan sent two athletes to the 1912 Olympic Games in Stockholm. Fifteen athletes were sent to the next Olympic Games in Antwerp in 1920 and won two silver medals. In 1928 forty-three athletes went to the 1928 Amsterdam games and 'Oda Mikio in the triple jump and Tsuruta Yoshiyuki in the 200 meter breast stroke both won gold medals. This was the first time that athletes from East Asia won Olympic gold medals' (Inoue 1998: 170).

20. Katsu Kaishū (1823–1899), also known as Katsu Rintarō and Katsu Awa, or indeed, as in the film *The Last Days of Edo*, as Katsu Yasuyoshi, was a statesman active in the transition from the Tokugawa shogunate to the Meiji government.

21. This film should not be confused with the 1958 re-make of the same Japanese title starring Mifune Toshirō. Subtitled prints of this version are in circulation and listed under the title *Rickshaw Man*.

22. *Dai Anke-to ni youru Nihon Eiga Besuto 150*, 1992.

23. A similar but perhaps more sophisticated sequence is in the 1928 French/German co-production *L'Argent*, directed by Marcel L' Herbier, when just before the hero is about to depart on his historic solo flight he is held in a frontal medium close-up shot saluting. The camera then cuts to a fluttering tricolour, the object of his gaze, before cutting back again to the hero still saluting as the tricolour is superimposed over his body. The hero is thus infused with a national sensibility. In narrative terms this sequence also serves to underline the motivation of the hero, which is clearly positive in that he is attempting to further national goals while the bank manager who has financed the expedition is clearly the villain, being motivated by money as in the film's title.

24. In this section I am focusing on Manchuria and Taiwan and to a lesser extent Korea. However, it should not be forgotten that Japan took control of Indonesia in 1942, establishing a film company in 1943 headed by Ishimoto Tōkira (1907–

1977) to produce newsreel films. Later they took control of the studios set up by the Dutch and, drawing on local actors, actresses and technicians, began producing entertainment films. Also in 1942 Japan took control of Manila and by 1943 Japanese films were being imported and screened.

25. Film attendance figures quoted for 1934 at 458,812 are cited as proof of the relative success of the colonial film policy (Japanese sources also quote a figure of sixty percent of the native population able to speak Japanese by 1943) (Satō 1995 vol. ii: 112).

26. The Manchurian Railway Company had long held interests in the film industry, building the first cinema in Dairen, the Denkikan, in 1909.

27. In *Orientalism* Said describes the West's response to the Oriental world in terms of an often negative sexuality, as he observes when discussing Flaubert. 'Woven through all of Flaubert's Oriental experiences, exciting or disappointing, is an almost uniform association between the Orient and sex. In making this association Flaubert was neither the first nor the most exaggerated instance of a remarkably persistent motif in Western attitudes to the Orient' (Said 1991a: 188).

28. Under the terms of the Total Mobilization Law of 1938, the Nihon Theatre Stage Review, which had been instigated by Hara Toyokichi (1873–1956), underwent a major change. Hara Toyokichi, before joining Tōhō, worked in the Berlin office of Mitsubishi where he had the opportunity to study Western popular theatre. Prior to taking up a senior management position in the Takurazuka Theatre in 1940 he had been instrumental in establishing a Western-style dance review programme at the Nihon Theatre, known as the NDT—'Nihon Theatre Dancing Team' (*Nihon Gekijo Danshingu Tīmu*). In the late 1930s with the rise in anti-Western sentiments, this review was changed, under the auspices of Hara, to the 'Japanese National Dance Review' (*Nihon Minzoku Buyō*) and a series of programmes were put on under the collective title 'The Japanese Peoples Native Lands' (*Nihon Minzoku no Kyōdo*). This series of reviews clearly located the colonies within Japan's 'native lands'—in 1939 Ryūkyū Islands Review and the Chosen Review, and in 1940 Yaeyama Islands Review and the Taiwan Review. These reviews clearly came under the *kominka* policy of assimilation by taking traditional elements of regional folk dances and incorporating them into the hegemonic structure of the nation-state. Added to this was the incorporation of indigenous cultural forms within the modern context of a Western-style review format.

## Chapter Three

1. This is a quotation originally taken from a thirteenth-century work, *An Account of My Hut* by Kamo no Chōmei (1155?–1216). The original reads, 'The flow of the river is ceaseless and its water is never the same. The bubbles that float in the pools, now vanishing, now forming, are not of long duration: so in the world are man and his dwellings' (translated by Donald Keene 1956: 197).

2. Ishiwari (2000) in his more recent account of these events implies that Makino was artistically inhibited by Nikkatsu at this time. He argues that Onoe Matsu-

nosuke's *kyūha* style of acting was limiting Makino's artistic expression, hence his
move to establish his own company.

3. Nava argues that the burgeoning number of cinemas in America and Europe
caused concern. 'By 1909 there were over 340 movie houses and nickelodeons in
New York City with an estimated 2 million visits per week. Paris had two cinemas
in 1907 and by 1913 it had 160. In Germany the number of cinemas rose from two
in 1900 to 2,446 in 1914. In Britain in the same year the number of cinemas was
estimated at 4,000 with a weekly audience of 7–8 million' (Nava 1996: 61).

4. Here I am translating '*tsūzoku kyōiku*' as 'popular education' but in fact *tsūzoku* as used in this context carries stronger class connotations, being perhaps more
accurately translated as 'vulgar'.

5. Under this provision, the producers of a 1925 adaptation of a novel by Kikuchi Kan (1888–1948), *The Second Kiss* (*Daini no seppun*), were forced to
change the title. Kikuchi Kan took up this issue in a series of articles arguing that
the novel had been released for print under the original title as had the earlier serialized version. (For a detailed account of this incident see Makino 1991.)

6. *The Times,* in an article published in September 1915, observed 'that, because so many of those who went to the cinema were young men of military age,
appropriate films could make a dramatic impact on military recruitment' (quoted
in Reeves 1999: 28).

7. Tatebayashi kept detailed diaries throughout this period and the editors of
the NHK study (1995) made extensive use of them.

8. As a student in Germany, Kawakita was taken to the opera to see *Madam
Butterfly*. He was reportedly shocked by the low level of European understanding
about Japan. According to his autobiography, this is what inspired him to work in
cinema as he felt this was one of the best mediums for the promotion of intercultural understanding.

9. For the complete list of regulations under the 1939 Law see Sakuramoto
1993: 7–19.

10. Similar shots of wheat fields are evident in Alexander Dovzhenko's (1894–
1956) *Earth* and Vsevolod Pudovkin's (1893–1953) *Storm Over Asia: the Heir of
Genghis Khan* (1928). Kurosawa Akira used similar shots of long grass billowing
in the wind in the final judo bout in *Sanshiro Sugata*.

11. This film should not be confused with the 1953 Kinoshita Keisuke film of
the same title. To avoid confusion I shall refer to Kamei's film as *The Tragedy of
Japan* and to Kinoshita's as *A Japanese Tragedy*.

12. The critic, historian and producer of *The Tragedy of Japan*, Iwasaki Akira,
was attacked by two sword-wielding right-wing fanatics angry at the treatment of
the emperor in the film. He had also been head of the Japan Motion Picture and
Drama Employees Union, which was established to expose war criminals (Anderson and Richie 1959: 163).

13. At this point, it is perhaps useful to define 'democracy' within the American
historical and political tradition. Noam Chomsky in *Necessary Illusions* briefly
traces the development of the term from the Founding Fathers to the present and
concludes, 'For us democracy is . . . narrowly conceived: the citizen is a consumer,
an observer but not a participant. The public has the right to ratify policies that

originate elsewhere, but if these limits are exceeded, we have not democracy, but a "crisis of democracy", which must somehow be resolved' (Chomsky 1993: 14).

14. The Potsdam Declaration (26 July 1945) had been ambiguous on the point of the Imperial House. When the Japanese government asked for clarification, President Truman, ignoring the wishes of China, the Soviet Union and Australia, but with the support of Britain, replied that, '[T]he authority of the Emperor and the Japanese government to rule the state shall be subject to the supreme Commander of the Allied Powers' (quoted in Horsley and Buckley 1990: 6). The Japanese government interpreted this to be an implicit acceptance of the emperor's position and the future role of the Imperial House in Japanese politics, and by extension, the continuance of the *kokutai*. According to Kosaka Masataka, this 'permitted the Japanese to interpret [the Potsdam Declaration] in a way that made a face-saving surrender possible' (1982: 40).

15. To what extent MacArthur was influenced by Yoshida is impossible to know. MacArthur dealt almost exclusively with Yoshida, refusing to see other Japanese representatives. What appears certain is that MacArthur and the occupation government came to see the Imperial system as a bulwark against a left-wing opposition.

16. There is some disagreement as to when precisely the first 'kiss' actually appeared on Japanese cinema screens. However, it is generally attributed to the 1946 Shōchiku production *Twenty Year Old Youth* (*Hatachi no seishun*) when, in the final scene, the two actors kiss through gauze in front of the camera. Just prior to this Daiei had released *One Night's Kiss* (*Aru yo no seppun*), but the filmmakers balked at the final moment and an umbrella slipped down to obscure the actual kiss.

## Chapter Four

1. The All Japan Film Employees Union Association (*Zen Nippon Eiga Jūgyōin Kumiai Dōmei*), which was founded in January 1946, was later disbanded as the film and theatre unions merged to form the All Japan Film and Theatre Workers Union (*Zen Nippon Eiga Engeki Rōdō Kumiai*) in April (Iwasaki 1958a: 112).

2. The charter for the International Tribunal for the Far East included the following: 'Neither the official position, at any time, of an accused, nor the fact that an accused acted pursuant to order of his government or of a superior shall, of itself, be sufficient to free such accused from responsibility for any crime with which he is charged' (quoted in Minear 1971: 42–43).

3. According to Ooms's analysis, Yamazaki Ansai (1618–1682) believed that the Truth existed in the world before humans and that a person's role was that of transmitter and not creator of the Way. 'The Way [transcends] all ages, was not man-made but Heaven-ordained—*tenri no shizen*—and regulated the life of man and the universe' (Ooms 1989: 200). Yamazaki's method of extrapolating the Truth was simple: he looked for latent significations in the exegesis of Confucian texts and in the early chapters of the *Nihongi* through native readings (*kun yomi*) of Chinese characters. The exposition of the 'Truth' embedded in these texts led to the

emergence of what Ooms has called an 'anthropocosmic' worldview, that is, 'the refusal to recognize separate realms of reality that respond to different laws of formation . . . These parallels all point to the political order that is therefore presented as an instance of the cosmic coherence of things. In this mental construct through "gulliverization" and "gigantization", *tenchi* (Heaven and Earth) becomes an intimate substance and man coterminous with the universe . . . Not analysis, but identification of similitudes is the explanatory procedure . . . This procedure decenters man, even if he is *analogum princeps*. He finds his self in the protected unity of the world and the cosmos. *This discourse refuses to recognize man as a source of initiative other than for action confirming that general order*' (emphasis in original Ooms 1989: 94–95).

4. Ooms makes the point in a footnote that, 'Modern scholarship on Ansai and his schools reached its peak in the 1930s and 1940s within a general political and intellectual climate that interpreted Ansai as the first in a long line of imperial panegyrists and ideologues of the *yamatodamashii* or Japanese spirit' (Ooms 1989: 195).

5. The Shin-Tōhō breakaway group was lead by Ōkōchi Denjirō (1898–1962), and included Hasegawa Kazuo (1908–1984), Takemine Hideko (1924–), Hara Setsuko (1920–) and the director Watanabe Kunio (1899–1981).

6. Second place, *War and Peace* (*Sensō to heiwa*); third place, *Once More* (*Ima hitotabino*); fifth place, *Actress* (*Joyū*); sixth place, *One Wonderful Sunday* (*Subarashiki Nichiyōbi*); seventh place, *Silver Snow* aka *Snow Trail/To the End of the Silver-capped Mountains* (*Ginrei no hate*) and in eighth place, *Four Stories of Love* (*Yotu no koi monogatari*).

7. Satō (1995 vol.ii: 243) argues that management in the major studios used the GHQ anti-Communist policy (the Communist party of Japan was banned in 1950) to crush the film unions.

8. Dower makes the following observations regarding the more general 'Red purge' that reached its apotheosis by 1949: 'By 1949, "Red purge" had become one of the fashionable new terms of the occupation, appropriately expressed in Japanized English (*reddo pāji*). Initially referred to within GHQ simply as a "troublemaker purge", the Red purge involved close collaboration among occupation officials, conservative politicians, government bureaucrats, and corporate managers. A major objective was to break radical unions at the company and industry level, and to this end some eleven thousand activist union members in the public sector were fired between the end of 1949 and the outbreak of the Korean War on June 25, 1950. After the war began, the purge was extended to the private sector (including the mass media), resulting in the dismissal of an additional ten to eleven thousand leftist employees by the end of 1950. Side by side with the "Red purge" came the "depurge"—a reference to the return to public activity of individuals previously purged "for all time" for having actively abetted militarism and ultranationalism' (Dower 1999: 272).

9. Dower writing on the annual figures for tuberculosis gives the following statistics: 'The annual tuberculosis death count had increased steadily from the mid-1930s. The disease claimed 130,763 lives in 1935, 160,398 in 1942. Impressionistic evidence suggests even greater numbers over the next four years. In 1947, when

official statistics resumed, 146,241 were reported to have died of TB, and it was not until 1951 that total annual deaths dropped below 100,000 . . . Following surrender, the total number of TB cases annually was probably well over a million' (Dower 1999: 103).

10. The post-defeat period saw a substantial increase in crime, 'in 1934, 2,126 persons were arrested for robbery and 724,986 for theft, whereas the comparable average yearly figures for the period from 1946 through 1949 were 9,485 and 1,177,184' (Dower 1999: 109).

11. The correct translation would be frog, as Satō is making a play on the word for 'frog', *kaeru*, which he links to *après-guerre* by mispronouncing it as *après-gaeru*. Frogs are heard croaking in the background throughout the scene.

12. *Until the Day We Meet Again* was ranked number one in the *Kinema Junpō* top-ten list for 1950.

13. For a more complete analysis of this film see Isolde Standish, *Myth and Masculinity in the Japanese Cinema: Towards a Political Reading of the Tragic Hero* (Curzon Press: London, 68–96).

14. Okada Eiji starred with Emanuelle Riva in Alain Resnais's *Hiroshima Mon Amour* (1961).

15. So popular was the film that a sequel to the *Diary of a Policeman* was released in the same year under the title *Diary of a Policeman Continued* (*Zoku keisatsu nikki*).

16. Dower quotes from a February 1948 report by the Ministry of Health and Welfare on orphaned children: '[T]he number of orphaned and homeless children combined [was] 123,510. Of this number, 28,248 had lost their parents in air raids; 11,351 were orphaned or lost contact with their parents during the traumatic repatriation process; 2,640 were identified as "abandoned"; and an astonishing 81,266 were believed to have lost their parents, or simply become separated from them, in the turmoil that accompanied the end of the war' (Dower 1999: 62–63).

17. Although released in three parts the film is actually divided into six sections following the structure of the original novel.

18. For a more detailed account of *The Human Condition* see chapter three in Isolde Standish, *Myth and Masculinity in the Japanese Cinema: Towards a Political Reading of the Tragic Hero.*

19. Gomikawa Junpei won the *Kikuchikan* literary prize in 1978 for his war novels.

20. This same ethos would again be co-opted by the novelist Mishima Yukio (1925–1970) in his short story 'Patriotism' and his exposition of the *Hagakure—On Hagakure: The Samurai Ethic and Modern Japan.*

21. The anthropologist Joy Hendry stresses that in marriage, even in postwar Japan, the emphasis is placed on the continuance of the *ie* rather than on the happiness of the individuals concerned. She concludes that '[M]arriage in a village like Kurotsuchi involves much more than a contract between individuals. Even for a couple living alone, . . . or a newly formed branch house, marriage immediately established the house head as a member of the village assembly, and various obligations follow for the household' (Hendry 1989: 228).

22. In the opening sequence Michiko does express the desire to have a child by Kaji. However, this should be read in terms of Michiko's expression of her desire for Kaji in the sense that if he is killed she would have the child as a token of their love, rather than the articulation of her express wish to bear a child.

## Chapter Five

1. In this chapter I am focusing primarily on the films and writings of Ōshima Nagisa (1932–) as representative of his generation of the avant-garde film movement of the 1960s. My reasons for doing this are twofold: first, Ōshima's films have been widely distributed in the West and, second, he has been a prolific writer and critic of Japanese cinema.

2. In his book *An Experiential Discussion of Postwar Film*, Ōshima mentions having met Susan Sontag at Cannes. Also it is clear from his discussion that he is familiar with Sontag's influential monograph *On Photography*.

3. The title of this article was taken from the *Weekly Asahi Magazine History of the Shōwa Period* (1989 vol. iii: 120), a compilation of articles published in the magazine in 1956.

4. Literally they refer to his style as that of an 'amateur' (*shirōto*). However, within the context of this discussion, the translation as 'natural' is closer to the original Japanese sense, which carries none of the negative connotations often implicit in the English use of the word 'amateur'.

5. In his book, *Ōshima Nagisa 1960*, Ōshima is adamant that, when approached by Shōchiku to make a sequel, he would not make *Cruel Story of Youth II*. I would suggest that this was a way of maintaining artistic integrity and of resisting the studio mentality of the series, so successfully exploited by the industry.

6. For the use of the term 'oxymoronic quality' I am indebted to Emma Dexter who uses it in her introductory essay, 'Photography Itself', to the Tate Modern Exhibition catalogue *Tender and Cruel: The Real in the Twentieth-Century Photograph*.

7. It was Max Weber who first defined the State as the agency that possesses the monopoly on legitimate violence.

8. It should be noted that Maureen Turim's analysis of *Death by Hanging* in her study *The Films of Ōshima Nagisa: Images of a Japanese Iconoclast* is marred by a mistranslation of these intertitles as, 'Graphics introduce a poll dated June 1957 that gives Japanese attitudes toward capital punishment: 71 percent for the abolition of capital punishment, 16 percent against the abolition, and 13 percent undecided'. She continues, 'While these numbers look refreshing from a U.S. standpoint nearly forty years later, with large numbers of the population clamoring for more death sentences, they are even more impressive as a measure of Japan's postwar antiviolence, its aversion to its traditional military and state codes of punishment' (Turim 1998: 68). The use of the double negative in Japanese is a common pitfall for students and in this case resulted in serious consequences for reaching any sort of understanding of the film under discussion.

9. He rejected the use of flashbacks other than in his last film of 1960, *Night and Fog in Japan*, which is built entirely around a discussion and analysis of past events.

10. Yamada, Yōji (1978) (ed.) *Kido Shirō: wa ga eigaron* (Tōkyō: Shōchiku Kabushiki Kaisa).

11. See Satō 1995 vol. ii: 324.

12. As with many of Ōshima's films, *In the Realm of the Senses* is based on an actual incident. In 1936 Abe Sada, a geisha/prostitute, was arrested for the murder and mutilation of her former employer. During the course of the investigation leading up to her arrest, it was revealed that Sada and Kichi had spent a week of intense sexual activity ensconced in an upper room of a restaurant frequented by geisha and their clients. Sada, after killing Kichi and severing his genitals with a knife, inscribed her name in blood on his limbs and the phrase 'Sada and Kichi alone together' (*Sada, Kichi futarikiri*) on his torso. The following morning she left the room ordering a taxi. An hour later she telephoned the restaurant, explaining that Kichi had stomach cramps and was sleeping; he was to be woken at three that afternoon, at which time the body was discovered (*Shūkan Asahi Shōwashi* 1989 vol. i: 152–153). As a result of the reported orgiastic nature of her sexual relationship with her lover, culminating in her act of murder and mutilation, Abe Sada achieved folk-hero status within the popular imagination, a position she continued to hold well into the postwar period, her story forming the basis for at least four films. The most famous is Ōshima Nagisa's 1976 version *In the Realm of the Senses* (*Ai no koriida*), which, filmed as 'hard-core', exploits the apparent excesses of desire through a series of fictional sexual encounters between the couple during the week of their confinement.

13. Another example, this time from the 1970s also dealing with prostitutes, is the 1974 Nikkatsu production released in the U.K. as *Streets of Joy* (*Akasen Tamanoi nukeraremasu*), directed by the master of the *romanporuno* genre, Kumashiro Tatsumi (1927–1995).

14. Jane Ussher defines the function of pornography for Western men in the following terms: 'Like other forms of representation constructed within the masculine gaze, pornography acts to deny or alleviate temporarily men's sexual anxiety through identification with phallic mastery. It counters man's underlying fear of woman—his fear of not being good enough, or hard enough, both literally and metaphorically. A fear of the devouring, consuming "woman", with her apparently insatiable sexuality; of being rejected, laughed at. In heterosexual pornography, where "man" is positioned as active subject and "woman" as responsive object, she becomes not a person, but a hole to be penetrated. The symbolic representation of "woman" in porn acts is to denigrate her, to dismiss her and to annihilate her power. She is fetishized in the most obvious manner—split into part object (breast, vagina, mouth) rather than whole object—and the fears she provokes in man (castration, not being big enough, of not being "man") are contained' (Ussher 1997: 197).

15. See Mikiso Hane's book *Reflections on the Way to the Gallows: Rebel Women in Prewar Japan* (University of California Press, 1993).

16. The Chinese character (*kanji*) *tai*, used to refer to the physical 'body', is the same as that used in the compound *kokutai* referring to the 'body politic'.

17. In 1958 attendance figures were in excess of one billion with each person attending the cinema on average a record twelve times during the year, but by 1961 audience numbers were in sharp decline, reaching an all-time low in 1996 when attendance dropped to just over one hundred million with each person attending a cinema once a year (Murakami and Ogawa 2000: 12).

## Chapter Six

1. Shōchiku produced Japan's first colour film in 1951, and Tōei produced Japan's first wide-screen film in 1957, *The Bride of Phoenix Castle* (*Ōtorijō no hanayome*), directed by Matsuda Sadatsugu (1906–2003).

2. *The Shōgun's Retainer, a Man of Leisure* series is based on the novels by Sasaki Mitsuzō (1896–1934) first serialized in 1929. Tōei made twenty-two films in the series between 1950 and 1963.

3. The fictional character of Tōyama no Kin*san* is based on the historical figure Tōyama Kinshirō (1793–1855). Tōyama Kinshirō was the magistrate for the northern part of Edo and was renowned for his wise and impartial judgements.

4. The character Mito Kōmon is loosely based on the historical figure Tokugawa Mitsukuni (1628–1700). A grandson of Tokugawa Ieyasu, he was the second lord (*daimyō*) of the Mito domain. He is renowned for being the originator of a history of Japan, the compilation of which began in 1657 and was completed in 1904.

5. *The Case Notes of Zenigata Heiji* series is based on the serialized novels published by Nomura Kodō (1882–1963) between 1931 and 1958. The Edo detective Heiji and his assistant, Hachigorō, were inspired by Sherlock Holmes and Watson. Daiei made fifteen films in the series between 1951 and 1961.

6. Kikuchi Kan (1888–1948) was a novelist and critic. He was instrumental in the founding of two of Japan's most prestigious literary prizes, the Akutagawa Ryūnosuke Literary Prize and the Naoka Sanjūgo Literary Prize. *The Gates of Hell* (*Jigokumon*), based on a novel by Kikuchi Kan and directed by Kinugasa Teinosuke after his move to Daiei in 1950, won the Grand Prize at Cannes in 1953. The year before Daiei also had success at Cannes with *The Tale of Genji* (*Genji monogatari*) directed by Yoshimura Kōzaburō (1911–2000).

7. Kawaguchi Matsutarō (1899–1985) was the author of the hugely popular serialized novel *Love-Troth Tree* (*Aizen Katsura*), which Shōchiku produced in 1938—see chapter one.

8. Mizoguchi Kenji continued the studio's success at Venice in 1952 with *The Life of Oharu* (*Saikaku ichidai onna*), in 1953 with *Ugetsu* (*Ugetsu Monogatari*) and in 1954 with *Sansho the Bailiff* (*Sanshō taiyū*).

9. As Ikegami Eiko points out, in the Tokugawa period, 'There was no *organized* intervention by religious-ideological power representing transcendental values that institutionally challenged samurai practices in any fundamental fashion . . . Rather, religious authorities tended to accommodate the spiritual needs of the sam-

urai as they inevitably confronted violent and painful death in the course of their occupational functioning' (Ikegami 1995: 190).

10. Other films listed under this subgenre include *Three Samurai (Sanbiki no Samurai)* (1964) directed by Gosha Hideo for Shōchiku, *Bushido: Samurai Saga (Bushidō zankoku monogatari)* (1963) directed by Imai Tadashi and *Cruel Story of the Bakumatsu Period (Bakumatsu zankoku monogatari)* (1964), directed by Katō Tai and produced by Tōei.

11. Hashimoto (1989) also links the 'cruel boom' to the novelist Nanjō Norio (1908–), who published a collection of short stories under the title *Cruel Stories (Zankoku Monogatari)* in 1959.

12. In the early 1960s Tōei released a double bill that consisted of one *jidaigeki* film and one *ninkyō* yakuza film in time for the main holiday seasons. However, in 1965 they released the *Kantō Wanderer/Kantō nagaremono* directed by Ozawa Shigehiro (1922–) and starring Tsurota Kōji with the first of the *Abashiri Prison* films *(Abashiri bangaichi)* starring Takakura Ken.

13. Within the Japanese lexicon there are various words used to designate the 'wanderer' *(matabimono)* or 'drifter' *(nagaremono)* in both *jidaigeki* and later yakuza films. In the first episode of the *Zatōichi* series *(Zatōichi monogatari)* (1962) directed by Misumi Kenji (1921–1975), Zatōichi refers to himself in the metaphorical sense as a *tabigarasu*, which literally means a 'migratory bird', but within these genres carries the same connotations of 'wanderer' and 'drifter'.

14. Daiei continued to produce the *Zatoichi (Zatōichi)* series from 1960 until the studio went into liquidation in 1971. Katsu Shintarō continued to produce films in the series through his own company, Katsu Productions (Katsu Puro). In all some twenty-six films were produced in the series between 1960 and 1989. The series was also transferred to television and more recently, in 2003, Beat (Kitano) Takeshi (1948–) released yet another film version.

15. A *koku* is a measure of volume or capacity used for rice. In the Edo period a *koku* of rice equalled approximately 5.12 bushels. Theoretically it was thought that one *koku* of rice was sufficient to sustain one person for one year.

16. For a detailed analysis of how this film series fits into the 'tragic hero' tradition of Japanese film culture see chapter four, 'Facts, Fictions and Fantasy', in Isolde Standish, *Myth and Masculinity in the Japanese Cinema: Towards a Political Reading of the Tragic Hero*.

17. The *Abashiri Prison* series closely followed the release in 1964 of the first film in the *Japanese Chivalrous Gambler (Nihon kyōkakuden)* series. Eleven films were made in this series. Makino Masahiro (1908–1993) directed the first nine films of the series. Yamashita Kōsaku (1930–1998) and Ozawa Shigehiro (1922–) each directed one film. Nine films were produced in the *Remnants of Chivalry in the Showa Era (Shōwa zankyō-den)* series, which ran from 1965–1972. Five were directed by Saeki Kiyoshi (1914–2002), three by Makino Masahiro and one by Yamashita Kōseku.

18. It should be noted that the first film in the series was re-released on DVD in the U.K. in 2002 under the title *Yakuza Papers*.

19. Eight films were made in the series starring Fuji Junko (1945–), the daughter of the principal Tōei Studios producer of *ninkyō* yakuza films, Shundō Kōji.

20. The two former prewar *jidaigeki* stars Arashi Kanjurō and Kataoka Chiezō both made the successful transition to the *ninkyō* yakuza genre in the 1960s. Arashi Kanjurō, as this chapter argues, was intrinsic to the *Abashiri* series, but he also made numerous guest appearances as the moral *oyabun* in *The Scarlet Peony Rose Gambler* (*Hibotan bakuto*) series starring Fuji Junko. Kataoka Chiezō also appeared as a guest in the following series, *Remnants of Chivalry in the Shōwa Period* (*Shōwa zankyō-den*), *Japanese Chivalry* (*Nihon kyōkyaku-den*) and *The Scarlet Peony Rose Gambler*.

21. The 1973 film ostensibly based on the autobiography of Taoka Kazuo, *The Third Leader of the Yamaguchi Gang* (*Yamaguchigumi sandaime*), and starring Takakura Ken, draws on similar conventions. Food is the metaphor that binds the young Taoka to the gang and his *oyabun*. This film also draws on flashbacks of Taoka's deprived childhood at the hands of a cruel stepmother who denies him food.

22. For a more detailed analysis of the stylistic structure of these films, refer to chapter four, 'Facts, Fictions and Fantasy', in Isolde Standish, *Myth and Masculinity in the Japanese Cinema: Towards a Political Reading of the Tragic Hero*.

23. The first series of the *War Without Morality* films were released in five episodes between 1973 and 1974. These were all directed by Fukasaku Kinji from scripts by Kasahara Kazuo (1927–2002). Due to the great popularity of this first series, the Tōei Studios produced a second series under the title *New War Without Morality* (*Shin jingi naki tatakai*); four films were released in this series between 1974 and 1979. Fukasaku Kinji directed the first three films and Kudō Eiichi (1929–2000) the fourth.

24. Second ranking in the *Kinema Junpō* award for 1973 went to the first film in the series *War Without Morality* and the eighth ranking went to the third film *War Without Morality: War by Proxy* (*Jingi naki tatakai: dairi sensō*). The fourth film in the series, *War Without Morality: High Tactics* (*Jingi naki tatakai: chōjō sakusen*), was ranked seventh in 1974.

25. One of the best English language accounts of these films is Mick Broderick (ed.) *Hibakusha Cinema: Hiroshima, Nagasaki and the Nuclear Image in Japanese Film*.

26. Referring to the first film in the series Schilling states, 'The film had a difficult birth, however. When producer Goro Kusakabe and scriptwriter Kazuo Kasahara approached Mino about making a movie—his writings about the Hiroshima gang war had been a basis for the *Shukan Sunday* articles—he flatly refused permission. Criticized by his fellow gangsters for his revelations about the gangs' inner workings, Mino didn't want any trouble. Using patient persuasion, Kusakabe and Kasahara were able to change his mind—the fact that Mino (sic) and Kasahara had been in the same navy unit as Mino helped, as did a declaration by a powerful Hiroshima gangster that anyone who touched Mino would have to answer to him' (Schilling 2003: 214).

27. The disclaimer at the beginning of the films, which usually just states that the work is fiction and any likeness to any actual person is unintentional etc., was altered for the *War Without Morality* series to read, 'This film is a creation based on the writings of Iiboshi Kōichi, the names of people and yakuza organizations

are fiction and not based in fact'. As Ōshima points out, this statement is ambiguous, leading the spectator to the conclusion that it is indeed based on a 'true account' as Iiboshi's best-selling writings had been marketed as 'true accounts' (Ōshima [1975] in *Best of Kinema Junpō* 1994: 734). This same disclaimer was again utilized by Tōei at the beginning of the *Gangster Wives/Women* films with the exception that the name has been changed to Ieda Shōko, whose novel inspired the film series.

28. Katō Tai directed three films in the series: the first, *The Scarlet Peony Rose Gambler: Showdown at Cards/Hibotan bakuto: hanafuda shōbu* (1969), the second, *The Scarlet Peony Rose Gambler: Oryū's Visit/Hibotan bakuto: Oryū sanjō* (1970), and the third in 1971, *The Scarlet Peony Rose Gambler: I've Come for Your Life/Hibotan bakuto: oinochi itadakimasu.*

29. In *Remnants of Chivalry in the Shōwa Era*, Takakura Ken's tattoo is of the lion and peony rose of the title of the theme song that runs throughout the series.

30. The last scene in Kurosawa Akira's production *Sanjurō* is an excellent illustration of this point. After order within the clan has been restored, Sanjurō is confronted by the Tatsuya Nakadai character, who insists on a duel. There is no logic to the scene, just a hubristic display of competitive individualism between two equals.

31. Two excellent examples of this ethic are seen in the second film in the *Gangster Women* series when the heroine (Toake Yukio 1942–) falls in love with a handsome lone yakuza and decides to go abroad with him, only to turn back on the way to the airport, resolved to pay back the organization's debts and maintain the honour of the gang. The other example comes in the sixth film in the series, *Gangster Women: Resolve!* (1993), when the heroine (Iwashita Shima), after having avenged the murder of her husband, still refuses to leave with the man she loves.

32. In 1967 with the release by the Tōei Studios of the war-retro film based on the experiences of the wartime *kamikaze* pilots, *Flowering Cherry Blossoms (A' dōki no sakura)*, the tragic pathos of the heroes of the *ninkyō* yakuza films transferred to the war genre as Takakura Ken took the lead. This marked a conservative shift in the war genre from the humanist style to a more defiant reclamation of an heroic nationalism.

33. Kasahara Kazuo was involved in the screenplays for many of the Tōei *ninkyō* films series including *Tales of Japanese Chivalry (Nihon kyōkaku-den)* and *The Scarlet Peony Rose Gambler (Hibotan bakuto)* before going on to write the screenplays for the series *War Without Morality (Jingi naki tatakai)*.

34. From the opening sequences of *I Want to Be Reborn a Shellfish (Watashi wa kai ni naritai)*, the principal character, Shimizu (Tokoro Jōji), is cast as an inconsequential figure caught up in world events. The opening shots of Shimizu with his wife and child collecting driftwood on the beach are merged through superimpositions over the sea of a series of iconic documentary still photographs taken from major wars. The first is taken from the Gulf War of 1990, symbolized by shots of oil-coated seabirds, followed by scenes from the civil war in Sudan in 1984, the Vietnam War of 1965 represented by a shot of a military helicopter and peasants,

the Korean War of 1950 with shots of refugees and soldiers, ending finally in a résumé of the major events of the Pacific War as depicted in newsreel footage.

35. Here I think it is important to make a distinction between these fictionalized portrayals of General Tōjō and Kobayashi Masaki's epic documentary reconstruction of *The Tokyo Trial* (*Tōkyō Saiban*) produced by Kōdansha in 1983.

36. Twenty-six films were made in the *Kurama Tengu* series between 1927 and 1942, and the series was revived in 1950 and continued until 1954 during which time another fourteen films were released.

37. Stuart Galbraith's assessment of Okamoto Kihachi's *Daibosatsu tōge* (*Sword of Doom*) in *The Emperor and the Wolf* provides a wonderful example of the importance of pre-knowledge of the narrative and genre conventions to the enjoyment of these films. '*The Sword of Doom* is no masterpiece. Despite its impressive set pieces, it isn't half the film *The Age of Assassin* are (sic), nor is it even up to the level of Okamoto's best crime and war pictures . . . Shinobu Hashimoto's uncharacteristically choppy script is confused and disjointed, jerking from one subplot to another, promising much but delivering little . . .' (Galbraith 2002: 398). He continues in much the same vein for the next two pages, totally missing the point of the film's ending (that it is only the first part of what is usually filmed as a trilogy), and that the so-called 'choppy script' only appears so if one is not conversant with the many subplots that are interwoven around the main character.

38. Ōshima, writing in *Kinema Junpō* in 1975, links this pleasure in the performative quality of the stars to the historical development of the yakuza genre from its beginnings in the indigenous oral *kōdan* storytelling and dramatic traditions, both of which were based on accounts of actual historical figures. 'Yakuza stories and theatre, which were from the first derived from "actual accounts" (*jitsuroku*), became fixed in particular patterns according to skills in storytelling and acting. Due to this process they were no longer "true accounts", but became universal dramatic forms. Spectator interest changed from an interest in the reality of these amazing yakuza, to an appreciation of the aesthetics of how beautifully the dramatic patterns are expressed. As this occurred, in order to express these dramas beautifully, stars began to appear. The spectator, already very familiar with the story, was interested in how beautifully a particular star expressed a role. At this point, the spectator lost interest in the story. Accordingly, if the star loses the ability to express the drama beautifully, he is abandoned. And a new star appears and performs in the same drama' (Ōshima, *Best of Kinema Junpō* 1994: 736).

39. Kitano Takeshi originally started his professional career as one half of a stand-up comic duo called the 'Two Beats'. As such he has retained the stage name Beat Takeshi. In order to make a distinction between his comic TV persona and his role as a director of international renown he tends to divide the two roles, reverting to Kitano Takeshi. However, in the context of this chapter I refer to him as Kitano Beat/Takeshi.

40. In Hollywood this trend is represented in the films of Quentin Tarantino, Oliver Stone and David Lynch. In the former two examples, it is clear that there are intertextual connections between the Japanese and more general East Asian depictions of violence and these directors' own representations—particularly so in *Natural Born Killers* (1994) and more recently in the *Kill Bill* (2003/04) series.

## Reflections

1. Michel Foucault goes into this aspect of modern life in some detail in *Discipline and Punish: the Birth of the Prison* (Vintage, 1995).

2. To quote Hansen in more detail, 'If this vernacular has a transnational and translatable resonance it was not just because of its optimal mobilization of biologically hardwired structures and universal narrative templates, but more important, because it played a key role in mediating competing cultural discourses on modernity and modernization, because it articulated, multiplied, and globalized a particular historical experience' (Hansen 2000b: 340–341).

3. As Dyer makes clear in his study of stars, '[S]tars articulate . . . ideas of personhood, in large measure shoring up the notion of the individual but also at times registering the doubts and anxieties attendant on it. In part, the fact that the star is not just a screen image but a flesh and blood person is liable to work to express the notion of the individual' (Dyer 2004: 9).

4. Taylorism is defined as: 'the theory and practice of organizing industrial production for maximal efficiency, by standardization of products, specialization of labouring tasks, etc. . . Named after the US engineer Fredrick Winslow Taylor (1856–1915), commonly regarded as the originator of scientific management' (Mautner 2000: 557).

5. The documentary filmmaker Hara Kazuo (1945–) made a film based on the same book in 1987 titled *The Emperor's Naked Army Marches On* (*Yukiyukite shingun*), which won a prize at the Berlin festival in the same year.

6. *Blade Runner* (Ridley Scott [1982]) is cited by David Harvey in *The Condition of Postmodernity* as a quintessential postmodernist film.

7. The 1997 film attendance increase is the first seen since the peak in 1958 when over a billion people went to the cinema. In comparison with 1996, an all-time low when the figure stood at just 120 million, the 1997 figure had increased to 140 million and to 150 million by 1998.

8. During the Reaganite era of deregulation in the 1980s, Hollywood majors were once again permitted to merge interests in distribution and exhibition. This merger of interests, as Acland points out, 'led to Hollywood's increasing reliance on global markets throughout the 1990s. This reliance includes the exportation of certain approaches to cinemagoing, and special cinema spaces, to select locales around the world' (Acland 2003: 18).

9. As an example, in May 2000 Shōchiku sold the Ōfuna Studios to the Kamakura Women's College for a reported US$117 million. The movie theme park Kamakura Cinema World, also run by Shōchiku, had already been closed in December 1998 after the company president Okuyama Tōru and his son Okuyama Kazuyoshi were deposed after the company suffered heavy financial losses (Cazdyn 2002: 224). In the summer of 2004 Jay Sakomoto, the grandson of Kido Shirō, was appointed as the new president of the company.

# SELECT FILMOGRAPHY

*Abashiri Prison* Series (*Abashiri bangaichi*/網走番外地) Tōei Studios Tokyo
1965–1973

*Abashiri Prison* aka *A Man from Abashiri Prison* (*Abashiri bangaichi*/網走
番外地)1965 Director: Ishii Teruo

*Abashiri Prison: Continued* (*Zoku Abashiri bangaichi*/続・網走番外地)
1965 Director: Ishii Teruo

*Abashiri Prison: Homesickness Episode* aka *A Man from Abashiri Prison:
Going Home* (*Abashiri bangaichi: bōkyō-hen*/網走番外地・望郷編)
1965 Director: Ishii Teruo

*Abashiri Prison: The North Sea Episode* (*Abashiri bangaichi: hokkaihen*/網
走番外地・北海編) 1966 Director: Ishii Teruo

*Showdown in the Wilderness* (*Abashiri bangaichi: kōya no taiketsu*/網走番
外地・荒野の対決) 1966 Director: Ishii Teruo

*Showdown in the South Country* (*Abashiri bangaichi: nankoku no taiketsu*/
網走番外地・南国の対決) 1966 Director: Ishii Teruo

*Showdown in the Frozen Wilderness* (*Abashiri bangaichi: daisetsugen no
taiketsu*/網走番外地・大雪原の対決) 1966 Director: Ishii Teruo

*Abashiri Prison: Duel at Thirty Degrees Below Zero* (*Abashiri bangaichi:
kettō reika sanjūdo*/網走番外地・決斗零下３０度) 1967 Director: Ishii
Teruo

*Abashiri Prison: Evil Challenge* (*Abashiri bangaichi: aku e no chōsen*/網走
番外地・悪への挑戦) 1967 Director: Ishii Teruo

*Abashiri Prison: Combat in a Blizzard* (*Abashiri bangaichi: fubuki no tōsō*/
網走番外地・吹雪の斗争) 1967 Director: Ishii Teruo

*New Abashiri Prison* (*Shin Abashiri bangaichi*/新網走番外地) 1968
Director: Makino Masahiro

*New Abashiri Prison: Duel at Exile Promontory* (*Shin Abashiri bangaichi:
Runin misaki no kettō*/新網走番外地・流人岬の血斗) 1969 Director:
Furihata Yasuo

*New Abashiri Prison: The Drifter from the Remote Parts* (*Shin Abashiri
bangaichi: saihate no nagaremono*/新網走番外地・さいはての流れ者)
1969 Director: Saeki Kyoshi

*New Abashiri Bangaichi: Duel in the Forest* (*Shin Abashiri bangaichi: daishinrin no kettō*/新網走番外地・大森林の決斗) 1970 Director: Furihata Yasuo

*New Abashiri Prison: the Stray Wolf in the Blizzard* (*Shin Abashiri bangaichi: fubuki no hagure ōkami*/新網走番外地・吹雪のはぐれ狼) 1970 Director: Furihata Yasuo

*New Abashiri Prison: the Stormy Shiretoko Promontory* (*Shin Abashiri bangaichi: arashi o yobu Shiretoko misaki*/新網走番外地・嵐を呼ぶ知床岬) 1971 Director: Furihata Yasuo

*New Abashiri Prison: Escape in the Blizzard* (*Shin Abashiri bangaichi: fubuki no daidassō*/新網走番外地・大脱走) 1971 Director: Furihata Yasuo

*New Abashiri Prison: Stormy Jingi* (*Shin Abashiri bangaichi: arashi yobu dampu jingi*/新網走番外地・嵐呼ぶダンプ仁義) 1972 Director: Furihata Yasuo

*An Actor's Revenge* aka *The Revenge of Yukinojo* Trilogy (*Yukinojō henge*/雪之丞変化) 1935–1936 Director: Kinugasa Teinosuke, Shōchiku

*Actress* (*Joyū*/女優) 1947 Director: Kinugasa Teinosuke, Tōhō

*The Air Aquadron at the Final Battle* (*A' kessen kōkūtai*/あ'決戦航空隊) 1974 Director: Yamashita Kōsaku

*Akagaki Genzō and the Night Before the Attack on Kira's Mansion* (*Chūshingura Akagaki Genzō uchiiri zen'ya*/忠臣蔵　赤垣源蔵・討入り前夜) 1938 Director: Ikeda Tomiyasu, Nikkatsu

*Akanishi Kakita* (*Akanishi Kakita*/赤西蠣太) 1936 Director: Itami Mansaku, Chiezō Productions

*Army* (*Rikugun*/陸軍) 1944 Director: Kinoshita Keisuke, Shōchiku

*An Autumn Afternoon* (*Sanma no aji*/秋刀魚の味) 1962 Director: Ozu Yasujirō, Shōchiku

*Aviators* (*Chōjin*/鳥人) 1940 Director: Marune Santarō, Nikkatsu Kyoto

*The Bad Sleep Well* aka *The Worse You Are, the Better You Sleep/A Rose in the Mud* (*Warui yatsu hodo yoku nemuru*/悪い奴ほどよく眠る) 1960 Director: Kurosawa Akira, Kurosawa Productions and Tōhō

*The Bases Where the Maidens Are* aka *Girls of the Air Base* (*Otome no iru kichi*/乙女のゐる基地) 1945 Director: Sasaki Yasushi, Shōchiku

*The Battle for Nihyakusankōchi* (*Nihyakusankōchi*/二百三高地) 1980 Director: Masuda Toshio, Tōei Kyoto

*Battle Royale* (バトル・ロワイアル) 2000 Director: Fukasaku Kinji—Battle Royale Seisaku Iinkai

*Battle Royale II Requiem* (バトル・ロワイアル鎮魂歌＜レクイエム＞) 2003 Director: Fukasaku Kinji—Tōei, Fukasakugumi, Terebi Asahi, WOWOW, Gag Communications, Nihon Shupan Hanbai, Tokyo FM, Sega and Tōei Video

*Beneath the Battle Flag* (*Gunki hatameku moto ni*/軍旗はためく下に) 1972 Director: Fukasaku Kinji—Tōhō and Shinsei Eiga

*Beyond the Clouds* (*Kumo nagaruru hateni*/雲ながるる果てに) 1953 Director: Ieki Miyoji

*Bicycle Thieves* 1948 Director: Vittorio de Sica

*The Big City: Labour* (*Daitokai: Rōdōhen*/大都会・労働篇) 1929 Director: Ushihara Kiyohiko, Shōchiku Kamata

*A Billionaire* (*Okuman chōja*/億万長者) 1954 Director: Ichikawa Kon, Seinen Haiyū Club

*Black Film* Series (Industrial Espionage) Daiei 1963–1964:

    *The Black Test Car (Kuro no tesutoka*/黒の試走車) 1962 Director: Masumura Yasuzō

    *The Black Challenger (Kuro no chōsensha*/黒の兆戦者) 1964 Director: Murayama Mitsuo

    *The Black Trump Card (Kuro no kirifuda*/黒の切り札) 1964 Director: Inoue Umetsuku

*Black Rain* (*Kuroi ame*/黒い雨) 1989 Director: Imamura Shōhei, Imamura Productions

*Blade Runner* 1982 Director: Ridley Scott

*Boy* (*Shōnen*/少年) 1969 Director: Ōshima Nagisa, Sōzōsha and ATG

*Branded to Kill* (*Koroshi no rakuin*/殺しの烙印) 1967 Director: Suzuki Seijun, Nikkatsu

*Bride of Phoenix Castle* (*Hōjō no hanayome*/鳳城の花嫁)1957 Director: Matsuda Sadatsugu, Tōei Kyoto

*The Brilliance of Life* (*Iki no kagayaki*/生の輝き) 1919 Director: Kaeriyama Norimasa

*Brothers and Sisters of the Toda Family* (*Todake no kyōdai*/戸田家の兄妹) 1941 Director: Ozu Yasujirō, Shōchiku

*Carmen Visits Home* aka *Carmen Comes Home* (*Karumen kokyō ni kaeru*/カルメン故郷に帰る) 1951 Director: Kinoshita Keisuke, Shōchiku

*Case Notes of Umon* Series (*Umon torimonochō*/右門捕物帖.) Twenty-three films were made between 1929–1945 starring Arashi Kanjurō.

*The Case Notes of Zenigata Heiji* (*Zenigata Heiji torimono hikae*/銭形平次捕物控) Series 1949–1961 (eighteen films in series) Daiei Kyoto (*Zenigata*

*Heiji*/銭形平次) 1951 Director: Mori Kazuo (second in series)

*The Case Notes of Zenigata Heiji: the Fake Mansion (Zenigata Heiji torimono hikae: karakuri yashiki*/銭形平次捕物控・からくり屋敷) 1953 Director: Mori Kazuo (fifth in series)

*The Case Notes of Zenigata Heiji: the Spider (Zenigata Heiji torimono hikae: hitohada gumo*/銭形平次捕物控・人肌蜘蛛) 1956 Director: Mori Kazuo (tenth in series)

*The Case Notes of Zenigata Heiji: the Speckled Snake (Zenigata Heiji torimono hikae: madara hebi*/銭形平次捕物控・まだら蛇) 1957 Director: Kato Bin (eleventh in series)

*The Case Notes of Zenigata Heiji: the Eight Brides (Zenigata Heiji torimono hikae: hachinin no hanayome*/銭形平次捕物控・八人の花嫁) 1958 Director: Tasaka Katsuhiko (thirteenth in series)

*The Case Notes of Zenigata Heiji: the Beauteous Shark (Zenigata Heiji torimono hikae: bijin zame*/銭形平次捕物控・美人鮫) 1961 Director: Misumi Kenji (eighteenth in series)

*Children of the Bomb* aka *Children of the Atom Bomb (Genbaku no ko*/原爆の子) 1952 Director: Shindō Kaneto, Kindai Eiga Kyōkai and Gekidan Mingei

*(Chūshinguragaiden Yotsuyakaidan*/忠臣蔵外伝　四谷怪談) 1994 Director: Fukasaku Kinji, Shōchiku

*Chūshingura: The Heavenly Scroll and the Earthly Scroll (Chūshingura: ten no maki, chi no maki*/忠臣蔵　天の巻、地の巻) 1938 Directors: Makino Masahiro and Ikeda Tomiyasu, Nikkatsu Kyoto

*Crazed Fruit* aka *Affair at Kamakura/Juvenile Passion/This Scorching Sea (Kurutta kajitsu*/狂った果実) 1956 Director: Nakahira Kō, Nikkatsu

*Crossing That Hill (Ano oka koete*/あの丘越えて) 1951 Director: Mizuho Shunkai, Shōchiku Ōfuna

*Crossroads* aka *Shadows of Yoshiwara (Jūjiro*/十字路) 1928 Director: Kinugasa Teinosuke, Kinugasa Productions and Shōchiku Kinema

*Cruel Story of the Bakumatsu Period* aka *Bushido: Samurai Saga (Bakumatsu zankoku monogatari*/幕末残酷物語) 1964 Director: Katō Tai, Tōei

*Cruel Story of Youth* aka *Cruel Tales of Youth (Seishun zankoku monogatari*/青春残酷物語) 1960 Director: Ōshima Nagisa, Shōchiku Ōfuna

*Days of Youth (Gakusei romansu: wakaki hi*/学生ロマンス若き日) 1929 Director: Ozu Yasujirō, Shōchiku Kamata

*Dead or Alive II (DEAD OR ALIVE 2:tōbōsha/ DEAD OR ALIVE 2*・逃亡者) 2000 Director: Miike Takashi, Daiei, Tōei Video

*Death by Hanging* (*Kōshikei*/絞死刑) 1968 Director: Ōshima Nagisa—Sōzōsha and ATG

*Desperado Outpost* Series (*Dokuritsu gurentai*/独立愚連隊) Tōhō 1959–1965 Director: Okamoto Kihachi

*Desperado Outpost* (*Dokuritsu gurentai*/独立愚連隊) 1959

*Desperado Outpost West* (*Dokuritsu gurentai nishi e*/独立愚連隊西へ) 1960

*Blood and Sand* (*Chi to suna*/血と砂) 1965 Tōhō and Mifune Productions

*Destiny's Son* (*Kiru*/斬る) 1962 Director: Misumi Kenji, Daiei Kyoto

*Diary of a Policeman* (*Keisatsu nikki*/警察日記) 1955 Director: Hisamatsu Seiji, Nikkatsu

*Diary of a Policeman Continued* (*Zoku keisatsu nikki*/続警察日記) 1955 Director: Hisamatsu Seiji, Nikkatsu

*Diary of a Shinjuku Thief* (*Shinjuku dorobō nikki*/新宿泥棒日記) 1969 Director: Ōshima Nagisa, Sōzōsha

*Disturbance* (*Dōran*/動乱) 1980 Director: Moritani Shirō, Tōei

*Double Suicide* (*Shinjū tenno amishima*/心中天網島) 1969 Director: Shinoda Masahiro, Hyōgensha and ATG

*The Downfall of Osen* aka *Osen of the Paper Cranes* (*Orizuru Osen*/折鶴お千) 1935 Director: Mizoguchi Kenji, Daiichi Eiga

*Dragnet Girl* (*Hijōsen no onna*/非常線の女) 1933 Director: Ozu Yasujirō, Shōchiku Kamata

*Drunken Angel* (*Yoidore tenshi*/酔いどれ天使) 1948 Director: Kurosawa Akira, Tōhō

*Duel at Takadanobaba* (*Kettō Takadanobaba*/決闘高田の馬場 aka *Chikemuri Takadanobaba*/血煙高田馬場) 1937 Directors: Makino Masahiro and Inagaki Hiroshi, Nikkatsu

*Early Spring* (*Sōshun*/早春) 1956 Director: Ozu Yasujirō, Shōchiku Ōfuna

*Early Summer* (*Bakushū*/麦秋) 1951 Director: Ozu Yasujirō, Shōchiku Ōfuna

*Earth* (*Tsuchi*/土) 1939 Director: Uchida Tomu, Nikkatsu Tamagawa

*Earth* 1930 Director: Alexander Dovzhenko

*East of Eden* 1955 Director: Elia Kazan

*The Emperor's Naked Army Marches On* (*Yukiyukite,shingun*/ゆきゆきて、神軍) 1987 Director: Hara Kazuo, Shissō Productions

*Everyone's Doing It!* (*Mina yatteruka!*/みんな一やってるか！) 1994 Director: Kitano Takeshi, Office Kitano, Bandai Visual

*The First Emperor* (始皇帝暗殺) 1998 Director: Chon Kaikō (陳凱歌) joint
  production Japan and China—Nihon Herald and Kadokawa Shoten
*Fistful of Dollars* 1964 Director: Sergio Leone
*The Five Scouts* (*Gonin no sekkōhei*/五人の斥候兵) 1938 Director: Tasaka
  Tomotaka, Nikkatsu Tamagawa
*The Flower of Patriotism* aka *A Patriotic Flower* (*Aikoku no hana*/愛国の花)
  1942 Director: Sasaki Keisuke, Shōchiku
*Flowering Cherry Blossoms* (*A' dōki no sakura*/あ'同期の桜) 1967 Director:
  Nakajima Sadao, Tōei Kyoto
*Four Stories of Love* (*Yotsu no koi monogatari*/四つの恋物語) 1947 Director:
  Toyoda Shiro, Tōhō

*Gangster Women* Series (*Gokudō no /onna tachi*/極道の妻たち) Tōei Studios
  Tokyo 1986–2001
  *Gangster Women* (*Gokudō no onna tachi*/極道の妻たち) 1986 Director:
    Gosha Hideo
  *Gangster Women II* (*Gokudō no onna tachi II*/極道の妻たち II) 1987
    Director: Dobashi Tōru
  *Gangster Women: the Third Leader* (*Gokudō no onna tachi: sandaime ane*/
    極道の妻たち・三代目姐) 1989 Director: Furuhata Yasuo
  *Gangster Women: the Final Battle* (*Gokudō no onna tachi: saigo no tatakai*/
    極道の妻たち・最後の戦い) 1990 Director: Yamashita Kōsaku
  *New Gangster Wives/Women* (*Shin gokudō no onna tachi*/新・極道の妻た
    ち) 1991 Director: Nakajima Sadao
  *New Gangster Women: Resolve!* (*Shin gokudō no onna tachi: kakugoshiiya*/
    新・極道の妻たち・覚悟しいや) 1993 Director: Yamashita Kōsaku
  *New Gangster Women: Love Is Hell* (*Shin Gokudō no onna tachi: horetara
    jigoku*/新・極道の妻たち・惚れたら地獄) 1994 Director: Furuhata
    Yasuo
  *Gangster Women: the Scarlet Fetters* (*Gokudō no onna tachi: akai kizuna*/
    極道の妻たち・赤い絆) 1995 Director: Sekimoto Ikuo
  *Gangster Women: the Dangerous Gamble* (*Gokudō no onna tachi: kiken na
    kake*/極道の妻たち・危険な賭け) 1996 Director: Nakajima Sadao
  *Gangster Women: Resolution* (*Gokudō no onna tachi: kejime*/極道の妻た
    ち・決着＜けじめ＞) 1997 Director: Nakajima Sadao
  *Gangster Wives/Women: The New Series* (*Gokudō no tsuma/onna tachi:
    shin shiriizu*/極道の妻＜おんな＞たち新シリーズ) Takada Jimusho,
    Tōei Video and Tōkyō Hōsō

*Gangster Wives/Women: Murderous Intent* (*Gokudō no tsuma/onna tachi: akai satsui*/極道の妻＜おんな＞たち・赤い殺意) 1998 Director: Sekimoto Ikuo—Takada Jimusho, Tōei Video and Tokyo Hōsō

*Gangster Wives: I've Come for Your Life* (*Gokudō no tsuma/onna tachi: shinde moraimasu*/極道の妻＜おんな＞たち・死んで貰います) 1999 Director: Sekimoto Ikuo – Takada Jimusho, Tōei Video and Tokyo Hōsō

*Gangster Wives/Women: Revenge* (*Gokudō no tsuma/onna tachi: ribenji*/極道の妻＜おんな＞たち・リベンジ) 2000 Director: Nakjima Sadao, Tōei Video

*Gangster Wives/Women: a Companion on the Road to Hell* (*Gokudō no tsuma/onna tachi: jigoku no michizure*/極道の妻＜おんな＞たち・地獄の道づれ) 2001 Director: Sekimoto Ikuo, Tōei Video

*The Gates of Flesh* (*Nikutai no mon*/肉体の門) 1948 Director: Makino Masahiro, Yoshimoto Eiga

*The Gates of Flesh* (*Nikutai no mon*/肉体の門) 1964 Director: Suzuki Seijun, Nikkatsu

*The Gates of Flesh* (*Nikutai no mon*/肉体門) 1988 Director: Gosha Hideo, Tōei

*The Gates of Hell* (*Jigokumon*/地獄門) 1953 Director: Kinugasa Teinosuke, Daiei Kyoto

*Gohatto* (*Gohatto*/御法度) 1999 Director: Ōshima Nagisa—Shōchiku, Kadokawa Shoten, Imajika, BS Asahi and Eisei Gekijō

*The Golden Demon* aka *The Usurer* (*Konjikiyasha*/金色夜叉) 1937 Director: Shimizu Hiroshi

*Good Morning* aka *Too Much Talk* (*Ohayō*/お早よう) 1959 Director: Ozu Yasujirō, Shōchiku Ōfuna

*The Great Bodhisattva Pass* Trilogy (*Daibosatsu tōge*/大菩薩峠) 1957–1959 Director: Uchida Tomu, Tōei

*The Great Bodhisattva Pass* Trilogy (*Daibosatsu tōge*/大菩薩峠) 1960–1961 Parts One and Two, Director: Misumi Kenji; Part Three, Director: Mori Kazuo, Daiei

*The Great Bodhisattva Pass* aka *The Sword of Doom* (*Daibosatsu tōge*/大菩薩峠) 1966 Director: Okamoto Kihachi, Tōhō

*The Great East Asian War and the International Tribunal* (*Daitōa sensō to kokusai saiban*/大東亜戦争と国際裁判) 1959 Director: Komori Kiyoshi, Shin Tōhō

*The Great Emperor Meiji and General Nogi* (*Meiji taitei to Nogi shōgun*/明治大帝と乃木将軍) 1959 Director: Komori Kiyoshi, Shin Tōhō

*The Great Japanese Empire* (*Dainihon teikoku*/大日本帝国) 1982 Director: Masuda Toshio, Tōei

*The Great Slaughter and the Serpent* (*Daisatsujin Orochi*/大殺陣　雄呂血) 1966 Director: Tanaka Tokuzō, Daiei Kyoto

*Hanabi* (*HANA-BI*) 1997 Director: Kitano Takeshi—Bandai Visual, Terebi Tokyo, Tokyo FM and Office Kitano

*Harakiri* (*Seppuku*/切腹) 1962 Director: Kobayashi Masaki, Shōchiku Kyoto

*He and Life* (*Kare to jinsei*/彼と人生) 1929 Director: Ushihara Kiyohiko, Shōchiku Kamata

*High and Low* aka *Heaven and Hell* (*Tengoku to jigoku*/天国と地獄) 1963 Director: Kurosawa Akira—Kurosawa Productions and Tōhō

*Hiroshima Mon Amour* 1961 Director: Alain Resnais

*Horse* (*Uma*/馬) 1941 Director: Yamamoto Kajirō, Tōhō Tokyo

*The Human Bullet* (*Nikudan*/肉弾) 1968 Director: Okamoto Kihachi—ATG and Nikudan Tsukurukai

*The Human Condition* Series (*Ningen no jōken*/人間の条件) 1959–1961 Director: Kobayashi Masaki

　*Human Condition Parts I and II: No Greater Love* (人間の条件　第1部・純愛篇/第二部・激怒篇)—Ninjin Club and Kadokawa Shoten

　*Human Condition Parts III and IV: The Road to Eternity* (人間の条件　第三部・望郷篇/第四部・戦雲篇)—Ningen Productions

　*Human Condition Parts V and VI: A Soldier's Prayer* (人間の条件　第五部・死の脱出/第六部・曠野の彷徨)—Shōchiku Ōfuna, Bungei Productions and Ninjin Club

*The Human Torpedoes* (*Ningen gyorai kaiten*/人間魚雷回転) 1955 Director: Matsubayashi Shūe, Shin-Tōhō

*Ichi the Killer* (*Koroshiya ichi*/殺し屋1) 2001 Director: Miike Takashi—Omega Project, EMG, Starmax, Alfa Group and Excellent Film

*If I Had a Million* 1932 Director: Ernst Lubitsch

*The Inferno of First Love* (*Hatsukoi: jigokuhen*/初恋・地獄篇) 1968 Director: Hani Susumu—Hani Productions and ATG

*Insect Woman* (*Nippon konchūki*/にっぽん昆虫記) 1963 Director: Imamura Shōhei, Nikkatsu

*In the Realm of the Senses* aka *Empire of the Senses* (*Ai no koriida*/愛のコリーダ) 1976 Director: Ōshima Nagisa—Anatole Dauman/Argos Films Paris, Ōshima Nagisa Productions and Tōhō Tōwa

*Intolerance* 1916 Director: D. W. Griffith

*I Want to Be Reborn a Shellfish* (*Watashi wa kai ni naritai*/私は貝になりたい) 1994—TBS

*I Was Born But . . .* (*Umarete wa mita keredo*/生まれてはみたけれど) 1932 Director: Ozu Yasujirō, Shōchiku Kamata

*A Japanese Tragedy* (*Nihon no higeki*/日本の悲劇) 1953 Director: Kinoshita Keisuke, Shōchiku Ōfuna

*Japan's Longest Day* (*Nihon no ichiban nagai hi*/日本のいちばん長い日) 1967 Director: Okamoto Kihachi, Tōhō

*Kantō Wanderer* (*Kantō nagaremono*/関東流れ者) 1965 Director: Ozawa Shigehiro, Tōei

*Katō's Falcon Fighters* (*Katō Hayabusa sentōtai*/加藤隼戦闘隊) 1944 Director: Yamamoto Kajirō, Tōhō

*Kikujiro* (*Kikujirō no natsu*/菊次郎の夏) 1999 Director: Kitano Takeshi— Bandai Visual, Tokyo FM, Nihon Herald Eiga and Office Kitano

*Kill Bill vol I* 2003 and *vol II* 2004 Director: Quentin Tarantino

*Kurama Tengu*/鞍馬天狗 Series. Multiple directors including: Makino Masahiro and Matsuda Teiji. Series ran between 1927–1942 and 1950– 1954. Nikkatsu Kyoto

*The Last Days of Edo* (*Edo saigo no hi*/江戸最後の日) 1941 Director: Inagaki Hiroshi, Nikkatsu Kyoto

*The Last Samurai* 2003 Director: Edward Zwick, Warner Brothers

*The Life of Muhō Matsu* aka *The Rickshaw Man, The Life of Matsugorō the Pure, Matsu the Untamed* (*Muhō Matsu no isshō*/無法松の一生) 1943 Director: Inagaki Hiroshi, Daiei Kyoto

*The Life of Oharu* aka *The Life of a Woman by Saikaku* (*Saikaku ichidai onna*/西鶴一代女) 1952 Director: Mizoguchi Kenji, Shin-Tōhō

*Listen to the Roar of the Ocean* (*Kike wadatsumi no koe* aka *Nihon senbotsu gakusei no shuki: kike wadatsumi no koe*/日本戦歿学生の手記きけわだつみの声) 1950 Director: Sekigawa Hideo, Tōyoko Eiga

*Living* (*Ikiru*/生きる) 1952 Director: Kurosawa Akira, Tōhō

*The Longed for Voyage to Hawaii* (*Akogare no Hawai kōro*/憧れのハワイ航路) 1950 Director: Saitō Torajirō, Shin-Tōhō

*The Love-Troth Tree* aka *The Compassionate Buddha Tree* (*Aizen katsura: sōshūhen*/愛染かつら・総集編) 1938 Director: Nomura Hiromasa, Shōchiku Ōfuna

*The Loyal Forty-seven Ronin* aka *The Forty-seven Ronin of the Genroku Era* (*Genroku Chūshingura*/元禄忠臣蔵) 1941–1942 Director: Mizoguchi Kenji, Shōchiku Ōfuna

*The Magnificent Seven* 1960 Director: John Sturges

*A Man Vanishes* (*Ningen jōhatsu*/人間蒸発) 1967 Director: Imamura Shōhei, Imamura Productions, ATG and Nihon Eiga Shinsha

*Manual of Ninja Martial Arts* (*Ninja bugeichō*/忍者武芸帳) 1967 Director: Ōshima Nagisa, Sōzōsha

*Marching On* aka *The Army Advances* (*Shingun*/進軍) 1930 Director: Ushihara Kiyohiko, Shōchiku Kamata

*Memorial to the Lilies* aka *Tower of Lilies* (*Himeyuri no tō*/ひめゆりの塔) 1953 Tōei and 1982 Geiensha, both versions directed by Imai Tadashi

*The Million-Ryō Secret* (*Hyakuman-ryō hibun*/百万両秘聞) 1927 Director: Makino Shōzō

*Mister Pu* (*Pūsan*/プーサン) 1953 Director: Ichikawa Kon, Tōhō

*Mito Kōmon*/水戸黄門 Series 1954–1961 Tōei Studios Kyoto. Fourteen films in the complete series.

> *Mito Kōmon: Travel Sketches* (*Mito Kōmon: man'yūki*/水戸黄門・漫遊記) 1954 Director: Igayama Masamitsu (first in series)

> *Mito Kōmon*/水戸黄門 1957 Director: Sasaki Yasushi (eleventh in series)

> *Mito Kōmon*/水戸黄門 1960 Director: Matsuda Sadao (thirteenth in series)

> *Mito Kōmon: Suke and Kaku and the Great Disclosure* (*Mito Kōmon: Sukesan Kakusan ōabare*/水戸黄門・助さんと格さん大暴れ) 1961 Director: Sawashima Tadashi (last in series)

*Miyamoto Musashi* Series 1954–1956 Director: Inagaki Hiroshi, Tōhō

> *Miyamoto Musashi* (*Miyamoto Musashi*/宮本武蔵)1959

> *Miyamoto Musashi: Duel at Ichijōji* (*Zoku Miyamoto Musashi: Ichijōji no kettō*/続・宮本武蔵　一乗寺の決闘) 1955

> *Miyamoto Musashi: Duel at Ganryū Island* (*Miyamoto Musashi: kettō Ganryūjima*/宮本武蔵・決闘巌流島) 1956

*Miyamoto Musashi* Series 1961–1965 Director: Uchida Tomu, Tōei

> *Miyamoto Musashi* (*Miyamoto Musashi*/宮本武蔵) 1961

> *Miyamoto Musashi: Duel at Han'nyazaka* (*Miyamoto Musashi: Han'nyazaka no kettō* /宮本武蔵・般若坂の決斗) 1963

> *Miyamoto Musashi: Enlightenment with the Two Swords* (*Miyamoto Musashi: nitōryū kaigan*/宮本武蔵・二刀流開眼) 1963

> *Miyamoto Musashi: Duel at Ichijōji* (*Miyamoto Musashi: Ichijōji no kettō*/宮本武蔵・一乗寺の決斗) 1964

*Miyamoto Musashi: Duel at Ganryū Island* (*Miyamoto Musashi: Ganryū-jima no kettō*/宮本武蔵・巌流島の決斗) 1965

*Modern Times* 1936 Director: Charles Chaplin

*The Most Beautiful* (*Ichiban utsukushiku*/一番美しく) 1944 Director: Kurosawa Akira, Tōhō

*The Mother He Never Knew* (*Banba no Chūtarō mabuta no haha*/番場の忠太郎瞼の母) 1931 Director: Inagaki Hiroshi

*Mount Hakkōda* (*Hakkōdasan*/八甲田山) 1977 Director: Moritani Shirō, Tōhō

*Mud and Soldiers* (*Tsuchi to heitai*/土と兵隊) 1939 Director: Tasaka Tomotaka, Nikkatsu Tamagawa

*My Favourite Plane Flies South* aka *Our Planes Fly South* (*Aiki minami e tobu*/愛機南へ飛ぶ) 1943 Director: Sasaki Yasushi, Shōchiku

*Natural Born Killers* 1994 Director: Oliver Stone

*Navy* (*Kaigun*/海軍) 1943 Director: Tasaka Tomotaka, Shōchiku Ōfuna

*The Neighbour's Wife and Mine* aka *The Lady Next Door and My Wife* (*Madamu to nyōbō*/マダムと女房) 1931 Director: Gosho Heinosuke, Shōchiku Kamata

*Nemuri Kyōshirō* Series (眠狂四郎) Daiei Studios Kyoto 1957–1969

*Nemuri Kyōshirō: Manual of Killing* (*Nemuri Kyōshirō: sappōchō*/眠狂四郎・殺法帖) 1963 Director: Tanaka Tokuzō

*Nemuri Kyōshirō: Showdown* (*Nemuri Kyōshirō: shōbu*/眠狂四郎・勝負) 1964 Director: Misumi Kenji

*Nemuri Kyōshirō: the Crescent Moon Cut* (*Nemuri Kyōshirō: engetsu kiri*/眠狂四郎・円月斬り) 1964 Director: Yasuda Kimiyoshi

*Nemuri Kyōshirō: the Entrancing Sword* (*Nemuri Kyōshirō: joyōken*/眠狂四郎・女妖剣) 1964 Director: Ikehiro Kazuo

*Nemuri Kyōshirō: the Sword Inflamed with Emotion* (*Nemuri Kyōshirō: enj ken*/眠狂四郎・炎情剣) 1965 Director: Misumi Kenji

*Nemuri Kyōshirō: the Demon Sword* (*Nemuri Kyōshirō: mashō ken*/眠狂四郎・魔性剣) 1965 Director: Yasuda Kimiyoshi

*Nemuri Kyōshirō: the Wanton Sword* (*Nemuri Kyōshirō: tajōken*/眠狂四郎・多情剣) 1966 Director: Inoue Akira

*Nemuri Kyōshirō: the Villainous Sword* (*Nemuri Kyōshirō: buraiken*/眠狂四郎・無頼剣) 1966 Director: Misumi Kenji

*Nemuri Kyōshirō: the Impostor and the Skin of the Enchantress* (*Nemuri Kyōshirō: burai hikai mashō no hada*/眠狂四郎無頼控・魔性の肌) 1967 Director: Ikehiro Kazuo

*Nemuri Kyōshirō: the Woman's Hell* (*Nemuri Kyōshirō: onna jigoku*/眠狂四郎・女地獄) 1968 Director: Tanaka Tokuzō

*Nemuri Kyōshirō: the Lure of the Spider* (*Nemuri Kyōshirō: hitohada gumo*/眠狂四郎・人肌蜘蛛) 1968 Director: Yasuda Kimiyoshi

*Nemuri Kyōshirō: the Hunt of the Evil Woman* (*Nemuri Kyōshirō: akujo gari*/眠狂四郎・悪女狩り) 1969 Director: Ikehiro Kazuo

*The New Publication of the Trials of Magistrate Ōoka* aka *Ōoka Trials* (*Shinpan Ōoka seidan*/新版大岡政談) 1928 Director: Itō Daisuke

*Night and Fog in Japan* (*Nihon no yoru to kiri*/日本の夜と霧) 1960 Director: Ōshima Nagisa, Shōchiku Ōfuna

*The Night Before the Outbreak of War* aka *On the Eve of War* (*Kaisen no zen'ya*/開戦の前夜) 1943 Director: Yoshimura Kōzaburō, Shōchiku Ōfuna

*No Consultations Today* aka *The Doctor's Day Off* (*Honjitsu kyūshin*/本日休診) 1952 Director: Shibuya Minoru, Shōchiku Ōfuna

*No Regrets for Our Youth* (*Waga seishun ni kuinashi*/わが青春に悔なし) 1946 Director: Kurosawa Akira, Tōhō

*Once More* (*Ima hitotabino*/今ひとたびの) 1947 Director: Gosho Heinosuke, Tōhō

*One Night's Kiss* aka *A Certain Night's Kiss* (*Aru yo no seppun*/或る夜の接吻) 1946 Director: Chiba Yasuki

*One Wonderful Sunday* (*Subarashiki Nichiyōbi*/素晴らしき日曜日) 1947 Director: Kurosawa Akira, Tōhō

*The Only Son* (*Hitori musuko*/一人息子) 1936 Director: Ozu Yasujirō, Shōchiku Ōfuna

*Osaka Elegy* (*Naniwa erejii*/浪華悲歌) 1936 Director: Mizoguchi Kenji, Daiichi Eiga

*A Page of Madness* aka *A Page Out of Order* (*Kurutta ichipeiji*/狂った一頁) 1926 Director: Kinugasa Teinosuke, Shinkankakuha Eiga Renmei

*Paisàn* 1946 Director: Roberto Rossellini

*Passing Fancy* (*Dekigokoro*/出来ごころ) 1933 Director: Ozu Yasujirō, Shōchiku Kamata

*Pigs and Battleships* (*Buta to gunkan*/豚と軍艦) 1961 Director: Imamura Shōhei, Nikkatsu

*The Pleasures of the Flesh* (*Etsuraku*/悦楽) 1965 Director: Ōshima Nagisa, Sōzosha

*The Pram* aka *The Baby Carriage* (*Ubaguruma*/乳母車) 1956 Director: Tasaka Tomotaka, Nikkatsu

*The Quiet Duel* (*Shizukanaru kettō*/静かなる決闘) 1949 Director: Kurosawa Akira, Daiei Tokyo

*Rashomon* (*Rashōmon*/羅生門) 1950 Director: Kurosawa Akira, Daiei Kyoto

*Rebel Without a Cause* 1955 Director: Nicholas Ray

*Record of a Living Being* aka *I Live in Fear/ What the Birds Knew* (*Ikimono no kiroku*/生きものの記録) 1955 Director: Kurosawa Akira, Tōhō

*Remnants of Chivalry in the Shōwa Era* Series (昭和残侠伝) 1965–1972 Tōei Studios Kyoto

    *Remnants of Chivalry in the Shōwa Era* (*Shōwa zankyōden*/昭和残侠伝) 1965 Director: Saeki Kiyoshi

    *Remnants of Chivalry in the Shōwa Era: the Lion and the Peony Rose* (*Shōwa zankyōden: karajishi botan*/昭和残侠伝・唐獅子牡丹) 1966 Director: Saeki Kiyoshi

    *Remnants of Chivalry in the Shōwa Era: the Lone Wolf* (*Shōwa zankyōden: ippiki ōkami*/昭和残侠伝・一匹狼) 1966 Director: Saeki Kiyoshi

    *Remnants of Chivalry in the Shōwa Era: the Bloodstained Lion* (*Shōwa zankyōden: chizome no karajishi*/昭和残侠伝・血染の唐獅子) 1967 Director: Makino Masahiro

    *Remnants of Chivalry in the Shōwa Era: the Jingi of the Lion* (*Shōwa zankyōden: karajishi jingi*/昭和残侠伝・唐獅子仁義) 1969 Director: Makino Masahiro

    *Remnants of Chivalry in the Shōwa Era: the Slaying Lion* (*Shōwa zankyōden: hitokiri karajishi*/昭和残侠伝・人斬り唐獅子) 1969 Director: Yamashita Kōsaku

    *Remnants of Chivalry in the Shōwa Era: I Have Come for Your Life* (*Shōwa zankyōden: shinde moraimasu*/昭和残侠伝・死んで貰います) 1970 Director: Makino Masahiro

    *Remnants of Chivalry in the Shōwa Era: the Roaring Lion* (*Shōwa zankyōden: hoeru karajishi*/昭和残侠伝・吼える唐獅子) 1971 Director: Saeki Kiyoshi

    *Remnants of Chivalry in the Shōwa Era: the Broken Umbrella* (*Shōwa zankyōden: yabure kasa*/昭和残侠伝・破れ傘) 1972 Director: Saeki Kiyoshi

*Rome, Open City* 1946 Director: Roberto Rossellini

*The Sacrifice of the Human Torpedoes* (*Ningen gyorai kaiten*/人間魚雷回転)
1955 Director: Matsubayashi Shue, Shin-Tōhō

*The Sad Whistle* (*Kanashiki kuchibue*/悲しき口笛) 1949 Director: Ieki Miyoji,
Shōchiku Ōfuna

*Samurai Assassins* (*Samurai*/侍) 1965 Director: Okamoto Kihachi—Mifune
Productions and Tōhō

*Samurai Rebellion* (*Jōi uchi hairyō zuma shimatsu*/上意討ち・拝領妻始末)
1967 Director: Kobayashi Masaki, Mifune Productions/Tōhō

*Sanjuro* (*Tsubaki Sanjūrō*/椿三十郎) 1962 Director: Kurosawa Akira,
Tōhō/Kurosawa Productions

*Sanshiro Sugata* (*Sugata Sanshirō*/姿三四郎) 1943 Director: Kurosawa Akira,
Tōhō

*Sansho the Bailiff* (*Sanshō tayu*/山椒大夫) 1954 Director: Mizoguchi Kenji,
Daiei Kyoto

*Sayon's Bell* (*Sayon no kane*/サヨンの鐘) 1943 Director: Shimizu Hiroshi,
Shōchiku

*The Scarlet Peony Rose Gambler* Series (*Hibotan bakuto*/緋牡丹博徒) 1968–
1972 Tōei Studios Kyoto

   *The Scarlet Peony Rose Gambler* (*Hibotan bakuto*/緋牡丹博徒) 1968
   Director: Yamashita Kōsaku

   *The Scarlet Peony Rose Gambler: One Night's Accommodation and One
   Night's Food* (*Hibotan bakuto: isshuku ippan*/緋牡丹博徒・一宿一飯)
   1968 Director: Suzuki Norifumi

   *The Scarlet Peony Rose Gambler: Showdown at Cards* (*Hibotan bakuto:
   hanafuda shōbu*/緋牡丹博徒・花札勝負) 1969 Director: Katō Tai

   *The Scarlet Peony Rose Gambler: the Leadership Succession* (*Hibotan
   bakuto: nidaime shūmei*/緋牡丹博徒・二代目襲名) 1969 Director:
   Ozawa Shigehiro

   *The Scarlet Peony Rose Gambler: the Tale from the Gambling Joint*
   (*Hibotan bakuto: tekkaba retsuden*/緋牡丹博徒・鉄火場列伝) 1969
   Director: Yamashita Kōsaku

   *The Scarlet Peony Rose Gambler: Oryu's Visit* (*Hibotan bakuto: Oryū
   sanjō*/緋牡丹博徒・お竜参上) 1970 Director: Katō Tai

   *The Scarlet Peony Rose Gambler: I've Come for Your Life* (*Hibotan bakuto:
   oinochi itadakimasu*/緋牡丹博徒・お命戴きます) 1971 Director: Katō
   Tai

   *The Scarlet Peony Rose Gambler: Remaining Steadfast to One's Morality*
   (*Hibotan bakuto: jingi tōshimasu*/緋牡丹博徒・仁義通します) 1972
   Director: Saitō Buichi

*Season of the Sun* (*Taiyō no kisetsu*/太陽の季節) 1956 Director: Furukawa Takumi, Nikkatsu

*The Serpent* (*Orochi*/雄呂血) 1925 Director: Futagawa Buntarō, Bantsuma Productions

*The Seven Samurai* (*Shichi-nin no samurai*/七人の侍) 1954 Director: Kurosawa Akira, Tōhō

*The Shōgun's Retainer, a Man of Leisure* Series (*Hatamoto taikutsu otoko*/旗本退屈男) 1950–1963 (thirty films in the series) Tōei Studios Kyoto

    *The Shōgun's Retainer, a Man of Leisure: Entrance into Edo Castle* (*Hatamoto taikutsu otoko: Edojō makari tōru*/旗本退屈男・江戸城罷り通る) 1952 Director: Ōsone Tatsuo (thirteenth in series) Shōchiku Kyoto

    *The Shōgun's Retainer, a Man of Leisure: the Mystery of the Serpent Princess' Mansion* (*Hatamoto taikutsu otoko: nazo no hebihime yashiki*/旗本退屈男・謎の蛇姫屋敷) 1957 Director: Sasaki Yasushi (twenty-second in series) Tōei Kyoto

    *The Shōgun's Retainer, a Man of Leisure* (*Hatamoto taikutsu otoko*/旗本退屈男) 1958 Director: Matsuda Sadatsugu (twenty-third in series—a special all-star episode made to commemorate the 300th film of the lead actor, Ichikawa Utaemon) Tōei Kyoto

    *The Shōgun's Retainer, a Man of Leisure: the Mystery of the Band of Assassins* (*Hatamoto taikutsu otoko: nazo no ansatsutai*/旗本退屈男・謎の暗殺隊) 1960 Director: Matsuda Sadatsugu (twenty-seventh in series) Tōei Kyoto

    *The Shōgun's Retainer, a Man of Leisure: the Mystery of the Palace of the Seven Colours* (*Hatamoto taikutsu otoko: nazo no nanairo goten*/旗本退屈男・謎の七色御殿) 1961 Director: Sasaki Yasushi (twenty-eighth in series) Tōei Kyoto

    *The Shōgun's Retainer, a Man of Leisure: the Mystery of the Coral Mansion* (*Hatamoto taikutsu otoko: nazo no sango yashiki*/謎の珊瑚屋敷) 1962 Director: Nakagawa Nobuo (twenty-ninth in series) Tōei Kyoto

    *The Shōgun's Retainer, a Man of Leisure: the Mystery of Ryūjin Promontory* (*Hatamoto taikutsu otoko: nazo no Ryūjinmisaki*/旗本退屈男・謎の竜神岬) 1963 Director: Sasaki Yasushi (thirtieth in series) Tōei Kyoto

*The Silver Snow* aka *Snow Trail/ To the End of the Silver-capped Mountains* (*Ginrei no hate*/銀嶺の果て) 1947 Director: Taniguchi Senkichi, Tōhō

*Sisters of Gion* (*Gion no kyōdai*/祇園の姉妹) 1936 Director: Mizoguchi Kenji, Daiichi Eiga

*Sonatine* (ソナチネ) 1993 Director: Kitano Takeshi—Bandai Visual and Shōchiku Daiichi Kōgyō

*The Spy Is Still Alive* aka *The Spy Isn't Dead Yet* (*Kanchō imada shisezu*/間諜
    未だ死せず) 1942 Director: Yoshimura Kōzaburō, Shōchiku

*Spy Sorge* (スパイ・ゾルゲ) 2003 Director: Shinoda Masahiro, Spy Sorge
    Seisaku Iinkai

*The Storm Over Asia; the Heir of Genghis Khan* 1928 Director: Vsevolod
    Pudovkin

*The Storm Over the Pacific* aka *I Bombed Pearl Harbour* (*Hawai Middōei
    daikaikūsen Taiheiyō no arashi*/ハワイ・ミッドウェイ大海空戦太平洋
    の嵐) 1960 Director: Matsubayashi Shūe, Tōhō

*The Story of an Adventurer in Troubled Times* (*Fūunji: Nobunaga*/風雲児信長)
    1940 Director: Makino Masahiro, Nikkatsu

*The Story of Floating Weeds* (*Ukikusa monogatari*/浮草物語) 1934 Director:
    Ozu Yasujirō, Shōchiku Kamata

*The Story of the Last Chrysanthemum* (*Zangiku monogatari*/残菊物語) 1939
    Director: Mizoguchi Kenji, Shōchiku Kyoto

*The Story of a Prostitute* aka *Joy Girls* (*Shunpu-den*/春婦伝) 1965 Director:
    Suzuki Seijun, Nikkatsu

*Stray Dog* (*Nora inu*/野良犬) 1949 Director: Kurosawa Akira, Shin-Tōhō and
    Eiga Geijutsu Kyōkai

*The Street Magician* (*Machi no tejinashi*/街の手品師) 1925 Director: Murata
    Minoru

*A Streetcar Named Desire* 1951 Director: Elia Kazan

*Streets of Joy* (*Akasen Tamanoi nukeraremasu*/赤線玉の井・ぬけられます)
    1974 Director: Kumashiro Tatsumi, Nikkatsu

*The Streets of Masterless Samurai* (*Rōningai*/浪人街) Trilogy 1928–1929
    Director: Makino Masahiro, Makino Eiga

*Submarine Number One* (*Sensuikan ichigō*/潜水艦一号) 1941 Director:
    Igayama Masamitsu, Nikkatsu Tamagawa

*Suchow Nights* (*Soshū no yoru*/蘇州の夜) 1942 Director: Nomura Hiromasa,
    Shōchiku

*Summer Soldiers* (サマー・ソルジャー) 1972 Director: Teshigahara Hiroshi

*The Sun of Shitamachi* (*Shitamachi no taiyō*/下町の太陽) 1963 Director:
    Yamada Yōji, Shōchiku Ōfuna

*The Sunny Hill Path* (*Hi no ataru sakamichi*/陽のあたる坂道) 1958 Director:
    Tasaka Tomotaka, Nikkatsu

*The Sun's Burial* (*Taiyō no hakaba*/太陽の墓場) 1960 Director: Ōshima
    Nagisa, Shōchiku Ōfuna

*Swallow Tail* (スワロウテイル) 1996 Director: Iwai Shunji—Pony Cannon,
    Nihon Herald, S Pictures and Fuji Television

*The Tale of Genji* (源氏物語) 1951 Director:Yoshimura Kōzaburō, Daiei

*Tales of Japanese Chivalry* Series (日本侠客伝) 1965–1972 Tōei Studios Tokyo

*Tales of Japanese Chivalry* (*Nihon kyōkakuden*/日本侠客伝) 1964 Director: Makino Masahiro

*Tales of Japanese Chivalry: the Osaka Episode* (*Nihon kyōkakuden: Naniwahen*/日本侠客伝・浪花篇) 1965 Director: Makino Masahiro

*Tales of Japanese Chivalry: the Kantō Episode* (*Nihon kyōkakuden: Kantōhen*/日本侠客伝・関東篇) 1965 Director: Makino Masahiro

*Tales of Japanese Chivalry: Duel at the Kanda Festival* (*Nihon kyōkakuden: kettō Kanda matsuri*/日本侠客伝・血斗神田祭り) 1966 Director: Makino Masahiro

*Tales of Japanese Chivalry: Duel at Kaminari Gate* (*Nihon kyōkakuden: Kaminarimon no kettō*/日本侠客伝・雷門の決斗) 1966 Director: Makino Masahiro

*Tales of Japanese Chivalry: the Sakazuki of the Naked Blade* (*Nihon kyōkakuden: shiraha no sakazuki*/日本侠客伝。白刃の盃) 1967 Director: Makino Masahiro

*Tales of Japanese Chivalry: the Attack with Drawn Swords* (*Nihon kyōkakuden: kirikome*/日本侠客伝・斬り込み) 1967 Director: Makino Masahiro

*Tales of Japanese Chivalry: Severing Relations* (*Nihon kyōkakuden: zetsuenjō*/日本侠客伝・絶縁状) 1968 Director: Makino Masahiro

*Tales of Japanese Chivalry: the Flower and the Dragon* (*Nihon kyōkakuden: hana to ryū*/日本侠客伝・花と龍) 1969 Director: Makino Masahiro

*Tales of Japanese Chivalry: the Rising Dragon* (*Nihon kyōkakuden: nobori ryū*/日本侠客伝・昇り龍) 1970 Director: Yamashita Kōsaku

*Tales of Japanese Chivalry: the Dagger* (*Nihon kyōkakuden: dosu*/日本侠客伝・刃) 1971 Director: Ozawa Shigehiro

*Tange Sazen and the Story of the One Million-Ryō Vase* aka *The Million-Ryō Pot* (*Tange sazen yowa hyakuman-ryō no tsubo*/丹下作善餘話・百萬両の壺) 1935 Director: Yamanaka Sadao, Nikkatsu Kyoto

*Tange Sazen* Series (丹下作善) 1953–1954 Daiei Studios Kyoto

*Tange Sazen* (*Tange Sazen*/丹下作善) 1953 Director: Makino Masahiro

*Tange Sazen Continued* (*Zoku Tange Sazen*/続・丹下作善) 1953 Director: Makino Masahiro

*Tange Sazen and the Vase* (*Tange Sazen: kokezaru no tsubo*/丹下作善こけ猿の壺) 1954 Director: Misumi Kenji

*Tange Sazen* Series (丹下作善) 1958–1962 Tōei Kyoto Studios

*Tange Sazen* (丹下作善) 1958 Director: Matsuda Sadatsugu

*Tange Sazen: Raging Billows Episode* (*Tange Sazen: dotō-hen*/丹下作善・怒涛篇) 1959 Director: Matsuda Sadao

*Tange Sazen: the Sword of the Wet Swallow* (*Tange Sazen: yōtō nuretsubame*/丹下作善・妖刀濡れ燕) 1960 Director: Matsuda Sadao

*Tange Sazen: the School of the Wet Swallow Sword* (*Tange Sazen: nuretsubame ittō-ryū*/丹下作善・濡れ燕一刀流) 1961 Director: Matsuda Sadao

*Tange Sazen: the Tale of the Ken'un and the Konryū Swords* (*Tange Sazen: ken'un konryū no maki*/丹下作善乾・雲坤竜の巻) 1962 Director: Katō Tai

*Tange Sazen: the Swordsmanship of the Flying Swallow* (*Tange Sazen: hien iaigiri*/丹下作善・飛燕居合斬り) 1966 Director: Gosha Hideo, Tōei Studios Kyoto

*The Tearstained Doll* (*Nakinureta ningyō*/泣きぬれた人形) 1951 Director: Chiba Yasuki, Shōchiku Kyoto

*Tenchu* (*Hitokiri*/人斬り) 1969 Director: Gosha Hideo—Fuji Television and Katsu Productions

*Time of Pride and Destiny* (*Puraido unmei no toki*/プライド　運命瞬間＜とき＞) 1998 Director: Itō Shun'ya—Tokyo Eiga Seisaku and Tōei

*That Fellow and Me* aka *That Guy and I* (*Aitsu to watashi*/あいつと私) 1961 Director: Nakahira Kō, Nikkatsu

*Theatre of Life* (*Jinsei gekijō, Hishakaku*/人生劇場・飛車角) 1963 Director: Sawashima Tadashi, Tōei Tokyo

*There Was a Father* (*Chichi ariki*/父ありき) 1942 Director: Ozu Yasujirō, Shōchiku Ōfuna

*The Third Leader of the Yamaguchi Gang* (*Yamaguchigumi sandaime*/山口組三代目) 1973 Director: Yamashita Kōsaku, Tōei Kyoto

*The Thirteen Assassins* (*Jūsannin no shikaku*/十三人の刺客) 1963 Director: Kudō Eiji, Tōei

*Three Samurai* (*Sanbiki no samurai*/三匹の侍) 1964 Director: Gosha Hideo, Shōchiku, Samurai Productions

*Throne of Blood* (*Kumonosujō*/蜘蛛巣城) 1957 Director: Kurosawa Akira, Daiei

*Tokyo Chorus* aka *Chorus of Tokyo* (*Tōkyō no kōrasu* aka *Le Chorus de Tokyo*/東京の合唱) 1931 Director: Ozu Yasujirō, Shōchiku Kamata

*Tokyo Drifter* (*Tōkyō no nagaremono*/東京の流れ者) 1966 Director: Suzuki Seijun, Nikkatsu

*Tokyo-ga* 1985 Director: Wim Wenders

*Tokyo Kid* (*Tōkyō kiddo*/東京キッド) 1950 Director: Saitō Torajirō, Shōchiku Ōfuna

*Tokyo Story* (*Tōkyō monogatari*/東京物語) 1953 Director: Ozu Yasujirō, Shōchiku Ōfuna

*Tokyo Trails* (*Tōkyō saiban*/東京裁判) 1983 Director: Kobayashi Masaki, Kodansha

*Toro-san: It's Tough Being a Man* (*Otoko wa tsurai yo*/男はつらいよ) Series 1969–1996 Director: Yamada Yōji, Shōchiku Ōfuna

*Town of Love and Hope* (*Ai to kibō no machi*/愛と希望の町) 1959 Director: Ōshima Nagisa, Shōchiku Ōfuna

*Tōyama no Kinsan* Series (遠山の金さん) 1950–1962 Tōei Studios Kyoto (seventeen films made in series)

*Tōyama no Kinsan: the Falcon Magistrate* (*Tōyama no Kinsan: hayabusa bugyō*/遠山の金さん・はやぶさ奉行) 1957 Director: Fukada Kin'nosuke (tenth in series)

*Tōyama no Kinsan: the Fireball Magistrate* (*Tōyama no Kinsan: hinotama bugyō*/遠山の金さん・火の玉奉行) 1958 Director: Fukada Kin'nosuke (twelfth in the series)

*Tōyama no Kinsan: the Whirlwind Magistrate* (*Tōyama no Kinsan: tatsumaki bugyō*/遠山の金さん・たつまき奉行) 1959 Director: Makino Masahiro (thirteenth in series)

*Tōyama no Kinsan: the Tattooed Magistrate* (*Tōyama no Kinsan: gozonji irezumi hangan*/遠山の金さん・御存じいれずみ判官) 1960 Director: Sasaki Yasushi (fifteenth in series)

*Tōyama no Kinsan: the Gambling Dice Magistrate* (*Tōyama no Kinsan: saikoro bugyō*/遠山の金さん・さいころ奉行) 1961 Director: Uchide Kōkichi (sixteenth in series)

*Tōyama no Kinsan: the Cherry Blossom Magistrate* (*Tōyama no Kinsan: sakura hangan*/遠山の金さん・さくら判官) 1962 Director: Ozawa Shigehiro (seventeenth in series)

*The Tragedy of Japan* (*Nihon no higeki*/日本の悲劇) 1946 Director: Kamei Fumio

*Triad Society* Trilogy (*Kuro shakai*/黒社会) 1995–1999 Director: Miike Takashi, Daiei

*Shinjuku Triad Society* (*Shinjuku kuro shakai: chaina mafuia sensō*/新宿黒社会　チャイナ・マフイア戦争) 1995

*Rainy Dog* (*Gokudō kuro shakai reiniidoggu*/極道黒社会　レイニードッグ) 1997

*Ley Lines* (*Nihon kuro shakai LEY LINES*/日本黒社会　LEY LINES) 1999

*Twenty-four Eyes* (*Nijūshi no hitomi*/二十四の瞳) 1954 Director: Kinoshita Keisuke, Shōchiku Ōfuna

*Twenty Year Old Youth* (*Hatachi no seishun*/はたちの青春) 1946 Director: Sasaki Yasushi, Shōchiku Ōfuna

*226* 1989 Director: Gosha Hideo

*Ugetsu* (*Ugetsu monogatari*/雨月物語) 1953 Director: Mizoguchi Kenji, Daiei Kyoto

*Until the Day We Meet Again* aka *Till We Meet Again* (*Mata au hi made*/また逢う日まで) 1950 Director: Imai Tadashi, Tōhō

*Violence at Noon* aka *The Daylight Demon* (*Hakuchū no tōrima*/白昼の通り魔) 1966 Director: Ōshima Nagisa, Sōzōsha

*Violent Cop* (*Sono otoko, kyōbō ni tsuki*/その男、凶暴につき) 1989 Director: Kitano Takeshi, Shōchiku Fuji

*Virgin of Fukuyama* (*Fukuyama no otome*/深山の乙女) 1918 Director: Kaeriyama Norimasa

*Walk Cheerfully* (*Hogaraka ni ayume*/朗かに歩め) 1930 Director: Ozu Yasujirō, Shōchiku Ōfuna

*The Wandering Gambler* (*Hōrō zanmai*/放浪三昧) 1928 Director: Inagaki Hiroshi, Chiezō Productions

*War and Humanity* Trilogy (*Sensō to ningen*/戦争と人間) 1970–1973 Director: Yamamoto Satsuo, Nikkatsu

　*War and Humanity: Part I Prelude to Destiny* (戦争と人間　第一部・運命の序曲) 1970

　*War and Humanity: Part II The Mountains and Rivers of Love and Sadness* (戦争と人間　第二部・愛と悲しみの山河) 1971

　*War and Humanity: Part III Conclusions* (戦争と人間　第三部・完結編) 1973

*War and Peace* (*Sensō to heiwa*/戦争と平和) 1947 Directors: Yamamoto Satsuo and Kamei Fumio, Tōhō

*The War at Sea from Hawaii to Malaya* (*Hawai Marei okikaisen*/ハワイ・マレー沖海戦) 1942 Director: Yamamoto Kajirō, Tōhō

*War Without Morality* Series aka *Battles Without Honour and Humanity* (*Jingi*

naki tatakai/仁義なき戦い) 1973–1976 Director: Fukasaku Kinji, Tōei Studios Kyoto

*War Without Morality* aka *Yakuza Papers* (*Jingi naki tatakai*/仁義なき戦い) 1973

*War Without Morality: Mortal Combat in Hiroshima* (*Jingi naki tatakai: Hiroshima shitōhen*/仁義なき戦い・広島死闘篇) 1973

*War Without Morality: War by Proxy* (*Jingi naki tatakai: dairi sensō*/仁義 なき戦い・代理戦争) 1973

*War Without Morality: High Tactics* (*Jingi naki tatakai: chōjō sakusen*/仁義 なき戦い・頂上作戦) 1974

*War Without Morality: the Concluding Episode* (*Jingi naki tatakai: kanketsuhen*/仁義なき戦い・完結篇) 1974

*New War Without Morality* (*Shin jingi naki tatakai*/新仁義なき戦い) 1974

*New War Without Morality: the Head of the Leader* (*Shin jingi naki tatakai: kumichō kubi*/新仁義なき戦い・組長の首) 1975

*New War Without Morality: the Leader's Final day* (*Shin jingi naki tatakai: kumichō saigo no hi*/新仁義なき戦い・組長最後の日) 1976

*Warm Current* (*Danryū*/暖流) 1939 Director: Yoshimura Kōsaburō, Shōchiku Ōfuna

*Waterloo Bridge* 1940 Director: Mervyn LeRoy

*What Is Your Name?* (*Kimi no na wa*/君の名は) in three parts 1953–1954 Director: Ōba Hideo, Shōchiku Ōfuna

*Where Are the Dreams of Our Youth?* (*Seishun no yume ima izuko*/青春の夢い まいづこ) 1932 Director: Ozu Yasujirō, Shōchiku Kamata

*The Wild One* 1953 Director: Laslo Benedek

*A Woman Called Abe Sada* aka *The True Story of Abe Sada* (*Jitsuroku Abe Sada*/実録・阿部定) 1975 Director: Tanaka Noboru, Nikkatsu

*Woman of the Dunes* (*Suna no onna*/砂の女) 1964 Director: Teshigahara Hiroshi, Teshigahara Productions

*Women of the Island* aka *Island Women* (*Shima no onna*/島の女) Early 1920s Director: Henry Kotani

*Women of Tokyo* (*Tōkyō no onna*/東京の女) 1933 Director: Ozu Yasujirō, Shōchiku Kamata

*Women Pirates* (*Onna to kaizoku*/女と海賊) 1923 Director: Nomura Hotei

*Yakuza Graveyard* (*Yakuza hakaba kuchinashi no hana*/やくざの墓場・くち なしの花) 1976 Director: Fukasaku Kinji, Tōei Kyoto

*Yojimbo: the Bodyguard* (*Yōjinbō*/用心棒) 1960 Director: Kurosawa Akira—Tōhō and Kurosawa Productions

*Zatōichi* (座頭市) 2003 Director: Beat/Kitano Takeshi—Bandai Visuals, Tokyo FM, Terebi Asahi, Saitō Entertainments and Office Kitano

*Zatōichi the Blind Swordsman* (座頭市) Series, Daiei Kyoto Studios. Twenty-six films were made between 1960 and 1989 starring Katsu Shintarō.

*Zigoma* 1911 Director: Victorin Jasset

# SELECT BIBLIOGRAPHY

Abe, Kashō. 2001. *Nihon eiga ga sonzai suru*. Tokyo: Seidosha.

Acland, Charles. R. 2003. *Screen Traffic: Movies, Multiplexes, and Global Culture*. Durham and London: Duke University Press.

Anderson, Benedict. 1993. *Imagined Communities: Reflections on the Origin and Spread of Nationalism*. London: Verso.

Anderson, Joseph L., and Donald Richie. 1959. *The Japanese Film: Art and Industry*. Tokyo: Charles E. Tuttle.

Anderson, J. L. 1992. 'Spoken Silents in the Japanese Cinema; or, Talking to Pictures: Essaying the *Katsuben*, Contextualizing the Text.' In *Reframing Japanese Cinema: Authorship, Genre, History*, ed. Arthur Nolletti and David Desser. Bloomington and Indianapolis: Indiana University Press.

Barrett, Gregory. 1989. *Archetypes in Japanese Film: The Sociopolitical and Religious Significance of the Principal Heroes and Heroines*. Selinsgrove, PA: Susquehanna University Press.

Beasley, W. G. 1990. *The Rise of Modern Japan*. London: Weidenfeld and Nicolson.

Benjamin, Walter. 1992. *Illuminations*. London: Fontana Press.

Berman, Marshall. 1993. *All That Is Solid Melts Into Air: The Experience of Modernity*. London: Verso.

Bordwell, David. 1997. *On the History of Film Style*. London: Harvard University Press.

———. 1995. 'Visual Style in Japanese Cinema, 1925–1945.' *Film History*, vol. 7, no. 1: 5–31.

———. 1990. *Narration in the Fiction Film*. London: Routledge.

———. 1988. *Ozu and the Poetics of Cinema*. London: British Film Institute.

Bordwell, David, and Kristin Thompson. 1980. *Film Art: An Introduction*. Reading, MA: Addison-Wesley Publishing Company.

Bordwell, David, Janet Staiger, and Kristin Thompson. 1999. *The Classical Hollywood Cinema: Film Style and Mode of Production to 1960*. London: Routledge.

Boyd, James. 1927. *Marching On*. New York: Charles Scribner's Sons.

Broderick, Mick. 1996. *Hibakusha Cinema: Hiroshima, Nagaski and the Nuclear Image in Japan*. London and New York: Kegan Paul International.

Buehrer, Beverley Bare. 1990. *Japanese Films: A Filmography and Commentary, 1921–1989*. London: St James Press.

Burch, Noël. 1979. *To the Distant Observer: Form and Meaning in the Japanese Cinema*. London: Scolar Press.

Carr, E. H. 1990. *What Is History?*, ed. R. W. Davies. London: Penguin Books.

Cazdyn, Eric. 2002. *The Flash of Capital: Film and Geopolitics in Japan.* Durham and London: Duke University Press.

Charney, Leo, and Vanessa R. Schwartz, eds. 1995. *Cinema and the Invention of Modern Life.* Berkeley, Los Angeles and London: University of California Press.

Chomsky, Noam. 1993. *Necessary Illusions: Thought Control in Democratic Societies.* London: Pluto Press.

Comolli, Jean-Louis. 1986. 'Technique and Ideology: Camera, Perspective, Depth of Field.' Parts 3 and 4 in *Narrative, Apparatus, Ideology*, ed. Philip Rosen. New York: Columbia University Press.

Davis, Darrell William. 1996. *Picturing Japaneseness: Monumental Style, National Identity, Japanese Film.* New York: Columbia University Press.

Deguchi, Takehito. 1991. '*Nani ga hakujin konpurekkusu o umidasitaka.*' In *Nihon eiga to modanizumu 1920–1930*, (ed.) Iwamoto Kenji. Tokyo: Libro.

Dexter, Emma, and Thomas Weski, eds. 2003. *Tender and Cruel: The Real in the Twentieth-Century Photograph.* London: Tate Publishing.

Dore, R. P. 1963. *City Life in Japan: A Study of a Tokyo Ward.* London: University of California Press.

Dower, John. 1999. *Embracing Defeat: Japan in the Aftermath of World War II.* London: Allen Lane, The Penguin Press.

———. 1988. *Empire and Aftermath: Yoshida Shigeru and the Japanese Experience, 1878–1954.* London: Harvard University Press.

———. 1986. *War Without Mercy: Race and Power in the Pacific War.* London: Faber and Faber.

Dyer, Richard. 2004. *Heavenly Bodies: Film Stars and Society.* London: Routledge.

———. 1993. *The Matter of Images: Essays on Representations.* London: Routledge.

———. 1992. *Stars.* London: BFI Publishing.

Eagleton, Terry. 2003a. *Sweet Violence: The Idea of the Tragic.* Oxford: Blackwell Publishing.

———. 2003b. *After Theory.* London: Allen Lane, The Penguin Press.

———. 1996. *Heathcliff and the Great Hunger: Studies in Irish Culture.* London: Verso.

Eco, Umberto. 1984. 'The Myth of Superman.' In *The Role of the Reader: Explorations in the Semiotics of Texts.* Bloomington: Indiana University Press.

Fiske, John. 1991. *Television Culture.* London and New York: Routledge.

Foucault, Michel. 1993. 'A Preface to Transgression.' In *Language Counter Memory and Practice: Selected Essays and Interviews by Michel Foucault*, ed. Donald F. Bouchard, trans. Donald F. Bouchard and Sherry Simon. Ithaca, NY: Cornell University Press.

———. 1992a. *The Archaeology of Knowledge*, trans. A. M. Sheridan Smith. London: Routledge.

———. 1992b. *The Order of Things: An Archaeology of the Human Sciences.* London: Routledge.

———. 1991. *Discipline and Punish: The Birth of the Prison*, trans. Alan Sheridan. London: Penguin Books.

———. 1990. *The History of Sexuality, vol. 1, An Introduction*, trans. Robert Hurley. London: Penguin Books.

Frisby, David. 1985. *Fragments of Modernity: Theories of Modernity in the Work of Simmel, Kracauer and Benjamin*. Cambridge: Polity Press.

Frye, Northrop. 1957. *Anatomy of Criticism: Four Essays*. Princeton: Princeton University Press.

Galbraith, Stuart IV. 2002. *The Emperor and the Wolf: The Lives and Films of Akira Kurosawa and Toshiro Mifune*. London and New York: Faber and Faber.

Gellner, Ernest. 1999. *Nations and Nationalism: New Perspectives on the Past*. Oxford: Blackwell.

———. 1998. *Nationalism*. London: Phoenix.

Giddens, Anthony. 1990. *The Consequences of Modernity*. Cambridge: Polity Press.

Girard, René. 1979. *Violence and the Sacred*, trans. Patrick Gregory. Baltimore: Johns Hopkins University Press.

Gombrich, E. H. 1998. *The Sense of Order: A Study in the Psychology of Decorative Art*. London: Phaidon Press.

———. 1996. *Art and Illusion: A Study in the Psychology of Pictorial Representation*. London: Phaidon Press.

Hagen, Margaret. 1986. *Varieties of Realism: Geometries of Representational Art*. Cambridge: Cambridge University Press.

Halford, Aubrey. S., and Giovanna M. Halford. 1983. *The Kabuki Handbook*. Tokyo: Charles E. Tuttle.

Hamada, Yoshihisa. 1995. *Eiga hyakunen, sengo gojūnen: Nihon eiga to sensō to heiwa*. Tokyo: Issuisha.

Hane, Mikiso. 1993. *Reflections on the Way to the Gallows: Rebel Women in Prewar Japan*. Berkeley and Los Angeles, CA: University of California Press.

Hansen, Miriam Bratu. 2000a. 'Fallen Women, Rising Stars, New Horizons— cultural influence of Hollywood film in Shanghai, China, in the 1920s and 1930s.' *Film Quarterly*, vol. 54 no. 1: 10–22.

———. 2000b. 'The Mass Production of the Senses: Classical Cinema as Vernacular Modernism.' In *Reinventing Film Studies*, eds. Christine Gledhill and Linda Williams. London: Arnold, a member of the Hodder Headline Group.

Harvey, David. 1992. *The Condition of Postmodernity: An Enquiry into the Origins of Cultural Change*. Oxford: Basil Blackwell.

Hashimoto, Mitsuru. 1998. '*Chihō*: Yanagita Kunio's Japan.' In *Mirror of Modernity: Invented Traditions of Modern Japan*, ed. Stephen Vlastos. London: University of California Press.

Hashimoto, Osamu. 1989. *Kanpon chanbara jidaigeki kōza*. Tokyo: Tokuma Shoten.

Henderson, Brian. 1976. 'The Long Take.' In *Movies and Methods*, vol. 1, ed. Bill Nichols. London: University of California Press.

Hendry, Joy. 1989. *Marriage in Changing Japan*. Tokyo: Tuttle.

High, Peter B. 2003. *The Imperial Screen: Japanese Film Culture in the Fifteen Years' War, 1931–1945*. Wisconsin: University of Wisconsin Press.

Hirano, Kyoko. 1992. *Mr Smith Goes to Tokyo: Japanese Cinema Under the American Occupation 1945–1952*. Washington and London: Smithsonian Institution Press.

Hitaka, Seiichi, ed. 1994. *Ishihara Yūjirō Eiga Korekushon*. Tokyo: Kinema Junpōsha.

Hobsbawm, Eric. 1997. *On History*. London: Weidenfeld and Nicolson.

———. 1992. *Nations and Nationalism Since 1780: Programme, Myth, Reality*. Cambridge: Cambridge University Press.

Hobsbawm, Eric, and Terence Ranger, eds. 1992. *The Invention of Tradition*. Cambridge: Cambridge University Press.

Hoffmann, Hilmar. 1996. *The Triumph of Propaganda: Film and National Socialism, 1933–1945*, trans. John A. Broadwin and V. R. Berghahn. Oxford: Berghahn Books.

Horsley, William, and Roger Buckley. 1990. *Nippon: New Superpower, Japan Since 1945*. London: BBC Books.

Iguchi, Rickihei, Tadashi Nakajima, and Roger Pineau. 1958. *The Divine Wind: Japan's Kamikaze Force in World War II*. Annapolis, MD: United States Naval Institute.

Ikegami, Eiko. 1995. *The Taming of the Samurai: Honorific Individualism and the Making of Modern Japan*. London: Harvard University Press.

Inoue, Shun. 1998. 'The Invention of the Martial Arts: Kanō Jigorō and Kōdōkan Judo.' In *Mirror of Modernity: Invented Traditions of Modern Japan*, ed. Stephen Vlastos. London: University of California Press.

Irokawa, Daikichi. 1985. *The Culture of the Meiji Period*, trans. and ed. Marius B. Jansen. Princeton, NJ: Princeton University Press.

Ishii, F. 1994. '*Tsukue Ryōnosuke to Nemuri Kyōshirō "Kyomu" o Seotta Otokotachi*.' In *Rekisi Dokuhon Tokubetsu Zōkan '94–11 Supeshiyaru [Ichikawa Raizō Botsugo 25 nen Kinen] Raizō: Nemuri Kyōshirō no Sekai*, no. 48. 102–107.

Ishiwari, Osamu, ed. 2000. *Nihon eiga kyōbō: Makino ikka*. Tokyo: Wides Shuppan.

Itami, Mansaku. 1961. '*Sensō Sekininsha no Mondai*.' In *Itami Mansaku Zenshū*, vol. 1. Tokyo: Chikuma Shobō.

Ivy, Marilyn. 1993. 'Formations of Mass Culture.' In *Postwar Japan as History*, ed. Andrew Gordon. Oxford: University of California Press.

———. 1995. *Discourses of the Vanishing: Modernity Phantasm Japan*. Chicago: University of Chicago Press.

Iwamoto, Kenji, ed. 1991. *Nihon eiga to modanizumu 1920–1930*, Tokyo: Libro.

Iwamoto, Kenji and Tomonori Saiki, eds. 1988. *Kikigaki kinema no seishun*. Tokyo: Libro.

Iwasaki, Akira. 1958a. *Gendai Nihon no eiga: Sono shisō to fūzoku*. Tokyo: Chūō Kōronsha.

———. 1958b. *Nihon eiga sakaron*. Tokyo: Chūō Kōronsha.

Jameson, Fredric. 1992. *Signatures of the Visible*. London: Routledge.

Jeffords, Susan. 1989. *The Remasculinization of America: Gender and the Vietnam War*. Bloomington and Indianapolis: Indiana University Press.

Johnson, Chalmers. 1964. *An Instance of Treason: Ozaki Hotsumi and the Sorge Spy Ring*. Stanford: Stanford University Press.

Kaeriyama, Norimasa. 1916. *Kinema Record*.

Kasahara, Kazuo. 1973a. 'Jingi Kangae.' *Shinario* (October): 138.

———. 1973b. *'Jingi naki tatakai Hiroshima shitōhen e no Purorōgu: Yamanaka Mitsuji Shōden.' Shinario* (June): 141–171.

———. 1974. *'Jitsuroku Shinario Taikentekidan Jingi naki tatakai no Sanbyaku Hi.' Shinario* (February): 106–114.

Kasza, Gregory J. 1993. *The State and Mass Media in Japan 1918–1945*. Berkeley: University of California Press.

Keene, Donald, ed. 1956. *Anthology of Japanese Literature from the Earliest Era to the Mid-Nineteenth Century*. London: George Allen and Unwin.

Kido, Shirō. 1956. *Nihon eiga fu: eiga seisakusha no kiroku*. Tokyo: Bungei Shyunjyū Shinsha.

Kinema Junpō. 1994. *'Chūshingura Eizōno Sekai.' Kinejun* 25 (October 1994).

———. 1994. *Best Kinema Junpō 1950–1966*. Tokyo: Kinema Junpōsha.

———. 1994. *Best Kinema Junpō 1967–1993*. Tokyo: Kinema Junpōsha.

———. 1991. *Nihon eiga haiyū zenshū: Danyūhen*. Tokyo: Kinema Junpōsha.

———. 1991. *Nihon eiga haiyū zenshū: Joyūhen*. Tokyo: Kinema Junpōsha.

———. 1988. *Nihon eiga teribi kantoku zenshū*. Tokyo: Kinema Junpōsha.

Kinmonth, Earl H. 1981. *The Self-Made Man in Meiji Japanese Thought: From Samurai to Salary Man*. London: University of California Press.

Kinoshita, Keisuke. 1953. *Nihon no Higeki Shinario*. Tokyo: Eigataimususha.

Kobayashi, Kyūzō. 1999. *Nihon eiga o hajimetta otoko: Kido Shirō den*. Tokyo: Shinjinbutsu Ōraisha.

Komatsu, Hiroshi, and Charles Musser. 1987. 'Benshi Search.' In *Wide Angle*, vol. 9, no. 2: 72–90.

Kosaka, Masataka. 1982. *A History of Post-war Japan*. Tokyo: Kodansha.

Lecourt, Dominique. 2001. *The Mediocracy: French Philosophy Since the Mid-1970s*, trans. Gregory Elliott. London: Verso.

Lee, Young-il. 1988. *The History of Korean Cinema: Main Currents of Korean Cinema*. Seoul: Motion Picture Promotion Corporation.

Lehmann, Jean-Pierre. 1982. *The Roots of Modern Japan*. London: Macmillan.

———. 1987. 'Oshima: the Avant-Garde Artist Without an Avant-Garde Style.' *Wide Angle*, vol. 9, no. 2.

Lehman, Peter. 1993. *Running Scared: Masculinity and the Representation of the Male Body*. Philadelphia: Temple University Press.

———. 1980. 'The Act of Making Films: An Interview with Oshima Nagisa.' *Wide Angle*, vol. 4, no. 2.

MacCabe, Colin. 1991. Introduction to *The Geopolitical Aesthetic: Cinema and Space in the World System*, ed. Fredric Jameson. London: BFI Publishing.

McDonald, Keiko I. 2000. *From Book to Screen: Modern Japanese Literature in Film*. Armonk, NY: M.E. Sharp.

———. 1994. *Japanese Classical Theatre in Films*. London: Associated University Press.

Makino, Mamoru. 1991. '*Ken'etsu to Nihon eiga no modanizumu.*' In *Nihon eiga to modanizumu 1920–1930*, ed Kenji Iwamo. Tokyo: Libro.

Makino, Masahiro. 1977. *Eiga tosei: Ten no maki*. Tokyo: Heibonsha.

———. 1977. *Eiga tosei: Chi no maki*. Tokyo: Heibonsha.

Matsushima, Toshiyuki. 2000. *Nikkatsu Romanporuno Zenshi: Meisaku, Meiyū Meikantoku-tachi*. Tokyo: Kōdansha.

Mautner, Thomas, ed. 2000. *The Penguin Dictionary of Philosophy*. London: Penguin Group.

Miller, Toby, Nitin Govil, John McMurria, and Richard Maxwell. 2001. *Global Hollywood*. London: BFI Publishing.

Minear, Richard H. 1971. *Victors' Justice: The Tokyo War Crimes Trial*. Princeton, NJ: Princeton University Press.

Mishima, Yukoi. 1977. *On Hagakure: The Samurai Ethic in Modern Japan*. London: Penguin.

Moeran, Brian. 1989. *Language and Popular Culture in Japan*. Manchester: Manchester University Press.

Morris, Ivan. 1980. *The Nobility of Failure: Tragic Heroes in the History of Japan*. Harmondsworth: Penguin Books.

Murakami, Yoshiaki, and Norifumi Ogawa. 2000. *Nihon Eiga Sangyō Saizensen: Japan Movies Now*. Tokyo: Kadokawa Shoten.

Myers, Ramon H., and Mark Peattie, eds. 1984. *The Japanese Colonial Empire, 1895–1945*. Princeton, NJ: Princeton University Press.

Nagy, Margit. 1991. 'Middle-Class Working Women During the Interwar Years.' In *Recreating Japanese Women, 1600–1945*, ed. Gail Lee Bernstein. Berkeley: University of California Press.

Nakane, Chie. 1972. *Japanese Society*. Berkeley: University of California Press.

Nakayama, H. 2003. '*Fukasaku Kinji to Tomo ni Takatta Otokotachi Dokyumento [BRII].*' *Kinema Junpō* 1385 (July 2003): 32–40.

Nava, Mica. 1996. 'Women, the City and the Department Store.' In *Modern Times: Reflections on a Century of English Modernity*, eds. Mica Nava and Alan O'Shea. London: Routledge.

Neale, Steve. 2000. *Genre and Hollywood*. London and New York: Routledge.

———. 1987. *Genre*. London: BFI Publishing.

*Nihon Eiga 100nen: Misono Korekushon*. 1995. Tokyo: Asahi Shinbunsha.

NHK, ed. 1995. *Nihon no sentaku: Puropaganda eiga no tadotta michi*. Tokyo: Kadokawa Shoten.

Nolte, Sharon, and Sally Ann Hastings. 1991. 'The Meiji State's Policy Toward Women 1890–1910.' In *Recreating Japanese Women 1600–1945*, ed. Gail Lee Bernstein. Oxford: University of California Press.

Okamoto, Hiroshi. 1958. '*Yūjirō to Ichijikan.*' In *Best of Kinema Junpō 1950–1966*. Tokyo: Kinema Junpōsha.

Okuzaki, Kenzō. 1988. *Yukiykite Shingun no Shisō*. Tokyo: Shinsensha.

Onuma, Yasuaki. 1986. 'The Tokyo Trial: Between Law and Politics.' In *The Tokyo War Crimes Trial: An International Symposium*, ed. C. Hosoya, N. Ando, Y. Onuma and R. Minear. Tokyo: Kodansha.

————. 1993. *Tōkyō Saiban kara Sengo Sekinin no Shisō e*. Tokyo: Tōshindō.

Ooms, H. 1989. *Tokugawa Ideology: Early Constructs, 1570–1680*. Princeton, NJ: Princeton University Press.

Orr, John. 2003. 'The City Reborn: Cinema at the Turn of the Century.' In *Screening the City*, ed. Mark Shiel and Tony Fitzmaurice. London: Verso.

Osborne, Peter. 1992. 'Modernity Is a Qualitative, Not a Chronological, Category.' *New Left Review* 192.

O'Shea, Alan. 1996. 'English Subjects of Modernity.' In *Modern Times: Reflections on a Century of English Modernity*, eds. Mica Nava and Alan O'Shea. London: Routledge.

Ōshima, Nagisa. 1994. '*Jingi naki tatakai-ron: Yakuza Eiga wa Kanashii Eiga de aru*.' In *Best of Kinema Junpō 1967–1993*. Tokyo: Kinema Junpōsha.

————. 1993. *Ōshima Nagisa 1960*. Tokyo: Seidosha.

————. 1992. *Cinema, Censorship, and the State: The Writings of Ōshima Nagisa*, trans. Dawn Lawson. Cambridge, MA: MIT Press.

————. 1979. *Ai no korīda*. Tokyo: Sanichi Shobō.

————. 1978. *Taikenteki sengo eizōron*. Tokyo: Asahi Shinbun-sha.

————. 1975. '*Jingi naki tatakai-ron: Yakuza Eiga Kanashii Eiga de aru*.' In *Best of Kinema Junpo 1967–1993*. Tokyo: Kinema Junpōsha.

————. 1968. *Ōshima Nagisa sakuhin: kōshikei*. Tokyo: Shiseidō.

Peattie, Mark R. 1984. 'Japanese Attitudes Toward Colonialism, 1895–1945.' In *The Japanese Colonial Empire, 1895–1945*, eds. Ramon H. Myers and Mark R. Peattie. Princeton: Princeton University Press.

Powell, Brian. 1990. *Kabuki in Modern Japan: Mayama Seika and His Plays*. Basingstoke, Hampshire: The Macmillan Press Ltd.

Reeves, Nicholas. 1999. 'Official British Film Propaganda.' In *The First World War and Popular Cinema: 1914 to the Present*, ed. Michael Paris. Edinburgh: Edinburgh University Press.

Richie, Donald. 2001. *A Hundred Years of Japanese Film: A Concise History*. Tokyo: Kodansha.

————. 1974. *Ozu*. Berkeley: University of California.

Said, Edward W. 1991. *The World, the Text and the Critic*. London: Vintage.

————. 1991a. *Orientalism: Western Conceptions of the Orient*. London: Penguin Books.

Sakaguchi, Ango. 1986. 'Discourse on Decadence,' trans. Seiiji M. Lippit. *Review of Japanese Culture and Society* (October): 1–5.

Sakuramoto, Totomio. 1993. *Daitōa sensō to Nihon eiga: Tachimi no senchū eigaron*. Tokyo: Aoki Shoten.

Sansom, G. B. 1983. *Japan: A Short Cultural History*. Tokyo: Charles E. Tuttle.

Sartre, Jean-Paul. 1964. *Saint Genet: Actor and Martyr*, trans. Bernard Frechtman. London: W. H. Allen & Company.

Satō, Tadao. 2000. *Ozu Yasujirō no geijitsu*. Tokyo: Asahi Bunko.

————. 1995. *Nihon eigashi 1896–1940*, vol. 1. Tokyo: Iwanami Shoten.

————. 1995. *Nihon eigashi 1941–1959*, vol. 2. Tokyo: Iwanami Shoten.

————. 1996. *Nihon eigashi 1960–1990*, vol. 3. Tokyo: Iwanami Shoten.

————. 1996. *Nihon eigashi*, vol. 4. Tokyo: Iwanami Shoten.

————. 1989. *Nihon Eiga to Nihon Bunka*. Tokyo: Miraisha.

————. 1987. *Ōshima Nagisa no sekai*. Tokyo: Asahi Bunko.

————. 1987. *Currents in Japanese Cinema*, trans. Gregory Barrett. Tokyo: Kodansha.

————. 1976. *Chūshingura: Iji no keifu*. Tokyo: Asahi Shinbun-sha.

————. 1974. '*Jingi naki tatakai Shiriizu no Omoshirosa.*' *Shinario* (August): 100–103.

————. 1968. '*Kōshikei.*' In *Āto Shiyatā* 55 (February): 4–10.

Schilling, Mark. 2003. *The Yakuza Movie Book: A Guide to Japanese Gangster Films*. Berkeley, CA: Stone Bridge Press.

Screech, Timon. 1996. *The Western Scientific Gaze and Popular Imagery in Later Edo Japan: the Lens within the Heart*. Cambridge: Cambridge University Press.

Shiba, Tsukasa, and Sakae Aoyama. 1998. *Yakuza Eiga to Sono Jidai*. Tokyo: Chikuma Shinsho.

Shimizu, Akira. 1994. *Sensō to eiga: Senjichū to senkyōka no Nihon eigashi*. Tokyo: Shakai Shisōsha.

Shohat, Ella, and Robert Stam. 1996. 'From the Imperial Family to the Transnational Imaginary: Media Spectatorship in the Age of Globalization.' In *Global Local: Cultural Production and the Transnational Imaginary*, eds. Rob Wilson and Wimal Dissanayake. Durham: Duke University Press.

*Shūkan Asahi no Shōwashi*. 1989. Vols. 1, 2 and 3. Tokyo: Asahi Shinbunsha.

Shundō, Kōji, and Sadao Yamane. 1999. *Ninkyō Eigaden*. Tokyo: Kōdansha.

Silverberg, Miriam. 1991. 'The Modern Girl as Militant.' In *Recreating Japanese Women, 1600–1945*, ed. Gail Lee Bernstein. Berkeley: University of California Press.

Slaymaker, Doug. 2002. 'When Sartre Was an Erotic Writer: Body, Nation and Existentialism in Japan after the Asia-Pacific War.' *Japan Forum*, vol. 14, no. 1: 77–101.

Smith, Anthony. 2000. 'Images of the Nation: Cinema, Art and National Identity.' In *Cinema and Nation*, eds. Mette Hjort and Scott MacKenzie. London: Routledge.

Sontag, Susan. 1983. 'Against Interpretation.' In *A Susan Sontag Reader*. New York: Vintage Books.

Sorlin, Pierre. 1999. 'Cinema and the Memory of the Great War.' In *The First World War and Popular Cinema: 1914 to the Present*, ed. Michael Paris. Edinburgh: Edinburgh University Press.

Stacey, Jackie. 1994. 'Hollywood Memories.' In *Screen* vol. 35, no. 4 (Winter): 317–335.

Stam, Robert, and Ella Habiba Shohat. 2000. 'Film Theory and Spectatorship in the Age of Posts.' In *Reinventing Film Studies*, eds. Christine Gledhill and Linda Williams. London: Arnold.

Standish, Isolde. 2000. *Myth and Masculinity in the Japanese Cinema: Towards a Political Reading of the 'Tragic Hero.'* Richmond, Surrey: Routledge/Curzon.

Suzuki, Kazutoshi. 1984. *Aizen Katsura to Nipponjin*. Tokyo: Jyōhō Sentā Syppankyoku.

Takizawa, Seinosuke. 1996. *Motto Natsukashimu Jidaigeki Gaido: Tsūkai Hiirō to Edo Chisiki.* Tokyo: Dōbunshoin.

Tanizaki, Jun'ichirō. 1986. *Naomi,* trans. Anthony H. Chambers. London: Pan Books.

Tayama, R. 1966. '*Abashiri bangaichi: Nagaremono no erejii.*' *Shinario* (October): 134–137.

Thompson, Kristin, and David Bordwell. 1994. *Film History: An Introduction.* London: McGraw-Hill, Inc.

Tsutsui, Kiyotada. 2000. *Jidaigeki eiga no shisō: nosutarijī no yukue.* Tokyo: PHP Shinso.

Turim, Maureen. 1998. *The Films of Oshima Nagisa: Images of a Japanese Iconoclast.* Berkeley: University of California Press.

Usui, Hiroshi. 1998. *Terebi ga Yume o Miru Hi.* Tokyo: Shūeisha.

Ussher, Jane M. 1997. *Fantasies of Feminity: Reframing the Boundaries of Sex.* London: Penguin Books.

Vidal, Gore. 2003. *Dreaming War: Blood for Oil and the Cheney-Bush Junta.* Forest Row, U.K.: Clairview Books.

Vlastos, Stephen. 1998. 'Tradition: Past/Present Culture and Modern Japanese History.' In *Mirror of Modernity: Invented Traditions of Modern Japan,* ed. Stephen Vlastos. Berkeley: University of California Press.

Washitani, Hana. 2001. '*Ri Kōran: Nichigeki ni arawaru: utau Daitōa Kyōeiken.*' In *Ri-Kōran to higashi ajia,* ed. Inuhiko Yomota. Tokyo: Daigaku Shūpankai.

White, Hayden. 1985. *Tropics of Discourse: Essays in Cultural Criticism.* London: Johns Hopkins University Press.

Williams, Linda. 1991. *Hard Core.* Pandora: London.

Williams, Raymond. 1977. *Marxism and Literature.* Oxford: Oxford University Press.

Winston, Brian. 1995. *Claiming the Real: The Griersonian Documentary and its Legitimations.* London: BFI Publishing.

Yamada, Yōji, ed. 1978. *Kido Shirō: wa ga eigaron.* Tokyo: Shōchiku Kabushiki Kaisa.

Yokochi, Takeshi, and Fusako Aida. 1999. *Man,ei kokusaku eiga no shosō.* Tokyo: Pandora Gendai Shokan.

Yomota, Inuhiko. 2001. '*Inshu: Ri-Kōran o Motomete.*' In *Ri-Kōran to higashi ajia,* ed. Inuhiko Yomota. Tokyo: Daigaku Shūpankai.

———. 1999. '*Genroku Chūshingura ni okeru joseiteki naru mono*' (The Feminine in Genroku Chūshingura). In *Eiga kantoku Mizoguchi Kenji,* ed. Inuhiko Yomota. Tokyo: Shinyō-sha.

Yoshida, Shigeru. 1996. *The Yoshida Memoirs: The Story of Japan in Crisis,* trans. Kenichi Yoshida. London: Heinemann.

Yoshimoto, Mitsuhiro. 2000. *Kurosawa.* Duke University Press.

Young, Louise. 1998. *Japan's Total Empire: Manchuria and the Culture of Wartime Imperialism.* Berkeley: University of California Press.

Yun, Yundō. 1968. '*Shikeiba ga Bokura o Matte iru*' In *Āto Shiyatā* 55 (February): 18–19.

# INDEX